I love Sarah Harnisch's book, Gamep[ ]
YOUR road map on how to be succe[ ]
Oils. She lays out everything for you in her no-nonsense fashion,
from finding your why to developing your skills to using social
media to learning the Compensation Plan to scripts and closes ...
every nuance of what's necessary to advance up the ranks as she
has done. A lot of my downline are teaching from this book and
loving it! When you read it, YOU GET IT!!

Diane Mora
Young Living Crown Diamond

To be successful in this business you need three things: passion,
consistency and strategy. Gameplan gives you the strategy
you need to make your business grow. It is simple, easy, and
duplicatable for the whole team. I have watched Gameplan turn
struggling, frustrated distributors into successful business owners.
If you want strategy and easy duplication, get Gameplan. It works!

Mary Starr Carter
Young Living Diamond

This is the best book on the market, giving you the tools you
need to rock your business. Whether you are a new or a seasoned
business builder, you will be able to take this book and apply it to
help you and your team grow. If you ever get the chance to meet
Sarah in person, don't pass it up!

Lorene Allen
Young Living Platinum

To:

_____

From:

_____

Date:

_____

GAMEPLAN

The Complete
Strategy Guide
to go from
Starter Kit to Silver

Sarah Harnisch
Young Living Platinum

Gameplan

© Copyright 2016 by Sarah Harnisch, All Rights Reserved

Edited by Trina and Jeremy Holden

Layout and cover art by Jeremy Holden

Content editors: Diane Mora, Kathryn Caywood

DEDICATION

The dedication for this book is incredibly easy to write. I knew before I put the first word on the page that every thought was focused on you and you alone, Young Living Distributor.

I know what it felt like to start my business without a script, a vision, or a lot of direction. I have been in a place where I plateaued—and I didn't know my next move. Heck, I went through the first six months of my business not even realizing I had a business at all. I had no idea how to inspire and train leaders. I have had moments of panic as I watched my volume dip. Unintentionally, I have made just about every mistake imaginable with the FDA. I got over the initial fear of the unknown with my first class, then had ten-thousand questions on what happened next. I have been lost, overwhelmed, and exasperated, and elated, invigorated, and blown away all on the same day. I have been disappointed in leaders, disappointed in my own leadership, and then stood back and saw that despite our mistakes we were catapulting to Platinum. I realized there is a strategy—there is a method, a way of doing this business. If someone wrote that down, it would bless thousands and thousands of people trying to navigate the network marketing world.

If you're brand new, great! You have just as much of a chance at making Diamond as someone who is a Platinum. If you're a Diamond and on the cusp of losing rank, this will give your leaders new energy and focus. Wherever you are, this book is dedicated to your tenacity, your hard work, your diligence, your fight, your climb, your drive and focus, your days of weariness and desire to quit, and your days of fist-bumping your team in raging success in the final minutes at the end of the month. This book is for all of it, your high days and your low days and your in-between days. I am standing there, rallying right beside you. Because some days, it takes a little shouting with joy for us to move.

I'd never have found my "shout" if it hadn't been for my Lord and Savior, Jesus, who gave His life for me on the cross. If you hear joy in these pages, my joy comes from Him. If you hear passion and hope, my Hope is in the Lord. May this book inspire you to grow a business and grow your faith. I know it's done both for me. And because of that, because God is my center, this book is also for Him.

Thank you for your commitment to ingest all that's on these pages. I want you to know that whether you're on my team or not, you are worth fighting for. Your dreams matter. Today is the day you stop chasing them, and you start to see them through. It's Gameplan day.

Contents

STRATEGIES FOR BUILDING YOUR TEAM

EXPAND YOUR INFLUENCE: SECRETS TO GREAT LEADERSHIP

IT WORKS: THE VIEW FROM THE TOP

APPENDIX: SARAH'S SCRIPTS AND MORE

How To Use This Book

A PERSONAL NOTE FROM SARAH

You've picked up this book up for one of four reasons:

1) You're brand new and want to learn how to get your oils for free (that's very doable!)

2) You are a seasoned oiler that is now interested in the business. You love earning free oils, but now you want to start making some money!

3) You are a business builder that has been taking it seriously for months or years but don't understand why you aren't growing as quickly as those around you.

4) You have already been successful at the business, but reached a plateau and you're not quite sure where to go next.

This book is for every single one of you. The title is deceiving. I began writing it as a resource for newbies who want to get to Silver, but I have seen even Diamonds benefit from it because we can all learn from each other. When you stop learning, you stop growing. As I sit and write this thing, I'm constantly gleaning new ideas from odd places and from every rank to use on my own team.

If you're just getting started

To the new oiler or new business builder: if you are just getting started, promise me something. Teach at least one class before you try to digest this whole book. Ninety percent of your fear is simply fear of the unknown. Grab the simple 101 Script in the appendix of this book, gather a few friends and read it aloud. Go through the motions of what a class looks like. Once you have gone through one business cycle of inviting to a class, sharing the 101 Script, closing confidently, and touching base afterward, return to the book.

Before you've held a class, the information in this book will seem overwhelming. But what I found was after that first class experience, there were a thousand legitimate questions:

"How do I navigate the Virtual Office?"

"Someone wants to sign up, but where do I place them?"

"No one is coming to class!"

"How do I deal with no's?"

"Where do I find leaders?"

"How do I get people on Essential Rewards?"

Once you are asking those questions, you are ready for this book. It's a game plan. It's a strategy guide. It's not a feel-good, vision-casting book—it's a nuts and bolts, how-to book. It's here to help you navigate the chessboard of network marketing. You absolutely can succeed at this, because it simply requires will. If you have will, even distractions and crisis cannot keep you from your end game long-term. This book is to show you it can be done by anyone who sees where Young Living goes, despite personality, income, time, resources, location, or friend circles.

This book is not fluffy inspiration—it's a proven set of instructions that work. But it's not overwhelming—most chapters are just a couple of pages, and written in a down-to-earth, easy-to-understand format. Take it at your pace, apply what you learn, and utilize the appendix. (I always skip the appendix in other books—but that's where the gold is in this book!) Then find an accountability partner, fill out the monthly accountability worksheets and you're off and running.

If you're tired or stuck

If you have leveled off in your growth and need new perspective or fresh wind—this book is written for you, too. You will be energized by the many tips and tricks assembled here from a very active, diverse, and creative team.

A word of caution: Gameplan is extremely dense. I'm a researcher and compiler by nature, and 17 years as a news anchor perfected my ability to pack the most essential info into the shortest amount of time. I'm trained to do election coverage, to listen to seven hours of tape on every major network,

ingest it, and condense all of it into 30 second stories that are easy on the ear.

When I went to train my oils team for the first time, I found there were many incredible resources, but they were in too many places. If I wanted to get someone off the ground, I had to purchase several dozen books for them!

This book is a summary of what I've experienced at my personal classes, what I've learned from my own leaders, cross-line friend's tips for growth, what I have gleaned from my Diamond and Platinum friends on Young Living trips, what I have read for personal growth, and more. It is the best of the best, every page packed with practical action points intended make the transition into a Young Living business fast and successful.

The Gameplan system will keep you on track if you stick with it. When life knocks you over, get back up, pick the book back up and start again where you left off. The only time you lose at network marketing is when you get off the horse and don't return. Stay on the horse.

If you're Silver or higher

If you are in higher leadership, take this book and run. Read it, digest it, apply what you need, and fly. You have been doing this long enough that you know the drill and you know what it takes to rock this thing. But maybe there aren't good training materials on your team—this book provides you with a proven system to train your leaders. My upline Diamond leadership and crossline Diamond friends have used it successfully with their teams, and we have had a powerful outcome from Gameplan on the Oil Ability Team.

Maybe you're a rock star leader who truly has it all totally together. You have ranked at record speed, your classes have standing room only, you pick up leaders everywhere and set them on fire, and you are a master at getting people on Essential Rewards. But here's the thing: every leader has a breaking point. We all have a place where we're worn so thin, and there are a thousand things we want to pour into someone, but there is no space in our life to do it.

That's what this book is for. It's for the things you want to tell your brand new budding Diamond, on level 47, but you don't have two weeks to spend with them alone on an island uninterrupted. This is your time saver. This allows you to pour into every leader with the same tenacity and content, without killing yourself or robbing your family of time.

Whatever the reason is that you are reading this, thank you for picking up Gameplan! My goal is to see as many individuals and families rise to Diamond as possible. My vision is to break the cycle of poverty, whether you're on my team or a crossline team. We're all part of the same Young Living family!

I can't wait to walk alongside you in the following pages and pour my heart into your business. Thank you for the honor of your time. This book is rich and dense and full of my mistakes to save you time, and I pass it off with prayers of blessing, multiplication, application, favor and fun. This is your year to explode! As I say to my Oil Ability leaders, you are a #diamondrising!!!

——Sarah

PART ONE

GETTING STARTED: WHAT YOU NEED TO BEGIN

As someone who had just gotten a kit and knew **nothing**, *Gameplan gave me a vision and understanding- from the beginning- of how to grow , where to go to keep growing and how to understand Young Livingese (OGV, PV, ER, etc.). Without it, I would still be playing with my oils and enjoying them for myself, thinking I had to know everything before passing on the blessings to others! (Thank you for all your hard work!)*

Jacquelyn Cook

Your book has given me a very detailed "how to" on how to succeed. It also has been an encouragement to just keep going, within the business and without.

Kimberly Slack

Gameplan gave me a layout and understanding of the amazing company we work for. I'm new to building my business and have proudly began to build my team using the knowledge from Gameplan. I have ten people on my team and have ranked Star!

Amanda Welch

CHAPTER 1

WHY LAUNCH A YOUNG LIVING BUSINESS?

Welcome! My name is Sarah Harnisch. I'm a Young Living Platinum and the leader of the Oil Ability Team.

With God's complete grace, I attained Platinum rank in Young Living 17 months after getting my starter kit, while homeschooling my five children, rearing a special needs son, anchoring news full time starting at 4:00 a.m., and cooking gluten-free, sugar-free, and dairy-free meals for seven people with allergies.

For more than a decade and a half I have been a news anchor, which meant depleting my body of sleep and robbing my husband and children of time. Although I love radio, and never took a day in the anchor chair for granted, it was extremely hard on my body, like running a marathon every single day. I retired from full-time radio on August 27, 2015—after just 14 months with Young Living.

When I launched my Young Living business, I lived in a new state, in an extremely rural and impoverished area with poor internet, and had no circle of friends. I'd love to say that running a network marking company is easy, but the road has been full of curves and obstacles, and I'm still learning, every single day.

I do believe that with Christ as the center of your business, and tenacity, *anyone* can run a Young Living business. It has nothing to do with who you know, how famous you are, how you look, what your personality is, where you live, or how much income or time you have. If I can pull this off—*you* can pull this off.

This book is about showing you the things I've picked up on my journey.

WHY START A YOUNG LIVING BUSINESS?

That's the question I get more than any other. Here's the short answer: it's better than any job you've ever had, including a job you love. (I love anchoring news!) Why?

Freedom.

If you can show your leaders and potential business builders that this is better then what they are doing right now, you will have a lifelong business builder. They have to see that how they are spending their time at this moment will not get anything crossed off their bucket list in the next five years. The minute they spot that, they have vision.

I didn't see the business right away. In fact, it took a good six months before my husband finally sat me down and asked, "What are you doing?? You're making more with these little weekly oils classes then you are at your full time job!"

That's when I realized I needed to take it seriously. The Lord had put something in my path to pull me out of the bondage of my 4 a.m. high-stress anchoring job, and I didn't even see it. It took my husband's wisdom for me to snap out of my routine and my patterns to realize this was a viable job that could really bless our family.

Once I saw it, I made a list of pro's to doing my Young Living business based on what I'd seen over our first six months. Was it truly worth it? When I weighed the options, that's when Young Living blew me away. This is that list.

Sarah's Why Do A Young Living Business Pro's List

1. THERE IS NO INCOME CEILING

In four months flat, I made more with Young Living than in 16 years of anchoring news. Two years out, I have multiplied the highest income I ever made in my life by five—and the best is yet to come.

If you look at the Income Disclosure Guide in a couple of pages, you'll see the average Diamond's monthly income is well over what most people usually make in a year. I know the people that are living that dream, dozens of them are our close friends. John and I are living that dream. It's possible. The only ones that don't get to the top are the ones that give up.

2. THE TIMING HAS NEVER BEEN BETTER

Many people say that timing is everything, and that you can't be successful in a network marketing company unless you get into the business early. But my story and many others disproves that. I didn't get into Young Living until the company was almost 20 years old! But in months I had surpassed nearly every person ahead of me, save my Diamond upline. There are hundreds of Diamonds, hundreds of Platinums, thousands of Golds, and thousands upon thousands of Silvers, and the company continues to experience radical growth even as you read this. It's rare for any network marketing company to cross the 1-billion-dollar threshold in sales. Young Living has done it and continues to grow.

The date that you sign up for your premium starter kit has no bearing on where Young Living will go for you. How do I know? Because the current market has never been more open to what you have to offer. In just the past five years, Panera Bread has cut all chemicals from their salad dressings. Kraft Mac and Cheese has cut all dyes from their sauce. Chipotle has vowed to cut all GMO's from their menu. People are demanding better food and better products. You're seeing more and more items on store shelves that are "simple" or "natural" versions—peanut butter with peanuts and salt instead of hydrogenated oils and soy products. And the stuff is selling.

This world has started to dramatically change. No longer do we accept at face value that everything in a store is safe simply because it made it past the government. We are starting to flip over the bottles and boxes of the foods that we consume and the things we clean our home with, and the personal care products we scrub our teeth with and slather on our armpits and say "I think there's a better way to do this." The companies that are keeping up with that trend are thriving. Those that don't will lose. Young Living is ahead of the game in every single field: personal care, oils, cleaning supplies, supplements, and more. They are a total wellness company. Wellness means you stay above the line of disease.

Do you ever get frustrated that it seems doctors are always treating the symptoms instead of the cause? That they chase inflammation, pain, headaches, and a plethora of other ailments instead of finding out what's underneath all that and stopping it? You're not alone.

That's what Young Living is about. It's about stopping the cause before it happens by supporting all the systems in your body without chemically overloading them. It's not about treating disease, it's about staying ahead of it: preventative maintenance.

The average woman applies 80 chemicals to her body before breakfast daily through four types of products: makeup, hair care, skin care, and soap. And we wonder why our livers are taxed and we are tired and have hormonal issues! It's the yuck in our life. We are in constant chemical exhaustion.

That means that if you meet any person who has not banned that stuff from the threshold of their doors, any person who is not label-reading every product in their home—you have just found a potential oiler. You have a market that is one hundred percent wide open, because literally every person you know needs oils. It's not like a pan or lipstick or a book or a skirt. It's about your health. It's about your life and your family's lives. That's what makes this company the best.

And I believe with all my heart that Young Living will continue to absolutely boom—because they have what everyone wants: health freedom. It is what wellness is all about: getting ahead of your health by saying "no" to the things you allow across the threshold of the door to your home. You are the gatekeeper. And if you will teach others to be a gatekeeper, you have the secret to unlocking an explosive business with unlimited customers.

3. YOU ARE YOUR OWN BOSS AND SET YOUR OWN HOURS

I had no idea how much I appreciated this until I had no boss! I dictate my own schedule every single day. And to a weary momma who has been getting up hours before the sun rises for years, you can't put a price tag on that.

One of my best moments was a few days after I retired. I woke up to the sun in my face, and stumbled out into the living room to watch the sun rise over the fields behind our home. I had not seen the sun rise in nearly 10 years. I had my weekends off, but from sheer exhaustion, I always slept well past the sun coming up. I got to be home with my kids and see the sun rise every day. Some of the smallest things bring the greatest joy. To me, a sunrise means freedom.

4. WILLABLE INCOME (THE BEST PERK EVER!)

Once you make $3,000 a month and write a personal will, then connect with Young Living and fill out their paperwork, the income your business generates will go to your spouse and kids *forever*. So, say you have 5 kids (like me), and are making $15,000 a month as a Platinum—that's $3000 a month for each child! My kids will never grow up without food in their stomach or a roof over their head. Young Living brings peace of mind. That's the biggest perk to me. It's a legacy income, not a 401K that disappears when the cash is gone.

Outside of network marketing, there is no job on the earth where you can pull that off. If I passed away while working in radio, two weeks after my death, my final news anchor check would show up. My family would be out of luck. The $17,000 I saved in my 401K over nine years would be gone in about six months. A Young Living business doesn't work like that. This isn't some account somewhere with cash in it—it's a real, living, growing business that generates capitol—cash that goes to your family every single month.

Young Living is like setting up a storefront in your hometown and having employees run it for you. It keeps generating income even after you're gone. If you have a will, your rank in the Young Living hierarchy doesn't disappear after your death; it goes to your family.

5. YOU CAN TAKE TIME OFF—AND STILL GET PAID!

If you were in a car accident tomorrow and missed three months of work, your paycheck at a regular job would drop off within a few weeks, right? Even with disability insurance it would be a fraction of what it usually is. But with network marketing, if you are in a season where you can't share the oils, the powerful team beneath you is still working.

This was one of my wow moments, where I really grasped the power of network marketing for the first time. John and I have a special needs son on the autism spectrum. When he was 14, we had to have him placed in a school on the other side of the country. We had homeschooled all five of our kids together for 12 years, and it was extremely painful to split the Harnisch herd up. Gabe was at that school for an entire year. For 12 months, save a visit at Christmas, we did not see him, and had to get by with a 20-minute weekly phone call. At Christmas the next year, he came home. It was a huge milestone for our family. We had missed him terribly!!

These are our two oldest sons, minutes after Isaiah saw his older brother.

When Gabe returned, I felt convicted that all of my time needed to be spent on assimilating him back into the family. So I committed to take 30 straight days off Young Living: no phone calls, no training, no classes, not even Facebook posts. I put all my attention on him, and reintegrating him into the house  and our routines. From December 6th until January 9th 2015, I didn't do a thing for my business. I figured it would be a period of famine for us that year, but it was more important to focus on Gabe than on work. We'd just have to get through.

But four days before Christmas, I got a Young Living check in the mail that was higher than my monthly income from my full time job. I itched my head, took it to John, and told him "I didn't do anything this month!" I hadn't anchored news either, and I had no paycheck come from the radio station. I had only been doing Young Living for five months and hadn't even taught any classes in December, but I still got paid because the team underneath me was still out there selling. This was the power of network marketing at work for our family! When I was at my low point, my team (and my paycheck) were still there!

I will tell you I came back more excited than ever, and started a firestorm of teaching after January 9th when Gabe was comfortable at home and had enrolled in college. That firestorm led us to Gold rank just 12 weeks after his return.

There will be seasons in your life that make it tough to do Young Living well. It's okay. When the season passes, keep going. And in the interim, you have the strength of the team under you. It's the best structure of any job there is.

6. RELATIONSHIPS: THE SURPRISE BENEFIT

I had no idea how small my circle of friends was until I got involved in network marketing. You get into a groove with a nine-to-five job, or with homeschooling or public schooling, or with running your home, and simply forget that the Lord created us for relationships and that we thrive when we're in community. Some of us need many, many friends, while others are fine with just a couple of them. But we need to take time to connect with the women and men that inspire us and make us better people.

Until two years ago, I had very little contact with the outside world save trivial relationships, because I was either anchoring or homeschooling. That has completely changed for me now because of Young Living. In 24 months, I have a team of over 3000 in all 50 states and several countries and have developed some serious relationships that I know will last my lifetime. Hundreds of them would drop everything and open their home to me in an emergency. I look forward to my girl time at our Oil Ability Silver and Above Retreats and Oil Ability Beach House Retreats, and our adventures at convention. Even outside of my own team, I have true friendships around the entire world. And best yet, I get to see them at corporate events, Silver retreats, Gold retreats, Platinum retreats, leadership events, training seminars, Oil Ability team events, and convention. We grow and laugh and make memories together each time we see one other.

There are members on my team that run their business for the sole reason of developing deeper relationships. And that's a great "why." Young Living has an incredible way of networking us with people when we need to be poured into, and allows us to be a spigot to pour into others. This is an aspect of the business that I completely underestimated that has blessed me more than I can put on paper.

7. GUARANTEED BONUSES

Young Living is a generous company that has built in bonuses and perks for every level in the business. If you do the work, you will be rewarded. What are some of these perks?

Stars and Senior Stars get a bigger paycheck.

Executives get a pin, a certificate, and a larger check.

Anyone who holds Silver rank goes to the largest essential oils farm in the world—Young Living at Mona, Utah—for three days. The company pays to fly you there, puts you up in a posh hotel, loves on you with a swag bag worth a few hundred dollars, and feeds you like a king. You'll make friends from around the world and catch the vision of where Young Living goes.

Golds get the same thing, but make a trip instead to the first Young Living farm, in Saint Maries, Idaho.

Platinums head to the farm in Ecuador and see Ylang Ylang and Dorado Azul and Copaiba—and the work of the Young Living Foundation, which has built a 200-million-dollar school for impoverished kids.

There are trophies for every new rank from Silver and up each year at convention.

Diamond retreats are in different locations every year. They also get new products before they are released, front row seating at convention, and are paid a hefty Diamond bonus every month for attending the Diamond retreat or convention. Young Living wants their top leaders there and gives generously to have them come. They also get regular conference calls from Young Living to get the latest inside information from the company (which is my favorite Diamond perk!).

And if none of those reasons rock your world, how about this one: you can earn a ridiculous paycheck!! Check out the 2015 income disclosure guide. These are average incomes from all Young Living distributors!

YOUNG LIVING 2015 WORLDWIDE INCOME DISCLOSURE STATEMENT

As a direct selling company selling essential oils, supplements, and other lifestyle products, Young Living offers opportunities for our members to build a business or simply receive discounts on our products.

Whatever your interest in the company, we hope to count you among the more than 1 million Young Living members joining us in our mission to bring Young Living essential oils to every home in the world.

What are my earning opportunities?

Members can earn commissions and bonuses as outlined in our Compensation Plan. As members move up in the ranks of Young Living, they become eligible for additional earning opportunities.

This document provides statistical, fiscal data about the average member income, average hours worked per week, and information about achieving various ranks.

RANK	AVERAGE HOURS WORKED PER WEEK[2]	PERCENTAGE OF ALL MEMBERS[3]	MONTHLY INCOME[4]				ANNUALIZE AVERAGE INCOME[5]	MONTHS TO ACHIEVE THIS RANK[6]		
			Lowest	Highest	Median	Average		Low	Average	High
Distributor	3	23.1%	$0	$2,643	$0	$1	$15	N/A	N/A	N/A
Star	8	4.4%	$0	$834	$39	$79	$948	1	12	240
Senior Star	9	1.5%	$0	$7,092	$200	$253	$3,030	1	18	239
Executive	11	0.6%	$0	$12,404	$463	$549	$6,492	1	23	233
Silver	16	0.3%	$306	$27,026	$1,789	$2,221	$26,652	1	32	228
Gold	24	0.1%	$1,952	$39,655	$4,879	$6,042	$72,504	1	53	239
Platinum	33	<0.1%	$3,064	$80,603	$12,043	$14,710	$176,500	2	65	238
Diamond	31	<0.1%	$13,871	$144,369	$29,846	$38,750	$465,000	10	83	221
Crown Diamond	39	<0.1%	$31,093	$204,917	$62,624	$74,335	$892,000	14	91	236
Royal Crown Diamond	37	<0.1%	$53,723	$241,324	$144,985	$141,851	$1,702,212	17	126	230

The income statistics in this statement are for incomes earned[7] by all active worldwide members in 2015. An "active" member is a member who has purchased at least 50 PV in the previous 12 months.[8] The average annual income for all members in this time period was $28, and the median annual income for all members was $0. Forty-two percent of all members who enrolled in 2014 and 54 percent of all members who enrolled in 2013 did not remain active members with Young Living in 2015.

Please note that compensation paid to members summarized in this disclosure does not include expenses incurred by a member in the operation or promotion of his or her business, which can vary widely and might include advertising or promotional expenses, product samples, training, rent, travel, telephone, Internet, and miscellaneous expenses. The earnings of the members in this chart are not necessarily representative of the income, if any, that a Young Living member can or will earn through the Young Living Compensation Plan. These figures should not be considered as guarantees or projections of your actual earnings or profits. Your success will depend on individual diligence, work, effort, sales skill, and market conditions. Young Living does not guarantee any income or rank success.

[1] Based on a count at the end of December 2015.
[2] Based on a survey of Young Living members in December 2015.
[3] Because a member's rank may change during the year, these percentages are not based on individual member ranks throughout the entire year. They are based on the average distribution of member ranks during the entire year.
[4] Because a member's rank may change during the year, these incomes are not based on individual member incomes throughout the entire year. They are based on earnings of all members qualifying for each rank during any month throughout the year.
[5] This is calculated by multiplying the average monthly income by 12.
[6] These statistics include all historical ranking data for each rank and are not limited to members who achieved these ranks in 2015.

YOUNG LIVING
ESSENTIAL OILS

8. FINANCIAL FREEDOM

Young Living is a vehicle to financial freedom. But it's about so much more than the money. Let me explain.

Not only are my husband and I nearly debt free (including $70,000 in student loans), but I have had the honor of watching many of my closest friends and family members do the same thing with their Young Living paycheck. If you're going to get rich, do it beside your friends and family! It's been incredible to watch friends pay cash for their wedding, watch my mom buy a home, see my downline members invest in missions, become debt free, give to the needy, let jobs go and stay home with their kids, retire their spouses, go on family vacations before their teens leave for college, cross things off their lifelong bucket lists, travel, and chase their dreams.

Many of my friends have asked me if Young Living is a prosperity gospel or a get-rich-quick scheme. No, it's not. If you think it's a get-rich-scheme, you're making the assumption that a Young Living business is handed to you. Let me tell you, new business builder, you will work and you will work hard! If anyone tells you otherwise, you're being fed a lie. There is no outstretching of your hands and waiting for the cash to fall from the sky. Sometimes it's difficult. People won't come to your classes. Leaders will drive you batty. But my worst day in Young Living has been better than my best day at 40 other jobs I've held.

Are you willing to stick it out and see where it goes? Do you have the tenacity to pull this off? If you look at that Young Living Income Disclosure chart—and truly believe where it goes—isn't it worth the push to keep going? Heck, I would work at a Dollar Store for 10 years if I knew I could make $30,000 a month eventually! That's what this is. No other job I've ever worked has had a chart like that. It's raw truth. Those are the stats. That's where people land when they push through the tough times with Young Living—the months where sales are down. The times when people said no to Essential Rewards. But for every no, it means you were out there working, you were doing it, and there are yes's on the horizon. Stick it out and create your dream! Keep fighting and never give up. Some will make it to Diamond in two years, and some in twenty years. But Diamond is Diamond. And it's worth every no, every no-show, and every dissident leader. Don't give up too soon! Be so busy teaching classes that you don't have time to notice the no's.

So many people are afraid of abundance. I scratch my head on that one! When the Lord gives you more, it means you are able to give more. It means you've been trusted with wealth. Some of God's favorite people were wealthy: David, Solomon, Abraham, and Job. Wealth is a blessing that gives you time, peace of mind, resources, and the ability to love more generously on others. And if we fear it, that's not of the Lord. He's the one that owns the cattle on a thousand hills; my Lord is the creator of wealth. And He loves to love on His children. You just have to accept His gift and be willing to roll up your sleeves in obedience when He calls on you to act. I am really enjoying this season of giving when I see a need, and knowing I'll still be able to put dinner on my table that night. There is something beautiful in coming beside someone hurting or in financial pain and making a difference, even anonymously. That is waiting for you with this business: the ability to silently bless.

You Can't Free Others When You're in Bondage

God wants abundance for His people. How are you supposed to take care of the widows, the sick, and the poor when you have a blown head gasket on your car, $100 in your account, and are short for your electric bill this month?

We love Dave Ramsey's financial advice and have taken Financial Peace University. He says to save $1000, make a list of all your debts from the smallest to largest, and start paying them off, beginning with the smallest debt first. We had done that so many times. But the reality is that when you and your husband are working four minimum wage, full-time jobs just to make ends meet, you just don't have the income to pull it off. We'd save that thousand, then blow the transmission in our car. We'd save it again, then the water heater would go out in our home. We found that we could never, ever get ahead, and that's how we lived for nearly two decades. Save it, lose it. Save it, lose it. How can you help others when you are in that place?

You can't serve when you can't even stand.

That is why we are here—to serve. You can't serve when you can't even stand. John and I were technically middle class, but we were drowning. We are not drowning any more, and we will never drown again. We live by Dave Ramsey now and can actually do his debt reduction strategy, because the crisis period in our lives has ended. Even as a middle class family in the richest nation on earth, we could not breathe with our regular jobs. You'll hear me say it so many times in this book: Young Living is a way out. The Lord has sent you a boat. Get on it and get off that island where you're financially stranded.

It's Not About Fame and Fortune

As a radio anchor I've had my name in millions of homes, so I know what it's like to be famous. I've had my name and face on many a banner and billboard. As a Platinum in Young Living I've received recognition, been on stage, and traveled the world. But I'll tell you—freedom is better than being famous. Why? Because I can be home with my kids. I have time to take care of my husband and take care of my body. I have the ability to run with my teenagers in the woods in the morning and stay up late watching their soccer games and talking into the night about their relationships and their faith, without having to rise at 3 a.m. to anchor news. I have the ability to wake up and have a candlelight breakfast with my husband and do devotions without interruption. I have the ability to give, and that drives me. I have the ability to see others set free—especially struggling families. Those are my "why's".

Money doesn't drive me. Freedom does.

Let me tell you how I found my "why". I fell in love with oils the first week I got my kit and saw them work. My primary focus in starting to teach was selfish. I just wanted to get them into my home and use them on my own children and husband. I had no other reason. But when I saw them work, I started wanting my friends and family to have them, too, so I taught. My husband said if I wanted every oil in the catalog, the only way that was going to happen was if I was out teaching. So I taught some more. And pretty soon, my "why"—my purpose for sharing the oils—was to see the stories of people who had used them successfully. It was incredible! I was on a high, having a front row seat to see the Lord work right in front of me. But honestly, that's not why I do it now.

Sharing Freedom

Now I share Young Living to break the cycle of poverty where I see so many families living. How can you do what you were called and created to do when you're constantly in survival mode? You can't. And that is where the business comes in. That little ripple in the pond of my oils business became a tsunami throughout New York and Pennsylvania, and I started seeing something I didn't expect to see as I got out there and taught. People weren't just experiencing wellness—they were becoming financially free!

First it was a mom on my team, able to stop working and stay home with her children.

Then my own mom's check surpassed her full time job.

Then a Silver on my team, married to a legally blind husband, was able to quit her $10/hour desk job that she'd had at different offices for 15 years.

Then my own sister, who had worked three jobs for 20 years, retired from one job, then two, then a month before her wedding, retired from her third and final job.

One by one, people were seeing freedom. At the beginning, it was just a few people sharing the oils. Then in 18 months, we had 800 leaders. One in every five people on my team were sharing. Most were just getting their oils for free, but many were able to make game-changer decisions with their life: retire themselves, retire their spouse, or pay off copious amounts of debt.

At the time of publishing this book, dozens of leaders on our team have either cut back or fully retired from their jobs. Those families have been forever changed because of a news-anchor homeschooling mom of five freak who was exhausted, living in a rural area, and thought she couldn't make a difference for anyone.

Raising Diamonds

Now, my "why" is to raise as many Diamonds as I can. If you are on my team, that's a blessing, because you may be a close friend or a family member and I have the honor of getting to watch amazing things happen in your life. But if you are not on my team, that's part of my purpose too. You matter. It's because Young Living isn't just about me or my family. I got outside that circle with my very first class. It's about abundance, wellness, and purpose.

Abundance means you're financially free *and* have the time economy to do the things the Lord has called and created you to do. How do you do that when you are tied down at a 40-hour/week job and have nothing in the bank? That's not freedom. That's slavery. I am no longer a slave!

Wellness means you are educated on the product and living a life where you make conscious choices to take care of yourself.

Purpose means you take that healthy self of yours and pour into the people around you with the same passion that was poured into you. Keep the spark going. Show others how to be free. You are a hope-bringer. You are a path-changer. And you were born for Diamond.

My goal with Gameplan is to show you how to get your own freedom. I'm here to train you how to start that ripple in your pond, and then how to fight for it. I want to see as many Diamonds packed onto that Young Living stage as possible.

IT'S TIME TO START

Remember the Income Disclosure Chart earlier in this chapter? John and I are Platinums on that chart! Crazy, huh?? And it happened in 17 months. This is doable. You just have to understand the strategy of how to pull it off. And that's what this book is about. It's a meat and potatoes, get-from-point-A-to-point-B book.

Read it, re-read it, highlight it and make your own personal game plan by filling in the Gameplan workbook (which customizes this entire book for your team) and the Accountability Worksheet in the appendix of this book. Read Gameplan once a year to regroup. Read it again if you plateau. Order Gameplan books (at oilabilityteam.com) for your leaders and get them on the same page. Use the scripts in the back to rock this thing. This is your guide book. This will fill your head with ideas and you will see network marketing from a different, doable perspective.

That's what this book is—thousands of hours of study, trial and error in our own business and fool proof tips that work, all in an easy-to-understand format. You'll find tips on how to fill classes, how to do this if you're shy, how to find new friend circles, how to do follow up, and how to raise leaders. And all of it is in one simple place. You don't need 10 books to learn how to start this trade. Just one. This one.

A Young Living business is a mathematical certainty because the oils work

---

A Young Living business is a mathematical certainty because the oils work. The only thing that is uncertain is your commitment and dedication to see it through. The neat thing is that you are the one who controls commitment. You control your ability to dig out. So share the oils with people! A few will get a kit. Share again. A few more will get a kit. Share again the same month and follow up with the first few you talked with, and you'll have more people on your team and even a few who will share the oils with others. It grows and grows. Hold onto your hat, mentally prepare yourself for the abundance that's coming, and brace yourself for what's ahead!

You were made to be free. So call it out, speak life over yourself, and run! It's time to move. The place you are now is not giving you the results you're looking for. Your bucket list will remain unchanged in five years if you don't regroup, refocus, and make a gameplan. You are the only one with the power to alter the outcome.

This is your year to get your game on.

CHAPTER 2

SARAH'S STORY

So what does it take to rock a Young Living business? Do you have to already be successful in sales, have a huge circle of influence, or a background in natural health? I hope not, 'cause I don't have any of those.

You simply need a strong enough why.

For you to see the power of a personal why, you need to hear my story. To see why I'm so passionate about leading others to wellness and financial freedom, you have to understand a bit about where I came from. And maybe as you read you will begin to see that your past does not have to define you, but can be the fuel that drives you to succeed in this business.

A Rough Start

I grew up in suburban Chicago in a townhouse in a poor family. My father was an alcoholic and car mechanic, and my mother pretty much raised my three siblings and me single-handedly. My dad has been in more DUI crashes then I can count, is a convicted felon, and has lost his driver's license for life. The abuse was hard. I was the oldest of four children, and when the yelling got bad, I'd take my siblings into my bedroom and we'd have Amy Grant concerts, singing into a plastic ice cream cone as a microphone and cranking up the music so we could not hear. Many times I remember my mom waking us up, putting us in the car, and driving away—and I wasn't sure if I'd see my dad again. Once, when I was in 4th grade, we stayed away for a full six months, living with my grandparents and aunt, and I had to enroll in a different school. But we always returned.

The neighborhood we lived in wasn't the greatest, either. I remember coming home from school one day on the bus and there was a drug raid going on in a home in our subdivision. Our bus had to sit there for 45 minutes as a helicopter flew overhead and SWAT teams entered that house. Our subdivision was the drug trading ground for two gang communities on either side of us.

I became engaged to my husband John when I was 16 years old, and we were married three years later. For the first 10 years of our marriage, we had babies every two years, while holding down four minimum wage jobs and full-time college courses. We lived off student loans, racking up $70,000 in debt.

The first year we were married, John worked eight hours a day for minimum wage at a gas station. He also worked another full-time job at a competing gas station across the street eight hours a night on the overnight shift. He'd leave for one shift at 7 a.m., work till 5 p.m., come home and sleep four hours, and then go work another 8 hour shift overnight. Then he would repeat it.

I typed addresses eight hours a day for a book publishing company (it's still the least favorite job I've ever had) and worked part time for a Christian bookstore at night. I had a 21-hour course load in college as night classes, and was pregnant with our first son. That was our first year of marriage.

Below the Poverty Line

Just about every month, we got an eviction notice. Even with four jobs, we could not maintain our rental, so we hunkered down and moved in with my parents for three years. Then we lived in government housing in Dixon, Illinois, and then in government housing in DeKalb, Illinois.

We were on public aid for everything: our medical card, LIHEAP heating assistance, the LINK food card, three food pantries, WIC food, government housing assistance, gas cards through our church for gas, and even with four jobs, were still getting disconnect notices. When you make $5/hour, it's really hard to make an $800/month rent. If anything, we knew it wasn't a handout. We physically could not take on more than four jobs between us. For a 12-year period we lived in extreme poverty, balancing full time college coursework with multiple jobs, toddlers, and nursing.

During that time, I had 11 different jobs in the world of food service, until I caused the evacuation of a restaurant after setting a microwave on fire. *Twice.* (Food was not my niche!) Amidst all of that, I was prompted by a friend to apply for a job at a local radio station. I was hired there to work every other Saturday for three hour shifts, at $4/hour. My first month's check was $21 after taxes. (I kept my day job!)

John and I adjusted to poverty, even while I was entering the world of radio. At the first government housing projects where we lived in Dixon, there were "water bugs" (cockroaches) crawling on the floors. We had almost no furniture, and the kids slept on mattresses on the floor because we could not afford beds for them.

Feasting From the Food Pantry

We went through the transmissions in four used cars in six months. We'd go a few days with no food in the house, digging for a quarter to get a loaf of bread so the kids could eat, while John and I went hungry. We'd literally not have a morsel of food in the house, because when you have to choose between food or gas in your car to get to work, you pick the gasoline. I remember running out of meat for two weeks, waiting for the next food pantry to open. When I arrived, they were out of meat also, but had plenty of chocolate pudding. So we ate chocolate pudding for a couple of days until our next food card went through.

We lived from food pantry to food pantry. We had more eviction notices and utility disconnect warnings then I can count, but the Lord always came through. A check from a relative would come within hours of our power being shut off. We'd use birthday card money to stave off eviction. After a few years of college and a few years in radio at a tiny station in a trailer in a corn field, I was offered a job in downtown Chicago anchoring news for an all-news station. It had an audience of seven million people. I thought I had arrived! My check was $35,000 a year!

What I didn't count on was that taxes, gas to drive 72 miles one-way into work each day, tolls, and parking in Chicago would take half my paycheck, and our family of seven would be living off $16,000 a year, and still on food stamps. I was on the air with personalities who were making millions of dollars a year, and we didn't have enough food for our children.

We had done it right. John worked full time and put me through college. I worked full time and put him through college. We both graduated with honors and took white collar jobs and started repaying $70,000 in student loans. We had followed the system, and we were drowning. It's been 12 years since I graduated college, and I still owe $18,000 dollars on my student loan, and my oldest son has already started college himself. This is the American life??! This is living the dream??

Weary worker, I know you have been there. Many of your stories are even harder than ours. That's why you *have* to take this seriously. You don't need to work this hard.

Dream Job

After John and I graduated, I was offered a position with a Christian radio network in upstate New York.

It was a wonderful ministry, but it meant leaving everything we knew behind: our family, our friends, our church, and the doctors who had delivered our babies. It was crazy hard. But there was the possibility of work for my husband, who had looked for a job for 15 months in Chicago without a single serious offer. And I had prayed for 11 years to work in Christian radio on morning drive so I could be home during the day to homeschool my kids. This was my dream job.

I remember a few nights before Christmas, days before the move from Chicago to upstate New York, I'd tossed my name into a lottery with the Salvation Army. We hadn't had a paycheck in six weeks—and had borrowed from the station for the move. Food was scarce. Christmas wasn't even on the radar. We had just a few dollars in our bank account. That morning, I got a call that our family's name had been chosen in a lottery, and I was to come in and pick out new gifts for our kids.

I walked into that high school gym and saw all the things people had donated—brand new gifts—piled high three-quarters of the way up the gym wall. I was allowed to pick out a new jacket, boots, hats, and gloves, a board game, and three presents for each child. I walked out with three 44-gallon garbage bags of the best toys my kids had ever owned and a turkey for Christmas dinner.

I sat in my car with all those new gifts in the backseat and lost it. Twelve years of poverty caught up with me. I wept harder then I'd ever had—tears of joy at the gifts of strangers, and how they'd made our Christmas that year, and tears of fear—that I didn't know how long our money famine was going to continue. We worked so hard, yet there we were, with $70,000 in student loans, a car payment, a van payment, credit cards, and absolutely nothing to show for it at the end of the day but an empty stomach, five little blue-eyed faces trusting us to take care of them, and a government-subsidized townhouse. I was so overwhelmed.

Praying Like Moses

That was when I prayed a prayer I'll never forget. I took several minutes and thanked God for every single gift in that car, for the turkey on my front seat, and for all that He had provided. We always had just enough. And we made it because of Him and Him alone. I thanked Him for how He loved us. But then I got bold, and I asked for something more. I asked to be totally rich—beyond my wildest dreams. I asked to make more than I could spend. I prayed for the Moses blessing. Moses waited for 40 days on that mountain to see God, and when He appeared, His glory was so great that Moses was face down on the ground. He never even got to see Him. I asked for the blessing to be so great, we couldn't even use it all or see the swath of what the Lord had given.

It wasn't because John and I wanted to own our own jet or mansion—it was because every single person we knew lived just like us. There was no way out. There was no hope. And for 12 years of our marriage, all we'd done was take from people out of desperation. I was asking the Lord to be the giver. I wanted to be able to give as much as people had given to me, and I couldn't do that when we barely had food. I wanted to live on 10% of my income and give the rest of it away.

Seven years later, God answered that prayer. For my 36th birthday in 2014, a Young Living premium starter kit showed up on my door. This is the box that started it all!

A New Adventure

My husband told me if I wanted to get oils every month, I'd have to teach a class and have a few people sign up under me. So without any strategy and without any sales background, I started teaching oils classes. I grabbed a bunch of aromatherapy encyclopedias and from them wrote a little three-page 101 script chronicling all the things I'd love to know about oils: the who, what, when, where, why and how of oils. Then I gathered a few friends to the couch in my living room and read it. I have given that script 206 times all over the country now—it is the number one reason we hold the rank we hold. (The script is in the appendix of this book!)

But for my first class, on July 18th 2014, I was completely terrified. I'd done radio for nearly two decades, but that meant staring at a wall six hours a day in a room all by myself. I never had to look at the people I was talking to, so this was a whole new ball game! Gone were the days of wearing pajamas to work and anchoring news barefoot. (People looked at me quite strangely when I tried to pull that off in an oils class!) If you had seen my knees knocking, you would have thought it was comical with my work background. (So don't beat yourself up if you have butterflies! Even famous people that talk to millions of people get butterflies! You're not human if you don't have a little fear!) How did I get through it? I doused myself in Valor oil (Stress Away works, too!), prayed a lot, and just read the script.

After I taught my first class, three people signed up. I was in total shock. I didn't think anyone would listen to a word I had to say! Three others who couldn't make it for the class met me for lunch, and by the end of the month I was off and running—I had a team of six and was a Young Living Star. My goal that month was to make $50 so I could get on Essential Rewards and get my oils for free. But my first paycheck was enough to pay my husband back for the starter kit, get on Essential Rewards, and still have nearly half my check to invest in the business!

I realized pretty fast that I wasn't going to be able to teach during the week, because I was still anchoring news at 4 a.m. every day. A 7 p.m. class was impossible for me because that was my bedtime, so I committed to Friday night and Saturday classes, four classes a month. I'd teach a Friday night and a Saturday morning, then take the next weekend off. In August, I taught four classes total. That was a commitment of 8 hours a month. I did another two hours of follow-up calls to people. That month, my check was enough for my mortgage payment—and my oils!

Eight weeks into my business, I made Executive. Eighteen days after Executive, I made Silver. In 12 weeks, I had surpassed 16 years of anchoring income by working fewer than a quarter of the hours. Five months later I was Gold. Eight months after that, Platinum! How? By slow, steady classes and a commitment to treat this business as a business, not a hobby.

Retired From Radio

In January, my husband asked me when I was going to start taking the business seriously, and I told him, "I don't know, Harnisch. You told me to teach oils classes to get my oils for free, so I'm teaching classes, just like you told me!"

But my soft-spoken, gentle-spirited husband replied with, "Are you paying attention? You are making more and working less! I know how much you love it, but it's time to let go of your anchoring job." It took me nine months to get up the courage to step off full time radio. (I still fill in, just because I *love* radio so much.) But almost exactly a year after I started Young Living, I was able to retire with no previous network marketing experience. I took a photo of my face the last day I anchored full time and a photo of my face three weeks later—with eight hours of sleep each night. I look like a totally different person!

Less stress, more family time, better balance in my mommy life.

Please understand, never will I take my years anchoring news for granted. Never do I take the generosity of the radio ministry for granted, or their graciousness in allowing me to step off morning drive and yet still fill in. Never will I take any job for granted, really—no matter where the Lord leads me. But to have such a large prayer answered—I have no answer for that, save the grace of God.

I have learned so much in that first year. I made a lot of mistakes. I've been discouraged, and I've been blown away. I've grown and been stretched and have been loved and hated. I'm starting to learn what matters and what to let go. I've picked up pieces and put them together again and then dropped it all on the floor once more. And I have ten thousand mistakes and ten thousand victories ahead of me. This book would have saved me over and over and over again, had it been written. This is my game plan. This is how I ranked.

I know that each person is different and has different gifts and talents. I know my road may not be your road, that my pace may not be your pace, and my tactics may not work for you. But I also know there are tools in this book that will save you a lot of time. There are resources here that took me quite a while to find, and if I couldn't find them, I wrote them. If I can save you time, you may have a shorter path to Diamond than I. One of my life goals is to help every person I possibly can to become financially free. When you are financially free, you have time economy and wealth to invest in the lives of those around you. The best way I can help other people to avoid the life I had is to give them the tools to stand.

Read, be blessed, pass this book on, and teach others what you have learned. Don't let the secrets of this book sit on a shelf. Share it. Hand it off to a budding leader. Hand it off to a leader who needs inspiration, a leader who is frustrated, stuck, desperate, or who needs a way out. One of the things that makes Young Living so wonderful is that it's about helping other people. You thrive when your leaders soar. I have had so many people ask me who this book was written for. It's not just for my team or my friends' teams. It's not even just for those in Young Living. It's for anyone who has a dream and wants to see that their dream is possible. Any team, any person, any dream, anywhere.

So take this book and fly!

I just wanted to tell you, I'm sitting outside in the sunlight reading the Gameplan book. I just read the first two chapters and started crying. I'm sitting outside because my electric was just shut off. I was doing a great job for years putting on a front to everyone that everything is just great. Lately I've been just too exhausted to keep up the front. My husband is permanently disabled and many days can't get out of bed, therefore needs someone here pretty much 24/7. He has been falling a lot lately and has fewer and fewer good days where he can actually walk with his walker. It's sad, but everything comes down to money. He'd have a better life, my four kids would have a better life and I would as well. Anyway, as I'm reading your story I just lost it and cried. Just knowing I'm not the only one who has gone through this, that I'm not a bad mom even though my kids don't have everything they need, that I'm not a bad person. Reading this has given me so much hope, a light at the end of the tunnel. If I work for it, it WILL pay off. Not in 20 years, but now. So I just wanted to thank you, thank you for sharing your story. Now on to chapter 3! I need to learn the right way, most effective and efficient way to work this business! Thank you, again.

Nancy

CHAPTER 3

A YOUNG LIVING QUICK-START TRAINING GUIDE

I told you earlier that the number one question I'm asked is "Why do a Young Living business?" If that's the most common question, the second thing I hear is, "how?"

This is going to be the quickest training you've ever seen! It's just two steps.

1) Photocopy the 101 Script out of the Gameplan Appendix. Read it a few times.

2) Open your calendar, schedule a class, get a few people to your couch, and read the 101 Script.

You are off and running! Book over! (Just kidding!) If you like, we can add a third step: "rinse and repeat."

It's the repeat that will get you to Diamond. So it's simple, but it will require diligence. Let's dig deeper into what that day-to-day diligence looks like.

RINSE AND REPEAT

I tell my business builders if you do the above steps 4-6 times a month, that's generally enough volume to reach the rank of Silver in six months, depending on your class size. If your classes last two hours with setup and tear-down, that's a commitment of 12 hours a month. A Silver income is usually $2000 to $3000 a month. Fewer than 3 hours of work a week for that check is not a bad deal! If you can commit 40 hours a week—160 hours a month—to a job that will not give you freedom, surely you can commit 12 hours a month to a weekly 2-hour class and follow up, for a business that will grow and set you up for retirement.

At the beginning, it's tough. You're pushing a snowball up a hill, you're launching your team, and you're going to have to run your Young Living business alongside your life. You'll have to wiggle it in where it best fits. For me, that meant no weeknight classes, because my job had me up at 3 a.m. to prep for the start of that 4 a.m. shift. But as your check grows, you can start kicking a few things off your plate.

A year into my Young Living journey, one of the things I could let go of was my full time job. There are people on my team who drop second jobs and third jobs. Some add services to save time. For example, one woman on my team added a cleaning service at $25 a week. Some have used the extra income to have organic food delivered twice a week through a service so they can answer emails instead of cook. Others have paid mommy helpers $20 a week so they have time carved out for their business.

Ultimately, any choice creates more space for Young Living. Once you reach Silver, that snowball is starting to roll down the hill on its own. It means more time to step away, to be with your family, train leaders, rest, and regroup.

I now limit myself to three classes a month and a leadership training every Tuesday night online. That's six hours of work, plus a couple hours a week of follow up and answering emails. It's pretty sweet for a Platinum income! Admittedly I work harder during Oil Ability retreats, boot camps, or when I'm doing things like writing a Gameplan book, but those are short, rare bursts of work. My average workweek now is about 10-15 hours. My average anchoring week was closer to 40, with 60-hour spikes, starting at 4 a.m. I believe I got the better deal with Young Living.

KNOW YOUR WHY

The critical thing to nail down as you begin is your "why". In layman's terms, you have to know why it is that you're doing this. Sit down and think through your reasons. If it's to replace an entire income, you should be teaching 4-6 classes a month. If it's to get your oils for free or double your grocery budget or go on a vacation, one class a month would be enough. If you treat this business as a business, you'll get paid as a business. If you treat it as a hobby, you'll get paid as a hobby. Make a commitment, set your hours, and run for it! Then watch it grow. A word of caution: it grows *fast.*

If you treat this business as a business, you'll get paid as a business.

Here's your action step for this chapter: sit down, grab a sheet of paper, and write out why you want this. If you're crafty, clip a few photos out of some magazines and make a photo collage vision board to show where you want to end up. (It sounds like a waste of time, but it truly does work! It's about keeping tangible goals front and center, every single day.) You can even run to a Walmart or Michaels or Hobby Lobby and pick up a canvas board to glue your pictures on, but it doesn't have to be fancy.

I'd encourage you to put specific, tangible goals on the board, goals for your OGV, for your rank, and for your paycheck. Don't just cut out photos—pick words of life that you want spoken over your business, and add them to the board, too.

Put your vision board in a place where you'll see it, like a bathroom or bedroom wall. Pray over it. Revisit it a few months into your business and see if your why has changed.

As I shared in Chapter One, my first why was simply to afford oils. Then it became paying off debt. Then my goal was to get my kids on the Global Leadership Cruise to Venice. Since all of those things have happened (the things I put on that board *always* seem to happen!) now, my vision board is to see all of my friends become financially free. Our vision board keeps changing because we keep reaching the goals!

Gameplan

You will meet your goals if you see them every day and every day work toward your goal. There is power in the spoken word. It changes the direction of your feet and your mind when you deliberately speak life over yourself out loud.

PART TWO

MAKING YOUR FIRST
CLASS SUCCESSFUL

I have never sold anything in my life before. Never had the desire to do so until Young Living Essential Oils changed my life. I didn't know where to start, didn't understand the ways of MLMs, and didn't understand how to navigate through the YL website very well. Gameplan was a lifesaver! While continuing to work my full-time employment, I started selling YL in June of this year.. From June 2016 I have gone from 3 members, no one on Essential Rewards, no legs and $800 in sales to 16 members, 5 on essential Rewards, $2000 in anticipated sales, and two legs——all with the help of Gameplan!

Angie Rogers

*Being a little bit on the quieter side, the scripts in Gameplan helped me sell four kits at my **first** party! Thank you Sarah!*

Dawn Courtney

Having "Gameplan" in my hands is like having a leader from my upline right there with me! From determining my next move, class prep, great class scripts to a powerful close… BOOM! It's all in your book—and so much more! Thank you for sharing a solid, concise business plan-of-action to take us from starter kit to success!

Joy Cooke

CHAPTER 4

AVOIDING PITFALLS:
THE SIX MISTAKES EVERY STAGNANT
BUSINESS MAKER MAKES

Why are we talking about mistakes before we've hardly started? Because if I point them out, you can avoid these pitfalls from the very beginning of your business.

In the first 18 months I launched my business and hand-trained about 800 business builders. Some are now Gold rank and beyond. Many are Silvers. Many more are Executives and Senior Stars. When you train that many people, a pattern starts to form. Every time one of my business builders is stagnant, they fall into one of these six categories:

1) They don't have a strong close to wrap up their lecture. "Tell me how to buy Young Living!" This book is full of training and scripts to help you share the oils with confidence and have a strong close.

2) They keep tapping into the same friend circles. I tell you how to avoid this mistake in Chapter Eight.

3) They don't market enough, or give enough lead time before a class. Again, Chapter Eight has your answers with a complete plan for marketing your classes.

4) They don't have a system for following up with people who came to class or bought a kit. Check out Chapter Ten for all the tools you need.

5) They don't treat their business as a business. They vision cast, read leadership books, and go to events, but never get out and actually teach.

You can't grow a business without teaching in some form, even if it's handing out CD's or DVD's. Step outside your comfort zone. (See Chapter Five to decide how to teach that first class!)

The Lemondroppers, a powerful group of Young Living distributors, call this "hustle." I met Lindsay Moreno on the YL Global Leadership Cruise to Venice in 2014 and was blown away by her strength in getting her Lemondropper leaders moving using hustle. In fact, you can learn hustle from just about any YL distributor who is Silver or above; they all have a story.

Two of my favorites are Royal Crown Diamonds Christa Smith and Adam Green. Christa has 15 children and works one day a week, while Adam, at age 24, became the youngest Royal Crown Diamond in Young Living history! Watch the greats, then copy.

6) They get distracted. This one is so important that I wrote a whole chapter on it at the end of this book. Check out Chapter 23. Distraction will kill your business.

Wake up every day with a list of three business goals and attack them. Don't bite off more than you can chew. Learn to gently say no to things that rob your time. Commit time to your business every day, even if it's an hour. And don't pour into things that don't grow your business.

What is distraction? Making a store instead of raising leaders. Attending tons of leadership training but never actually holding classes. Going for an aromatherapy certification. Getting on Facebook to connect with your team and then wasting time instead, scrolling. Doing crossline classes but never growing your own legs. Those are distractions, and I have done them all! Are the things you're doing actually pouring into your business or pulling from it? How do you spend your time? Is it productive?

Make a list of what you need to do to get to the next rank, and then do it and nothing else.

If you can learn the six things listed above (and this book will walk you through each of these mistakes), you can have a flourishing business.

Now don't get me wrong—this list isn't about when you have to take a break. If you have a major family emergency, you are living through a crisis. It has nothing to do with weak follow up. Just as you would at a regular job, you take time off. In the same breath, I'll tell you that if you don't go to work every week at your 40-hour-a-week job, you get no paycheck. When the crisis ends, return to your Young Living business. How can you grow a paycheck without working your business? Don't wait for it to come to you. Fight for it!

But for people who are actively holding classes and yet not seeing growth, it's 100% of the time one of the six items above. So identify your weakness and follow the plan to avoid those pitfalls!

CHAPTER 5

OVERCOMING EXCUSES AND FINDING YOUR NICHE

I cannot tell you how many times people come up to me and make one or more of the following excuses:

"I don't know any people."

"I live in a rural area."

"I am not a news anchor."

"I don't have the influence you have." "

"I don't have the time you have."

"I don't have the money to start a business."

"I can't stand in front of people."

"I have children and no babysitter."

"I work too many hours."

"I don't want anyone in my house."

"I don't like to sell stuff."

Yes, I pulled out my inner momma bear and I used the word "excuses". Because that's exactly what those are. When you want something, you find a way around the mountain without complaint. You find someone who did it before you and learn from them. If their way doesn't work for you, find another person with a way that does. You fight for it. And you dig out of where you are.

Let's tackle these challenges head on.

LOCATION

My strongest teams live in extremely rural areas with limited resources. My Eldred, PA team regularly draws 100 person crowds for classes, but you have to drive 12 miles from the highway to get a cell signal in Eldred. It's in the middle of the Alleghany forest, that runs half the length of western Pennsylvania.

On the opposite end of the coin, I regularly hear that people can't hold classes in a certain town because of "saturation." Saturation??? That's what happens when you put too much butter on your popcorn. It's not a concept that affects your Young Living business. I've been told that they can't teach in a certain area because too many people in that town are holding classes.

One woman, who lives in a town of 12,000, gave me the same story. I told her there are 3000 people on my team, and that as soon as we cross 12,000 and every member on my team was from that town, then it's officially saturated. The issue is tapping into new friend circles, not market saturation. We'll attack that in a later chapter.

I also have had quite a few people tell me they really don't want anyone in their home. That's fine. Either find a free location within 20 minutes or so (libraries, fire halls, community centers, churches)—or ask a friend to loan you their living room. If you want this, you will find creative ways to make it work. One woman on our team even used the local state park's picnic pavilions for six months when it was warm enough, until she had found a better location.

MONEY

There's no overhead with Young Living, save a starter kit. It's the cheapest business on the planet to start! Franchises cost about $200,000 to $500,000 per store. Not Young Living. There's no store front, no rent to pay, no employees to pay, no insurance, no utilities—the oils literally go straight from the Young Living farms and warehouses to people's homes. There's just you, your starter kit, and your 101 Script. That's all this takes.

I'll be honest with you: it took me about five weeks to save for my kit. A bunch of times I kept asking myself why I was putting cash into a box for oils instead of getting some more food for the house or taking my van in to figure out what the knocking sound was. I'll tell you now that Young Living was the best financial decision I've made in my life! I wish I'd made it when I was 20 years old.

The investment of the kit is a fraction of what you'd pay to launch any other small business. I had one friend in a different multi-level marketing company that had to stock $5,000 of product in her home, then transport it from site to site for her classes. That's crazy! All the ordering is done through Young Living's site. You don't need to stock a thing for anyone else—just show up with your own personal kit. Your job is to get that kit in front of as many people as you can. No inventory required.

Do whatever it takes to get that starter kit in your hand—hold a yard sale, tuck $30 a week away out of groceries (that's what I did), pick up some babysitting or some extra house cleaning jobs—just pull it off. You'll be so glad you did.

INFLUENCE

Right now, this month, I have more than 800 active sellers who aren't news anchors, and they are doing just fine. They're all growing at their own pace. Some are Gold and some are Stars, but their rank doesn't matter much to me. The fact that they are out there running their business without being famous is what matters. Some of my top leaders are the most-soft spoken people on my team.

It's not fame that grows a business. It's rolling up your sleeves and holding classes! I don't know people, either. I moved from Chicago to rural upstate New York, and the largest population center in my town is the county jail. Again, it comes down to friend circles—not who you know. It's who your friends know. Our Oil Ability system for filling classes works (see Chapters Seven and Eight). Influence is not necessary. Tenacity is.

TIME

So many people come to me and tell me they want to do this. I hand train them and then four months go by and they've added two people. When I contact them and ask what's up, they tell me, "I just don't have the time." Seriously? Young Living is *your way out*. Look at all the things going on in your life right now that consume all you have. Young Living is time economy.

I tell people all the time when I train them that the Lord isn't going to bless you with more time if you aren't using the time you have now wisely. It's a gift. It's one of the greatest gifts, actually. If you're not a good steward of your time, you'll always need more time.

Look at your schedule, find two hours for a class each week, and make it happen. Cut other things out to make it fit. Bring your kids with you if you have to (my oldest four have taught 206 classes faithfully by my side!)

As your team and your income grow, you'll be able to re-evaluate other places where you can save yourself more time. Yes, it's a juggling act. This mom of five who was working 40 hours a week and homeschooling gets it. If you want out, you have to make your doorway and walk through it. No excuses.

Here's the deal: you can either start the business or not start the business. If you speak life into your business, you'll flourish and grow. If you speak death and talk of all the reasons you can't pull it off, you'll never get off the ground. Start each day by knowing where you're going and run for it. Make a plan. Then do it. No excuses. (In the same breath, don't over-plan. Jay Carter, my Diamond upline, makes a list of three business items each morning. When those three are done, he's done for the day. Make it manageable.)

"I DON'T WANT TO SELL STUFF"

This is the statement that irritates me the most. I've never sold a starter kit in my life! From day one, from the very first class in my living room, to today—when I speak to auditoriums of thousands of people, it's always been about education. I have a passion to help people live a chemical free life. Every oil they're using a chemical they're not using.

Let me share why chemical-free living means so much to me.

When I was 12 years old, I had my first migraine headache. It was debilitating. By age 22, I was having them monthly, and they lasted 10 days, and followed the bell curve of my cycle. With each child I had in my 20's, they got worse and worse. I worked with 13 neurologists and was on 16 families of migraine medicines over the space of twenty-four years. By age 32, the headaches were so crippling that I would lay in bed, grabbing my knees writhing in pain in a room of total darkness. I would get into cycles of vomiting and tremoring from the pain and would get dehydrated.

Most months, I went to the local emergency room for a migraine cocktail, a trio of three drugs given intravenously—a pain medicine, an anti-inflammatory and a drug to stop throwing up. They started doing yearly MRI's on me, and found that every time I had a migraine, the blood vessels on my head would swell and cause tiny, pin-prick brain bleeds. Each year, I had about 30-40 more spots of dead tissue on the surface of my brain. And every month, the right side of my face would droop and half my body would go numb until the migraine was gone.

The last neurologist I saw wanted me on six medications: all the ones listed above as well as a steroid and two medicines to counteract the side effects of the first four medications I'd be on. The steroid alone had two pages of warnings, most heart-related. I told the neurologist I felt like I was choosing between a heart attack and a stroke. He said "You are. But if it was me, I'd choose the heart attack. If you have a stroke, you'll watch your kids grow up but will never be able to communicate with them. That would be worse than just being gone." I remember driving away thinking, *"How dare you make that choice for me?"*

I took the medications home and lined them up on my counter. I was going to be on drugs every two hours for the rest of my life. John and I are not anti-pharmaceutical, and I have over 45 nurses on my oils team, but something about this specific situation just didn't sit right. I did not have peace.

So I started using what I knew about researching news and applied it to researching my own health. Was there anyone out there who had been cured of migraine headaches? I stumbled on a neurologist named Natasha Campbell-McBride. She had cured thousands of people in her office of neurological and digestive disorders simply by changing their diet and cutting all sugar, gluten, and dairy. Her website is called gapsdiet.com. I started her diet (which I'm convinced is the most masochistic thing on the earth) in January of 2013.

The first month, I still had the drooping in my face and the numbness on my right side. But I had no pain. I remember telling my husband "if this is as good as it gets—it's good enough for me! I don't remember what a life of no pain feels like!"

The second month I had no drooping, no weakness and no pain, and I'm proud to say that I've been completely migraine free for nearly four years. I have not taken a single medication since 2013, after over 20 years on meds. I did it solely by changing what I was eating.

The foods I'd been eating were loaded with processed garbage, hydrogenated oils, soy, nitrates, dyes, preservatives, synthetic, enriched vitamins and chemicals. Those ingredients, over time, punctured holes in my gut lining until my body couldn't function the way it was designed. For me, it metastasized as migraine headaches. For others, it's food allergies, IBS, Crone's Disease, unexplained inflammation or pain, or a host of other illnesses. What I was eating was literally killing me.

I'd love to say that oils had a hand in eradicating my migraines, but I was healed of them long before I got my starter kit. What it did do, though, was open my eyes to what's out there. Not everything that's in a store is safe. Not everything that has "FDA approval" is safe. If gluten, sugar, and dairy (we're talking a bowl of ice cream and a sandwich), could puncture holes in my gut lining, what about my bright blue chemical-laden dish soap that I wash my dishes with and then eat off of? What about the chemical cleaning supplies with ingredients I can't even begin to pronounce, that I wipe my butcher block with, in the name of sanitizing? Then I read the bottle and it says "Don't eat, poisonous, not for human consumption." Three days later, I am dicing strawberries and eating them right off the same butcher block that smells like chemical cleaner. We're oblivious. And we're poisoning ourselves.

This is why it's so critical that you take oils seriously, and you share them with every person that you meet. Start the swap from chemical cleaning supplies first if you're not sure where to begin. Young Living's Thieves cleaner alone replaced every cleaner under my kitchen sink—and it's made of plants! There's no yuck!

I am passionate about oils because I have lived through the other side of slowly poisoning myself and my family. And I will do everything I can, even teach a million classes, if it saves one family from what I have gone through. For me, it's all about education—it's never been about sales. I'm bold and tell them where I started my journey and I have no fear of walking them through ordering a Young Living starter kit. There's passion behind the purpose: it's to save them. This is serious. And there is a haste to it, because with each passing day someone out there is getting hurt. You can't do what you were called and created to do if you have lost your health.

Always know the place where your student is coming from—the place you were when you first got your kit. Return to that place and walk them through so they see the dangers in their own home. This isn't about selling. It's absolutely always about education.

Now with those excuses out of the way, I'll give you one get-out-of-jail-free pass.

THE ONE LEGITIMATE EXCUSE

There is one legitimate excuse, and it's the "I can't stand in front of people" line. God made us all with unique talents. We're different. And that means we all have creative ways of sharing Young Living. If you would rather *die* than stand in front of a room full of people, let me encourage you with some of the stories from my team, and give you some creative ideas to help you find your unique way of sharing Young Living.

Myrna: grew her team to 10,000 OGV a month (a Silver in Six)—simply by mailing our Oil Ability 101 DVD to her friends and doing great follow up one-on-one. We now offer an audio CD of the 101 class that people can listen to in their cars. Here's a what Oil Ability leader Bethany says about the CD:

> "Sarah, I LOVE your CD's!!!! In my opinion, hands down, the best tool you've given us yet! I sold a kit today with one...I gave it to a lady at church and by the time I got home she had ordered her kit!!! People can listen in their car.... it's so easy to do!!"

(Pick the audio CD's up at oilabilityteam.com).

Robyn: runs her entire business by looking for people she can bless. Her focus is on those who need the income the most. She has never taught an in-person class, but every time I do a Teacher Training in her area, it's loaded with potential business builders. She has an eye for talent, and for those in need.

Stephanie: grows by putting the oils on people. She loves handing out samples and letting people see how the oils can support their systems. Her team cracked Star in a month using only this method. She is also a genius at seeing a need for people to have a good income and raises as many leaders as she does 101 classes. She is extremely gifted at edifying her leaders and recognition, and people will go the world for Stephanie because of her strong leadership.

Rachael: works three jobs and is new to the area. She held 11 classes and no one came to the last five classes. So she started meeting people one-on-one over lunch. Using that method only, she rose to a Senior Star. When I did our marketing training with her, she implemented it and had a class with eight people and a class with 20. She also raised up four new leaders in a week, and they are now off the ground with their own Young Living businesses. By August of 2016 she was able to retire from all three jobs! Rachael is now a strong Silver on her way to Gold!

Joel: just moved to North Carolina and he's a brand new first time dad. And he's young—just 21 years old. But he's determined to beat Adam Green (sorry, Adam!) and become the youngest Royal Crown Diamond in

Young Living history by age 24. He grows fast by putting up flyers in health food stores and bulk food stores and Salvation Army stores. He makes contacts with chiropractors to have places to teach across the area and markets to areas already clean-living driven, areas that will get excited about Young Living. He enrolled nine people his first month.

Theresa: does vendor events where she can talk to people one-on-one, because she's personable and loves sharing knowledge. Her goal is to help people understand how they can use the oils. She is education driven. She's also a very gifted writer and her blog has taken off on-line. She thrives on seeing others "get" concepts and then apply them to live a chemical-free lifestyle. But her greatest strength is leadership. She writes a weekly newsletter and connects with her team on the oils and oily products on Young Living's site. She raises leaders and builds intimate relationships with them. When I met her, she was living in a trailer with her family and had to make a choice between medicine for her non-verbal autistic son and club foot surgery for another son. She had no stove in her home. She is now a solid Silver with a powerful and dynamic team of leaders, en route to Gold, and she is planning for her husband's retirement. This was a total game changer for her family. Poverty: 0. Theresa's family: 1.

Sharon: is a genius at follow up. Though shy, she's incredible at hand-written notes and resources and spends hours at her desk each week putting something personable together for her team members. She mails out Oil Ability DVD's with hand written notes. Her OGV just cracked 30,000 and despite her quiet personality, she's on her way to Gold this year. She was married for 40 years to an abusive, alcoholic husband with multiple DUI's. After a year and a half in her Young Living business, Sharon is now financially free and dependent on him for nothing. Her Young Living check is now twice her pay at her full time job! She just purchased her own home after renting for more than eight years and trying to get on her feet.

Aaron: plays to his gifts. A natural salesman, with a decade and a half in sales but he had a hard time making the jump from a brick and mortar store to network marketing. Then he had an idea of Aaron's car kits, so he started there—marketing to the people in his work circle. His car kit included a premium starter kit, Thieves cleaner, a rag, and an orb diffuser—everything you need for a new vehicle. He plays to businesses, because he understands business. It took him a while to warm up to the oils and then to warm up to the business side. But his warm personality allowed him to start sharing the oils with his inner friend circle and then his circle of clients from his brick and mortar job. Now he is catapulting into the world of network marketing and is on his way. His heart's desire is to be home with his wife and two babies so they can enjoy more family time. His average time at the sales job was 12 hours daily and 16 hours during peak sales times like Black Friday. His Young Living "why" is freedom.

Angela: holds 101 classes, but her focus is on prayer and where God can use the money. She prays heavily and mightily over her business. She just made Silver in Six and donated her entire check to a cancer patient for treatment and to a family in poverty (and a few other charities!). When you keep Christ as the center of your business and lean on Him for every decision, He multiplies your efforts.

By the way... I used each person's real name (with permission). These are real people like you and me. They are all members of the Oil Ability team. Most have just started in the past six months, and they're thriving in Young Living.

Here's the trick: each person has a niche. Maybe it's teaching—either lecture style, in front of people, or by playing hostess and simply popping my 101 DVD in the T.V. and letting me teach for you. It could be in front of 1 or 10 or 50 people. Maybe it's strong follow up, with hand written cards and personalized letters and notes. Maybe it's vendor events or make-and-take classes. Maybe it's one on one's over lunch. Maybe it's online work—building your business through social media and blogging and video. Maybe it's a theme—you love animal aromatherapy or biblical aromatherapy or beauty school classes with full orchid facials with Young Living products.

Whatever your gift is, play to it. Delegate your weaknesses to others. But above all, pray and give your business to the Lord and keep Him as your center. Then watch it grow!

CHAPTER 6

YOUR GREATEST TOOL:
A DETAILED TOUR OF THE
YOUNG LIVING VIRTUAL OFFICE

This is the part of the book where we really start getting into the meat and potatoes. How do you actually run a Young Living business? By this point, you should have found the 101 notes at the end of this book (or at oilabilityteam.com) and picked a location and date for your first class. After you hold it and get past that fear of the unknown, read the next few chapters of this book. I will walk you through one entire cycle of a Young Living business: marketing, filling classes, holding classes, and follow up. By the time you're done, you'll be a pro!

This chapter is pretty neat, because Young Living has done a lot of the work for you online. You don't really need any costly business tools, because just about all of it is offered through the Virtual Office. This is where you track your online presence, your team, your rank, and more. All of it can be viewed online by going to www.youngliving.com, clicking on "Sign In," and using the username and password you set up when you got your starter kit. If you're not sure what those are, you can phone Young Living and they will send you new ones.

Once you have logged in, you'll be looking at your Dashboard, which looks something like this:

There are three tabs across the top. Those are Summary (which takes you back to the main page), Rank Qualification, and Getting Started. Then there are a bunch of buttons down the left side of the page. I'd really encourage you to spend an afternoon just exploring all the information and resources here! I'll give you a little explanation of each, but I'll go in depth on the two most important buttons—how to watch yourself, and how to watch your team. Let's start with the top tabs.

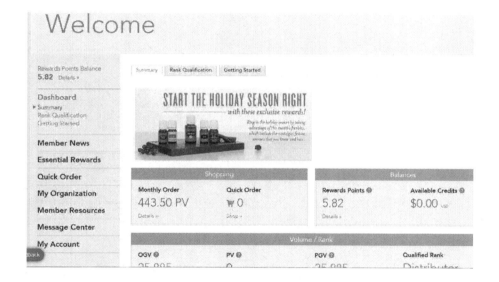

"GETTING STARTED"

The "Getting Started" tab is fantastic and gives you a series of short, 3-minute videos that tell you exactly who Young Living is and what we stand for. Watch them all. My favorite is the Seed to Seal page with videos on why Young Living is so different from other oils companies. It's what sets us apart.

"RANK QUALIFICATION"

Next click on Rank Qualification. This is the all important "How to Watch Yourself" button. It looks like this:

| Qualified Rank | Platinum |
| Volume | 794.06 PV   104,242.98 OGV   9,170.81 PGV |

Distributor	Star	Senior Star	Executive	Silver	Gold	Platinum ✓	Diamond
50 PV	100 PV	100 PV	100 PV	100 PV	100 PV	100 PV	100 PV
	500 OGV	2K OGV	4K OGV	10K OGV	35K OGV	100K OGV	250K OGV
		2 x 1K OGV Legs	2 x 4K OGV Legs	3 x 6K OGV Legs	4 x 8K OGV Legs	5 x 15K OGV Legs
				1,000 PGV	1,000 PGV	1,000 PGV	1,000 PGV
				29,026.19	17,373.06	9,170.81	6,052.76

If you look across the top, you'll see all the ranks you saw in the income disclosure guide at the front of this book. These are the ranks in Young Living: Distributor, Star, Senior Star, Executive, Silver, Gold, Platinum, Diamond, Crown Diamond, and Royal Crown Diamond.

Understanding How You Rank

There are four requirements to move up to the next rank. Two are crazy easy to get, and the other two require persistence and strategy.

Line 1: PV:

The first requirement is that you spend 100 PV once you rank. The good news is that you never need to spend more just because your check goes up—it stays at 100 PV all the way to Royal Crown Diamond.

(People ask me all the time why Young Living requires them to purchase 100 PV in product to get a paycheck. Honestly, I'm grateful for it. The products I've ordered have made me much more familiar with the company and what they offer. I could never talk knowledgeably about Pure Protein Complete if I hadn't had it in my glass of raw milk this morning. You can't talk about what you don't know. It also supports your team and your check. If all your leaders are spending 100 PV, it contributes greatly to the team volume.)

One word of caution: I have had people on my team place an order under 100PV, and are poised to lose their check at the end of the month. Make sure you're always checking your leaders the last week of the month to see if they have spent their 100PV so they get paid. Sometimes, it's just a lack of knowledge at what's required. Many leaders on your team will only sell one or two kits in their Young Living lifetime, and just don't know the rules. It's your job to do the PV scan at the end of the month and take care of your leaders. Shoot them a quick message and let them know their hard work won't be rewarded unless they meet the minimum requirements for their check: 100PV.

By the way, as a bonus for getting through this chapter, which is the most technically challenging in the book, I'll pause for a moment and give you a knockout smoothie recipe using Young Living's Pure Protein Complete Vanilla Spice powder. Best. Breakfast. Ever

SARAH'S FAVORITE MANGO CREAM SMOOTHIE:

In a Ninja, Vitamix or Blendtech blender, combine:

2 cups frozen fruit (I like mangoes best, but strawberries are good too)

2 cups ice

When mixed, add:

½ quart of Stoneyfield organic whole-milk French Vanilla yogurt (it has to be this brand, this flavor. Oh my word it's good. Don't ever buy low-fat anything—they replace the fat with chemicals.)

1 cup of raw honey (no corn syrup synthetic yuck)

2-4 ounces of Young Living's NingXia

3 scoops Young Living's Vanilla Pure Protein Complete

2 tablespoons pure vanilla

1 cup water or unseasoned bone broth until it's your desired thickness. I like my spoon to stand in this sucker!

1 pinch of Himalayan or Celtic sea salt for minerals (no iodized salt!)

If you're up for it, break up a little organic kale and toss it in. Blend it all until it's amazing goodness. Oh. My. Word. It's so much better then sugar-laden cereal. Even organic cereals can have about four days' worth of sugar. Eggs are great, but Pure Protein Complete has 25 grams of protein in it. That's like having steak, hamburgers, fish, eggs, chicken, and more steak for breakfast. Protein helps you think clearly and lose weight. It's a win-win.

Now go make yourself one so you can finish this chapter!!!

We were talking about the four lines in the Virtual office tab under "Rank Qualification." Once you understand this tab, you know how to rank. Now that you've eaten your power smoothie, you can take on the world. Here we go with Line 2!

Line 2: OGV

Organizational Group Volume. These are your purchases and the purchases of everyone under you. To rank as a Star, your OGV must be at least 500. A Senior Star must have an OGV of 2000; an Executive, an OGV of 4000, a Silver, 10,000. Every month, it resets to zero. At first, you will cry when the first of the month appears, but as you grow in rank, it starts getting really fun to watch it. I remember rolling my eyes when a Platinum in line in front of me at convention said he reached Gold by the third day of the month. Now we are there too, and it's awesome to see your leaders lead and be blessed financially. Your work raising them up blesses you and them!

Line 3: Legs

This is where the strategy comes in. This third requirement is all about legs. A "Leg" is one person with a bunch of people underneath them. To rank as an Executive, you need two, people under you, and each of their legs must have an OGV of 1000. The overall volume of your entire team—your purchase and everyone else's—must be at least 4000 OGV, but half of that must be under two people. Why? It sets the stage for you to grow long-term. You don't just make a big paycheck at the beginning and then lose it. You don't have to work 15 years to get a decent check. The growth is consistent as you build your team first deep and then wide. Young Living is a company with tenure. The average network marketing company fails within seven years, but Young Living has been around more than three times that length. With this business model, you are building a business legacy, one that will last far beyond your lifetime.

So what's the strategy to it? Start with two. Pick two business builders from the get-go and teach classes under them. These must be people who are committed to spending 100 PV a month to get a paycheck, and Lord willing, also to manage their own teams and host their own classes—so you don't end up with an entire leg you have to manage with no strong leader on it. Once you have your two and one is well trained, start your third leg. You should always be thinking two legs ahead. If you're a Star, be thinking as an Executive. If you're a Silver, be planning as a Platinum—with 4 legs. You never want to have your OGV and be caught without your legs.

Line 4: PGV

Personal Group Volume. PGV is how much of your OGV belongs to you–it comes from the people you sold kits to that have not ranked. When your leaders rank, they will break off into their own teams, and that volume will disappear from your PGV. But if you look closely, a Royal Crown Diamond has an OGV of 1.5 million dollars a month. Only 1000 of that must be from them as sponsor.

Sign everyone under you for the first two months, or eight classes. The goal is to reach 1000PGV in volume so you never have to worry about it again, all the way to Royal Crown Diamond. You need 1000PGV to hit Silver.

This one is easy to get–it happens organically if you are sharing the oils. If you have three or four people on Essential Rewards that are not building their own team, you'll always hit this. I qualify from people I signed from my first class over two years ago.

Overview of Rank Qualification

Is that all as clear as mud? Let me break it down one last time in uber simple terms:

Line 1: PV: spend 100 PV to get a paycheck.

Line 2: your OGV—organization group volume. Your purchase and the purchase of everyone under you.

Line 3: Legs. For Executive, 2 legs at 1000 each. For Silver, 2 legs at 4000 each. For Gold, 3 legs at 6000. For Platinum, 4 legs (people) at 8000 each. Got it?

Line 4: PGV. At least 1000 of your entire volume must be from you. You can't get carried along in the system from someone else's work.

Honestly, I check the rank qualification page at least once a day. If you scroll under the green chart, you'll see all the perks you get for that rank. Below that, it breaks down your OGV. I love that because it tells you exactly how much more is sitting in people's carts, so you can see if you're close to hitting the next rank.

2 ORGANIZATION VOLUME 250,000 OGV

56,371.83 OGV completed orders

37,184.75 OGV pending auto-ship orders

Need additional **156,443.42** OGV to reach 250,000 OGV

Below that, it breaks down your legs so you can see how much you have to go on each leg.

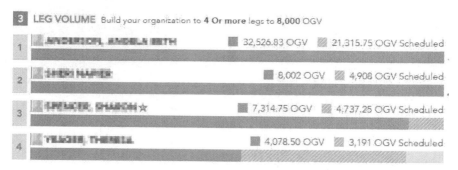

You can see from this peak at my Virtual Office that at the time of this screen shot I needed four legs at 8000 to reach Platinum. My first two were already there. My third leg was at 7300, but that's nothing to worry about because there's still 4700 sitting in people's carts as Essential Rewards. And my last leg, my Platinum leg, looks great—it's only halfway through the month and it's sitting at 7200 with processed and unprocessed orders. I have 12 leaders on that team and they still have three weeks to sell eight kits. I didn't have to worry about Platinum this month. This month shows me it's time to focus on my Diamond team and let my leaders lead.

Now you know how to keep an eye on your rank—watch your numbers, watch the volume on Essential Rewards and strategize on how to grow your team—all through the Rank Qualification button. That means we've hit all three buttons across the top of the page. Next we'll zoom in on the boxes in the middle of your screen.

"SHOPPING"

Monthly order:

The order amount you have sitting in essential rewards right now (which will not process until the day you have selected for it to ship.)

Quick order:

The order amount you have sitting in your cart under quick order right now (which won't process until you log in and pay for it.)

"BALANCES"

Rewards points:

How many points you have accrued in Essential Rewards

Available credits:

These are credits to your account that are accrued through many ways: for example, if you check was under $25 dollars, it would be credited to your account. If you are unsure what it is from, give Young Living a call.

While we are on that topic, you may notice under your "my account" tab that there are adjustments to your commission. Young Living has a fee that goes through each month (just a few dollars) that covers the cost of your check being mailed or direct deposit. It is called a "maintenance" fee.

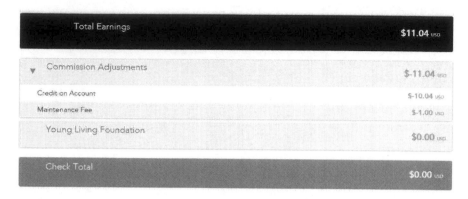

Total Earnings	$11.04 USD
▼ Commission Adjustments	$-11.04 USD
Credit on Account	$-10.04 USD
Maintenance Fee	$-1.00 USD
Young Living Foundation	$0.00 USD
Check Total	$0.00 USD

"VOLUME/RANK"

OGV:

Is your organization group volume, the amount of total sales from your purchases and all those under you.

PV:

Is personal volume. It's how much you spent. It's the number I gently sneak past my husband each month....

PGV:

Is personal group volume. It's how much volume is outside your legs. You need 1000 PGV to attain the rank of silver—volume outside your legs.

Qualified rank:

Is what your rank is at this moment. If you have not spent your 100pv, you will be listed as a distributor until it goes through. Once it clears, your rank will be displayed. I like to place my Essential Rewards order early in this month just for that reason!

OGV history:

This shows the history of your business in a bar graph. If you are holding 4-6 classes a month and getting people on essential rewards through follow up, your peaks and valleys will be much smaller. There is always a bit of an up-and-down in network marketing, but the overall trend is up. Don't ever compare from one month to the next, compare this October to last October. If you are up, you are doing something right.

"MY ORGANIZATION"

Downline accounts:

This tells you how many people are in your organization

Leaders:

This tells you how many leaders have ranked Silver or above for the month. It will change as the month goes on, especially the last week, as your leaders uprank.

New members:

Tells you how many people have been signed to your team, by you or your distributors, as of the first of the month.

About to go inactive:

If you sell someone a starter kit and they never purchase again, one year after that kit sale their account will go inactive and their name will disappear from your downline. To keep them active, have them place an order of 50PV or greater.

Now let's do a brief tour of the buttons down the left side of your dashboard.

"MEMBER NEWS"

Here's where you'll find the latest Young Living news. It may be a new book, a new oil, a new promotion, the Essential Rewards promos for that month, a new contest or philanthropic trip. My favorite feature on this button is the "Products Currently Out Of Stock" button. It will tell you which Young Living products aren't available, why, when they'll be back in, and what you can use instead.

"MESSAGE CENTER"

This is for your leaders or Young Living to write to you directly in your Virtual Office.

Rewards Points Balance
14.56 Details »

Dashboard

Member News

Message Center

My Organization

Quick Order

Essential Rewards

Member Resources

My Account

"MY ORGANIZATION"

This is the other super important button we're going to look at most closely. This is the "How to Watch Your Team" button.

At the top, you can see the number of members on your team. At the time of this screen shot, ours was at 1599.

On the right, you can change the month you're looking at and go all the way back to the start of your business.

The top of the downline is you. You'll see your rank to the left of your name—mine is P for Platinum. You'll see your distributor number, so if someone needs you to look up their member number, this is where you'd look. PV is what you have spent. OGV is what the whole team has spent.

All the little boxes are people on Essential Rewards. When it's got a green check mark, their order has gone through. A healthy, growing team has at least 30 percent of their members on Essential Rewards. If you have lots of kits and no checked boxes, you're not doing good follow up with your team and training them how to use the oils.

On the far right side, you'll see an envelope that allows you to write your team members. I usually just use my personal email, because many don't know how to log into their Virtual Office to see the messages.

The green square with the person's head in it is invaluable—that's how you do follow up. That lists their email, name, address, and phone number. That's how you touch base with your team.

The two heads together shows you their sponsor path—who that person is enrolled under. And the three bars show you their rank.

If you look at the left side of the page, you'll see a little plus sign next to each person's name. That allows you to expand the team and look under each of those leaders to look more closely at their team.

Remember: you are paid on the top five levels of your team. Anything leaders below five levels, you're training for free. That's why our team has developed this book and our website, oilabilityteam.com, loaded with videos to train oilers and leaders (even crossline leaders from other teams), just to give people a leg up on understanding the business without robbing our families of lots of time. You are welcome to use the system, too, to train your leaders at a fraction of the cost.

There are just a few buttons left, and our Virtual Office training is over!

"QUICK ORDER"

This is one way you can place an order. I recommend never using this button *unless* you're claiming Essential Rewards points or there's a really good promo that you want twice, so you place a 300 PV Essential Rewards order and a 300 PV Quick Order. Other than that, use it all on Essential Rewards, which is the button below. Why? You get 10%t back right away, 20% after 4 months and 25% after 25 months. You're literally getting paid to buy your laundry soap and Thieves cleaner! Double score! Save up your orders and get them all in one shot on Essential Rewards once a month to get up the most points.

"ESSENTIAL REWARDS"

Who doesn't love Essential Rewards? Getting free oils is pretty sweet! You earn a percentage back on each order placed through Essential Rewards. It starts at 10% right away which means if you spend 100PV, you're getting 10PV back in free oils. That's nearly a bottle of Lime oil or some Cedarwood, just for restocking your laundry soap!

This graphic lays it out visually if you need to see Essential Rewards in clear language:

Essential Rewards perks:

1) 10% back immediately, 20% after 4 months, 25% after 25 months

2) More economical shipping

3) Essential Rewards kits—like the NingXia and Thieves kits— make it much more affordable. You're basically buying in bulk.

4) Free oils. Like a LOT of free oils. In the past Young Living has given out diffusers, entire Everyday Oils kits, and many other perks. You get the oils for free (in addition to your 10, 20 or 25 percent back) for hitting certain benchmarks. Though it can vary occasionally, the typical breakdown of the Essential Rewards promos look like this:
190PV: 2 free oils
250PV: 2 free oils and a cash incentive (like 10% off a starter kit or 20 extra ER points)
300PV: 2 free oils, a cash incentive, and something else (like NingXia Nitro or a diffuser)

I recommend that every single business builder click on this button and get on Essential Rewards right away. Why? It's a smarter way of managing the cash from your business. If you have to spend 100 PV to get a paycheck, you might as well spend 90 PV, right? Also, it sets an example for your up and coming leaders to get on Essential Rewards. This month, our team has 75,000 OGV in Essential Rewards. That means that if all 450 leaders don't sell a single kit, we'd still be a Gold team with zero effort. That's the power of the snowball rolling down the hill. You get there by getting on Essential Rewards, encouraging your leaders to get on Essential Rewards, and then doing follow up after classes and getting your newbies on Essential Rewards as well. It truly is a fantastic program!

"MEMBER RESOURCES"

This is the button I told you at the beginning of the chapter to lose yourself in on a lazy Sunday afternoon. It's chock full of resources. Start with the Policies and Procedures button and immerse yourself in the ins and outs of network marketing. It'll explain all the rules and all the isms you may have never known before. Did you know you can't enroll your spouse and build a team under him/her? It's just good to know this stuff. Click on each button and absorb. When I am training my leaders, this (along with the Getting Started tab) is one of the buttons that I require them to read all the way through.

"MY ACCOUNT"

This is a pretty essential button! It allows you to set up direct deposit, to track your orders and see if they've shipped (and click on the tracking number to see how close it is). You can click on your commissions and see the breakdown of your paycheck, and who you were paid on. I'd recommend you do that at least once, just to understand the breakdown of your check.

That wraps up your Virtual Office tour! Why do you want to use your Virtual Office? First off, it's a free resource, and as a frugal momma of five, I'm all about free. Secondly, it's an opportunity to see everything in one place—your goals, your team, product that's shipping to you, the breakdown of your paycheck, training videos under the Getting Started tab, and addresses for follow up. Log into it daily and watch your team expand!

CHAPTER 7

YOUNG LIVING MARKETING 101: HOW TO SHARE THE OILS

I used to think that I could never do network marketing because I'd come off as salesy to my friends. I'd be begging my closest comrades to buy things off of me weekly—things I knew they couldn't afford. That's what we all think, right? That if you have a friend in an MLM you can expect to host parties, buy pans, makeup, and books—and be harassed constantly. We're going to debunk all of that in this chapter and make you unafraid of all things MLM, but especially about sharing Young Living.

THE TRUTH ABOUT MULTI-LEVEL-MARKETING

Let's start by talking about MLM's. When you walk into a grocery store chain, you're supporting that CEO's third house. When you buy from an MLM, you are literally putting food on your friend's table and gas in their car. It's the epitome of a small business, but without a storefront. It's no different from going to the downtown in your hometown and buying something in the store of your local gift shop.

I have had people tell me they can't take part in an MLM because it's a pyramid scheme. A pyramid scheme is illegal in the United States. It means you pay for something and it never shows up. To date, after two years with Young Living, I've never had an oil not show up at my door, which means this is *not* a pyramid scheme.

Amway was sued by the federal government in 1978, and was told that network marketing was not a valid business model. They won in court, and to this date, MLM's have thrived across the United States. The goal is to put as much cash in the distributor's hands as possible, and cut out the middle man. Instead of paying for lights, electric, health insurance for employees, and rent for a storefront—all that cash goes to the person selling. To debunk the entire argument against MLM's, I'll give you a video to watch. Go to YouTube and type in "I Still Think It's A Pyramid Scheme" by Pat Petrini. For three minutes, enjoy a pig and a bear, and then return to this chapter.

OVERCOMING OTHERS' OBJECTIONS TO MLM'S

A woman approached me a few weeks ago and threw back her head and laughed when she heard I was with Young Living. She said she "didn't do those pyramid things." I'll tell you, those "pyramid things" are genius! They are endorsed by Christian financial guru Dave Ramsey and by dozens of the top financial advisors around the world.

She said that it was a get rich quick scheme.

I told her that I multiplied my income by five in a year and a half, and I worked my tush off to do it—and it definitely wasn't a scheme, and it definitely wasn't easy.

She said you had to get in early to make cash.

I told her that Young Living had been around for 22 years, and that I'd been a part of it for a year and a half and was able to climb to be in the top 1% of income earners in the entire company. We sure haven't been doing it 22 years.

Then she said I was an exception to the rule and that the only reason I'd gotten that far was because I was a news anchor and everyone knew me.

I told her I took a survey of my team when we were Gold rank, and that only 5% of our team knew me from the radio. The rest were friends of friends of friends. Many were out of state. Several had no idea who I even was.

I also told her that we now have 800 leaders on our team and dozens have retired because of Young Living. More than 100 have experienced lifestyle changes where they can drop things off their plate and make their lives a bit simpler because of the extra income. Hundreds more on our team are getting their oils and their NingXia for free simply by holding one class a month. If that's a pyramid scheme, *sign me up!*

WHY YOUNG LIVING?

She then proceeded to tell me that Young Living can't possibly be the only pure oils company in the world.

I'll agree. It's not the only pure company. But I believe it is the *best* pure company, and I know it is a pioneer. I have far more oils to choose from than anywhere else that I go. I believe in what they do and how they do it, and that's enough for me.

I have so much respect for Gary Young and the groundwork that he's laid in studying the greats in France and then bringing that knowledge to the United States. His methods of distillation are copied all over the world.

There is a wonderful book about the path that Young Living took to become a billion dollar essential oils company. It's called "D. Gary Young:

The World Leader In Essential Oils." Get your hands on it and devour it, and you'll never look at Young Living the same way again. If you have any doubts as to Young Living as a company, you'll lose them in that book.

Young Living has the largest essential oils farms on the planet. I have used many other oils side by side without the same results, and the only explanation I can give is that the oils are distilled correctly—distilled at the right temperatures, at the peak of the harvest, and without any chemicals. They are hand weeded. There is integrity in the process.

There are over 140 single oils and blends Gary has developed, many by trudging through forests in the Amazon and smelling for aromatic plants. His passion for purity and integrity blows me away with every new farm I visit!

One of the other things I love about Young Living is that it's a totally transparent company. As a news anchor, I'm naturally curious. I remember as a grade-schooler, my mom had taken my three siblings and me to an ice cream shop. By the time she got the kids out of the car, she could not find me. I was downstairs in the basement of the ice cream shop interviewing the owner and asking for a tour of where the ice cream was stored. I have carried that far into the newsroom, interviewing presidents, governors, activists, Olympians, and hundreds of famous people over my career. (If you want to hear my interview with Young Living Ambassador and Olympic Gold Medalist Bryan Clay, go to Oil Ability with Sarah on Facebook and click "videos". Enjoy!)

I love that when I step onto a Young Living farm, there are no secrets. I can open any door, pull aside any employee, pop out my cell phone and shoot a video. And at every Young Living farm I attend, I get the same responses and the same answers from dozens of employees. "I've been here 'x' number of years, I love working for Gary. I love his mission for purity. This company is honest and good. They do oils the right way."

I love how simple the process is. Step out into a wide lavender field, never touched with weed killers or pesticides, pluck the plant at its peak value (they check it every hour around the clock as it gets close to harvest time, which you just can't do at a mom and pop oils distillery because you don't have the manpower), they distill it at the right temperature (that's where most companies make their mistake), and they use no solvents distilling, even though it is more expensive to distill without solvents. It's beautiful and simple and true. And the oils work.

When you stand in those fields and see it yourself, it takes your breath away! I was swept away at all the Lord has created. He really gets the glory for it all! He created the plants before He made us. They have been around since the dawn of time. It's only the last 150 years that we've forgotten how to use oils. It's time to take that knowledge back.

I am over the fear of MLM's and over the fear of Young Living as a powerhouse. They have earned that title and my respect. Multi-level marketing works or I wouldn't have been able to write this book.

PROUD TO BE AN ENTREPRENEUR

Let me put one more resource in your hands, because I'm a numbers cruncher and a fact hunter, one DVD really filled that void for me. Eric Worre has a wonderful DVD called "Rise of the Entrepreneur" that breaks down the numbers in network marketing. If you need facts and statistics that this truly works to show your spouse, your best friend, or to convince yourself that this is worth it, that's the place to go. You can find it at ericworre.com.

But even after you believe in the product, the company, and that MLM's are a legitimate vehicle for entrepreneurs to reach financial freedom, you may still struggle with the fear of selling. That's an easy one to tackle. I already shared my story for using oils: it's to live a chemical-free lifestyle. Now let me tell you how I share it in a compliant way.

WE'RE NOT SELLING OILS!

Never once have I sold a Young Living starter kit. I have empowered people to trust their instinct when something is off. I've shown them to pay attention to the amount of chemicals in their home.

Never once have I sold a Young Living starter kit.

I issue the three-cabinet challenge in my classes and tell them to go home, flip over the products in any three cabinets of their home and google the ingredients. If they don't know what it is, they shouldn't be slathering it on their body or cleaning with it. Then I encourage them to switch to chemical-free essential oils.

It's a journey. Some will go gung-ho and swap everything out as fast as they can, while others will take it one product at a time. Here's the way I look at it: neither way is wrong. Again, every oil they use is a chemical they're not using.

Never once since I started with Young Living have I felt salesy or that I'm pushing someone to do something they wouldn't do or can't afford.

I am training them to pay attention to their bodies, to be aware of the chemicals in their cabinets, and to start living a less toxic life. It's empowering to see people get healthy. It's a calling, not an occupation. If they say they can't afford health, they will pay for it in other areas—chemical use has a price. And the price is high. It's about creating an awareness so they start to take steps to swap chemicals out.

WHAT IT TAKES TO SHARE OILS SUCCESSFULLY

There are two things you need to do this business extremely well: passion and compassion. You need passion for the product, and if you have a Young Living starter kit in your home, you're likely in the process of developing the passion. Compassion is about meeting people where they are. It doesn't matter if they're a crunchy momma that does grass-fed pastured fermented organic everything or if they live on fast food five days a week. Meet them on their journey, without judgment, with passion, and walk them through.

Every person has a niche when it comes to oils. Perhaps the way to their heart is a diffuser for their new home. Some people put more into their pets then into their own health. Find that place where they can relate to the oils and share from that place. Be silent and listen to them, and then and you'll know where that place is.

YOU DON'T NEED TO BE AN EXPERT

What is one thing you don't need to market your classes? You don't need to be a certified aromatherapist. I have people come to me constantly saying they can't teach classes unless they are certified. They say they don't know enough.

I say it's not about what you know. It's about the resources you have from experts who have gone before you. It's about knowing where the tools are, and showing your team how to find them. There is a plethora of resources out there that will give them tips on how to oil up. You don't need to be the expert.

Let me repeat that: *you don't need to be the expert.*

This is actually a proven strategy in network marketing called "Third Party Validation." It's using a third party—a person or resource—to educate people instead of being the expert yourself. Connect your team with reliable outside sources. It gives credibility to what you are sharing and ensures that you have a duplicable system for them to follow. They don't need to be just like you. They don't need your gifts and talents. They don't need to be experts in business or aromatherapy. They just need to know where to point people when questions arise. They can be successful with their own gifts and talents. It's not about what you know, it's about knowing where to point people.

Empower people to do their own research and lead them to the right resources.

It is a simple process: instead of trying to be everything to the people you are trying to educate, rely on experts to train your team. Empower people to do their own research and lead them to the right resources. That is the secret to growing a team: allow your leaders to see a clear, simple path to follow in your footsteps.

Here is what it looks like to use Third Party Validation when sharing oils:

"I don't know the answer to that, but here's where I'd begin my research. Check out pubmed.com. It's loaded with studies that will help you find what you're searching for."

"I am still learning how to run my own business, but I have a great resource in the Gameplan book. The book walks you through step by step. Let me hook you up."

"What makes Young Living such a good company? Well, I haven't been with them since they started. But there is a book filled with photos and primary source documents that chronicles the entire story of Young Living that will blow your mind. It's called "D. Gary Young: The World Leader in Essential Oils." I read that book and walked away with a complete appreciation of what it takes to do oils right. You have GOT to check it out if you think buying cheap oil is a good idea."

What happens when you use tools? You are training your new oilers and your new business builders that they don't need to have all the answers. You are training them that it will take a lifetime to amass the education to answer every question, but tools can point them to the answers.

If you wait a lifetime to start oiling, you lose the benefit and blessing of the daily application of the purest substances on the planet. If you wait until you know it all to start your business, you lose the release from poverty, stress, and exhaustion.

And there's the thing: you'll never get to a place where you actually know it all. I hold six aromatherapy certifications from aroma chemistry to Biblical aromatherapy to Vitaflex. I've worked with thousands of people in the past two years either online or in person and in all 50 states and several countries. Yet still, when I stand in the presence of Gary Young, who built the distilleries from the ground up and developed more than 140 oils, and who trudged through rain forests to find Copaiba oil, I feel like I know nothing at all.

Wishing you were the expert is a problem with pride. It's trying to be all things to all people. Don't do that. Just train them how to look things up for themselves. It's always better to teach an oiler to fish then to fish for them. It will save you stress, frustration and time.

The other day a member of my team said "Sarah, I'm sure more people come to your classes because you throw the title 'certified aromatherapist' in your marketing material."

First of all, even as a Platinum, I still have classes of no-shows and low-shows... so don't beat yourself up too hard if that happens. It happens to every single rank occasionally, regardless of title. You are no less of a distributor if you have a bum class. Just pick yourself up, dust yourself off, and do better marketing. Get more personal with your invites. Talk to them individually and build a relationship.

To answer the question of whether an aromatherapy degree is needed, I just look at the facts. I had ranked Gold before I completed my aromatherapy trainings. I have personally enrolled several hundred people, but my team consists of over 3,200 oilers, most of whom I don't know. I didn't sign them. My team did. People come to your classes and sign up because they trust you—not because you have a title. Or they come to your classes because they trust the friend who invited them, not because of what is printed next to your name.

The majority of the people I've enrolled come because they want to learn about oils. Your team is not built on titles; it's built on relationships. Relationships will open more doors than any title.

Why do you want to be the expert? Fear. You have fear that people won't accept you because you're not educated enough. Ask yourself this: do you trust the person at Panera because they are educated in the science of making bread? No. Do you expect the person selling books at Barnes and Noble to have a working knowledge of all books ever published? No. Do you refuse to order coffee at Starbucks because the barista doesn't know the ins and outs of where the coffee beans were sourced? (You still buy coffee. Coffee is not negotiable.)

Why then do you need to be an aromatherapist to sell oils? You're a Young Living distributor. Wear the title with pride, and without fear of having every answer.

> *Relationships will open more doors than any title.*

Your greatest tool is not a title but your connection to others who have gone before you. Find someone who knows what you're looking for. Get good at locating tools and putting them in the hands of those asking the questions, and you'll grow like crazy without a title. You'll also build trust, which is far more important than any certification.

Release yourself from the pressure of having to be perfect. Release yourself from fear. And lean on what's already been written. If you get to a place where you're not sure where to point someone, that is what your upline is for. Every question you'll be hit with has likely already been asked. Don't miss the opportunity of a lifetime waiting on a certification.

You now know what you don't need to say and do to share the oils. The information and mindset from this chapter will make sure you're sharing the oils confidently and not turning people off. Next we'll discuss practical techniques to actually get people to come to your classes!

CHAPTER 8

THE OIL ABILITY MARKETING SYSTEM: HOW TO FILL CLASSES WITHOUT KNOWING PEOPLE

Some people will buy Gameplan solely for this chapter. This chapter has catapulted many a leader's business on our team. It's a strategy for overcoming one of the biggest challenges to sharing the oils: filling classes.

When I first began my business, I put a post on my Facebook page and 47 women showed up at my house. I did it again and got about 20. By the fifth class, I was out of friends and my classes were dwindling, so I asked a good friend who was a naturopath doctor to host a class for me. She had 60 women show up in a church gym. That worked out well for a while until that circle of people started to dwindle too. It was then when I realized that everyone has an end to their circle of friends.

Of all the questions I'm asked on the road or on Facebook, this is, hands down, at the top. "How do I get people to come to my classes? I post, but no one shows up. I don't know that many people."

Here's the thing—neither do I. Neither do the top leaders on my team. The trick isn't who you know. *It's who your friends know.* The trick to marketing isn't how many people you know. It's more about how many times you get outside your circle of friends!

Whether it's after your first class or your tenth, there will come a day when you will run out of people to fill classes unless you get out of your personal friend circle. You must tap into your friend's friends and that can happen from your very first class if you are strategic. Every person in that class knows someone outside your friend circle. In fact, the average person knows about a thousand people, if they were to sit down and write it all out. It's astounding.

Within my first 20 classes, different attendees had contacts in Germany, Italy, Thailand, Japan, Canada, and Mexico City. Guess where we now have teams? Did I know those people? Heck no. So take some pressure off yourself. It's going to take a lot more than just you to pull off a Young Living business. It takes a lot people doing the same thing you're doing. That is a network marketing company.

This is the formula that I follow for every single class that I hold. Each has the same pattern, and I still haven't run out of people to speak to.

THE OIL ABILITY EVENT MARKETING SYSTEM

1. Choose a date for your class

You should begin marketing a class at least 2 to 3 weeks in advance. People are busy. During the holidays or during wedding or graduation or vacation season, you may want to leave yourself even more lead time. If you give people 3 or 4 days' notice, you're going to have a low turnout. Most of the people who attend my classes are busy mommas. They have to know ahead of time if they're going to work it into their schedule.

2. Set up an event for your class on Facebook

It's free, and it reaches the widest swath of people. How do you set up an event? Go to your Facebook page. Look under your Facebook profile picture for a button that says "more." Click on that, then scroll down till you see "events." (Note: Not on Facebook? Get on it. Go to Youtube, go to the search bar, and type in "21st Century Social Media Trends" and watch a free 9-minute video on the power of social media that will blow your mind. One billion people are on Facebook. That's 1 in every 9 people in the world. Social media is where the people are—if you're running a network marketing business, you should be there too. Our team has used just about every marketing tool out there—radio, newspaper, flyers, word of mouth, texting—and hands down we've gotten the greatest return every time from Facebook events.)

Setting up an event is pretty simple. You'll be setting up "Private Event" which means only and those your friends invite will see the event (this keeps you from spamming the feeds of people who aren't interested as you update the event page). You'll fill in basic information, select a photo for the top of your event (google "Young Living banners" for some ideas), then put in the time and location and address, and an FDA compliant description of the class.

A note on writing: Wording matters on your events. Use power-packed action verbs that take them somewhere. For example, this is a snippet of an actual event invite that I saw online, before the English major and network journalist in me ran away, screaming in horror:

Bad: Please come to my essential oils class. I will have dessert. I will speak for 2 hours on oils. If you can bring someone, that would be good. We will have NingXia for an extra cost. If you can't come, I will teach another class.

Good: Do you want to learn how to kick toxic chemicals out of your home? I'll walk you through step by step and give *easy, simple, and affordable* tactics that anyone can do with the best essential oils on the planet. This class is totally FREE and will blow your mind! I come with an iced NingXia bar for weary mommas! Gear up for a fast-paced, ground-up lecture on everything oils, and have some fun and pampering in the process. I can't wait to see you! I'll have freebies at the door for those who invite 50 friends on the Facebook event. It's time to take control of the yuck in your home and kick it to the curb!

(Feel free to steal this if you can't write! It's all good! This book is full of resources for you at every turn.)

3. Invite three people to invite their friends

Once your event is live, here's the key to the whole thing: find three people on your Facebook friend list—any three who may have an interest in oils and live close enough to attend—invite them to the event and then ask *them* to go in and invite 50 people to the class.

Have them type a sentence in the event promoting you, for example, "This is my friend Sarah. She's a rock star! She made me a bottle of Thieves cleaner for a dollar and it did this to my sink in 3 minutes. It's chemical free. You can't get chemical free cleaning supplies that cheap in the store. Oils have so many other uses. You've GOT to come to this class!"

If you have 3 people each invite 50 people to the class, it means you'll have 150 people invited. Most people wig out at this point. Don't wig out. You *won't* be teaching a 150-person class, for sure! Standard network marketing numbers tell us that 20-25% will show. Of that, 20-25% will get the starter kits. So if you have 150 invited, with good marketing 20-30 will show, and 5 or 6 will get a kit.

4. Thank your hosts

When you have the event set up and 3 people have invited 50 people each to that event, make up a little basket to show your appreciation to your 'hosts'. Pop in some Thieves cleaner or lozenges or a peppermint roll-on. Add a couple of my oily education DVD's to the basket, and let them know you appreciate them. Keep the cost under five dollars, but hand deliver it with a thank you. If they aren't local to you, pop it in the mail. They will be surprised and delighted, and much more excited to help people get to your class!

5. Market the event

Once that event is up and people have been invited, market it. That means every single day you should be putting 1-2 posts up promoting the class. What does that look like? Pull FDA compliant photos off the Oil Ability with Sarah Facebook page and feel free to safely share those. Take a line out of the lecture and share that. Take a photo of the gift baskets you'll give away, the desserts at the class, how you're preparing for class. Let them know you're on your game and you're ready to rock their world. People's interest will be peaked. A word of advice: don't over post. Most of these people have never met you before. If you're putting 6 posts a day in that event, people are going to leave. Once or twice a day is more than enough.

6. Rinse and repeat

After the class, you'll have a few people purchase kits. Some may get it right at the class, and some may get them in the weeks after. Either is fine. To market your next class, dip into your downline. If you teach four classes a month, and four people get a kit at each class, it means that, in the first month alone, you have 16 people who can invite other people to your classes. You literally never, ever run out of friend circles. It goes on and on forever. We still haven't run out of friend circles, and I'm meeting new people every single week.

Overview of the Oil Ability Event Marketing System:

1) Set up a Facebook event 2 to 3 weeks ahead of the class.

2) Ask 3 people to invite 50 people to the event and make them a thank you basket.

3) Grab photos and lines from the script and market it every single day.

4) After class, tap into your new downline and ask three of them to invite 50 people to the class. Rinse and repeat. You have never-ending friend circles.

Encouragement from Silver In Six Oil Ability leader Rachael Spencer:

I held 11 classes in the first three weeks of my distributorship. I was so excited to build a team like Sarah's after spending several days with her on her Gold Retreat at the Saint Maries farm in Idaho! Unfortunately, I was not very well networked in New York and didn't understand how to fill classes with people outside my circle.

Since moving here from Illinois seven years ago, I had either worked 70+ hours a week as a salaried manager at Walmart or I had been working 40 hours a week at the credit union, 30 hours a week at Walmart as a cake decorator and I was taking 2 to 8 cake orders a week. I had very little free time to build a personal network.

Of the first 11 classes I held, 2 had 5 attendees, 4 classes had 1 or 2 attendees, and 5 were no shows. Rather than giving up, I changed my tactics!

At the credit union where I worked, I began meeting with co-workers one on one during my lunch breaks to build my team. I did that from August until January when I used Sarah's method for filling classes.

I ranked as Executive in February and am working to reach Silver this month. I am teaching classes nearly every weekend now, because I ask previous attendees or leaders on my team to invite 50+ of their Facebook friends and I give them an oily gift basket or sign people under their sponsor number.

Network marketing is like any other business—if you stick with it and are adaptable, you will be successful.

To the left is a shot of Rachael, after meeting Young Living Founder D. Gary Young.

I STILL CAN'T FILL A CLASS—NOW WHAT?

I want to take a moment and speak directly to the people who say this marketing system doesn't work. I'll shoot straight with you—it is rare, but I have seen this system fail before, and it always comes down to one of two things: confidence or gifting. I wrote an entire chapter on confidence, and this next section will give you even more creative ways to share the oils!

Each of us have different strengths and weaknesses. You may need to try this from a different angle. Maybe you don't have the comfort level to approach people to go into the event and invite 50 people. You may not have the writing ability to put together punchy FDA compliant marketing posts. None of the people in the event may connect with you as you post. The good thing is that there are many ways of sharing. There were many, many millionaire-level network marketers long before Facebook.

LISTEN TO YOUR WARM MARKET

Go through your entire Facebook friends list. (In network marketing, we call that your warm market—the people who you know personally. They may be an acquaintance, and that's okay—they know your face.) Go through your Christmas card list. Keep a tally of the people around you at work, at play dates, homeschool groups, sports teams, and extra-curricular activities.

You can be more deliberate about the people you contact. Look through the lists of the circles of friends you know and write down the name of any person who would be blessed by the oils and the name of any person who would benefit from a chemical free lifestyle. One by one, contact them, offer to do a personalized intro class, mail them some samples, and show them the passion you have. *Keep the focus on them.* Listen to them. Pause—instead of you doing the talking, hear where they are at and meet them there.

One of my favorite stories to tell is of my brother, Aaron. For a good year, I sent him Young Living samples, but he didn't use them. They stockpiled in his house. When I'd bring up oils, he'd check out. When I went to go visit him after he'd bought a new-to-him home and started in right away with Young Living, he asked me politely to stop. So I stopped.

As we toured his home, he expressed frustration that the basement, which was newly finished and gorgeous, had been the designated smoking room of the person who'd lived there before him. He couldn't get the smell out and was about to have it bombed, but that would mean leaving the house for three days so it could be sprayed with chemicals.

He asked if there was another way, and finally I had an open door! For stinky smells, I recommended Purification in the diffuser and the Thieves cleaner undiluted on every wall and rafter in the basement.

That weekend, the smell was gone, and without a $1000 bombing fee. Eight weeks later, my brother had a starter kit and was texting me about how to buy FCO (fractionated coconut oil) online so he could make his own blends. I jokingly told him he's not allowed to speak in oily acronyms until he's been using oils for at least 6 months.

The reason I was able to break through to Aaron was not because I was talking. It was because I stopped talking—and listened to where he was. I listened for the need. If people see your heart and that your desire is to help them, it becomes a totally different ballgame. Suddenly it's not about sales—it's about people. And that's what makes this a passion for most of the people doing this business. They are on the front lines to help people. So stop talking, and start listening.

HOST CLASSES IN A PUBLIC PLACE

Many people are uncomfortable about hosting their own friends in their home, much less a group of Facebook contacts their friends helped invite. Additionally, some guests might not want to come to the home of someone they don't know for an oils class. If you are having trouble finding people willing to book classes with you in their home, or with getting people to come to home classes, overcome this hurdle by scheduling classes in a room available to the public. People often feel more comfortable attending an event in a public place such as a room at a library, a conference room at a local restaurant, a community center, health food store. We've even had people on our team find that they could use the class room at the local craft store.

One word of caution: don't bite off more than you can chew financially. Don't book a 100-dollar room for a 5-person class. There are many resources available locally that you can tap into a for a fraction of the cost: the YMCA, your VFW, churches, fire halls, etc.

If the class is in a public building, you can still use the same Oil Ability marketing system to invite people--create a Facebook event and ask three people from your warm market to invite 50 of their friends. You may find that those who were unwilling to host or attend an in-home class would be more than willing to invite and attend if it's at a public place in their home town.

BE WILLING TO TRAVEL

Another tidbit of advice I can give you is to go where the people are. Most people have moved several times and they have friend circles in other towns. If you live in New York, but grew up in Chicago, take the tax deduction on mileage, make a trip home, and teach a couple of different classes at friend's homes. It's worth it! Tap into home plate. It's the neatest feeling to visit your friends and family out of state and feel like you're at home, with Thieves soap in the bathrooms, Thieves laundry soap in the laundry room, Thieves dish soap on the kitchen sink and a diffuser running in the background. Chemical-free living creates bonds. If you have to save three months of your check to pull off a trip of that size, do it—but not till you have it saved. Make sure you're not living outside your income.

It's also been a joy and a blessing to see my closest friends and family doing what I do. I couldn't pay them enough to anchor news! No one would touch the 39 radio stations I've worked for. This is the first time I've had the honor of working closely with the people I love the most, so start there, build a team, and do it together. My strongest teams have a network of friends and family close by who they can lean on during the frustrating days, and rejoice with during the victories. Network marketing can be an emotional roller coaster, but the payoff far outweighs the ride.

TEACH ONLINE CLASSES

This one I learned from one of my Diamond friends, Joanna Malone, who got to Diamond in under two years using this protocol. Joanna is a sheer genius and knows how to rock the social media world. If you are tech savvy (I'll tell you I am NOT—but was able to figure this one out!) you'll like this. Here are some simple steps:

HOW TO HOLD AN ONLINE CLASS

1. Record the 101 Script

Grab the compliant 101 script in the back of this book, and break it into bite size 3-minute chunks. Record those chunks on your cell phone in a place with good lighting. Make sure your first video tells your oils story (compliantly) and that your last one has a strong close, with where to order.

2. Upload the videos

I recommend the uploading the videos to vimeo.com because this allows you to password protect them all. I pay the yearly fee, (about $60) so that I can upload an hour of video in one sitting. You can skip the fee, but you'll have to upload the videos once a week for about a month until you hit your bandwidth limit.

3. Prepare your captions and photos

Write a little intro into each video and have it in a place where you can quickly copy and paste it into Facebook.

The trick to a successful online class is making sure you already have the content sealed and ready to go. I once did an online class with 22,000 people in it—and it took me three hours to do a one-hour class (that's bad—you'll lose people) because I got bombarded between generating the content and answering questions. Your content needs to be completely done before you head in, so all your time can go on answering questions and engaging with the class. Make sure you have taken and uploaded a few photos of the giveaways.

4. Market the class

Now you have all your content ready, and it's time to market your class. This is a class they can attend from their living room—in 30-45 minutes or less—so market it that way. It's easy for people to attend with no hassle. Say you will be doing giveaways, and keep the energy up. Use the same system as you would for a live class: set up a Facebook event: have 3 people invite 50 people, market it once a day for 2-3 weeks ahead of time. If you have leaders, asking them to share it to their page will really give you a big boost, too. I popped an online class up this evening and had 150 people going within an hour—all by offering a free bottle of lime oil to one person who shares it on their Facebook page. That's $11 advertising. And it's worth every penny.

5. Class day

Start on time and during the class, watch your clock, because the excitement of an online class can cause you to lose track of time. You want to hold them until the end so they know how to get the kit. If you can keep the class to 30 to 60 minutes, you'll retain the most amount of people. Pop up a little one-minute intro video so they know who you are, and you're off.

Every couple of minutes post a new video with the password to unlock it, and stand by to answer questions under each video. You're just posting and answering questions. Keep the answers compliant, and don't forget your giveaways every few posts.

6. Close strong

When you end, your close is just as important as in a live class. Make sure you've shot a video telling them where to get the kit, how to get the kit, and which kit you recommend. Have them IM you for more information. I like to post a link at the end of the class (Young Living has a link generator in the Virtual Office) which has your sponsor and enroller number already filled in. That makes it easy for people who are just starting to navigate the Young Living website.

7. Follow up

Leave the links up for a week or so for late-joiners. I like to leave my online classes up long enough to tease the next online class to the same crowd. You can really grow your audience size for the next class that way, because people will come to respect you and will come back for more.

Make sure you mail your giveaways out within a few days. I always use those as an opportunity to sell more kits, too. Inside, I put what I call my portable office—a 101 DVD, a flyer of the 101 premium starter kit with instructions on how to order, and an "oil revolution designs" booklet of the premium starter kit to get their attention. As with regular face-to-face classes... rinse and repeat!

I have done online classes for Beauty School, chemical-free home, 101's—and around each of the kits—Golden Touch (my 102 script), Oils of Ancient Scripture (my 103 script), Oils and the Family, Oil Affordability, and quite a few others. Look for the Oil Ability scripts online for more ideas for classes! We have a bundle of all the scripts to make it easy on you at oilabilityteam.com

ATTEND VENDOR EVENTS

I'll be straight up with you on this one. I stink at vendor events. I'm way too ADHD. I can't make myself stand still for hours in one place. As a matter of fact, when I brought this book to convention I actually paid my 17-year-old son to stand at the table and sell it for me. I'm too interested meeting new friends, wandering the halls, connecting, and networking to stay put. In radio, they gave up putting me behind the table for meet and greets. I'd constantly disappear when I saw something bright and shiny. In oils, it's much of the same for me. But just because it's not my gift doesn't mean it's not yours! So let me give you a few tips and tricks

I've picked up from Oil Ability members who have amassed quite a team using this method.

I'll tell you who is best at vendor events: the people who don't know anyone! This type of outreach works really well if you're new to an area or just have freakishly small friend circles (the kind where you don't know three people who can help invite to your class). Maybe you once had great friend circles, then you became a mom or dad, and all your friends dried up as you lived vicariously through your kids, shuttling them from activity to activity. You may have had an injury or illness that's kept you isolated for a while, or even a job that's so demanding you have no social life, and you really need a base starting point for your Young Living business. It also works if you're all tapped out and need new friend circles—and your business has plateaued. Whatever your reason, vendor events work. It just takes a bit longer then online or in person classes, so you have to be patient. But if you're committed and consistent, it will pay off.

TOP TIPS FOR VENDOR EVENTS

1. Make sure you have a starter kit on the table and the diffuser is running

The diffuser alone will draw people to your booth. (Bring an extension cord and make sure you ask for a site with electricity ahead of time.) My favorite reach-across-the-hall diffuser oil is peppermint. The starter kit should be the focal point of the entire table. It's where you want to drive their eyes. Don't lay out so many books or bottles that they miss the kit. It's the reason you are there.

2. Have something for sale

If you can't afford hordes of oils, at least make up some Thieves cleaner and give away samples or sell it for the cost of the supplies (the cleaner must be free, per Young Living's Policies and Procedures). You want them to take something home, use it, and fall in love.

3. Have a laptop set up

Just like at in-person classes, you want a place they can sign for a kit on site. (Before the doors open, make sure you have a strong internet connection.)

4. Do a drawing for a door prize

Go for it. Create a big, beautiful, oily basket and do a giveaway. Make them leave their contact info to win it. Contact info = leads for classes.

You should have a clipboard at the booth where people can sign up if they are interested in a class. Make it clear that it doesn't need to be at their home. Tell them it's free and short. Put the clipboard right next to that large, amazing gift basket they might win (if they fill out a form). On that clipboard, instead of one sheet, I have about a hundred. You can find this form, ready to photocopy, in Appendix H.

5. Everyone leaves with something

I like to hand out organza bags (you can get them on the cheap—10 for a dollar online—with a flyer in it, a sheet with step-by-step instructions on how to order a starter kit, and my business card. If you can afford it, the audio 101 lecture at oilabilityteam.com is a great giveaway too. That gets the lecture in their ears on the drive home from the event.

It's amazing how many people are interested in classes. One of my leaders walked away with 97 different leads from people checking the box that they'd love to host a class—from one 3-day vendor event. She also sold six kits. You just have to ask the right questions. People move past the booth swiftly, often only spending a few seconds before you. Capture as much of their information as you can and make it clear that you'll touch base with them on the form so they're not freaked out when you call.

Bonus Tip: Make It Eye Catching

There are a couple of relatively inexpensive things you can do that will up your game when it comes to presentation.

1) Have a Young Living tablecloth—they make you look sharp with minimal effort. Google "Young Living tablecloths" and pick one up at an online retailer. Expect to spend about $100 for a good one

2) Use height. Get your product off the table and at eye level. People are much more likely to stop if it's as tall as they are. I get wooden crates at Hobby Lobby for $9. They are a pain to haul, but they really look nice in a convention hall.

3) If you can swing it, have a stand up or table-top banner. I get mine at www.crowndiamondtools.com.

Do you need some examples of a good vendor event setup? These are shots from members of the Oil Ability team:

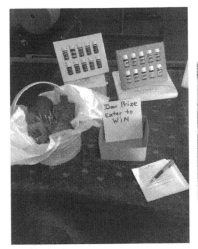

Hopefully that gives you a few ideas!

Vendor events are not my favorite way to grow because they're not as fast as in-person classes, and I have seen people give up their Young Living businesses because they are not ranking quickly enough. You just have to realize the purpose of vendor events. You rarely sell a lot of kits at them, because vendor events are designed to draw leads for in-person classes. If you go into it knowing that, you'll meet a lot of people and pick up many leads.

WHAT TO SAY WHEN YOU INVITE

Remember, this isn't about selling, it's about educating people about the oils themselves. Why would they want to come to a free oils class?

I'll tell you first that a lot of it depends on your own passion. Passion is infectious. If you love the oils and you know that they work, it will be hard to turn you away. Speak with authority and excitement. Let's go through a little role playing exercise.

This is an actual conversation I had with a prospective oiler:

Sarah: Hey Jessie! It's so good to see you! I feel like we haven't talked in ages!

Jessie: What have you been up to lately?

Sarah: Well, I am teaching classes on essential oils. It's really blessed my family!

Jessie: I have never even heard of them before. What are they?

Sarah: (Note: you have 30 seconds to get her attention. Keep it tight!) Essential oils are a bit different than the oil you buy in the store. They have incredible effects on the human body. I use them all over my home—to get rid of chemical cleaning supplies, calm my kids down, emotions, focus, stress—I use them in my toothpaste and deodorant and supplements. I have gotten really good at label reading, and I'll be straight up with you—I just don't like what I can't pronounce on the back of the bottles. I was poisoning my family with a lot of things that I thought were safe.

Essential oils are made of one thing: steam distilled or cold-pressed plants. No yuck. The only ingredient in lemon oil is lemon. If you flip the bottle over and can't pronounce what's on the label, you really shouldn't be slathering it on your scalp in the shower or putting it on your skin or eating it or washing your dishes with it. Did you know the number one poison in the family home is fabric softener? Right behind that—air fresheners. I've replaced both of them with oils.

Jessie: That's crazy. I had no idea. I still have a plug-in air freshener in my living room.

Sarah: I have class Saturday that's free. I'd love to see you there! If you come, I'll have some peppermint for you to try and you can smell nearly a dozen oils in a starter kit. It's how I began. Will you come?

BAM. Done. Give them meat and potatoes. Tell them how they can use it. Tell them why they need it. I always carry samples with me (peppermint is my favorite "wow" oil)—so they can take some right away. Then make sure you follow up and don't lose that contact.

I use the exact same approach when raising leaders. You just have to have an eye for the people who are dissatisfied at their job or the single mom who's trying to make ends meet at her second job. Look for the poor, the weary, and then show them that this way is better. Do the same among your family and friends. I want my top leaders to be my family and friends, and I want to see them financially blessed. Don't be timid.

Have the same conversation I just had above with potential business builders. Keep your "reason" for doing Young Living to 30 seconds or less and give practical information and substantial facts. If that doesn't seem to catch their attention, be quiet and listen! Listen to where they are. Then go from there, and based on what they are telling you, respond to their needs.

Here's a role play of a conversation with a potential business builder:

Grace: Hey Sarah! I don't usually run into you at the store at this time!

Sarah: I have switched jobs!

Grace: What are you doing?

Sarah: Network marketing.

Grace: Oh. You're selling stuff to people?

Sarah: I've never sold an essential oils starter kit in my life. What I do is teach people how to get chemicals out of their house and protect their families. Best. Job. Ever.

Grace: Yeah, I tried the oils thing, but it's really expensive.

Sarah: Not really. You can make Thieves cleaner for $1 a bottle. If grab a starter kit and host a class, I will come teach under you and you can work to get your oils for free. I don't pay for any of my oils.

Grace: It sounds interesting, but I'm really not interested in another job.

Sarah: So you like what you're doing right now?

Grace: Heck no. I work way too many hours and we barely make it.

Sarah: I worked 11 hours last week at my full time Young Living business. Maybe you should consider this.

Grace: But I don't like talking to people.

Sarah: It's as hard as grabbing a few people, sitting in your living room, and reading a 3-page script. Super crazy easy. And you're teaching people how to take care of their families.

Grace: It doesn't sound that hard.

Sarah: It's the best financial decision I've ever made. Do you have time next week for a Teacher Training?

Grace: Yes!

CONNECTIONS ARE ALL AROUND YOU

I actually had this exact same conversation, almost word for word, with a woman I met at the Young Living convention. I was sitting at the Diamond awards night and she was part of the catering company that was serving our food. She saw all the Diamonds going on the stage and turned to me and asked, "Is it real?" I said "Do you want to know how real this is?" Then I opened the Oily Tools on my cell phone and showed her my team stats. Her jaw was on the floor. I added her on Facebook immediately and made contact when I got home. That was someone I'd never met.

Be bold! I once sold a kit to a TSA agent on the way to my flight, another to the mail lady down at the post office, and two kits to some people who were on my zip lining tour for the Young Living Drive-to-Win Tour in Hawaii. You share because you love the oils, and you don't want people to be without them. Don't be afraid to speak to the everyday people around you. You come into contact with far more people then you realize!

Keep a running list of the people you run into during a week—and make sure you're not dropping the ball connecting, because connecting is key. You'll learn a thorough follow up system in Chapter 10. There are also follow up cards in the Gameplan Workbook. They are 3x5 cards that help you recall what you mailed out to whom, what oils they are interested in, and fills your new oilers with recipe ideas and resources. You can pick up the Gameplan Workbook at oilabilityteam.com.

I've now walked you through in-person connections and how to fill your classes, whether they are in person or online, big or small. It's time to get to the heart of what teaching a class looks like! Next I'll walk you through step-by-step, as if you're in one of my own classes. Let's go!

CHAPTER 9

ANATOMY OF A SUCCESSFUL CLASS

This is where the book gets interesting to write, because everyone has a different definition of what "class day" is. If you're primarily blogging or doing classes online, it will look quite different from someone who's meeting a person over lunch or someone who's teaching a class of 50 in a church gym. I will tell you this, whatever class style you prefer, try something new from this list. If you're a gifted blogger, try branching out with a bit of class time also. If you're doing it all in person, it's not a bad idea to also add in a little social media. It's like diversifying your 401k portfolio. Don't put all your eggs in one basket.

CLASS STYLES AND SIZES

Our team has the best success with face-to-face, in-person classes. It's how we've grown so fast. Why? You're building relationships.

I held my first online class in November 2015, and we had 22,000 people on the class. It resulted in two kit sales and two new business builders.

Then I held a class in the nearby tiny town of Hornell, New York, which is in a very impoverished area. This class was attended by eight people, and we sold eight kits that night and picked up two business builders. We had one hundred percent sales!

There's just something to be said for face-to-face relationships. It shows people you care, and that you're not just a line on a screen in front of them. You can do in-person classes one-on-one or you can do them in groups.

Large Classes

Very few people will actually stand in front of 40 or 50 people and teach; it's quite rare. But I'd encourage you to have classes of at least 5 to 10 people. If you have a competitive personality, I'll recommend that you get your class size to at least 20 people. You'll grow *very* fast that way if you are effective at following up.

Small Classes

If you are not competitive—in fact, you're downright shy—but you *really* want this to work, we have a game plan for you, too. Some of the top sellers on my team are introverted and soft-spoken. You don't need to be loud to do this, you just need to be confident.

If you're really nervous about reading the 101 script in front of people, simply play hostess. Invite them to your home, share your story briefly on how you got your kit, and pop our Oil Ability 101 DVD in your DVD player. (You can find it at oilabilityteam.com.) End by passing the kit around and telling them how to get started with Young Living.

Speak for 3 or 4 minutes before the DVD and 5 minutes after, and you'll have a powerhouse class! No lecture experience needed! We've seen tremendous success with this model, even among people on my team who are very timid and shy. A few of my Silvers-In-Six have used this model with great results.

One-on-One Classes

You can teach one-on-one classes, but just recognize that your pace of growth will be much slower. If that's what you can handle, go for it! It doesn't matter whether it takes you 10 years or 20 years to get to Diamond. It's still the best job on the face of the earth. (And the best paid job, too!)

The only thing you need to watch for with this type of teaching model is getting burned out. Some people will give up because they don't see results fast enough. If you can stick with it—one or two one-on-ones a week, every week—you'll get where you want to go.

Speaking of getting burned out—don't make your classes such a production that the very act of doing one drains you for the rest of the week! Keep it simple. Delegate. Have everyone bring a snack or a dish to pass. Hungry moms sit still when they have food in their gut! Do not make all the food yourself or spend a lot of money—that is not reproducible.

ANATOMY OF AN OIL ABILITY CLASS

Every class, big or small, should incorporate these 10 elements:

1. Tell your story

Introduce yourself and share a bit about your oils story, how you got involved in oils and why you're passionate to share them with others.

2. Introduce the chemical free lifestyle

Issue the Three Cabinet Challenge. Ask people to take a look at three cabinets in their home and get familiar with what they're slathering on their bodies or ingesting or cleaning with. The rule of thumb is if you can't pronounce it—don't use it. The shorter the list of ingredients the better. If you're not sure if it's safe, type the word into Google with the words "dangers of" in front of it and do a little research. Why learn about oils? Every oil you use is a chemical you're not using.

3. Play the Oily Scavenger Hunt video

This is a 3-minute icebreaker video which shows people what a home infused with essential oils looks like. It features my 5 children, the Harnisch herd. (Heads up—we had a bit of fun with it.) You can find it at www. oilabilityteam.com.

4. Launch into the lecture

It's just three pages long when printed out and runs about 35 minutes. You have a free copy of that lecture in the appendix of this book. Why give a lecture? Because it's important that people know essential oil basics—safety, how they hit the body, what they're used for, and purity. Of these, purity is the most important, because you don't want someone leaving your class and to buy essential oils in the grocery store! Don't let the lecture run too long or you'll lose interest.

5. Pass around the starter kit

Get the caps off and let people smell the oils. Why is this so important? Because the magic is in the oil. When they get the smell of Peppermint or Frankincense in their nose for the very first time, that's when the oils will get their attention, more so then any lecture. It's like trying to teach someone to drive without putting them in a car. Book learning will only take them so far, they have to experience the oils. I have said many times in this book that you only need two things to teach a class: a 101 Script and a starter kit. This is the second half of that sentence and it's critical. Let them experience the oils in the kit. Don't forget there are compliant descriptions of each of the oils in the 101 Script for you to rely on as you share.

6. End with a strong close

You've given them a lot of information and they may be unsure what their response should be. Tell them exactly what their best next step is. Say something like, "This is the only essential oils company I trust. I began my journey with a Young Living premium starter kit, and that's where I suggest you start your journey, too. It's as simple as going to 'YoungLiving.com', clicking on 'Become a Member', and entering my sponsor and enroller number. Thank you for blessing my family!" There are two strong closing scripts included in the Appendixes for you to work from.

7. Get their information

Make sure you grab their information on a clipboard so you can follow up with them after the class.

8. Give them resources

It is important that they have your information, too! I like to hand out what I call "purple bags"—organza bags with a one page photo brochure of the starter kit, a paper explaining how to order with my distributor number on it, and my business card.

I also hand out free 101 DVD's or audio CD's. I tell them there was likely someone they know who should have heard the class, and I ask them to pass the DVD or audio CD along. That way, you have just doubled your class size. Feel free to point them to the Oil Ability Facebook page and website for more videos to continue their education. It doesn't matter if you're a crossline member. If they are on your team and they watch our 101 class, they'll order more oils, and it will bless your OGV. We put those together as a resource for all oilers to use as they learn to grow.

9. Find the business builders

If you're a genius and want to spark business builders, you'll pop in the "How to Get Your Oils For Free" DVD for 10 minutes right at the close of your lecture. I'm always blown away at who sticks around to watch a 10-minute video on business building. I offer to show it by saying, "Would you like to learn how to get your oils for free? Watch this 10-minute video. You will love it. If you have any questions, I am at the back of the room." I truly believe this is one of the reasons we grew to 800 leaders in two years. I am always bold about the business in my classes, dropping line about it 5-10 times during the lecture, and showing this DVD after. You can find it at oilabilityteam.com

10. Don't let them leave without something oily

I like to have a table or two with make-and-take stations. That can be as simple as a spray bottle and a cap of Thieves cleaner. You can charge for your supplies, but you can never charge for open bottles of Young Living oil. That must be given away for free. I tell them to make up a bottle of Thieves cleaner—run home—and spray down their kitchens. Then call me in the morning.

DIFFERENT TYPES OF IN-PERSON CLASSES

The one-on-one

This is you and one person. Grab the three-page 101 script and have at it. You will be slower to grow than someone with a larger class, but growing is better than staying still. You will get there. Just do not be discouraged by how quickly people are ranking around you. There is nothing wrong with your style or your gifting, it just takes longer. And that's completely okay. Don't ever rate yourself against other people's gifts. The end game is all that matters. A Diamond is a Diamond.

The lunch and learn

Grab the 101 script, contact a local business, and speak to their employees over their lunch hour. Keep it short.

The couch class

Before I started renting halls and speaking to lots of people, I started right in my living room. My first class had 12 people on my couch and my knees were a-knocking. Start small till you get your rhythm.

"But I don't want people in my house." Then find a friend that will let you borrow their living room and have at it.

The big class

If you are expecting a crowd, you may need a larger space, a sound system, and a projector and screen. I have taught most of my larger classes in church gyms. Other ideas for venues: libraries, the "Y", community centers, senior centers, hotels, fire halls, churches, public schools after hours—I have taught in them all.

The connection class

This is a one-on-one I hold with the owner of a bulk food store, a dentist, a chiropractor, a massage therapist, or anyone I want to host classes for me in their business. I am leaning on their friend circles and business connections to fill classes. If they are willing, it's always wise to leave portable offices in their office—an organza bag with a DVD or CD, a flyer, a sheet on how to order and your contact info. I also ask if someone is willing to run the diffuser each morning, and I put up new banners in the office each month with topics I'll be speaking on. The diffuser alone is usually enough to generate interest in the class.

Gotta eat

This is a class I do with 3-10 friends over lunch or dinner. We pick a restaurant, I give my intro, we eat, I read the 101 Script. It's a great way to gain some weight! But it sells oils kits! I train a lot of leaders in this environment. It's different from a lunch and learn in that I usually do these with leaders.

Speed oiling

This is a type of class where you set up stations, usually with several of your leaders, who teach a 5-minute topical oils class like Oils for Fall and Winter, or Oils of the Bible. As long as you sneak a 101 in there somewhere, I'm down with it. Always push to the starter kit—and don't forget your close. Rotate every 5 minutes.

Make and Takes

In this class, you give a condensed (10-15 minute) 101 class, then create something. Themes I have done in the past: Spa, Chemical Free Home, It's All About That Base, Oil Your Man, and Make Your Own Diffuser Necklace + Diffuser Recipe Book.

The downside to this: it's better to push products that Young Living sells right on their site. People are only likely to make the make-and-takes once: in your class. If you want to build dedicated oilers, give them a reason to order on Young Living's site, rather than collecting supplies for their own DIY's off Young Living's site.

END YOUR CLASSES STRONG

Whatever your class style, you must not neglect a strong close. Remember the beginning of this book, where I gave you five mistakes that all stagnant business builders make? This is one of the most common mistakes I see.

I once had a woman teach a dozen classes and didn't sell a single kit at any class. I finally went to one of her classes and sat in the back of the room. She gave this beautiful 101 lecture, and then ended by saying, "You have just survived Essential Oils 101!" And that was it. No starter kit explanation, no laptop in the back of the room for people to sign, no instructions, no paper with her number as sponsor and enroller. Nothing. Those people left and got kits under someone else. One woman told me she didn't even realize that the lecturer was selling oils. Oy.

Why do we get so skiddish over our close? That's easy to explain. This is the part where we think we're selling something. It's the part where we feel like we're imposing on someone. We're forcing them to spend money they do not have. We are the solicitor at the door. Oh... and they might say "no".

Here's the thing we don't realize: these people gave up their time to come to this class! They wanted to learn about oils, they have a desire to swap out the chemicals in their home, and you failed to open the door to the start of that journey. They walked away from their families or their other obligations to attend your class. But you failed them because they have no knowledge on where to start and they left your class with absolutely nothing.

In the Appendix of this book, I have included closing scripts that lay out word for word what to say. But the gist of it is this: tell them that this is the company you trust, that this is where you began your oils journey, that this kit is the only thing on Young Living's site that's half off, so it's truly a bargain. Explain what comes in the kit and pass it around (11 oils, a diffuser, literature, NingXia samples, and 24% off your oils for life!).

As you close, tell them that you have a laptop in the back of the room and that anyone who needs help navigating the website can get assistance at a station in the room. Let them walk out with a purple bag on how to order at home. Make sure your contact information is in it. Go through that sheet. Tell them it's as hard as going to "youngliving.com," clicking on "Become a Member," and using your sponsor and enroller number. Select the premium starter kit with Home diffuser, and they're off.

Essential oils are the bridge to natural living.

Then you get the blessing of seeing where that goes. You get to field the texts of glee coming from them as they open the box. You get the updates as they discover the kits for themselves. You get to walk that journey alongside them and experience it all over again, as if it were your first week with the oils.

I tell people that if they're nervous about the close, imagine what you felt like when you knew absolutely nothing about oils. You were in darkness. You really didn't realize what a wonderful tool the Lord had given us. As you discovered them one by one, fear melted away and was replaced with confidence, joy, and the satisfaction of knowing that yet another chemical had been banned from your home.

They're so easy to use—easier than a tincture or an herb. I like to say essential oils are the bridge to natural living. Instead of having to learn about tincturing and fermenting for six weeks to begin their journey toward health, they can literally just grab a drop out of a bottle that's been expertly distilled. No prep required. The oils are powerful, they're accessible, and they have millions of uses. Find a way to share what you know with someone who was in the same place you were before you had the kit in your hands. Remember that place so you can communicate effectively with them.

If you can pull that off, you have had a very successful class. If you can can connect, educate, and train people how to research the uses of the oils for themselves and catch the vision of where Young Living goes, you will have a lifelong oilers!

PART THREE

AFTER THE CLASS: HOW TO FOLLOW UP

Your book helped us with our marketing techniques and our OGV soared. It also help us to get more people signed up for not only a membership, but the Essential Rewards program too!

Adrienne Evans

Gameplan improved our marketing technique and our followup. We are in touch with our downline more frequently which has doubled our our OGV and has gotten us more classes scheduled.

Audrey Newman

Gameplan has given me more focus for my business, as well as the confidence to know that I am "doing"it right for me. From first contact, through the class, to follow up with a rinse and repeat procedure...it is making my team grow!

Amy Metcalf

CHAPTER 10

THE OIL ABILITY FOLLOW UP SYSTEM

One of my team members approached me last week and said the last four people she's tried to sign to her team ended up on other people's teams. Do you know what causes that? *A lack of follow up.* You planted the seed, you got them interested in oils, and then *you walked away.*

You never touched base.

You never made the call to see why they weren't at class.

You never checked in to see how that Peppermint oil worked.

Consistent follow up is key to a successful business and the residual income that will bring true financial freedom to your family! You've got a system for filling classes and sharing the oils, and now I'm gonna give you...

THE OIL ABILITY FOLLOW UP SYSTEM

I'd love to say this concept was my idea, but it really wasn't. I first learned about 3-10-30 from Royal Crown Diamond Teri Secrest's materials. I had the opportunity to connect with her in person on the Global

Leadership cruise to Venice, and to pray with her and her incredible daughter Elizabeth Rose, my whitewater rafting buddy, at the Gold retreat. Their family is just wonderful. That's what I've found of all the Diamonds, though, is that they're just real people, like you and me, who have trudged through life, been poor, and found a better way. Teri's advice was fantastic and so is her book, "How Big Is Your Wave." Check it out!

This is a shot of Elizabeth (in the center) and me (on the left) rafting. (Whoever gave Young Living Corporate water guns to spray us as we came off the rapids, payback hurts!)

At about the time of this picture, I was frustrated trying to get people on Essential Rewards. That's where your residual income is—the income you don't have to hunt down in new starter kits month after month after month. It means that instead of starting from zero every month, you're starting from 300 when three people sign up for Essential Rewards. After you get 10 people on Essential Rewards, you're starting from 500 to 1000 or more OGV. Last month, we had 140,000 OGV in Essential Rewards—about 38% of our team. That means we could rank Platinum without any of our distributors selling a single kit, because the groundwork was already laid.

But how do you get people to follow through on their desire for a kit or to get Essential Rewards? You touch base with people. It's called follow up. Teri uses a fool proof system called 3-10-30. She checks in with attendees 3 days, 10 days, and 30 days after a class.

As you begin to follow up, you'll run into three types of people:

1) The type who wants nothing to do with you and asks you to leave them alone. This is the reason we all fear doing follow up after a class—we believe in our minds that 100% of the people we speak to will respond in this way, but this is extremely rare. These people came to a class to learn and they were grateful for the information. In the rare event that they react negatively, drop them and move on. Never call again.

2) The second type of people are those that say, "Oh man! I meant to get a kit when I was at class but I had to get Junior to soccer practice and have been running like crazy since then! Can you walk me through it?" Bam! You just sold a starter kit.

3) The third type of person is the one you're most likely to encounter. "Yes, I want to get a starter kit, but I just can't afford it right now."

What they're actually telling you is, "I don't know whether I need this." So it's your task to show them they need it. However, my first question isn't, "When can you afford it? When do you get paid?" That's rude and it's also counter-productive.

My first question is, "If you could wake up without one thing tomorrow—a feeling of frustration, stiffness, anything—what would that one thing be?" Write down that one thing and bring them an oil. Have them put it on and see how they feel. Most of my kit sales aren't from being pushy—they're from loving the people who came to the class and having a heart for them, wherever they are.

Follow up takes many forms. It can be a text message, a phone call, or a message on Facebook. It may be a face-to-face meeting or a Skype training to go through the kit for someone who lives far away or who has a busy schedule. I spend more time doing follow up and mailings than I do in the classroom, and follow up is one of the reasons why we have so many people on Essential Rewards.

So when you're making these calls, what do you say? There are two different types of calls. The first is for people who haven't got the kit and the second is for people who have. Let's start with the newbies.

FOLLOW UP FOR THOSE WHO DON'T HAVE A KIT

I'd tell them I'm calling to see how they liked the class and what stood out for them. I'd listen for a while in order to determine what they are interested in—perhaps they'd like oils for their pets. I'd ask if they'd like to get a kit. Then I'd talk them through how to order.

If they say not now, I'd ask if I can mail them some more resources. If they say yes to that, I'd slip a sample, a handwritten note, and one of my other lectures on DVD in the mail. But if they have said yes to getting a starter kit, I walk them through it and slip a similar package in the mail.

FOLLOW UP FOR THOSE WHO GOT A KIT

If they have already purchased the kit, the goal is to get them on Essential Rewards as a regular oiler. Then my first question is, "Did your kit arrive?" I'll ask them which oils they've used and which ones they haven't used. I'll ask if they know how to set up their diffuser. We'll talk about the

NingXia samples. I'll explain Essential Rewards and discuss the other products Young Living has on their site. Did they know they can swap out their laundry soap and dish soap and cleaning supplies as well? Do they know about the supplements? (Nitro. Oh. My. Word. It's a saving grace for tired moms!) Then I'll explain the Essential Rewards freebies for that month and give them the lowdown on Essential Rewards.

In the Gameplan workbook, I have included 12 months of graphics for Essential Rewards based on a 50PV order, 12 months of graphics based on a 190PV order, and 12 month of graphics based on a 300PV order. They include ideas like Bones and Muscles, Respiratory Support Kit, Oral Care, Chef Young Living, Conquer Emotions, Detox, Balance and Grow, Relax, Get Cleaning, and Intro to Supplements.

I have also put together a set of 3x5 cards for you to track your follow up by person. They tell you what to ask on each follow up call, give you checklists, and a place to write out what you have mailed. Find all those resources in the workbook at oilabilityteam.com.

Follow up takes a lot of time, at least an hour a week, depending on the size of your team. But if you are committed to it and train your leaders to follow your example, you'll see slow and steady growth. Another thing I do is to offer contests on my leadership page specifically for people who sign others on Essential Rewards.

The rise in numbers of people on Essential Rewards is rewarding in multiple ways. First, it's your ticket for periods of rest. Second, you get the joy of seeing more people on your team using the oils. And third, you get to see your leaders breathe a little easier, too, as their paychecks increase. It's a triple blessing. And best of all, you're developing relationships with the people who came to your classes—relationships which are built out of a love for oils and a passion to educate. You can't top that!

(I share even more strategies for how to educate your team onto Essential Rewards in Chapter 19!)

PLAN TO FOLLOW UP!

There's one more tip on follow up that our Oil Ability team members, Joy and Hans Hinterkopf, Young Living Golds, came up with. They were really struggling actually getting a hold of people after they'd purchased a kit. They'd call and call, and because the person on the other end didn't recognize their number, they would not respond. They'd email or text and get no response.

They found a simple way to fix that. When new people are signing up for their starter kit, *right then and there* set a date to go through the kit with them. Tell them you want to show them how to use their diffuser without frying it, how to utilize the oils in their kit in their home, and the benefits of NingXia. Tell them you'll train them how to look stuff up when they have questions and how to log into their Virtual Office to order more oils. Offer 30 minutes of time and set a date. Write down the date and time you'll be at their home (or if they're a distance away, will meet them on Skype) and put it in your planner. Then they are expecting that call.

There's one more critical thing to tell you about follow up. And it can be summed up in one word:

CONSISTENCY

Consistency is essential to every part of your business but it's especially crucial with follow up. You need to be consistently following up after each class or you won't see the rewards of all your other efforts.

I've found that I spend more time behind the scenes touching base with people than I do teaching. If you are aiming for Silver in Six and teaching 4-6 classes a month, with each class averaging 2 hours with setup and tear down, you're working 8-12 hours a month, based on class time only. That's about one day of work a month. But I probably spend another 5 hours a month, on average, doing follow up.

Consistency is essential to every part of your business but it's especially crucial with follow up.

Consistency will make or break your business. If you teach one class a month, you'll earn enough to get a free oil. If you want a sustainable, livable income, then the reality is that you must teach more than once a month. Would you expect to get paid $40,000 a year for a 40-hour-a-week job that you don't show up to? Then why would you expect to make

$10,000 a month for a Young Living business that you only work 2 hours a month, by teaching only one class?

If you want to grow, you have to be consistent! Let me show you what that looks like. On the next page are two snapshots, used with permission, of different members of the Oil Ability team.

The first held just one class, in the month of December. Every other month since then, they have privately added one or two people a month. What you'll see in the mapping of their business from the dashboard on their Virtual Offices is that they are all over the place. It's because there is no consistency to the way that they run their business. There's no game plan. And with no game plan, there's no solid execution. That means no steady income and no reliable business.

The second person regularly holds classes four to six times a month and follows up. That's 90 minutes a week of class time and a couple hours of follow up.

Person 1:

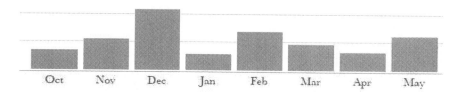

Person 2:

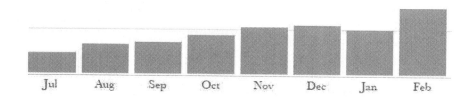

What I found to be most telling was the month of January. Team wide, that was a low month for all of us. But can you see how hard it hit the first person, versus the second? The second didn't take such a hard hit because they had consistently been signing people up on Essential Rewards. It wasn't as painful. This is how you build a multi-million-dollar home business—no excuses. Get out there and do it, and do it regularly, consistently, and with a game plan.

You have survived follow up 101. It's truly not painful! It's actually the fruit of your work because it's the place where you get to hear their stories and feel their excitement. Drop the fear and run for the relationship! It's the part of this that makes it all worth it.

CHAPTER 11

DEALING WITH DIFFICULT PEOPLE

As you follow up with people who have attended your oils classes, expect some opposition. In this chapter I want to equip you for what to say when people want just one oil, when they don't want to commit to a wholesale account, or when they are just plain negative.

PEOPLE WHO WANT JUST ONE OIL

Why would someone need just one oil? Because they don't know what the oils do. That's the only reason.

Every single person should be funneled through the premium starter kit wholesale option, because this kit trains them with 11 oils how to become oilers. You're going to get great at using lavender if that's the only oil you own, but I can't imagine a winter without R.C. for respiratory support or Thieves for immune support. When you allow people to order only individual oils, you are training them to be needy and they will have a lack of commitment.

If those in your friend circle just order a single oil off of you every few months, it's not their fault. You have not equipped them to buy, you have been enabling them. You drop things off at their door for them to try. You add oils to your order so they don't have to get on Essential Rewards. They pawn Thieves cleaner off of you when they are low. They are the "just watching from the sidelines" oiler, the "lack of commitment" oiler. But there is an easy solution.

Don't Enable—Educate!

Have a gentle conversation with them about all of the products they should be using daily, and should order themselves: NingXia, Pure Protein Complete, Thieves cleaning products like dish soap, dishwasher soap and Thieves cleaner, personal care products, etc... They are either serious about wanting a chemical free life, or they are not serious. If they are not serious, kick the dust off your feet and move to the line of people that are.

The one exception I'll make—and I only do it once for them. If they really want to try an oil but aren't sure they want the kit yet, I'll add one oil or one other product to my order and let them try it out. But I always encourage them to purchase the starter kit. I make sure they've heard the 101 class, either on audio CD or on DVD. I lay the groundwork for a chemical-free home. They get one freebie from me, and then they have to set up their own account. In the past, I have had at one time over 20 people wanting to place orders through me. I don't have the time to drop off all those orders! Stop enabling them to leach off your account and have them set up their own.

PEOPLE WHO DON'T WANT A WHOLESALE ACCOUNT

If you have gone through the process of enrolling someone with a starter kit, then you've seen the options they can choose when they enroll. They can be either a retail customer or a wholesale customer. Some people will shy away from the commitment of becoming a wholesale customer and want to just buy a few oils as a retail customer. This is simply lack of education, as we discussed above.

I'll tell you that to this day, I have never enrolled a single retail customer. I just don't believe in it. I am thankful Young Living has made the option for us, but I believe it's a cop-out for people who are trying to save cash. (There. I said it!) By saving cash on oils, they are inadvertently spending it in much more dangerous chemical-laden places. I never feel like I am pushing people to buy product they can't afford. I am far too passionate about getting the garbage out of their homes, the chemicals that are poisoning their families. It's all about showing them a better way.

Sometimes you have the people who ask about professional accounts. Those are accounts that you can set up if you're a small business with a storefront. It allows someone to purchase the oils at wholesale and sell them at retail in order to make a profit. However, people with professional accounts forfeit any right to a downline, which makes no sense, because your true money-making ability is in your downline. You never know who will come into their store and turn out to be a Diamond!

I would never, ever encourage someone to throw away the opportunity to have a successful business. I'd recommend skipping the professional account and just going with a regular wholesale account. Even if the store owner doesn't want to do the business side, they'll be blessed by those under them who do. Always leave that door open.

NEGATIVE PEOPLE

Now we'll talk about facing negative people. You will encounter them. Goodness, Christ encountered negative people. There are two types out there: the type that bashes your family business, and the type that bashes oils.

This is where one of my life verses comes in. "If anyone will not welcome you or listen to your words, leave that home or town and shake the dust off your feet." (Matthew 10:14)

There are so many people out there who need oils. In fact, every single person you come into contact with needs them, whether they're at the post office, Walmart, or Panera. (I have sold kits in line at each of those places! I even sold a kit to the TSA agent in Spokane, Washington when we were flying home from the Gold retreat!) There are more than enough people to keep you busy, so stop focusing on the ones who you want to be oilers, and speak to the people who are ready.

I know that some of the people you desperately want on your teams are your mothers, your best friends, and your sisters—but recognize one thing: just because they say no now, it does not mean the answer will always be no. It's impossible to be around an oiler and not have a positive oils experience at some point, especially if you're in regular contact with them. Let the oils and the success of your business speak for itself. They will see it when they are ready. Forcing it is one of the worst things you can do. It took some of my family members two years to warm up to oils (and a few of them I'm still working on!) Do not be discouraged. The field is wide and you have more time then you think you do.

If you waste all your time trying to convince everyone that oils are a great option, you're losing time with the people who are already eager to learn and sick of the chemicals in their home. So follow Biblical principles, kick the dust off your feet, move to the next person, and don't look back. Don't let it wear on you. It's better to be out there collecting no's then not moving and having a stagnant business. The trick is to prevent their response from hitting you emotionally. They're just not ready yet. Did you catch that? Because it's a critical principle if you want to have a successful business.

Emotionally detach yourself from the sale of the starter kit

If you're so busy holding classes and doing follow up, you have little time to notice those out there that gave you a resounding no. Move on, stay focused, and work with the scores of people attending classes. It sounds difficult to do if the person telling you no is a close friend, but it's truly not. You just need to refocus yourself. Let it sting for a second and then remember that the answer may not always be no—it's just no at this moment, and likely because they need to have an oils experience. They need to see them work. It may take a while. And in that time, redirect yourself, stay positive, and put one foot in front of the other.

"There is precious treasure and oil in the dwelling of the wise."

While I'm at it, let me throw another Bible verse at you, one I have on my wall at home: Proverbs 21:20: "There is precious treasure and oil in the dwelling of the wise." Oils in your house. Be wise. Oil up. And according to Scripture, have backup oils, too. When I am down about the loss of a kit, some of my favorite emotional oils are "Magnify Your Purpose", "Highest Potential", and "Forgiveness." Put a little of them on the back of your neck or in the diffuser for a few minutes and see how you feel. It's a great pick-me-up.

What about the family members that don't believe in multi-level marketing? Well, that's just ignorance. You can work 40 hours a week and survive or work 10 to 20 hours a week and make $10,000 a month or more in your Young Living business. If they are willing, I'd point them to Eric Worre's Rise Of The Entrepreneur DVD. For 50 minutes, it will throw out all sorts of facts and statistics for the non-believer. If they don't want to waste another second on your business, keep this in mind: you don't need their approval.

A year after getting my starter kit, I really struggled with coming off my anchoring shift, but I chose to retire. It was an emotional hit to me. All of my radio friends wrote and asked, "What are you doing!??! You have a morning drive position on a powerful network that broadcasts to 5 million people, and you're walking away??!? You waited 11 years for that job! Are you insane? No one gets morning drive jobs at 29 years old. Why would you leave radio to sell oils kits???!!!?"

I got it good and I got it from all angles. I got it from people I had worked with in Chicago and in New York. I got it from family members and some of my closest friends.

The secret to handling negativity

Here's the deal: my identity isn't as a news anchor. My identity isn't as a mom. My identity isn't even as a Young Living Platinum. My identity is in Christ, and if my eyes stay focused on Him, all else fades away. It really doesn't matter. I don't have to search for hope and meaning. I already have it through Jesus's death on the cross.

So if my identity isn't in speaking to 5 million people every morning, did it matter if I walked away? Nope.

I have a hope and future far beyond the whisperings of this world. The Lord has taken care of us. That one decision allowed me to multiply my income by 5 after I stepped off my full time anchoring job and now, two years out from my starter kit, my husband is retiring as well. We are blessed, despite the naysayers.

CHAPTER 12

No One is Coming to Classes—Now What?

In this book, we have hit on quite a bit of strategy. We've worked on English with writing for your classes, and now you'll get a class in the Psychology of Network Marketing. If you master this one skill, you will have cracked the hard outer shell of network marketing!

If you have ever heard anyone tell you network marketing doesn't work, it's likely because they never got past the psychology of it. It's one of the biggest pitfalls I see. I have had so many people come to me and say "I did that once. I told x, y, z. I never made more than..." Let's debunk exactly what happened to them. (Or maybe to you, with another network marketing company!) This chapter will change the entire way you look at your business and will take the pressure off of prospecting new people. Are you ready?

WHY ARE PEOPLE AVOIDING ME?

There are three reasons people avoid you. Only three. Here they are:

1) You are hunting them.

2) They are missing the education connection between coming to class and getting the kit.

3) You spew negativity and are not a leader they want to follow.

There is the possibility they truly have zero interest in oils, but because of their ten billion uses, that's likely not the case. It's more likely they truly don't understand what they can use them for, or they're overwhelmed and don't know where to start, and have paralysis by analysis. That falls under the education reason. I'm going to address each of these issues head on.

1. DON'T BE A HUNTER!

Don't go into every conversation with the eye on the prize of selling a starter kit, and don't give every person you pass your "pitch." You have to emotionally detach from each class, each person, and each conversation. Don't take it personally when people say, "no," and don't take it personally when they say, "not yet." The average person can only say no seven times—keep pursuing! It's easy to say but tough to do, so let me give you a trick.

You need to stay so busy scheduling 101 classes and so busy talking to everyone you meet about oils and getting them to classes, that you don't have the time to notice the people who are naysayers. Make sure you have good follow up, for sure, and don't leave people in the dust. But also don't take the time to dwell on those who say no. If your focus is always on educating people and teaching them to live a chemical-free life, your heart is always for the distributor. It's never for the sale. They will feel it. They'll feel your passion and your compassion—that it's for them, and that will build a relationship of trust.

Do you remember the story of my brother Aaron, from Chapter Eight? I really wanted him to be a Young Living distributor. He had worked in sales for nearly 20 years, and I knew he had the blood of a Royal Crown Diamond. I needed him for my business, but more than anything, I genuinely wanted him to succeed. He had a toddler and another baby on the way and was working 12 to 15 hour shifts. I did not want to see my brother so depleted.

I gave Aaron my pitch. I tried the chemical free home angle, telling him that he was poisoning his family with the cleaning supplies in his house. I sent him sample after sample after sample, but 18 months later, it was all in a cabinet, untouched, and he still didn't have a kit. It was not until I heard his heart telling me about his basement that smelled like smoke that I met him where he needed to be met—a stench in his house. Then he made the purchase. The oils worked, and now he is a die-hard oiler.

He didn't respond to my pitch because he knew he was being hunted. He is a salesperson! He knew my passion for the oils, but had no desire to join me. Why? Because I came across as coming in for the sale instead of building a relationship on trust, even with my own brother.

Focus on Relationship

In your 101 class, some people will be "on fire" from the start. They'll get the kit, run with it, and need little mentoring. There are some who will write you constantly, and you can refer them to places to do their own research. Then there will be some who you so desperately want to help, but they just aren't buying it.

For that last group of people, there are two options. If you truly desire to see them on your team, then engage in a gentle pursuit. Eric Worre has some wonderful training in one of my favorite network marketing books, "Go Pro." He uses the "If I, would you?" question.

If I give you this 101 lecture on DVD or audio CD, will you listen to it? If so, when? May I call you on Saturday to touch base afterward?

If I invite you to a free class, would you come?

If I set up a coffee break, would you have an hour to meet with me to talk oils?

"If I, would you?"

I love that concept. You're never just freely giving something away, you're always asking something in return. It's a give and take. It's a dance. You're not a hunter, you're in a relationship.

For the others who are constantly saying "no", I'd move on. There may be a time when they will listen, but it's not now. Don't take it personally.

If you have engaged in a way that's genuine and real and have built a relationship of trust with them, most of them will follow. Some will do it right away and some will do it after they have processed the conversation (or many conversations.) That's okay. Just make sure that your heart is always to educate, not to go in for the sale.

If you switch your philosophy about how you run your business, suddenly there's no pressure to perform! You're out there helping people. Do it more frequently and you'll grow more quickly. If you are not filling classes, it's because of how people are reading you. They don't like to be hunted, so change the way you present. They will read realness and rawness.

And don't dwell on the no's. Pursue relationships, not kit sales!

2. BE AN EDUCATOR

I want you to walk back in time with me for a second. Do you remember the place you were the moment you were in your first oils class? You hadn't had the oodles of experiences that you've now had that have made you so passionate.

That is the place where your almost-oiler is. You have to walk back into that place, connect with them, and find what piece of education they need for these to work for them. It may be smells. Or emotions. Or cleaning supplies. Or chemicals. Or supplements. Or pets. Or so many other places. Young Living now has a pain cream—and that little ditty alone has sold many a kit for me.

Start where they are. Meet them there. Don't give up on them because they are new. Don't walk away too soon. Drop it at their feet and wait. Then do it again and again and again. Some will pick it up right away, others will take longer. But if you walk into the blackness of a total lack of oils knowledge and pluck them from that place, by meeting them where their needs are, you will have won trust and developed an oiler. Educate.

3. DITCH THE NEGATIVITY

This is a hard one, because there are SO many reasons why it happens.

You may have been disappointed so many times you won't allow yourself the pleasure of believing that financial miracles can happen in your life.

You may have been hurt over and over and over again.

You may have had your trust crushed.

You may have been abused, and have built terrific walls that no one can break through. (If that's your story, I'd encourage you to get plugged into a church and a Christian counselor that can speak life and hope into you, and pray with you, and start to break down some of the barriers. A wonderful place to start is the ministry fln.org. Do a search for a Healing Journey group on their website--they are available throughout the north-eastern U.S.. The groups are incredible!)

Whatever your reason for spewing negativity or sarcasm, you're going to struggle building a business, because people do not want to follow that. People will look at you and see if you have something in your life that they want. If all your posts online are negative or divisive, they don't want to follow it.

Consider every word out of your mouth, every conversation with those around you, every post on any social media platform as an arena where you are studied. If you're not emulating Young Living values of abundance, purpose and wellness, people will run the other way. They have no reason to follow something they don't want in their life.

---

*Start with a simple step:
pause before you speak.*

Start with a simple step: pause before you speak. If what you are about to say is hurtful or negative, reconsider. If your heart's desire is truly to grow a thriving Young Living business, you have to do it in a way that lifts people up and encourages them. If people see nothing to follow, they will look for another team. Guard your words—words speak life. They either build up or tear down. Use them carefully.

If you can master these three skills, and have a genuine heart as you do them—being real and raw, you'll inspire people in all walks of life. It's about your growth as a leader. And you do that one step at a time, filling yourself with good things, and then projecting that through your friend circles and your team.

CHAPTER 13

KEYS TO CONFIDENCE

It would be a disservice to tell you how to launch a Young Living business without giving you a chapter on confidence. Why? Because there are two things you really need to know to do this well. First, you need to understand the ins and outs of Young Living—the Virtual Office, the 101 lecture, and your starter kit. This book walks you through just about every question you may have on launching a business, in depth.

But there is another element to pulling this off: confidence. If you do not have confidence, no one will trust what you are saying. It's the number one reason I see people unable to fill classes.

We have a saying in the newsroom—"fake it 'till you make it." If you don't know an answer, give them an honest response and either teach them how to look it up themselves (the better option) or tell them you'll ask your upline or Young Living corporate for guidance. There's nothing wrong with not knowing an answer. But I've seen people take a lack of confidence to extremes.

I had a woman on my team who held class after class after class—with zero attendees. Finally, I took a look at the wording she used for her events, and it went something like this: "If you want to learn more about essential oils, PLEASE come to my class. If not, it's ok. I will be holding other classes in the future, if you are busy."

Wuh?!? Who will follow leadership like that??

That's like saying, "If you want to douse yourself in chemical toxins for another two weeks until my next class, I'm totally okay with that. I don't have the confidence to tell you that you're poisoning yourself and your family." The people you do not speak to because of your lack of confidence will be hurt. These are people that have been placed in your path specifically for you to speak into their life. Do not be so timid that you steal their lifeline when they most need you.

A lack of confidence can come from a lot of places. If you set goals and repeatedly fail to reach them, you end up telling yourself you can't win. It can come from losing hope. It can come from being abused. Here's the thing: God didn't make you that way. I've never met a toddler who wasn't confident. It's a learned behavior. There was a point in your life when you weren't afraid, and that's who you really are.

Confidence is something that I can't teach in this book. But I can tell you where to go to learn it, with a system that works, because I've put dozens of my team members through this training. I put myself through this training. The month I went, my OGV had been stuck at 46,000 for five months. Five months later, it was at 152,000 and I was a solid Platinum, because I was no longer afraid.

There was a point in your life when you weren't afraid, and that's who you really are.

My favorite resource to get over emotional blocks in your business is from a gifted network marketer named Dani Johnson. She does a 3-day weekend intensive called "First Steps To Success" that will blow your mind. It addresses every block you may have, and she also teaches how to understand personality types on your teams, how to connect with your leaders, how to stop emulating a person who is afraid, how to stop making excuses, and how to get out there and execute. It is worth every penny. I continue to go several times a year and bring more leaders each time, because I'm letting Dani train them for me. And every time we go, our team grows.

Best. Investment. Ever.

If you opt to attend one of her conferences, tell her you heard about it in this book. And thank you for the blessing. I've never had one of my team members tell me they wish they hadn't gone, and I've seen some pretty incredible things out of it afterward. For example, an abused woman stood up to her husband of 40 years, a shy team member stood before a table of 25 people and spoke for the first time, and what followed was dramatic OGV growth as walls of fear were destroyed.

One of the things Dani speaks a lot about is excuse making. In fact, she spends her entire first day speaking about it. Early on in this book, we covered the typical excuses I hear from my team:

- I don't have time
- I don't have money
- I don't have the right personality
- I can't talk to people
- I don't know anyone
- I live in the middle of nowhere
- I am too tired
- I have no resources
- My upline stinks
- I can't find a place to teach
- I can't find anyone to watch my kids
- I'm not you
- I don't like "selling" stuff

Here's the deal. Do you like where you are? Do you have enough income? Do you have enough time with your spouse and your children? Are you able to bless other people and pour into their lives with your time and finances? Are you crossing things off your bucket list every single year, or are you waiting five more years for your dreams to happen? Those aren't just dreams—they are your heart's desires that God put there! You're supposed to be pursuing them!

If the answer is no to any of those—*get over your excuses and fix it.* My team includes software developers who are making $70,000 a month, a surgeon, a doctor, several dentists and chiropractors, a university researcher well respected in the field, and many other professionals, some with extremely high paying jobs. Just because your job pays well doesn't mean you have time economy or freedom. It also doesn't mean you have your retirement said and done. If don't like where you are, change it! It's as simple as that. Get over the confidence issues, stop making excuses, and do what you need to do to succeed, without distraction.

Another word I absolutely hate is "try." I'll "try" to do my business, but I can't make any promises. You're either in or you're not. I will work with people who show me they are serious and will work the business. If you're not serious about digging out of where you are, I move to the next person. I have a passion to raise people from poverty, but only those that want to be raised.

At the Young Living International Grand Convention in Salt Lake City in 2016, there was a wonderful demonstration with 22,000 people in the crowd. We were all asked to stand. Then we were asked to sit. Then we were asked if we "tried to stand" or "tried to sit". We didn't try, we did it. You don't try to do things. You either accomplish or you don't. Trying is an excuse as you look for a way out. If you want this, fight for it!

If you have a hard time drawing people to classes, I'd really encourage you to get to a Dani Johnson conference. One of the reasons people don't come to classes is because they feed off your negative energy. You say you believe in the business and believe in the oils, but your demeanor and tone may show something completely different. The first day of her "First Steps to Success" conference does a wonderful job in training you how to recognize excuses, how to build confidence and overcome negativity, no matter what you have been through. Check it out here: www.danijohnson.com.

Remember that you are not hunting. You are building relationships and educating. Always go in with the goal of education and not kit sales. That takes the pressure off of a sales mentality, and it makes it easier to teach. Detach yourself from the outcome. I believe a lot of our fears are fear of rejection and fear of what people think of us. None of that matters when you do a mental shift and focus on the person, not the sale. It's all about education. Then it's all about being so busy selling starter kits that you don't notice the no's. That is the key to confidence.

PART FOUR

STRATEGIES FOR GROWTH:
STAR AND BEYOND

Gameplan gave me simple directions to motivate and put into action what I need to do to propel my YL business. It has created a fire on my team as each member goes through the book and workbook and puts it into action. A fire can't burn with one piece of wood alone!

Dawn Harvey

Gameplan marketing works! I doubled my OGV and ranked up in one month just by implementing it.

Jaime Anderson

CHAPTER 14

YOUR BUSINESS TOOLKIT: OILY TOOLS, TAXBOT, AND MORE

At this point, you've walked through one full cycle of a Young Living business. You have practiced the 101 lecture diligently and you have set a date. You marketed the class heavily, invited 100 people and 15 showed. After that class you did great follow up, and four people got kits. Congratulations!

If you continue with that model, you're following in the footsteps of the Diamonds, Crown Diamonds, and Royal Crown Diamonds before you. If you're tenacious and don't give up, you will get there, and it won't take as long as you think! Rinse and repeat. If you rinse and repeat four to six times a month, most of my leaders reach Silver within six months. That's usually $2000 to $3000 in monthly income.

In my house, that was a game changer. That was me stepping off my job full time. It was letting a second job go. It meant paying off some serious debt. I love to see everyone reach the rank of Silver, because this sets the stage for Gold, Platinum, and Diamond!

I'd like to take a chapter and put some strategic resources in your hands. Hopefully you're fairly comfortable at this point with marketing and filling classes—you've checked out the Appendix and collected some scripts to help you with follow up and your close. And you're getting a bit more confident. Let's make you super confident. I promised you a meat and potatoes book. Here's the second helping.

RESOURCE NUMBER 1: OILY TOOLS

There are many gifted people involved with Young Living and they have created some pretty incredible things. Take Jake Dempsey, for example. Jake is a software developer like my husband. He's pretty amazing at it, actually. When his wife had a tough time calculating her Young Living paycheck, he made her a software app to do the math. It was so wildly successful that he made a cell phone version, and now thousands of us can accurately calculate our checks because of Jake. Jake is now a Young Living Crown Diamond, so the app was a pretty good motivator for his wife.

The neat thing is that you can use this app without a lot of effort. It's called Oily Tools. Download it from the Google play store or the Apple store. It's seriously awesome.

You can see your projected paycheck by rank, what your pace OGV is set to hit, how many people are ranking up, how much you have in Essential Rewards, and a money miser report for those that haven't spent their 100PV and won't get paid. It's awesome!If you're an English person like me, this man has incalculable worth to you. (That guy with the curly hair is Jake. Those other people in the picture are a couple of my kids. They are pretty amazing too).

RESOURCE #2: TAXBOT

Are you afraid of doing your taxes? It's not bad. Here are the rules: for every penny you make, save 20% and put it in a savings account and forget it's there.

Also, every time you get a receipt for absolutely anything, upload it to a program called Taxbot. It costs $5 a month for Young Living users. I spoke with the creator Stanley Botkin (who by the way does the taxes for Bill Gates) and he's a genius. He says the program makes you virtually audit proof. On each receipt, you type out the "who what when where why"- who you were with, what it was for, etc. Taxbot also syncs with your smart phone and tracks all the miles for your business—automatically. By satellite. It's pretty awesome, and completely worth the $5 a month.

They created their own page specifically for Young Living users and that gives you 50% off. You can find it here: https://taxbot.com/z/yl/

What are some items you can deduct? Here's a brief list.

- The room where you do you Young Living business (not your whole house, but a percentage of your home. For example, one room is your office. That room is 8x10 and takes up 10 percent of the square footage of your home. You can deduct 10 percent of your utilities, 10 percent of your taxes, etc.)

- The same percentage for each utility

- Your mileage. Check with the post office to see what the current mileage rate is

- Your business expenses. That would include things like Taxbot, Oily Tools, supplies that you order for a store or a vendor event, etc.

- Business trips, for example, costs of hotel rooms for business related events, including CONVENTION!

- Half of all business related meals

- Awards for your team, up to 25 dollars per person

- Oils you are using for your business and other Young Living products for your business

- Any employees you pay to help you with bookkeeping, mailings, follow up, and to help at events

The Taxbot website has some wonderful videos to explain the ins and outs of running a small business. Take an afternoon and check some of them out.

RESOURCE #3: IBLOOM PLANNER

This is my favorite planner for network marketers. It's where I store all my classes, receipts, and thoughts. It's how I track where I'm going next. They have a nice laminated planner or one that you can print for a discounted price. Of all the planners I've used so far, this one is definitely my favorite. (https://ibloom.co/free-ibloom-planner/)

RESOURCE #4: OIL ABILITY!

The Oil Ability team has put together some incredible DVD's, CD's, bootcamps, and books. They will take you through, step by step, how to grow your business or how to train your new members to use the oils. They're even more comprehensive than this book. There are scripts and downloadable videos to train your team and even a monthly newsletter with recipes and updates for classes that are near you. Check it all out at www.oilabilityteam.com.

We also have a knockout Facebook page thousands strong—just search for the "Oil Ability with Sarah" page!

RESOURCE #5: BRAIN FOOD

During the last 18 months, I have read over 200 books on aromatherapy, and if you want to know my favorites (they change weekly), you can shoot me a message online. For the sake of this book, which is meant to train business builders, let me give you my top three network marketing resources.

1) Eric Worre's Go Pro. This isn't Young Living specific, but it's a wonderful guidebook to all things network marketing—the very best I've seen. This is the one that I ask all of my leaders to buy.

2) Eric Worre's Rise DVD. This is 52 minutes of awesome! If you have any skeptics in your family who think that network marketing is a scam or doesn't work and that the 40-hour work week is the only true way to make a decent income, they MUST see this DVD. It's so loaded with stats and facts that you can't possibly ignore that it will blow your mind. As a news junkie who loves facts, this DVD really spoke to me about how much time we waste.

3) How to Win Friends and Influence People, by Dale Carnegie. Just read it. Wow!

It's said that you should commit one hour a day of your work day to stretching your brain, growing it, and thinking outside the box. With five children, I'll be straight up—it's about one hour a week for me. (Hey, it's more when they go to summer camp!) But even with that commitment, these resources have really made a big difference in how I lead my team, the negative talk over my business, how I pray for my distributors, how I spend my time, and what types of goals I set.

As a leader, it's important that you're being fed good food. Changing your brain is the first step toward digging out of the places you don't want to be. You have to believe you can make it, and if you believe and you speak life over yourself and your business, it's amazing the places you will go! Your feet will start to follow your mouth. You may go 37  years of your life without a single vacation, and then 18 months into your business find yourself in Hawaii with Young Living. It's happened before, so speak life!

CHAPTER 15

GROWING YOUR BUSINESS THROUGH BLOGGING

Okay, you've got me here. Although John and I were able to catapult to Platinum 17 months after our starter kit arrived on our door, I'll be the first to admit that I'm not tech savvy. I did not build my business online; I did it through in-person relationships developed at classes.

(I think I have five photos uploaded to Instagram. It was a leap for me, and I still don't get it. In fact, I'm kind of hoping that by the time this book is printed it's outdated so I don't have to learn it.)

But that's the neat thing about Young Living. There's no "wrong way" of sharing—online or in person. The trick is to be genuine and to use your gift set. I recognize that technology is an anomaly to me, but thankfully, I married a software developer, so I get a leg up occasionally. Unfortunately, said software developer isn't available for my every whim, so I had to hit up one of my friends to write this techie-geek chapter.

This is a good place to pause for a moment and talk about a quality that's critical to lead a team—knowing your weak spots and being willing to delegate them to others and defer to their strengths. It's just as important to have a teachable spirit. If you're unable to learn math or online social media platforms, at least smile and pretend that you know what's going on.

One of my Young Living crossline besties, Mary Souther Clendenin, has offered to write this chapter for me. Mary runs the blog "The Encouraging Home," which has over 100,000 followers. She is also a homeschool mom of boys and a treasured friend who loves the Lord. Because she has grown the bulk of her business online, reached the Gold rank primarily through her massive blog, (which she wrote while living in the boon-docks in North Carolina and surrounded by 800 cows), she commands an audience out of her sheer genius. Here is what Mary has to say about growing a Young Living business from your living room.

GROWING YOUR BUSINESS ONLINE

Word-of-mouth marketing is one of the most powerful ways to promote your products. But today, with the Internet, creativity, and planning, you can get the word out on a larger scale and at a faster pace.

It is about building relationships, gaining trust and caring about people. It is about letting them know that you are not just selling products to get a paycheck, but that you have a passion for helping others improve their lives.

It might take a little longer to get that across online as people are getting to know you, but it is possible and sometimes goes much faster than you think! That is the way I have grown my business, while still doing some local classes, but focusing mainly online.

Share your heart and your passions. Be cautious about what you post or share because this is all they know about you. They look at everything you share, not just what you post about essential oils. Be honorable and be the best you can be. People watch you closely online and you may never know it.

You want to brand yourself, not your company. Don't build your social media or blog around a company or a product. Build relationships. Compel people to ask what you do. Let people get to know you and it will take you far.

Always remember to stay compliant online. Watch your words, pictures, and the links you post. Keep up to date with policies and procedures. You can check under Member Resources in your Virtual Office for a hot word list and more.

SHARING VIA SOCIAL MEDIA

One of the fastest ways to start sharing is on social media. Facebook is the most popular. It is all about creating culture and sharing your stories. People aren't buying the product. They are trusting you.

Share real life pictures of your oils and diffuser. Share but don't spam. You will want to have a business Facebook Page with your blog or business name. Make sure you follow current Young Living policies about social media pages.

Your posts should be positive, encouraging, and motivational. People will be curious about you and want to get in on whatever makes you this happy person who is spreading joy, light and encouragement. You should be building relationships, just like in person. You create a culture. You post things that encourage, such as favorite quotes, simple recipes, asking them questions, throwing in some product education and every now and then, and posting about your product or sale that is going on.

Provide value every day.

While people follow you on social media to learn more about you and to be encouraged, they also want to know how you can help them. They aren't coming to see what you wore, what you ate, etc. You just have a few seconds to capture their attention before they click away, unless they are friends or have become faithful followers. Provide value every day.

There are other forms of social media that are great ways to share. I recommend getting proficient on one platform before adding another.

Instagram can be more personal and helps to connect you. Twitter is like text messages. It is great for business and getting your point across in 140 characters or less.

Don't get overwhelmed posting on all platforms. Choose one or two and get really good on those before adding more, if you choose to do so.

A word of caution...don't be on social media all the time. It can take over your life. Literally. And you will lose productivity and momentum, as well as precious family time. Use a scheduling platform like Hootsuite.com to schedule posts. It will simplify your life.

Get on social media several times a day to answer questions and monitor for trolls and rudeness. Use the delete and ban button if needed. Your social media platforms and blog is like your home. Would you allow people to enter your home and be rude or say ugly things? No, you would protect your family. The same is true for your online presence. You are protecting your name and your community that has put their trust in you.

SHARING WITH A BLOG

Another good way to grow your business online is with a blog or website. Creating one from scratch can take a little time, so if you want to start quickly, get a YLDist.com website. It is a nice, clean site that you can link to different pages on social media or when you email people. You can also add in the blog function when you are having classes and events. This can connect to your other social media platforms and is how people can get in touch with you. I have a blog at TheEncouragingHome.com, but I also have one of these sites that I love.

If you want to grow a larger online presence, a blog is a great way to do that. I personally built a blog about more than just essential oils, although I am very passionate about them.

Ask yourself some questions: What are you an expert at? What do you love? Decide on your niche and what you can talk about every day, or a couple times a week, besides essential oils. Who is your target audience that you are able to help?

Do you want your blog just to be about essential oils? Do you want to expand to other natural health areas? I recommend blogging about other things than just one focus. My blog is about inspiring hope, health and happiness at home. My target audience is moms who need encourage-ment in life, family, marriage, parenting, self-care, have a natural health interest and may be looking for work at home. Do others read my blog who don't fit into this category? Yes. Focus on providing quality content that can touch lives and that people will want to share with others.

6 STEPS TO STARTING A BLOG

1. Choose a name

Some people use their own name. My blog is The Encouraging Home. Either way, your name or a business name, will work. You are branding yourself and you can be successful with either. Don't build your blog around what you are selling. Be a resource and provide great content that can change lives!

2. Choose www.wordpress.org

I recommend a wordpress.org site so you own your blog and you also can sell on it. The beautiful thing about a blog is that it can lead into many directions and become income producing in a number of different ways. So make sure you start out with the right platform.

3. Choose a hosting company

I use Bluehost.com. You want one that provides excellent customer service and is available to help you anytime you need it. Other companies also provide this service, so do your research.

4. Choose a domain name

Check to see if it is available. Try to use one that ends in .com since that is the most popular. You can check this through your hosting company or just google to see if it comes up. You will need to renew this each year. Whether you use your name or not for your blog, I recommend purchasing it as well. You never know how big you might grow and you might want to use that sometime too.

5. Choose a logo

Check on your team to see if there are any graphic designers who can help you. There are many graphic designers out there who provide these services. This logo is something that shows what your blog is all about.

6. Create great content

I recommend writing several posts before you launch your blog so you have content ready to go. Try to blog at least once or twice a week. Perhaps one post can be about essential oils or practical ways to use oils, DIY projects, etc. The other weekly post can be something that adds value and encouragement to your readers.

A blog is also a great place to create resource pages for your team. You can upload files, images and videos for education and support. You can password protect these pages so only your team can access this.

Your blog can grow quickly or it can grow slowly and steadily, just like your Young Living business. Be careful not to allow your blog and social media to overtake your life. It is easy to get caught up in how many followers you have, or how many comments there are on your blog. It is easy to become distracted and take time away from your family and income-producing activities for your business.

While you want to blog regularly, life can happen. You can take some time off from blogging and just post on social media if needed for a little while. Or you can recirculate some great content from past posts when you need a break. Just like your Young Living business, it can continue to grow if you need a few weeks to breathe, but if you take your hands off for too long, it will slow down. Be careful not to get burned out in the online world and work at a steady pace.

THE IMPORTANCE OF AN EMAIL LIST

While social media platforms are the quickest way to start sharing, you do not own your friends' list or the community on your business page. They could disappear at any time. If you are blogging at wordpress.org, you own your platform but people come and go on your blog.

Which is why you need an email list. You own your list, people choose to subscribe to your blog and email list. There are several great email providers to choose from, but carefully read their Terms of Service to see if they allow work at home or MLMs. Contact their customer service with questions. Aweber is what I currently use. It is a paid program and people can opt into your emails/newsletter and give you permission to email them.

People must choose to be added to your email list. You can create a list in your email service and place a box on your blog. Don't randomly add emails. When people purchase a kit from you, they have given permission to be emailed.

You can create a free opt-in, a gift in exchange for their giving you their email address. This can be a one-page sheet, eBook, phone call, or video. Be creative and make it something valuable that is a taste of what your blog offers.

Remember to stay always stay compliant in everything you write, post, and share. You are responsible for it or where links lead to once they click through. Be safe and always check before posting. If in doubt, delete for your protection and for Young Living.

SUPPORTING YOUR TEAM ONLINE

Facebook groups provide an excellent place to support your customers and members. You can create secret or closed groups and post product education, team news, company news, host contests, and giveaways and provide a place of community for your team. It is a great place to build relationships and support each other. You will most likely find that this helps your team become like a family and that it provides a venue in which they can encourage each other in many areas of their lives, not just Young Living.

You can create learning groups for product education, as well as business groups for those wanting to do the business and learn how to share. Really use these groups to encourage, educate, support, and lead your team.

One of the newest features at the time of this printing is the Live Video for groups. You can do live videos and connect with members at different times of the day. You can set a time that you will do the video and use that as a team training.

Help your team become a family.

It can be hard to keep things organized in Facebook groups due to the fast pace of questions, comments, and new posts. To help with the organization, go to "Files" and "Create Doc." Grab the links you posted that month. Or you can create different topics, like "Essential Rewards" or "Team Calls". To grab the permalink to include in the document, click the date and time under the name of the person who posted. Then grab the URL and put that in the document. This will help some with organization and making things easier to find.

Encourage members to use the search function and help them be independent. You do not want the support groups to become a place to keep you hopping. Encourage leaders and team members to help answer questions and point people in the direction to find answers. Create learners and researchers.

Set the rules that you want for your group. Most people are great but you will need rules, and "no drama" is one of them. No bashing the company or others.

As with everything we do, be sure to stay compliant online in social media, your blog, even in your private groups. Set a good example for your team and let them know where they can find their own answers and that you will have to delete non-compliant questions and answers.

The world is a huge place and building online allows you the opportunity to reach more of it than you think possible. This can open many new doors for you. Have fun and be creative while you are helping your family and others.

These are just a few tips to help you grow your business online. If you would like more information on growing your business online, visit: www. theencouraginghome.com/ylbiz.

CHAPTER 16

STAYING LEGAL:
COMPREHENSIVE FDA TRAINING

I can't write a book for business builders without a chapter on how to protect your businesses. By protection, I'm referring to the Food and Drug Administration and what you're legally allowed and not allowed to say about essential oils.

First off, I want you to know I wrote this because I'm really good at screwing it up. I've made just about every mistake you can possibly make. My business was flagged twice in 2015 for non-compliance. That meant no paycheck, no Virtual Office so you can't contact or watch your team, and no ability to order oils. The third time it happens, your downline disappears and you're banned from Young Living for a year. Then after you petition a board for approval, you must start over again, from scratch, as if your original account never existed. Young Living has to have a system in place for its members who are breaking federal law, or it could force the entire company to shut down. Then everyone loses their oils because of a few that aren't compliant.

Because I'm on strike two, it means that I've had about 50 hours of training directly from corporate either on the phone with their conduct and education department or from trainings on the Leadership cruise or the retreats. So I'm passing along what I've learned in order to save you the stress of trying to log into your Virtual Office and discovering that you've been locked out for non-compliance.

Why is the FDA going after Young Living? That's not really accurate. They're not going after anyone. The rules that are being broken have been broken since they were written back in the 1930's. They are not new rules. They are in place for our protection because unfortunately, there are a lot of companies out there that sell vitamins filled with wood chips instead of actual vitamins and weight loss supplement gimmicks. We want the FDA, because they are there for our benefit. Unfortunately, this means good companies like Young Living are restricted in what they say about what their oils.

Why doesn't Young Living just become FDA certified? It's because then the oils would be considered to be a drug, and to get a drug, you have to go to the doctor, get a prescription, and have it filled at the drug store. Young Living wants oils to be for everyone—every home in the world—regardless of how good your health insurance is. But unfortunately without that approval, we can't speak about the oils as drugs. Oils are not about curing disease, they're about supporting systems. Respiratory support. Immune support. Don't live in the land of sickness, live in the land of health. You need to learn a new language!

Young Living wants oils to be for everyone

I shared my migraine story with you for more than one reason. I wanted you to trace my path to oils, but also one of my greatest frustrations with the medical world: it's always chasing symptoms. When I spoke with my final neurologist, I asked him why he didn't look for the source of the migraines. He said it was too complicated and instead gave me pills for swelling, pills for pain, pills for vomiting, and pills to counteract the side effects of the other pills.

One of the things that makes Young Living so amazing is that it's a wellness company. Wellness is exactly what I was searching for with that neurologist. It's about preventative maintenance. It's about putting your body's systems in a place where they are well-supported. It's the first time I've seen a company go after the root causes: your body needs to be strong. How do you get it to that place? You take supplements like NingXia and Pure Protein Complete and Life 9 for gut health. You take Thieves Vitality internally if you feel you need a little immune support on a day you're just off. It's about setting the stage for your body to have all the resources it needs. And if you keep your dialogue about Young Living in that place, you will never run into non-compliance, because you're not curing people.

My goal with this training is to make it as simple as I possibly can. FDA compliance training is kind of like studying grammar. You think you have the rules down, but then you realize there are rules you may have missed. I'll give you one rule to trump them all and put your mind to ease:

Don't talk about the oils to treat disease.

If you can buy it at the drug store, don't talk about an oil for it. The product at the drug store is likely FDA approved, and comparing oils to that will get you into trouble. That includes things that seem ok, like bug spray and sunscreen.

Let's get specific.

HOW TO STAY COMPLIANT WHEREVER YOU ARE

We'll start with online posts, because that's where marketing for your classes begins. When you're online, everything is out there forever, so here are some tips to make sure you're following the rules.

Facebook

1) Only pull graphics from Young Living's Virtual Office or the Young Living Blog. Both have been run past a team of lawyers for compliance.

2) If you are running a Facebook page, do not post any links that people can click on. The article you're posting might be compliant, but the FDA doesn't just look at the article. They click through the entire website, so any article from any button on that site that isn't compliant can get you in trouble. It's not safe to post links that take you other places—to other blogs, websites, or even other Facebook pages.

3) Liking a post: if it's not compliant it's going to get you in trouble, because you're affirming the comment. You're agreeing with it. If it were my page, I'd contact the person who posted it and let them know that I appreciate them, but had to delete the comment so my page stayed in FDA compliance.

4) When you're writing posts: don't imply anything. Talking about fibromyalgia without using the word fibromyalgia is still not compliant. The FDA is looking for your intent. Are you intending that people use the oils as a drug? The rule of thumb is, if it's something you can buy at Walgreens, it's probably FDA approved. Sunscreen, bug spray, and the more obvious—asthma inhalers, eczema cream—all of that can be bought at the store. Don't talk about the oils as drugs or even make implications.

5) Don't ask leading questions that can get you into trouble. What are you using your diffuser for today? What's your favorite use of Pan Away? You will end up having to delete a lot of comments.

6) The FDA will look at every single thing on your page. It's not just your wall. Pictures, the "about me" section, videos, they will read the reviews on your Facebook page. For your own safely, I would delete non-compliant reviews or comments. Every single button on your business page and personal page is fair game. Even if you have a secret or a closed group, they can see that too, as well as personal IM messages. Everything on the internet can be checked out.

Other forms of social media

Twitter, Instagram, Periscope, blogging—the rule of thumb is to talk about how you are using the oils, but not what you're using the oils for. For example, "today I'm diffusing R.C. It smells great! I love eucalyptus!" is a better post than "Upper respiratory infection, broke out my oils." One is completely compliant, the other—you're dead meat. As for photos, I snapped a picture at the lavender farm that I thought was totally okay, until I looked back at it and realized it had non-compliant speech on a sign, so I didn't post it. Pinterest. If you have a Pinterest oils folder, delete the entire thing. That's the safest advice I can give you. Unless you know with confidence that every button on every page is compliant, you are not safe. Pull from Young Living's blog or shareable graphics under the Member Resources button in the Virtual Office, and you'll always be compliant.

Oil Application

There is one more trick to sharing correctly, and it's the hardest one to master, so I recommend you lean on the experts by using the documents in the Virtual Office. We know that there are three ways to apply oils to the body—topical, aromatic, and internal—and sometimes we use one oil in multiple ways. But that doesn't make sense to the pharmaceutical world. You can't take an antibiotic capsule and smear it on your skin, so the FDA says that you can only talk about one use for each oil. It's either topical, aromatic, or digestive. A handful of the oils can be talked about in two ways. If you talk about taking lavender internally, you fall out of compliance because that's listed as a topical oil by the FDA. Young Living has made it easy for you to know how to speak compliantly and one way is with a new chart under the Member Resources tab in your Virtual Office. Stick to the chart and you're safe!

Don't talk about the oils to treat disease

Classes

These rules apply no matter what type of class you're doing—webinars, in a restaurant with one person, or before a class of 100. We have written an FDA compliant 101 class that you can use in your classes, and it's in the back of this book. Read from the script and you're safe. Do not share personal testimonies that talk about the oils as a drug, and do not use testimony photos.

If you hold a make-and-take class, the safest way to do it is simply to put the names of the oils on the containers. Lavender. Peppermint. Lemon. Don't write Young Living's name on it, and don't name blends. Just write the oils in the blend, for example, cinnamon, clove, rosemary and eucalyptus for Thieves. Don't have bins of pain cream and sunscreen or you're not compliant. When you are talking about cleaning supplies, all "anti-" and "dis-" words are banned, for example, antibiotic, antiseptic, disinfectant, anti-viral, anti-bacterial, etc. But you can pop a picture of your sink up before and after you cleaned it, and just say that you wiped it down with Thieves cleaner, and you're totally compliant.

Books

A lot of people ask me how you're supposed to educate your team on the oils. The FDA does allow you to have a table of books for sale at your classes, but there are two rules. First, keep them on a table separate from the oils and outside the room you're teaching in. Two, have more than one book for sale, because otherwise you're promoting only one author. It breaks federal law to give books away as an incentive for buying the starter kit, but you can absolutely have them for sale.

Teach people to fish instead of giving them fish. I've found this is a lot more freeing than answering non-compliant texts at 10:00 p.m. Point them to PubMed (a website featuring studies on oils) or a selection of reference guides. There is a ton of information out there on how to use them. They just have to do their own research. The minute you open a book and issue a recommendation, you have crossed the line!

A WORD OF ENCOURAGEMENT

Now, some encouragement. In March of 2015, my OGV was 46,000, and five months later, in August, it was 67,000. A few months later, it was 153,000 and I was a Platinum! That happened even though I'm teaching FDA compliant classes. I want you to know that you, too, can teach compliant classes and still grow.

In one year, I made it to the top one percent of income earners in the company, so it doesn't matter when you get in. It's all about getting out there and sharing—the right way. It's worth it, I promise. Just do it correctly to protect Young Living, to protect your family, and keep the purest oils in the world available to everyone.

PART FIVE

Strategies for Building Your Team

I am close to hitting Silver following the Gameplan way of running my business. I am doing much better at following up and loving on my team. I have the confidence to be a leader, thanks to Gameplan.

Tracy Fleet

In the past 3 months since reading Gameplan, I went from no 2nd leg to a 2nd leg with a solid 1000+ OGV. I went from a one-sided Senior Star to a solid Executive!

Paula Krueger

CHAPTER 17

THE YOUNG LIVING
COMPENSATION PLAN
IN LAYMAN'S TERMS

There have been *lots* of books written on this subject. As with anything I write, I'll read what's out there first, and I have a half dozen of these books next to me right now. I recommended several of them in the resources chapter earlier on. But I owe it to you in a business book on Young Living to at least not shove you to another book, so let me give the simplest, easiest way to understand the comp plan. Because I'm an English major, not a math major, this is the best you're going to get from a girl who's paid to talk for a living.

HOW YOU GET PAID

There are four parts to your check. Checks are paid out by mail or direct deposit on the 20th of the month and it represents your labor from the previous month. For example, your March 20th check will be from your work in the month of February. By the way, you can get direct deposit anytime by going to "Member Resources" and "Direct Deposit Instructions For U.S. Members".

The four parts of your check are as follows:

1) Starter kit Bonus: $25

2) Fast Start Bonus: $25 for each starter kit plus 25 percent of all purchases for the first 12 weeks after enrolling

3) Unilevel: You are paid 8 percent on your level 1's, 5 percent on your level 2's, and 4 percent on your level 3's, 4's, and 5's.

4) Other Bonuses: At the beginning, the Rising Star bonus is paid on groupings of OGV. (About $50 for every person with 1000 OGV, two people with 500 OGV each, or three people with 300 OGV each). As you rank higher, Generation Leadership Bonuses (paid on either your leaders ranked Silver and above, or a percentage of your OGV from Silver to Silver—generations deep) kick in. A Gold is paid on volume three generations deep or three Silvers deep.

A bit more detail...

Starter kit bonuses

For every kit you sell, you receive $50. That's pretty sweet, since the kit is already half price and you're getting a third of Young Living's profit. Of that $50, $25 is your starter kit bonus and $25 is your Fast Start Bonus. When you sign people for kits, one person is the sponsor and one person is the enroller. (Everyone seems to get the two mixed up. Here's an easy way to remember it: "E" comes before "S." The enroller is the higher rank, always.) If you try to switch them out, it won't work. Can you teach classes and sign one of your leaders as sponsor and enroller? Yes, but you're losing your check. Can you teach for a crossline member and share the sponsor and enroller numbers? No, they must be on your team.

Fast Start

When you first start with the company, most of your check will be Fast Start and starter kit bonuses. As you rank up, it'll be more Unilevel and Generation Leadership bonuses. Fast Start is an incentive to motivate people to order right away and not sit on their kit for six months before they place another order. For the first 12 weeks, you will get 25 percent of all they order above and beyond their kit. After 12 weeks, they slip into the Unilevel system.

Unilevel

A "level 1" is a person you have signed who is directly under you, for example, your mom. If your mom were to go and enroll her coworker, that person would be a level 2. If that coworker signed someone, they'd be a level 3. You're paid on your first 5 levels. The only way to make more than that is to be paid on your generations—which don't kick in until you're a Silver. As you rank up, this will become a large part of your check.

Generations

Once you reach the rank of Silver, you qualify for generations. These are nice, because they allow you to get paid on more than just the first 5 levels. You're paid a percentage of OGV from Silver to Silver. If you have a Silver who is 3 levels deep and the next Silver is 100 levels deep, you're paid a percentage on that volume. Generations are a HUGE part of my check, about half of it. It's how the Diamonds make 30-thousand dollars a month.

The second part of generations the leadership bonus. For that, you're paid per leader on all leaders ranking at Silver and above. I make about $160 per Silver. I know of some Golds who are paid more than Platinums because they have so many Silvers on their team. As soon as you reach Silver, definitely be developing your Platinum leg, but also be working hard to raise more Silvers on your team. That's the trick to a large paycheck – raise lots of Silvers.

If you want to take a closer look at the compensation plan, you can find it in the Virtual Office under "Member Resources" and "Compensation Plan."

In my next book for Silvers and above, I include strategies on how to help more people achieve Silver rank on your team. If you added just five Silvers to your team by the end of the year, your paycheck would go up by $800/month, solely for them holding rank. You're paid even more on your Golds and Platinums (as long as they haven't outranked you. You can only get bonuses for the rank that you are, i.e., you can't be paid on a Diamond downline if you are a Platinum). What I love about this is that you benefit when others are blessed financially by this business. There is a vested interest for you financially to help other people out. Network marketing is the best business model there is!! My bosses in any other field were never paid a higher check if I was better compensated.

ELITE EXPRESS BONUSES

Now that you get the paycheck, let's talk about rank for a few more moments. If you're a person who likes goals, and LOVES incentives—check out the "Elite Express" plan. (You can find a detailed explanation of it under the "Member Resources" tab in the Virtual Office.) For ranking up within specific time limits, you can earn a year's supply of NingXia, an Aria diffuser, and oodles of other gifts valued at nearly $10,000. Not only does Young Living reward with a free flight and hotel stay to the farms for holding Silver, Gold, or Platinum rank for three consecutive months, they also have benchmark gifts if you rank within a certain time period. If you need a tangible goal with a deadline, this is a good place to start.

These are the benchmarks, so you can keep them in front of you:

Executive in Three (Ei3)

Pre-qualifying Rank: Star (once you rank Star, the countdown begins on the first day of the next month)

Qualification Period: Three calendar months from first-time qualification as Star

Maintenance: Maintain Star or Senior Star rank during each of the three qualifying months

Reward: Seed to Seal® collection, featuring an Aria™ Diffuser and 5-ml Peppermint, Idaho Blue Spruce, and Ylang Ylang essential oils; Young Living-branded padfolio. Retail Value: $424 USD*

Silver in Six (Si6)

Prequalifying Rank: Executive

Qualification Period: Six calendar months from first-time qualification as Executive

Maintenance: Maintain Executive rank during each of the six qualifying months

Reward: Exclusive collection of 30 15-ml essential oils, FitBit Charge HR. Retail Value: $1,650 USD*

Gold in Six (Gi6)

Prequalifying Rank: Silver

Qualification Period: Six calendar months from first-time qualification as Silver

Maintenance: Maintain Silver rank during each of the six qualifying months

Reward: Year's supply of NingXia Red®; Thieves® collection, including 2-pack of Thieves Laundry Soap, 3-pack of Thieves Foaming Hand Soap, 2 32-oz. Thieves Foaming Hand Soap Refill, 2 64-oz. Thieves Household Cleaner, 2 15-ml Thieves essential oil blend; Gold iPad Mini. Retail Value: $1,835 USD*

Platinum in Five (Pi5)

Prequalifying Rank: Gold

Qualification Period: Five calendar months from first-time qualification as Gold

Maintenance: Maintain Gold rank during each of the five qualifying months

Reward: Premier Aroma collection, diffuser collection, including AromaLux™, Dewdrop™, USB, Rainstone™, and Dino Land™ diffusers; Branded Luggage. Retail Value: $4,265 USD*

BONUS: Elite Twenty (E20) (for hitting all the benchmarks)

Prequalifying Rank: Star

Qualification Period: 20 months from first-time qualification as Star

Maintenance: Must qualify for all four reward tracks within 20 months to qualify

Reward: 1,000 Essential Rewards points and free registration for the International Grand Convention. Retail Value: $1,230 USD*

If you miss one gift, you can still catch the next one. If you don't make Executive in three months, but you do make Silver in six months from ranking Executive. You will lose the ei3 gift, but can still earn Silver in Six.

I will tell you that if you don't hit these benchmarks, you can still earn your trip to the farm. There is no deadline for that prize. You must simply hold rank for three consecutive months. Three months at Silver gets you the Silver retreat, three months at Gold gets you the Gold retreat, etc....

John and I ranked before this program was in place, but had it been around when we started, we would have hit every benchmark. I love how generous Young Living is! Not only do they make it priority to fly you to the farms to see the purity of the oils and understand the process it takes to make them, but they also have a plan in place to reward you as you rank with considerable prizes. It felt like Christmas when our buttons appeared in the mail with a recognition letter. Young Living has so much love for their distributors.

CHAPTER 18

A YOUNG LIVING STRATEGY GUIDE ON WHERE TO SIGN NEW OILERS

I'm not the greatest at math, but I was able to hit Platinum pretty fast because I figured out the strategy. An MLM is a chess board. If you understand how the board is played, you know where to put your pieces.

This is probably one of the most common questions I get asked. "What's the strategy, Sarah? How do I place people? Where do I place people? I don't know what to do!"

First, open your bottle of Young Living Stress Away and slather it on. Then, follow these three simple rules:

1. Always think two legs ahead

It's never too early to think about legs. To rank Silver you need two legs at 4,000 OGV. Don't underestimate how fast your OGV can rise, and get caught without legs to stand on. You don't want a 10,000 Silver OGV, and have five legs at 1000.

You must remember as you work toward Silver that you're not the only one out there selling all those kits—it's the power of the team underneath you, and when they are motivated, hold on! You need to have your legs in place. The only way to do that is to always be thinking two legs ahead.

Stars and Senior Stars should be working on their legs for Silver right from the start. If you're a Silver, you should be actively building your Platinum leg. If you're a Platinum, you should be building your Crown Diamond leg.

A word of caution: *only* think two legs ahead. Otherwise, you'll be way too wide and it will take you much longer to rank up. New leaders will rise up as you're out teaching classes. Trust that your business will grow organically as you are out there teaching. If you're a Silver, you should have four legs going. If you're a Gold, five legs going. You don't need five legs as a Senior Star. It's a good way to wait a really long time for a great paycheck.

2. Teach with the proper ratios

Teach three 101 classes for every specialty class you teach. (Specialty classes include Beauty School, Make and Takes, Oil Affordability, Biblical Oils, etc. Why? Because the 101 Class is the class that sells the starter kit, and when you first start, you're looking for business builders. You don't find them with make-and-take classes. At make-and-take classes, 70% of the people who attend never order the oils and never make the product again. If your goal is to sell starter kits and raise leaders, focus on the class that does that.

As soon as you reach Silver you can flip your ratios. For every 101 lecture you give, you should be doing three Teacher Trainings. And that, my friend, is the secret to the entire chess board. It's not about how many starter kits you sell. It has everything to do with how many leaders you raise. If you teach a class on a Saturday, you'll go home at the end of the day with one completed class. If you have trained four others to teach, you will have just taught five classes in one day! It's the power of multiplication.

Don't lose sight of what got you to your rank in the first place, and never stop teaching 101 classes. If someone tells you that once you reach Diamond, you stop teaching 101's, they're off their rocker. You'll always have to run your business to keep it growing. But as a Diamond, you just have a bit more time and financial freedom, so you can take it at the pace you choose.

3. Go wide before you go deep

"But Sarah—I just started teaching. I'm not even a Star yet. How do I strategize that?"

If you have no team yet, that's the easiest team to strategize. Everyone goes under you. Teach like a madman and give every person your number as sponsor and enroller. But it won't be a long wait. If your enthusiasm for oils is infectious, you'll find that people turn around and share the kit with someone else pretty quickly. I tell people to watch their teams for someone that "pops." In the Virtual Office under "My Organization," you can watch your team closely. If you see a little plus sign next to someone's name, it means they have sold an oils kit to someone else. This means they are a potential leader!

So, when someone "pops", gauge their level of commitment. Do they want to manage a team? Do they want to hold classes? Will they commit to spend 100 PV a month? If the answer is yes, you have a business builder. Do the three-page Teacher Training with them in the Appendix of this book, and help them through their first class. Put a Gameplan book in their hands after class as a congratulatory gift. Once I see them teach their second class on their own, then I know they are committed and I will work closely with them.

How wide do you go while looking for leaders? Well, you only ever need 1,000PGV to hold rank, which equals 10 people who are spending at least 100PV a month (or 20 at 50PV). If you have that solid base and still haven't found any business builders, then look for someone on your team who orders faithfully and whom you would like to bless. Begin building a leg under them.

When you want to sign someone under one of your leaders so you can build a leg, then you would be the enroller and your leader would be the sponsor. For some reason, this gives people many headaches—understanding who is who—under "sponsor" and "enroller." It's very simple. E comes before S. E, enroller, is the higher rank. You can't place someone above you. It will not go through on the signup page. So if you're building a leg, you are the enroller (you get the starter kit Bonus and the Fast Start Bonus, while they get the OGV and the new person who pops up on their leg.) In 13 weeks, your leader will get the paycheck on that new distributor as they slip into the unilevel system.

What if you do classes for months, and no one "pops"? Start plugging the business in your classes more often, with little drops. See who is faithfully spending 100PV organically, and ask if you can build under them. Or in the worst case scenario (only because they may not choose to lead)—sign your mom or best friend, or someone you really want to see blessed, that you know will place orders, and build under them.

How do you know when to start to build under someone? Wait until you have the 1000PGV you need to rank Silver. That would be 10 people under you ordering 100PV a month on essential rewards. Or 3 or 4 order 300PV. If a leader buds on their own and you don't have the 1000PGV, it's ok. Help them take off, and slowly work at it simultaneously. It's better to build PGV right when you first start your business, because once you have developing leaders, you won't have the freedom to teach as many classes solely for yourself, you'll be training them. Take advantage of the beginning of your business to build PGV.

Summing it up: hold about eight classes. Sign everyone under you as sponsor and enroller until you hit 1000PGV, but plug the business side of Young Living at each class. If someone "pops" while you're building PGV, work on training them and building your level 1's at the same time. (So if you teach a class, half would go under you as sponsor and enroller, and half of the kits would go under your leader, with you as enroller and them as sponsor.) If no one pops and your PGV is in place, it's time to pick some distributors on your team to build as leaders, and start signing people under two clear legs.

But Sarah, if I do that, who gets paid??

Paycheck breakdown when you are enroller and your leader is sponsor:

Starter kit Bonus: goes to you

Fast Start Bonus: goes to you (it lasts for 12 weeks)

Unilevel: goes to your leader

Generations: go to your leader

If you are enroller and your leader is sponsor, where does the new distributor show up on your downline chart? They show up under your new leader. Look there to find them. They are still on your team, they're just not directly under you. You want the new oiler placed under a leader because it motivates them as they see their OGV rise, and the more they work their business, the more you are blessed.

Paycheck breakdown when you are enroller and sponsor:

Starter kit Bonus: goes to you

Fast Start Bonus: goes to you

Unilevel: goes to you

Generations: goes to you

But if you're trying to build your legs to rank, you'll get paid a lot more if this new oiler is placed under one of your committed business builders.

GROWING YOUR TEAM

So many come to me and say "Sarah, I can't find anyone to teach. No one is interested." I tell them I can't find anyone who doesn't want to share the oils. Seriously.

When I look over my friend pool and see what they're doing for a living, how they're investing their time, and what they'd rather be doing, I truly don't see a single person who wouldn't be blessed by Young Living. Instead of looking at who isn't out there, look at who is out there. We think no one has interest, but if we really knew how our friends felt about what they did 40 hours a week, I think we'd be far less timid in approaching them. Even people who absolutely love their jobs just like I did have moments when they come home, look in their children's eyes, and wish they had a bit more of themselves to give. That's where Young Living comes in.

When I look over my friends list—there are probably only one or two people on the whole thing who wouldn't be blessed by a Young Living business, solely because they are already millionaires in another MLM. The thing I've noticed from working this is that we never really know who will show an interest. It depends on the place they are in their life and what their desires are, and all of that constantly changes. Some people I'd never, ever imagine doing the business have completely blown me away. For example, people who are very timid are some of my top sellers and that's because it doesn't have much to do with personality. It has to do with drive and how much you want it. If they can catch the vision and see where this goes, you'll have an impassioned leader.

What's the benefit of Young Living over other MLM's? A consumable product that works. Instead of selling makeup, or a diet fad, or a pan or a book, oils are something that people use every single day, multiple times a day, for everything from cleaning to personal body care to emotions. It always needs to be replenished, and that makes it extremely easy to share with people. Educate and empower and you'll have a lifelong oiler! No one uses Thieves cleaner and then goes back to their $3 cleaner loaded with chemicals. They just don't. The passion is easy to ignite because moms and dads care about what they have in their home.

Nonetheless, it can be a bit daunting trying to raise leaders. Where do you start without coming off pushy or awkward? Our team planned for that, and we have a simple system. I've recorded a 10-minute DVD that we play right after every single 101 class, every make and take, and every Beauty School class. It's called "How to Get Your Oils For Free" (a.k.a.: Why Do a Young Living Business). It goes through every benefit we've already discussed, such as no income ceiling, you are your own boss, you set your own hours, etc. When we play that DVD, it's amazing how many people will sit there and watch it after the lecture. I believe it's the reason we've grown as fast as we've have.

One more thing: pray for leaders. I remember in 2014, before we made the DVD, I'd had a three-month dry spell where not a single leader had contacted me. So I contacted my upline in desperation. She asked me if I'd prayed for leaders. I told her no, not specifically, but I'd prayed to grow. She said that I needed to pray specifically over my business if I wanted specific answers. So I did, and within two hours, seven different people contacted me. Right now, four of them are top leaders in my organization. Prayer works!

A WORD ON UPLINE SUPPORT

While I'm on the topic of uplines (the members signed above you), there's one more thing I want to include in this chapter, since we're talking about strategy. Don't blame your upline if you don't feel you have support. That's another excuse. We bloom where the Lord has planted us.

All of the materials in this book I've written myself. My upline didn't compile it for me and I wouldn't have expected them to. Each of them are wonderfully gifted people trying to manage their own organizations, and it's not their job to manage mine. If my business is faltering, it's my responsibility to find my errors—perhaps look for others who have overcome them—and fix it.

Your upline does not need to provide you with resources or money or time or gifts or even training. Utilize the Gameplan book, pass it to your leaders, your crossline friends, and your upline. Apply it. You will blossom because you roll up your sleeves and work at it, not because you're gifted something in the mail.

If you always keep in the forefront of your mind that all this takes is a the 101 Script and a starter kit, there's no need to blame someone above you when you get stuck. Your feet and your feet alone will get you where you need to go. Even the best leadership in the world can't turn you into the rank you desire—it's all on you. If you're not happy where you are, fight for it. Roll up your sleeves, stop blaming others, get out there and bloom where you are planted. Switching teams or hunting down successful leaders won't make you a successful leader. You become a leader by getting in the trenches and getting good at connecting with people. The more you teach, the more you learn, the more you grow.

Stop the blame game and redirect your energy toward growing your business. Your upline has nothing to do with your success. They are not responsible for your stunning failure or stunning growth. You are.

You can do this. Just walk.

CHAPTER 19

THE KEY TO REACHING AND MAINTAINING RANK

I have touched on this lightly in a few areas of the book, but for the leader that keeps starting at zero OGV every month, this may be the part of the Gameplan book that saves your business. Let's go into deep detail on the importance of educating your team onto Essential Rewards, and why it's critical for you to rank.

THE KEY TO RANKING UP

It's terribly important that you don't let someone walk out of class and never touch base with them again. It is equally important that you don't help them through their starter kit purchase, shoot them a text or email on why they should be on Essential Rewards when their kit arrives, and move on impatiently when they don't respond.

The fact is, you could conceivably get to Silver completely on your own. You could find two friends, or sign your mom, and sell 40 kits on each leg and a few outside those legs and you could make it. Your pin will show up in the mail, you'll enjoy every moment of the Silver retreat gifted to you by Young Living knowing you literally earned every single drop of that rank single-handedly (which is not a good thing). Your two "leaders" spend their 100pv and you're off and running.

But that tactic will never work to hit Gold or even to maintain your rank as Silver. For that you need groundwork, and you need a team. I don't want you or the hard working leaders on your team to be unable to rank because your distributors are only ordering the one product they know about and spending 50PV a month. Or they ordered a kit and dropped off the planet.

After a year, because of my lack of follow up, I was losing 130 people a month. If your distributor orders a kit and then never orders again, they will go inactive and will disappear from your team after 12 months. It's incredibly difficult to maintain rank as that happens! John and I never lost Platinum, but it will take more than a year to get to Diamond—and my plateau was not necessary. The entire secret to the thing holding me back was Essential Rewards.

If you wait until Silver to start getting people on Essential Rewards, you will sit at that rank for a very long time. Or you'll get Gold and lose it over and over and over again. (You can lose Silver over and over and over again, or Star as well). It's because your path there was not solid and organic, based on relationships and trust. It was based on quick sales, and moving onto the next person.

Don't be so timid to touch base that you lose your business. Those people came to your class for a reason—they wanted to know about oils. So talk to them. A strong team will have at least 30% of their people on Essential Rewards. As you are growing from Star to Silver, I like to see that number closer to 50% or higher. You can check to see where it's at by logging into the Oily Tools app and clicking on "stats."

EDUCATING ONTO ESSENTIAL REWARDS

Here's the reality—if they didn't respond to your email about Essential Rewards, they didn't drop off the planet, you did. You'll never be able to hold rank without people placing orders regularly. It takes an OGV of 10,000 each and every month to maintain a Silvership!

Some of it will happen organically as your team flips through the catalog and their eyes land on Thieves laundry soap and they think of their Borax project in the back room, but most will need your nudge. And they need ideas. They have the kit, they believe in oils because you have passion and you passed it to them, but they really don't know what the next step is.

It's just as critical that you touch base with these people as it is for you to hold classes. Build time for follow up into your week just as you build a calendar of classes, and just as you build time to train your new leaders. My monthly calendar looks something like this:

Last week of the month: schedule all my classes for the next month

First week of the month: do mailings and follow up (I have found I tend to be more consistent with them if I do them in one batch, rather than try to dribble them in throughout the month. People get missed.)

Rest of the month: Schedule trainings with leaders and hold classes

Let's dive into the Oil Ability Strategy for getting people on Essential Rewards.

The first week of the month when you do follow up, your going to pull-from the list of names of people that got kits the previous month. Every person that I sign gets a follow up package in the mail. (Refer to Chapter 10 for follow up if they *didn't* get a kit.)

For those who have ordered a kit, the follow up package I send them looks something like this:

1) Diamond Jordan Schrandt's Welcome book (purposemeetshustle.com)

2) A sample of something not in their kit like a Thieves cough drop or some Cool Azul pain cream in a little container

3) One of my lectures on audio CD or DVD

4) A brochure or graphic that explains Essential Rewards

I love to keep them excited about learning. I will also tell them about upcoming classes. If they don't respond to that, I mail out something that looks a little bit like this:

1) A hand written note explaining how it's wise to get 10% off their cleaning supplies and personal care products, like toothpaste. I also mention that after four months they get 20% back!

2) A different sample (more ideas: a Thieves cleaner "stain stick" in a roller bottle, a Vitality oil, a packet of NingXia or Nitro, Thieves mints, Thieves hand sanitizer or spray, a small sample of the Satin Mint Facial scrub, a small sample of any oil that is not in the kit)

3) A visual idea of what three months of Essential Rewards would look like (we have many more of these graphics available—look for them at oilabilityteam.com)

4) A snapshot of the Essential Rewards program

Here's a photo of what one of my bundles looks like. (Just add a hand-written note explaining the little care package!)

OVERCOMING OBJECTIONS TO ESSENTIAL REWARDS

What if that doesn't work, Sarah?

Then I'd encourage you to call them and touch base. Find out what their reservation is. Maybe they can't afford a $300 a month commitment. Show them how they can make a difference in their home with just $50 a month. Fifty is enough to keep them on Essential Rewards, and still swap chemicals out of their home.

Maybe they just don't really understand how autoship works. I've had people drop out because they didn't realize that the same stuff in their cart will ship out if they don't change it every month. Help them understand how and why of it.

Why does Young Living ship what went out the month before? Many people order the same supplements each month, and it's a beast to add NingXia, Nitro, Master Formula and Life 9 to your cart every single month—over and over again. So instead you leave it in, and Young Living will send you an email notice two days before it will ship just to remind you to update your cart.

Most of the time, I've found the reason people are hesitant to get on ER is truly just a lack of knowledge. If they understand how Essential Rewards works: that they can cancel it at any time with a single phone call without penalty, that they can change the date if they are on vacation, that it's completely customizable to their family's needs—it's usually enough for them to get on board.

Make sure you are communicating all the details of the program with them: 10% back the first 3 months, 20% back on month 4, 25% back after 25 months. Young Living has the most generous, gracious rewards program of any company that I've ever seen. If your distributors love the oils, they will love getting them every single month. It truly is Christmas in a box, just for you.

Here is an idea of what a 50pv order looks like:

Three Months to a Chemical Free Lifestyle
using Essential Rewards

Month 1
$50.25

Three Months to a Chemical Free Lifestyle
using Essential Rewards

Month 2
$51.50

Three Months to a Chemical Free Lifestyle
using Essential Rewards

Month 3
$55.00

Here is an idea of what a 190pv order would look like:

3 Month Young Living Tour
with Essential Rewards

Month 1 $192.25
Essential Rewards Points Earned $19.23
Plus all the free oils on the 190PV Level of Essential Rewards freebies

3 Month Young Living Tour
with Essential Rewards

Month 2 $200.00
Essential Rewards Points Earned $20.00
Plus all the free oils on the 190PV Level of Essential Rewards freebies

3 Month Young Living Tour
with Essential Rewards

Month 3 $195.25
Essential Rewards Points Earned $19.53
Plus all the free oils on the 190PV Level of Essential Rewards freebies

WHY ER IS CRITICAL

Why is it so important that you and your team understand Essential Rewards? There are two reasons.

First, because you'll have a lifelong oiler. This is how they learn to incorporate the oils into their homes. This is how they learn to get rid of the junk. It's through simple, tiny steps. It doesn't all happen at once. I made an icebreaker video for classes called "Scavenger Hunt DVD" that's three minutes long, that shows what an oil-infused home looks like. It showcases dozens of Young Living products in a silly way, with my 5 kids bounding through rooms and opening cabinets (and even on the roof!) Find it at oilabilityteam.com. Share it with prospective oilers, in your classes, and with your leaders. This is why we do what we do.

The second reason that it's so critical that they get on ER is because that's one of the key secrets to going from Star to Senior Star to Executive to Silver and beyond. If you cry each month on the first of the month when your Virtual Office dashboard is reset to zero, this is your way out. Lay the groundwork that will help you rank. If two people on your team get on ER, the next month you may be starting at 300 or 4000GV instead of 0. It's much easier to rank up.

Train your leaders to do the same things with their own teams, and you have learned one of the key secrets to growing very quickly (and not getting burned out by trying to manage all your leader's legs). Show them how incredibly important it is. Make sure you show them what a follow up mailing looks like when you train them with the Teacher Training in the Appendix of this book.

I truly believe that alongside raising leaders, this is the one thing that people never understand about network marketing. It's one of the main reasons that they jump from MLM to MLM, saying the business model doesn't work. They have never laid an organic groundwork for their business, and every single month, they start from scratch. Could you imagine working on a project at your current job, and every month that you came in, it was as if the last month never existed? Then why do you do it to yourself with Young Living? Lay your groundwork. Touch base with your team. They WANT to hear from you.

They are looking for a chemical free life. And you have the answer for them. You have been given such a gift in all that you have learned already in the simple changes you have made in your own home. Remember—it's not sales, it's education. Drop ideas in their lap and stand back and see where they go. What have you already swapped in your house? Start there. Many of my "non" business builders, who swear they only wanted oils, ended up building businesses because they developed a passion from their monthly Essential Rewards order.

Essential rewards has many rewards. Be bold and talk about it like you talk about the oils. You'll develop deep friendships, get to know your team better, and will learn some cool things along the way on how others have used the oils in their own homes. And you'll explode your business. It's worth it.

PART SIX

EXPAND YOUR INFLUENCE:
SECRETS TO GREAT LEADERSHIP

Gameplan helped me to understand how to build my organization. I had little understanding of MLMs prior to reading it. It also helped me to tap into a bolder approach to my business. I am continually looking for opportunities to expand my team. For instance, I have called on chiropractors, done in- person classes, Facebook live classes and am attending health fairs. My growth has been slow thus far. However, I started from zero a couple of months ago and am laying a solid foundation that will most likely lead to huge dividends.

Dessie Leff

Gameplan book helped me to recognize and conquer distractions. Through the system I was able to increase my team's percentage on ER each month and ranked up to Executive.

Lisa Ammerman

CHAPTER 20

BALANCE, BOUNDARIES AND TREATING YOUR BUSINESS AS A BUSINESS

I must confess, I wrote this chapter for myself. Every distributor has an Achilles heel, and I know mine well. I have no boundaries. For example, I repeatedly tell my leaders, "Anything you need, anything at all, tell me, and I'll bend over backwards to make it happen." Then I realize that I've over scheduled my classes, yet again filled my calendar to the brim, and spent another night away from my littlest Harnisches. That's when mommy guilt overtakes me.

When I retired from anchoring news in August of last year, I was determined to get the balance back into my life. I didn't want the hours of my anchoring shift to get replaced by other things and filled for no reason. If I was going to give up something I loved as much as putting together a newscast and performing before millions of people every day, I wanted that time in my day to have purpose.

I wanted to wake up holding my husband's hand and seeing him off to work. I wanted to see the sun rise—something I'd missed for 16 years. I wanted to go on a run each day. I wanted to do devotions with my teens before the little ones rose, and get an early start on our homeschool day so I could work my business each afternoon.

Let me tell you what actually happened.

- The first week I slept. It felt SO good to sleep past 3 a.m.

- The second week, I woke up and made my husband an amazing breakfast a few times.

- The third week I started homeschool—with the hopes of finishing by 1:00 each afternoon and then pouring into my Young Living business. Well, we're on week 18 of school now, and I have yet to set hours each afternoon. Instead, I find that school runs until 4:00 or 5:00, then I become mom taxi and shuttle kids to sports, then run home and get dinner. Before I know it, it's bedtime and yet another Young Living day has escaped me.

So I let my full time job go—but I never made room for my business. Now what?

A few months ago, Jay Carter, a member of my Diamond upline, said something very convincing to me, and it was about over scheduling. As a Type A personality himself, I am pretty confident he could spot an over scheduler a mile away. He saw that I was a momma who tended to go with the flow—whatever seemed important, I'd let it take as long as it took, live in the moment, and try to fix it all later. That doesn't work when you're self-employed. When you are your own boss, you need discipline! Your business can't run itself, and if you don't commit time to it, you'll find you don't have a business. Or a family.

I recognized the issue pretty swiftly, but not before it cost me a wonderful personal assistant who was frustrated with my lack of boundaries. I took the entire month of December off and regrouped. I tried to get into a rhythm, but it eluded me, so I decided to commit some time to study and get better at time management. No matter what rank you achieve in Young Living, never lose your humility and always be willing to take it on the chin when you have made an error. You have to be willing to accept criticism or you'll never grow.

These were the resources I digested:

- Dani Johnson's Time Secrets Series (danijohnson.com)
- Lisa Terkeursts' "The Best Yes"
- Dr. Henry Cloud and Dr. John Townsend's "Boundaries"

Have I got it all down now? Absolutely not. But there is a pause to my step. In January, I had the opportunity to schedule 16 classes with some lucrative groups, but instead I committed to only two classes a month. John and I are in mega debt payoff mode right now, and the extra income would have been a great blessing to us, but I feel like I'm honoring the Lord more by staying behind the scenes this season. It also allowed some new leaders to take the limelight on my team, and I'm realizing how much I love seeing them shine. I am also loving the rest that is coming by letting others lead.

After reading those books, I looked at ways to be more efficient with the time I was spending on my business. I hired a woman to help me with mailings and follow up and committed that extra time to going on a run each day. By making that simple change, I've lost 22 pounds in three months and am sleeping better.

Then, to save time burning DVD's and to save money in the cost of mailings, I decided to put more of my lectures and content online. We're launching the oilabilityteam.com page, and it will be accessible to any team member—even our members in Thailand and Canada—without the cost of mailing packages. I've written this book to pass knowledge along to leaders who are a great distance away and harder for me to hand train in person. When I realized that each class I teach, especially the one-on-one classes, takes time away from my children, I started holding group Teacher Trainings.

Those are some of the changes that have really helped me get on track. But to be totally honest with you, I had to apply some of those tactics to my home life as well. We power clean different areas of the house for 15 minutes a day, with each child assigned a room that's visible to the visiting public. I save my deep cleans (and cleaning of hidden areas, like back rooms and master bathrooms) for Saturdays. I am pretty OCD about a clean house, but I had to let perfection go if I'm running a business and homeschooling.

I'm getting better at sticking to a schedule with our schoolwork and not going on so many rabbit trails that it costs me an entire day of work. Putting my littles in quiet time for an hour each afternoon made it possible to give my leaders more respect by using that afternoon hour to return their messages which came in while my phone was off that morning during homeschooling time.

I mentioned earlier that my Diamond upline, Jay Carter, told me he had a system for staying on track. He made a list of seven things he wanted to do every day (usually three or four were personal things, like working out. Three things were business related). When he has completed the list of seven, he makes time for his family and for fun. I'll get so wrapped up in writing books and lectures, reading, studying, training that I often forget to include the fun. I've lucked out though, because my husband is the master of fun. He's the one who's always bringing home new movies to watch and planning ahead with root beer float nights for the kids, while I'm tucked away in a corner typing as fast as I can. One of my goals this year is to pull my head out of my books and focus on some of the things in front of me—before my kids are grown.

I don't want to wrap up this chapter without speaking to the other crowd too, though. You know who you are: the crowd that doesn't start. The crowd who sees the task of the business, gets overwhelmed, and watches other leaders rise from afar, knowing it could have been you, if you'd make the commitment to begin.

Here's my admonition: start. Please, hear my heart, leader. This is the one thing you should be committing time to. All the other distractions in your life—look at them for what they are. They take your time away from something the Lord has placed right in front of you to bless you. He has sent your rescue. This is the thing that will buy you time with your family, financial freedom, and the dreams and wishes of your heart—whatever they may be, like supporting a missionary, going on missions trips yourself, taking care of a family member who's had nothing, visiting a friend that's far away because you can, anonymously writing a ridiculous check to someone in need, your first true family vacation. Through hard work and consistency, Young Living is the vehicle that will take you there!

Never in my wildest dreams would I have imagined that I'd be standing in the streets of Venice in 2015, 11 months after getting my starter kit, as one of the top Young Living leaders in the entire world. I had won the honor as a Silver, not as a Diamond.

I stood there in those ancient streets with my three oldest teens, looking at things we'd only read about in our homeschool books. We stood in a clock tower with a bell made by Galileo and walked the streets Lord Byron walked and saw the body of Mark who wrote the gospel of Mark in the Bible. We stood in the stadium in Ephesus, Turkey, where Paul gave his sermon before he was arrested.

We made a thousand memories together. Our first vacation, our first flight, our first overseas trip, our first cruise—all rolled into two weeks. We ate dinner each night with Young Living Diamonds, my children frolicked on the ship with a dozen Royal Crown Diamond children, and my oldest son hung out with Gary Young's son Jacob and wore his Shutran for the girls on the ship. They were the silliest, most bizarre Cinderella memories, and somehow, I was actually in them this time, and not watching from afar.

This is shot of the four of us in the Doge's palace in Saint Mark's Square in Venice, in the medieval torture chamber above the prison catacombs. If you had told me I'd take my children to Venice because of Young Living, I would have laughed at you. Yet, there we were.

May I give you a practical, hands-on tip on how to apply time management at its best? Start in your home. The Bible says if we're faithful in the small things, God will trust us with the bigger things. What order should that be in?

1) Your Lord and Savior

2) Your spouse

3) Your children

4) Your job

If it's out of order, God is not going to trust you with more. It's called time economy, and you do not have favor if your priorities are out of whack.

Christians really seem to understand the principle of tithing. If you take 10% of what you make and give it to your home church, the Lord blesses the other 90%. It seems as if you don't have enough to cover the bills, but somehow, God stretches and multiplies that last bit and you never starve.

It seems to be lost on us that God does it with time too. Just like we tithe our money, we need to be putting our priorities in biblical order so God will bless the work of our hands. If we're faithful with the small things—our relationship with Christ, our spouse, our children, and our job—in that order—God will multiply our time, just like He does with our money.

If we're faithful with the small things, God will multiply our time.

I tried this out at home this week. I'm one of those moms who has 52 plates spinning in the air. Every second can't get wasted—we're homeschooling, I'm anchoring news part time for fun, running kids to activities, cooking unprocessed food, etc. If I want one-on-one child time or a date, it has to be budgeted. Just as I started setting aside time to pray over my business, I started setting aside blocks of time as alone time with God, as date time with John, and as time with my children.

To give you a few examples, we played laser tag at 10:00 p.m. in our yard, I made out with my husband when he walked in the door from work, and after I took my 16-year-old son on a driving lesson, we stopped for a slice of pie. They were all little things, but when they were the priority and I wasn't on my phone running my Young Living business, somehow I still had time to send the messages I needed to send, write the lectures that needed to be written, contact the leaders that needed leading, and it all worked. I have no explanation except that God multiplied my time.

How do you start? Set aside a time each day for your business. Commit to that time. Maybe it's 6:00 a.m. to 7:00 a.m., or 1:00 to 2:00 p.m., or 4:00 to 5:00 p.m., but in this season, only once a week, with a class twice a month on Friday nights, commit to it and stick to the parameters. When the clock crosses 5:01, shut the phone off and prepare for your husband or your children. Then devote that time to them and see what the Lord does to the rest of your clock!

Here's a photo of me with the love of my life, who we call "The Harn." We got engaged three weeks after we met, when I was 16 years old, and we just celebrated our 18th wedding anniversary. Your spouse has to be a priority. If your marriage isn't right, set your business aside and fix that first.

I can't tell you what adventures you'll have with this company! It really depends on you and what you put into it. But I can tell you that if you make the commitment to truly run this as a business, that I have yet to meet anyone on my team who has regretted that decision. For John and me, it's the best financial decision we've ever made.

How do you get there? From point A to point B? It starts with a why. Write it down. "I want to take my children to Venice." "I want to pay off my credit cards and live debt free." "I want to take care of my mom without being in financial peril." "I want to buy grass-fed beef." Set goals and then commit to the business. Set aside time for four classes a month. That's eight hours a month of teaching. Then set aside an hour a day—at any time- to do follow up and practice your lecture and respond to messages. Pick two leaders and start building under them. Commit to that time, with discipline, every day. Pray and keep Christ as your center and number one on your priority list. Then stand back and watch your business grow and hold on, because it will completely surprise you! Your life will not look the same a year from now!

179

CHAPTER 21

ATTRACTING AND
MOTIVATING LEADERS

This is a pretty short chapter, because when you are practicing good leadership, you will naturally attract and inspire other leaders. There are a couple of practical tips I can give you for identifying and motivate leaders, but remember that *how you lead* will have the most impact.

Chase every 101 class with a "Why Do Young Living As a Business DVD," a.k.a., "How To Get Your Oils For Free." We have it available on the oilabilityteam.com page. It shows people why—the same reasons I gave you in Chapter One—this is the best job in the world.

When you do follow up mailings, mail that DVD (along with Oily Lifestyle) to all the people who got a kit. Show them how to get their oils for free. When you follow up with people who do not have a starter kit yet, include those same materials. I have people that know little about the oils who started sharing simply because they were drawn to the business side of things.

HOW TO SPOT POTENTIAL LEADERS

How do I find leaders? I look for those who are frustrated at work. Those that don't make enough to get by. Those that have no plan for retirement or nothing saved—or see no way out. I sit down with them and I train them with the Teacher Training script and get them off the ground, walk them through their first class, and touch base weekly.

How do you raise a leader? You vision cast with them. Once they see that how they are spending their time will not get them where they want to go, they will pursue the business with tenacity.

Never judge from the outside. I can tell you my upline never, ever had any idea that I'd walk away from radio to sell oils kits. When I started sharing, it blew her mind! She said, "You're famous! You talk to five million people every morning! I never thought you'd do this. I didn't even think to ask!" But when I looked over my life, it seemed wiser to have time economy and be home with my children than to be so depleted from the morning hour of my shift. I love radio with every bone in my body. Anchoring news is in my blood, and it will always be there, but I love my husband and children more.

I mentioned in the Virtual Office tour that you need two leaders for the first couple of ranks, so that's where I'd start. Whether you're a Distributor, a Star, or a Senior Star, it does not matter. But for Executive and Silver you need two strong legs. So start with two leaders, two people who'd be blessed by the income and blessed by the oils. If you don't know who they are, pray specifically for the Lord to reveal them to you. Ask for names, ask for the right people to cross your path. When I first started, it was all about free oils. But as our check grew, I couldn't walk into a Walmart without talking to the cashier. It's a smarter way of living, and anyone can share oils!

This is a shot of me with one of my Silvers-in-Six, Sheri Napier. We were on our way to teach a Beauty School and a Teacher Training. She had just driven from South Carolina to New York to teach for one day. That's commitment!

Once you see someone on your team has started sharing and a new member pops up under them, contact your new leader with the three-page Oil

Ability business training, which is in the Appendix of this book. Run them through it, train them on the Virtual Office, and check in with them once a week to see how they're doing. Give them this book after they teach their first class. Build a relationship, and as their check comes in, they'll get more and more excited about where Young Living goes! Cast the vision with them.

CONFIDENCE IS KEY

I'd say the biggest key to developing leaders is boldness. Most business builders I see who aren't raising leaders don't have confidence in themselves. If you truly believe Young Living is a crazy incredible income source, and when you see where it goes, wouldn't you want to share it with everyone around you? Wouldn't you want your mom and sister and best friend to be financially free? So share boldly and see what doors open up! I promise you you'll be very surprised at who takes leadership roles in your organization!

I have hinted earlier on in the book, but I'm going to give you a few more details on a little secret I'm working on just for you. I am just starting to write a sequel to this book, because I know you're going to rank and you'll need it! It's a "You're a Silver, now what?" book for people who have achieved that rank. Gameplan II will give you strategies for Silver and above, because as you rank up, your goals and your chess board change a bit, and you have to morph your strategy to fit your growing team. Some of the topics for that book: how to do retreats with your leaders, what is recognition and how to do it on the cheap (and have it work), specialty classes, top tips and strategies for getting 100-thousand-dollars in Essential Rewards, how on earth do I balance a team this large, and more. Gameplan II is coming! Watch for it at oilabilityteam.com!

CHAPTER 22

HOW TO PRAY OVER YOUR YOUNG LIVING BUSINESS

This should have been the first chapter of the book, because it's at the top of my priorities list. But honestly, I can't teach you how to pray over your business unless you're sure you want one first, so it was pretty important to tell you the "why" of a Young Living business at the beginning. We're about to get serious about all that vision casting right now.

The single most important thing you can do for your business is pray for it daily. Let me repeat that. The single most important thing you can do for your business is to pray for it daily. If you're not a prayer warrior or you don't like to pray with others or can't think of what to say, one of my favorite movies is "The War Room." To get some prayer strategies, go watch it!

This is a shot at one of our Oil Ability leaders' retreats in Myrtle Beach, South Caro-

lina. Fifty-three leaders were bowing together, praying specifically over their businesses.

As you practice, here are a few things I do that have really helped me.

START A PRAYER JOURNAL

You can dress it up and go to a bookstore and get something really nice in leather, or you can go to the corner store and grab a $1 notebook. Both work just as well.

Break the book into three sections: thanks, leaders, goals.

1. Thanks

In the first section, every single time you come across something you're grateful for, write it down. Keep that notebook close. For example, this week I trained my 60-year-old mom how to do follow-up on her downline. She called me twice in 24 hours to say that two people had gotten on Essential Rewards. She was giddy! Something she had done had impacted the lives of those families. A simple gesture of a mailing made all the difference. That went in my grateful column, grateful that more people will be impacted by the oils and that more people will be following Young Living's mission of getting oils into every home in the world. I was so grateful to hear the joy in my mom's voice, knowing that she had a made a difference.

2. Leaders

The second section is a bit trickier. It only works if you're keeping touch with your team. At first it will just be the people you come into contact with. Then it will be people at your classes and new leaders who are raised up. Get to know them and get to know their struggles. Write them down very specifically and pray for them. As your list grows, you may only be able to pray for three or four of them a day as your rotate through the list, and that's totally ok. Just commit to praying every day. I leave a little check box next to each name, because as the Lord answers those prayers, I love to see them checked off. It always floors me when I go back over a year and see how many checks there are. Sometimes you think the Lord isn't answering, but the truth is that you're just not watching.

3. Goals

Column three is the fun one! That's your goals column, the place where you write down, specifically, what you'd like to see happen in your business. And I mean *specifically*. Many of my leaders have frowned on this one because they feel like they have no place asking God for things, but I tell them that God LOVES to love His children! The Bible says to ask and you'll receive! So ask!

May I give you specific story from my own life on column three? Many people have asked me what John and I are doing with the Platinum income, and I'll be straight up with you. There are no jets or hot tubs in our future this year. We're laser focused on getting rid of debt. Then we want to pay off our house and build a crazy savings account, make a will, and invest. After that, we'll have more freedom and feel like we're in a place to start living on 10% and tithing 90%.

Because I'm OCD in setting goals, I made a list of all our debts and committed to paying off one thing a month this year. Last month, it was our car, and we owed $2500 on it. I looked over the classes I had scheduled and realized that was going to be a bit rough.

I got down on my knees and prayed that the Lord would raise up $2500 so we could pay off our car, to get closer to using our income to glorify Him.

I had two classes until the end of the month. At the first one, we had 100 people show up! It was crazy! It was the first large-scale Teacher Training I'd ever done. My little girl counted the cash on the way home from selling this book and my DVD's, and it was $1900. Then next morning we drove to Johnson City for an Oils-of-the-Bible class. There were only ten people there. At the beginning of the class, we formed a prayer circle with the team and prayed specifically for the last of the money. Even though there were only ten people, I had a total confidence that the Lord would raise it up.

We counted on the way home—$570. We had made $2,470 in 12 hours, which was unheard of for us! When John and I went to pay the car off the next morning, the payoff amount was less then what we had thought, and we had almost $200 left over!

That is the power of praying specifically.

PRAY SPECIFICALLY

How do you do it? Pray for OGV. Pray for leaders to be raised up under specific people you want to see blessed. Pray for full classes. Pray for many kits sold. Pray for motivation to accomplish tasks. Pray for clarity and wisdom on how to spend the time for your business that day. Pray for the right words to connect with your leaders. Pray for an open door to raise up leaders or grow your team. Pray for more people to get on

Essential Rewards and then give a number. Pray specifically over certain leaders and areas in which they need to be blessed. Pray with another leader on your team and commit to regular prayer time with them.

My prayers look like this. Right off the bat, it is 30% praise for the things I'm seeing the Lord doing that week. Next comes the 40% prayers over my team and my leaders, specifically. Last is the 30% vision casting with my Lord and praying specifically over our family business. End with thanks and gratitude at how the Lord is already moving.

Not sure how to pray? Just read right through your notebook. If it sounds silly, that's okay. God hears your heart. It's not about how you pray. It's that you pray. That's all that matters.

Commit and see what happens, and for even more fun, track it! One of my greatest joys is seeing the Lord move over my team!

If you do not have a personal relationship with Christ, there's a number you can call right now to speak with someone. Go online to www.needhim.org. You are not alone.

We'll end this chapter with a testimony from Brandee Gorsline, the woman who enrolled me in Young Living.

"I KNOW prayer is why I have been so successful! I am not as deliberate as what Sarah describes above, but I do pray over people and our businesses. I am blessed to have some of my best friends in the world on my team and I love them and their families, so praying for favor and abundance over them comes naturally. Can you imagine what our team will look like in a year if all the leaders took the time to pray like this? It's so exciting to think about! Goal setting with specifics is a proven strategy for success. It's amazing how often it turns out exactly as you planned. My team member, Mindy, had a goal of adding 22 team members in February, and on the last day of the month #22 logged on and bought a starter kit! It truly works and when backed with prayer and intention, WOW! There are only three commandments in the Bible: prayer, giving, and fasting. Can you imagine what would happen if we pray over our teams and our businesses and fast regularly for wisdom, action, and breakthrough? God wants to bless us in so many ways, and not just financially. My Young Living journey has been a blessing to me and my family in SO many ways, financially, friends, oils, health, and helping others. We need to remember that the enemy does not want any of this to happen, so we need to bathe our journey in prayer every day!"

CHAPTER 23

AVOIDING DISTRACTIONS

This is a big deal. Maybe you dive head on into your business, ready for it to explode. You're so serious about aromatherapy that you go for a certification and you read 192 aromatherapy and leadership books in a year. You go to every leadership training you can get your hands on. You even stop teaching classes so you can get more leadership training. Then you go train some more. You want everyone to experience the oils so you build a massive make-and-take store. Maybe you pay rent to sell the oils retail somewhere. You're on fire, but your business isn't growing!

Who am I talking to? Umm ... me. I did all of the above. I hold six certifications in aromatherapy, and I read all those books. I had a huge store in the ten bins I toted around with me; this is where I gave my Young Living oils away and sold the bases, like a cream base or a roll on base. This story was all me! I believe I would have been Diamond long before now, had I not been so distracted.

When I was on the Young Living Venice Global Leadership cruise, I was in a hot tub with a few other women. We were all Golds together, yet nine months later, they were all Diamond, and I was baby Platinum.

What happened? Distraction. Distraction will take your momentum and melt it into a puddle. You'll push and push and push—like a fish swimming against the current—and not get anywhere. You put in hours, but don't grow, and you don't know why.

Here's why. What you're doing isn't growing your business. Your attention is in other places. There are tasks each day that will grow you and tasks each day that will slow you down or do absolutely nothing to your magnify your business. What grows your business? Raising leaders, selling starter kits, and good follow up! That's it!

If it doesn't fall in either of those three categories, then don't do it. When you're raising leaders, if they're not on the leg you're building, it's counter-productive. Hand them this book, do a two-hour Teacher Training with them with the script in the back of this book, and let them loose. Work with the leaders on your weak legs. That's how you move up in rank, that's how you grow your income, that's how you get time freedom and financial freedom, and that's how you bless more people. Focus on you so you can get to the place where you can pour your attention into philanthropy. You're not there yet.

PITFALLS TO WATCH OUT FOR:

1. Spending more than you make

Hear me on this. If your check is $200 a month, you may have friends in Canada, but you don't make enough to travel to them. The Lord will not trust you with more unless you're faithful with the small stuff. You haven't grown enough to spend $700 on a flight to Canada. If you're set on that team, train them online. Mail them resources. Get creative. Find local leaders on other teams who will allow them into their classes. Mail my DVD's (oilabilityteam.com), but don't go there until you have the income to pull it off. That's not good stewardship.

I went without business cards for eight weeks because I just didn't have the income to do it yet. We were faithful, God provided, and I have knockout business cards now. Overspending is a distraction that can cause dissension in your marriage and pull your heart away from your business. Be careful!

This is a wonderful place to offer a rare resource. At convention, I met a friend and top Young Living leader named Steve Sheridan, who I consider to be the Dave Ramsey of Young Living. He's a gifted financial advisor. He and his wife Nancy have written a book called "Journey to Health and Wealth: 10 Step Plan to Wellness, Purpose, and Abundance," which takes you through the financial side of Young Living, including emergency funds, debt reduction, and investing. It's wonderful, and it will give you a good road map on how to handle your income as it rises. Pick up his book and check out his website at www.j2hw.com. Steve has written an entire chapter in Gameplan 2 for Silvers and above—watch for it!

2. Wanting education upfront

I mentioned this is earlier, but I want to go into more depth. Do you think doctors and lawyers have 20 years' experience the first month they start their practice? No way. Most of what I learned, I have learned from listening to distributors and hearing their heart on their oils journey, then teaching them to answer their own questions by researching and looking things up.

Is an aromatherapy certification good to have? Well, sure it is. But do you need it to grow your business? Absolutely not! That's what reference guides are for. That's why I make my CD's and DVD's available. Learn as you go and don't wait to start until you have an aromatherapy degree. That's a distraction and a waste of time as you are starting. As you grow, if you have the income, absolutely—go learn. You'll have time freedom and money. But right now, as you're building and trying to escape your 40-hour-a-week job in order to have time with your family, you don't need to nail aromachemistry. Wait for it. What am I saying? Trust the system. Learn your tools. Point people where they need to go and stand down. Don't be the expert.

If I could go back and do all those certifications again, I probably wouldn't. I did them because I was brand-spanking new at network marketing in 2014, and I thought that was what it took to build a business. But some of the fastest growth in my business happened before I ever even finished the education. I found some of my most powerful leaders before I took my final exams.

Is education important? Yes. Please don't read me incorrectly. I think personal development and reading books matters. I digest dozens of books a week just because I love learning. But should you put your business on hold because you don't "know" enough? Never. That could be the mistake that costs you your entire business. You will lose interest because you rank so slowly—and it's because you're not doing the things you need to do to grow.

What do you need to grow your business? A passion for oils! When you have a passion that is infectious, people will buy the kit! That doesn't require a degree. Anything else you need, you can look up, or better yet, train your downline to look it up themselves.

3. Getting Involved In More Than One Network Marketing Company

This one is a doozy, and I see a lot of people make this mistake. On my own team I've lost more than 20 members who got discouraged that they weren't ranking fast enough with Young Living, but at the same time, they were trying to run another business.

I was blessed to have a great upline that warned me of this early on. It is tempting in the beginning to host a jewelry party or a pots and pans party or a books party to bring in some extra cash. But when you do that, you confuse your team.

I'm not saying to avoid your friends in other MLM's. Go to their classes, buy their pans and books and makeup, and support and encourage them. Just don't market their classes on your social media as if it's your own class—that will really mess with the heads of your leaders. Attend the classes, don't host the classes.

Do you think it may harm your relationships with your friends? It may in the short-term, but only with the friends you have that are doing MLM's—which is a very small percentage of your pool of potential oilers.

I truly don't believe it's possible to successfully run two network marketing companies. One of them will suffer, or you or your family will suffer. For Young Living, I spend time each week with my leaders, I run two Facebook pages, teach classes, do follow up, mail packages, and do recognition with my team. A couple of times a year I'm also holding retreats and large Beauty Schools and Business Bootcamps. How can I do that for two MLM's? I can't do it well. If you commit to both, you will do both with mediocrity, and never rise to a rank of Diamond in either. You also confuse friends who are watching and see you as not committed (and they may have joined your team), as well as your leaders and oilers.

Focus on one thing and do it with excellence. Do not run two businesses.

4. Building a storefront

This is a big one, and many of my own leaders have fallen into this trap. First, it's against Young Living's rules to sell their oils if the bottles are opened. If you do that, you can get into big trouble. You can give anything away that you want, and Young Living even encourages that by giving you share-it bottles in your starter kit, but you can't sell their oils which have been opened. So having a store and making products out of the oils is a liability and a big distraction.

It's also time consuming. If you're making your own creams and roll-ons and selling them (which is illegal), then you're not training leaders and holding classes. If you want someone to experience an oil, give them a few drops of that oil, but don't make a store. You'll lose valuable, precious time while you're on fire and you need this fire to assemble and amass your team.

5. Getting on Facebook and wasting time

Okay, confession time. I *totally* still do this. I get on hoping to write a few messages to my leaders, and hour later I've commented on Billy's new toad, liked my friend's pillow fight photo, and posted a pic of me eating ice cream. Wow. That's an hour of my life I'll never get back!

Here's my tip (this goes back to the chapter on Balancing the Business): make a list of three things you *need* to do that day, three tasks that are critical to your business. Don't allow yourself free time until those tasks are done. Period. Just don't do it. If those tasks are not on Facebook, don't get on Facebook. Don't put yourself in places where you'll lose time. Then when those tasks are done, reward yourself with brainless scrolling!

6. Not setting regular business hours for yourself

I homeschool five children, so I get up at 7:00, go on a run, and set breakfast on the table. I start with the little ones and school them from 8:00 until 10:30, which is time for a snack, and then they go off and work on their homework. I homeschool my older children from 11:00 until 1:00, after which they do the rest of their work independently. I nap for an hour. Then I work my business from 2:00 until 5:00. After that we have family time.

Those business hours are when I answer all my team's questions, run my leadership page, and train leaders. That's when I do follow up, mailings, and recognition. One night a week I'm out of the house teaching, and one night a week I do a team wide leadership training online for 30 minutes. That's my life as a Platinum.

Even my little ones know not to disrupt me during business hours, or they will pay for it with a loss of their own personal time and some extra chores. That time is protected, and their time is protected, too. My phone is off during school and when I'm engaged with my children. You may try to write or call, but I will not answer. Set boundaries. Train your leaders that you're not available at 1 a.m., and that they shouldn't be, either.

Some days I can't get all three hours in because the children have dance or Boy Scouts. That's okay, because I'm consistent and I protect that time throughout the week, so that when we have seasons of recitals, my business is not suffering because of it.

One of the reasons our business has grown so quickly is because of committed, consistent time without distractions. Each night before you go to bed or each morning, make a list of the three most important business tasks, and set aside regular time to make it happen and do them! Make no excuses. Stay on course!

7. Training Other Teams

I also want to make a quick statement on raising leaders and crossline training. First off, if you're thinking of crossline recruiting (taking people from other teams)—DON'T. Even if they're your close friend and you missed your chance to sign them for a kit by a week. Why? It's a lack of integrity. The Lord won't bless you if you're pulling from other people's teams. When I see a crossline request to join our team, I delete it. I don't even respond. We have plenty of training tools online (oilabilityteam.com) for them to grow where they are planted. It does not honor the leader who poured into them by signing them to steal them for my team.

What about requests to speak for other teams? As you rank up, you'll get these more and more frequently. People will be drawn to your success. I'd definitely recommend against more than one or two crossline classes a year. It will burn you out, and this means that you're not pouring life into your own leaders. It is another form of distraction. Keep your eye out for burnout. If you're in a stage of life without a lot of family responsibility and can pull it off, you may be able to do more. But recognize that for every crossline class taught, that's a class you've lost for your team.

Apply that same principal to your family. Each class you're out teaching for your own team is time away from your spouse and children. Choose your classes carefully. Choose locations carefully. Always ask yourself if this is a class you must teach in person or if you can achieve the same results online or by delegating it to another leader. Don't overbook yourself. (I once taught four classes in 12 hours in three different states and pulled my children along with me. That is not good time stewardship.) Work in a way that's wise and that keeps your family above your business. Doing that will bring far greater blessings.

In the same breath, you can experience more growth by pouring your efforts into certain downline groups. If you have a leader who's knocking it out of the ballpark, send them encouragement, but let them lead. Don't step on their team. Focus your attention on the leaders who need more encouragement. If you have two legs that are under the OGV you need to rank, take six months and do all your classes under those legs and those legs alone. Don't get distracted. The faster you rank, the more people you can help!

8. Leadership training

For me, this falls under the same category as aromatherapy classes. It's great. You will grow, and personal growth is important. But if you're spending more time reading and attending seminars than you are in teaching 101 classes or training leaders, you're doing it wrong.

I once asked Adam Green how on earth he got to Royal Crown Diamond by age 24. I call it classes, and he calls them "meetings." He said, "Meetings meetings meetings. Hold a lot of meetings, and then hold more. Then do it again." This is a pattern among all the Diamonds. Even at that rank, they are out there teaching classes. Constantly. If you keep that right in front of you and make it your number one goal, you'll move up in rank. If you're doing more leadership training and reading books than teaching classes, you are upside down and will grow slowly.

Don't get distracted. Education is good, but not to the detriment of your ultimate goal, which is to build a business which is sustainable and sets you free. That includes the freedom to learn and the freedom for personal development.

I commit a little time each day for personal development, 30 minutes a day, sometimes 60 if I have more free time. Most of it is done by audio CD as I'm driving. (My children are well-trained too because of it!) But most of my attention is on classes. Because that's where it needs to be for you to grow. By the way, if you want this book on audio CD for your leaders, check it out at oilabilityteam.com.

Keep distractions down and classes up, because that's the secret to thriving!

CHAPTER 24

Encouragement for the Climb

I want to end with some encouragement. It's easy to close this book, look at your OGV, and quit. Even at Platinum rank I've had days with so much frustration that I wanted to walk away, so let me pass along a few words that really encouraged me in those moments.

COMPARISON WILL KILL YOU

First, don't rate your beginning by someone else's middle. Their life is like an iceberg; their bulk of their story is under the water of ocean waves. You have no idea what it took for that person to get where they are, and their journey may have been incredibly difficult. Don't rate your starting line with their mile 26. You're comparing apples and oranges, and you're putting yourself in a place where you're speaking death over your business.

Is that a term you've heard before? Speaking death or speaking life? It's Biblical. The Bible talks about the power of the words that we speak. God created the entire universe with His spoken words of life. When you walk around saying you can't do things, or that your business won't grow, or that network marketing can't possibly work, or that you'll never attain a certain rank or income, you're speaking death.

If you had $170,000 deposited into your bank account on the 20th of this month because you were a Royal Crown Diamond, would you carry yourself differently? Would you speak with more confidence? Would you make different choices? Carry yourself as if you're already there. Have passion, purpose, abundance, and meaning to your day. Speak life over the work that you do, and then watch your work and your attitude transform!

EMBRACE YOUR PACE

Second, each person has their own rate at which they grow, and that's okay. If it takes you 12 years to get to Diamond and it takes someone else two years to get there, your way was not wrong and their way was not right.

Each person has unique gifts, treasures, and personality traits that allow them to grow at different rates. It doesn't make them better at network marketing. In fact, network marketing guru Dani Johnson in her GEMS training says that across all network marketing companies, most of those who reach top the top ranks in their company have pearl personalities! These are the most laid back, peaceful, compassionate, loyal people out there. They aren't the ones in the spotlight or the ones that are loud—they're the ones that don't give up. Ever. They are tenacious, and they persevere. They are the ones that dominate this field. I am a ruby—a loud, obnoxious, uber-organized competitive limelighter, so some of us make it in too—but the pearls are more common! Rate each day against yourself, not anyone else.

It is my hope that if this book does nothing else, that it helps you see where Young Living goes. I hope you can walk away and really catch the vision. Young Living is the least amount of effort for the most amount of reward. It's time economy. If you were to commit 40 hours a week to your Young Living business, it would explode! But don't think that's the only way to succeed.

Commit what you are able.

Set boundaries, including boundaries over your business, and protect that time you've set aside just to work.

Don't give up, even when things don't go as planned. The only people who don't make it to Diamond are the ones that give up. When life throws you curve balls, collect yourself, get back on the horse, and keep moving. Pick up where you left off. That's how you become a Diamond.

Grow from your weaknesses and take criticism well.

Avoid the six pitfalls.

Know your why and revisit it often.

Pray specifically over your business, and pray over your leaders by name.

Connect relationally with your downline. Whatever you do, always keep the distributor at the center of your decisions. If your heart is always for them, the Lord will bless it.

Be a good steward of your time and your finances, and the Lord will give you more time and more finances.

PLANS TO PROSPER

I have no idea where the Lord will take our family business another year from now. But let me tell you what our family has seen in the past two years. I've stood in the fields of almost every U.S. Young Living farm. We took a trip every month from May through November last year. I've had a 20-minute private conversation with Gary Young. I've watched my daughter play with his horses for an entire afternoon, interviewed his employees and opened all the doors to the farms and peeked in each room, just out of news anchor curiosity.

I've made friends in Australia who I text and speak with daily—and also in Texas, Chicago, North Carolina, and more. I have grown closer to my family and watched my mother buy a home and my sister and sister-in-law quit their jobs and retire because of Young Living. In less than a year, I have seen over 100 leaders on my team walk the same path and they have similar stories. It's not just me.

I have interviewed nearly every major figure at Young Living Corporate, just so my team would have a chance to meet them. I have laid my hands on a thousand people and spread oils on their skin. I have stood before rooms full to the doorways and lectured for hours when people had no room to sit, and I've given the same lecture with four people in the tiny house of an elderly couple who opened their doors for a night to love some weary moms.

I've taught classes kayaking on the Aegean Sea off of Greece and walked in catacombs in Venice with my children and Young Living distributors who were the top sellers in the world. I sat at a table with half a dozen Diamonds at the Drive to Win in Hawaii and had a 5-hour breakfast, picking their brains on the secrets to their success.

I now manage a team of over 3000 people in all 50 states and several countries. We have team members who have made Silver or Executive in one month. The Oil Ability team added 430 people to our team in one month. That's not big by Diamond standards, but for a homeschool mom in the middle of nowhere—who moved across the country and didn't know anyone—and who had zero network marketing or sales experience- that's dynamic!

I was the one on welfare. I was the one who at age 20 who was pregnant, working two jobs, and taking a 21-hour college course load. I was the one living in public housing with no furniture and with cockroaches. I was the one who got my children's Christmas gifts at the Salvation Army. That was me at the beginning of the story.

I have one thing to say about that—one thing that's mighty, prophetic, and spoken over your life, too. "'For I know the plans I have for you,' says the Lord. 'Plans to prosper you and not to harm you. Plans to give you a hope and a future.'" Jeremiah 29:11. Claim your future. Stand on the hope that is promised to you. The photo below is of me in a rental car with the wind in my hair. I have Oola Grow oil on my hands. This was taken

at the Young Living Drive to Win contest in Hawaii. I had wanted to go to Hawaii for my wedding 18 years ago, and there I am! That trip was an answered prayer. It was only the second vacation I'd been on in my life. The first was Venice, last year, with my oldest 3 kids. All of it was paid for, courtesy of Young Living.

Do I share my story with you to brag? Goodness, absolutely not. I share all this with you because I believe with all my heart that you can do it too!

There is a part inside of you that looks at this story, shakes your head and walks away. But there's a part of you that knows that you have it in you to pull this off.

The time line doesn't matter.

The size of your friend circle doesn't matter.

The location doesn't matter or the resources.

The only thing that matters is your will, your passion, your consistency, your focus, your confidence, and your tenacity.

So here's your challenge. You have 24 hours. Sit down and write your vision. Write your goals. Make a Gameplan. Open your calendar and schedule a class. Ask three people invite others to your class. Don't just say you'll do it or think you'll do it—make it happen. Set a date for your first class *today*.

Then, share your story to inspire someone else. You have some wild adventures ahead! The stuff books are made of!

PART SEVEN

It Works: The View from the Top

Wow, the Gameplan book has given me the courage to speak to everyone about Young Living. It has also given me the answers to so many questions that I had. It's the best book ever for new business builders!

Jenn Merriam

Gameplan was essential for the launch of my business – it gave me practical, logical, simple steps and all the tools necessary to grow my Young Living organization quickly – as long as I put in the effort! It is a wealth of tips, encouragement, and solid training from someone who has DONE IT – who has navigated this road and distilled out all the important nuggets to be successful – that in itself makes it worth its weight in GOLD. I am a #diamondrising!!! Thank you Sarah Harnisch for sharing your knowledge with us!

Sue Maduro

Gameplan is a one-stop-shop business building goldmine, encompassing every tip and tool you need to become successful. Sarah is an amazing author, leader and giver; planting "oily" seeds in all who read her book. The power to make these seeds grow is within you and I.

Amanda Hickey

CHAPTER 25

CHEAT SHEET TO GO FROM
STARTER KIT TO SILVER

You did it. You just finished this whole book. That tells me you have the tenacity to do this business! This book is a hum-zinger! It's tough!! (Don't skip the Appendixes, they are the best part of the book!)

Now what do you do? Apply it! If you can't remember the last 100 pages, here's this book in a nutshell. Cross each line off as you complete it! (If you want a more comprehensive to-do list, go to oilabilityteam.com and grab our Gameplan Workbook. It's not fill-in-the-blank busywork. It actually customizes this entire Gameplan Strategy guide to fit your team, and help you put feet to your dreams.)

1) If you are brand-spankin' new, order your premium starter kit online (feel free to use my number, 1879195, if you have no team).

2) Photocopy Appendix A, the simple 101 Script, from the back of this book and practice it.

3) Make a list of all of your contacts *everywhere*. Grab them off Facebook, your Christmas card list, and even former

co-workers. That's your warm market. It is what you will draw from to start filling classes.

4) Set up a Facebook event for a class. (Click on "More" then "Events" to get to the page). Fill out the description. Use powerful verbs and make the lecture exciting! Put a photo on your event.

5) Ask three people off your warm market list to invite 50 of their friends to the class. They can't just share it to their page, they have go under the "Invite Friends" button in the event and invite people. Ask them to say something nice about you and the class. Make up a gift basket as a thank you.

6) Market the class for two to three weeks, with no more than one or two posts a day.

7) Open your doors and read the 101 Script to the people sitting on your coach. End with a strong close, and tell them where to get the starter kit.

8) Follow up. Call or mail a hand-written note to those who came. I don't do this by email, because that's too impersonal. Stay in contact. The average person can only say no seven times!

9) Rinse and repeat. Teach four to six classes a month if your goal is Silver-in-Six.

10) As someone on your team turns to the person next to them and sells their own kit, grab the Appendix tool "Teacher Training" and train them. Make sure you touch base with your new leader once a week. To get to Silver, build under two strong leaders. When your OGV crosses 10,000 and each leg is over 4,000, you have made it!

11) Don't hunt people. Don't get lost in the no's. Change the philosophy of how you see the business. You are collecting relationships, not starter kit sales. Don't take it personally when they don't order. Move on, and keep yourself so busy scheduling classes that you don't notice the no's. Keep the focus on education instead of sales.

12) Pray! Pray over your business and use Abundance oil abundantly. God has you and God has this. You were meant to be free. Go out there, world changer! Be bold, have confidence, and bless all those you meet.

13) Snag the Oil Ability Accountability Worksheet from the Appendix of this book. It will help you see each month laid out before you. Make a goal of getting that thing totally filled out by the 25th of each month, for the next month coming.

You can do this! I believe it with all my heart. After digesting all that this book has (I told you it was dense!), keep at the forefront of your mind that it really all comes down to three very simple things: schedule 4-6 classes a month, make sure you're doing good follow up afterwards, and train your leaders. Rinse and repeat those three things over and over and over again. As you rank, don't ever forget those three things, despite the title that follows your name. The day you forget them is the day your business stops growing.

CHAPTER 25

STORIES OF SUCCESS FROM THE OIL ABILITY TEAM

Do you think this is real? Do you think you can really do it? Perhaps it will help you if I share some true-to-life stories from our team. These stories aren't over yet, because each of these Oil Ability Team members is still ranking. But the best way to end this book is with the end game: stories of hope.

Angela is an Oil Ability Silver-in-Six and a school teacher with a lot of debt. She paid off over $30,000 of debt this year, as well as giving another $8000 to charity. She also got married completely debt free. Her goal is to be 100% debt free by 2018.

Rachael As a Young Living Silver in Six, she was able to retire from all three of her jobs. In fact, in August of 2016, she left her third job weeks before her wedding and is now fully supported by her Young Living income! She is no longer working 60 hours a week.

Sheena is an Oil Ability Gold who ran a wonderful natural health store in Eldred, Pennsylvania. She first came to a five-person class, then came again to the same class in a different town. Very soft spoken (but extremely competitive), she became convicted to take the business seriously when one of her downline members had a larger paycheck than she did. She went from Executive to Silver in 11 days (beating my team record of 18 days...that stinker!), and is now retired and home full-time with her two boys.

Theresa is an Oil Ability Silver-In-Six with a severely autistic, non-verbal son. She started taking her business seriously in May of 2016 and nearly doubled her OGV in 1 month. This soft spoken mom now runs a vendor booth at a large scale event called the Windmill in upstate New York every weekend and is leading a powerful team beneath her. She has connected and won the love and respect of the Oil Ability team because of her ability to organize, write, and educate. She is currently in the process of building her first home, after more than a decade in extreme poverty.

Sharon is an Oil Ability Silver-In-Six who endured 40 years of and physical abuse from an alcoholic husband. She separated from him and moved across the country to be near her grandchildren, and took a $10-an-hour job in Ithaca, NY. After 16 months with Young Living, her paycheck surpassed her full time income. She's now able to buy a home and be totally self-sufficient because of her Young Living paycheck. Sharon just moved this week into the first home in New York that she was able to buy entirely by herself.

These are some of the stories of the Oil Ability team, and they can be yours, too, because you have your Gameplan. You know how to do this!

Remember the 3 simple steps: hold 4-6 classes a month using the 101 script in the back of this book, do follow up after every class or event, and train your leaders. Every time someone sells a kit, read the Teacher Training in the appendix and give them a tour of the Virtual Office. Put Gameplan in their hands. Rinse and repeat.

Classes, follow up, leaders.

Get into a regular rhythm of your business cycle. If you can master those three things, you have what it takes to be a #Diamondrising. The only thing between you and becoming a Young Living Diamond is tenacity and consistency. The more often you teach, the faster you will rank, the more people you will help, and the sooner you will become free.

It's time to cross some things off that bucket list you have been making for years. Are the ways you are spending your time right now getting you to the places you want to be? If not, it's time to re-evaluate. It's time to put a new Gameplan into action.

It's time to start.

APPENDIX

SARAH'S SCRIPTS AND MORE

SIMPLE 101 SCRIPT

WHAT ARE ESSENTIAL OILS?

They are the most powerful part of the plant.

They are distilled from shrubs, flowers, trees, roots, bushes, fruit, rinds, resins, and herbs.

Oils consist of over 100 different natural, organic compounds.

In humans, they provide support for every system in the body: your skeletal system, your muscular system, circulatory system, endocrine system and your hormones, respiratory system and immune system. They support brain health and a healthy weight. They are used extensively for emotions and for spiritual support in your prayer life. An oil in a diffuser can soothe a child's tough day at school and provide a calming effect when you've had a stressful day at work. Oils can be used as an alternative to toxic cleaning chemicals in the home. You can literally start swapping out every single chemical cleaning toxin in your home to live a purer lifestyle, and you can do it without breaking the bank!

There are about 300 oils on the earth, but you only need ten to twenty of them to build a good kit.

You do not need to be an aromatherapist to use them. In most cases, just rub it topically into the skin. There are three main ways to get oils into your system: the English apply it topically—rub it on the skin; the French ingest and cook with it; the Germans diffuse and inhale, which can be the most effective method because it doesn't have to pass through the digestive system.

How do they enter—and how long do they last?

Tests have shown oils reach the heart, liver, and thyroid in three seconds when inhaled; they were found in the bloodstream in 26 seconds when applied topically. Expulsion of essential oils takes three to six hours in a normal, healthy body.

ESSENTIAL OILS HISTORY

They were first mentioned by name in the biblical book of Genesis, chapter 37, when Joseph was sold to the slave traders. They carried spicery, balm and Myrrh! Genesis ends with the burial of Joseph's father anointed with myrrh. Oils are mentioned 1100 times directly or indirectly in Scripture.

Some of the oldest cultures on earth used essential oils. The Babylonians placed orders for Cedarwood, Myrrh, and Cyprus. The Egyptians used essential oils for beauty and embalming and they have the oldest recorded deodorant recipe made with essential oils. Pakistan and Rome used essential oils in the communal bath houses.

They were even used by Christ! Jesus was given Gold, Frankincense, and Myrrh. Frankincense is sometimes referred to as "the coconut oil of essential oils" because it has over 10,000 uses.

Essential oils were used by the Medieval Europeans, many of whom brought oils back during the Crusades.

It was only after World War 2 when essential oils were "rediscovered," and the science on their uses grows with every single year.

DO ESSENTIAL OILS WORK?

I have used oils for six years. Lavender smelled nice in my bath, but never had any significant effect on my body. I used to buy my Lavender for $4 a bottle online, at farmers markets, or at bulk foods stores. In the United States, there is no rating system for essential oils. The closest we get is an FDA requirement that in order to label a bottle of essential "pure" or "therapeutic grade," the contents of that bottle must contain at least 5 percent essential oil!

All oils in the world fall into one of 4 catagories: Grade A, Grade B, Grade C and Grade D.

1) Grade A is therapeutic, made from organically grown plants and distilled at low temperatures.

2) Grade B oils are food grade, but may contain synthetics, pesticides, fertilizers, chemical extenders, or carrier oils.

3) Grade C oils are perfume oils that often contain adulterating chemicals. They usually use solvents, for example, hexane, to gain a higher yield of oil per harvest. Solvents can be cancerous, and are in many store bought oils. They may also be diluted 80-95 percent with alcohol.

4) Grade D is called "floral water," which is aromatic only and is usually a byproduct of Grade A distillation. After all the oil is pulled out, the leftover trash water is sold to companies which will fill 5 percent of the bottle with this

"leftover trash water," fill the rest with carriers, and label it "pure."

Grade A is the only true pure oil. Grade D would be like walking into your fridge, taking a glass of orange juice and diluting it 95 percent before you drank it! It wouldn't have the full benefits of orange juice. That's why you want Grade A oils. Before you purchase, check to see if the company grows their own plants, owns their own fields, and controls the entire process from Seed to Seal—from the farm to the sealed bottle. Pesticides, pollution, previously farmed land—all of it can affect the quality of an oil. Young Living's oils are Grade A. Why would you go the extra step of using an oil to get away from a chemical—and then use an oil laden with chemicals? It makes no sense.

One of the things that stands out to me is Young Living's Seed to Seal process. It's a promise of integrity. Gary Young has said that he never makes an oil for profit, he makes it for a purpose. Seed to Seal means each plant is hand-weeded, there are no pesticides used, no chemicals, and no weed killers. The plants are harvested at their peak. They're then put through a vigorous testing process. Then they go from the farm directly to your home. Seed to seed is not a slogan, it's a promise. You can learn more by checking out the Young Living story, and fall in love with the company as I have, at seedtoseal.com.

WHY DO OILS COMPANIES SELL OILS MORE CHEAPLY?

To save money. If you spray your crop with pesticides, you have more crop to distill. If you use a chemical solvent to extract the oil, you pull more out. If you dilute it with a cheaper oil or a carrier oil, you stretch the oil you have distilled. Most essential oils are sold more cheaply because companies cut corners.

HOW OILS ARE MADE:

It takes a great deal of work to produce a tiny amount of essential oil!

- 60 thousand rose blossoms provide only 1 ounce of rose oil
- Lavender is abundant—220 pounds will provide 7 pounds of oil
- Jasmine flowers must be picked by hand before the sun becomes hot on the very first day they open, thus making it one of the most expensive oils in the world! It takes 8 million hand-picked blossoms to produce 2.2 pounds of oil

- A Sandalwood tree must be 30 years old and 30 feet high before it can be cut down for distillation

But a little goes a long way. Most oils are $10 to $30 a bottle. A 5 ml bottle contains about 90 drops, and a 15 mL bottle contains about 250 drops. Each application is one to three drops, meaning even a small bottle will get you 45 to 90 applications. Thieves cleaner is made of plants only and costs about $1.50 a bottle to make. You can't even get that in the organic section at the grocery store! It replaces a multi-purpose cleaner, glass cleaner, and floor cleaner. The organic versions of those can run you $4 to $6 a bottle.

ARE THEY SAFE?

There are certain oils that are photosensitive, meaning you don't want to wear them and go outside. These are mostly citrus oils, like grapefruit, lemon, etc.

When using on your skin, always watch for redness and dilute with a carrier oil. Dilute oils on children, because their skin is more permeable and absorbs the oils more quickly. What is a carrier oil? It's a fatty oil like olive oil or coconut oil, and its molecules are much larger than those of essential oils. Using a carrier oil with an essential oil slows down the rate the body can absorb the essential oil, because it has to ping pong through the large molecules of the carrier oil to get into your skin.

Be wary of putting the oils topically near your eyes. Some oils, like peppermint, can cause a burning sensation. If you are placing an oil near your eye, apply the oil to a Q-tip instead of tipping the bottle toward your face.

You can become desensitized to an oil if you use the same one day after day, so I rotate my oils every three to four days.

What about internal use of essential oils? NAHA, one of the top aromatherapy schools in the United States, doesn't advocate essential oils for internal use. Why? Most oils companies don't carry any GRAS (Generally Regarded As Safe) essential oils which have been cleared by the FDA. NAHA also bases a lot of their decisions on the British model, which advocates topical use only. Many of the British studies are flawed, for example, done at extremely high doses or in ways the oils aren't used, like pouring a bottle inside the body. Young Living utilizes all three methods, British, French and German. The French have been safely using some essential oils internally for decades. Young Living has created a Vitality line with distinctive labels so you can easily recognize which oils are safe to take internally.

ON THE FLIP SIDE...

Look at the ingredient list of what you have in your bathroom and kitchen. Every day we put products on our skin, in our body, and breathe them, but many of these products contain damaging chemicals. The average woman applies over 300 chemicals a day to her body just through soaps, makeup, shampoos, and hair care products. Eighty of those products are applied every day before breakfast!

When you use Young Living's essential oils, you're using a product with one ingredient, like Lemon, Oregano, Tangerine – no additives and no chemical yuck.

Is all this a bit overwhelming? Let me tell you how I started my oils journey: with a Young Living starter kit. It's the only thing on the Young Living website that is half off! If you're a frugal momma like me, this is the best bang for your buck! It comes with 11 bottles of oil and a diffuser.

Pass around the Premium starter Kit with Home Diffuser, open the bottles and smell them:

- **Frankincense**. One of the top skin oils. Helps smooth the appearance of skin. A key ingredient in Young Living's "Brain Power" essential oil blend. Diffuse during prayer time to help with grounding and purpose.

- **Lavender**. Oil of relaxation. Diffuse for a calming, soothing aroma. Unwind by adding a few drops to a nighttime bath. One of the top oils to support healthy skin. Called the "Swiss army knife" of essential oils because of its many uses.

- **Peppermint**. Supports gastrointestinal comfort. Promotes healthy bowel function and enhanced healthy gut function. Helps maintain efficiency of the digestive tract. May support performance during exercise.

- **Purification**. Diffuse to freshen the air and eliminate odors. Add to a carrier oil to moisturize your skin or for a soothing massage on your feet. Use in a spray to enjoy an annoyance-free outdoor experience.

- **Thieves**. Helps support a healthy respiratory system and helps maintain overall wellness when taken as a dietary supplement. Add a drop to hot drinks for a spicy zing!

- **Stress Away**. Promotes wellness and may be an important part of a daily health regimen. One of the top emotion oils!

- **Lemon**. Its citrus flavor enhances the taste of food and water. A key ingredient in Thieves and NingXia Red. May help support the immune system.

- **PanAway**. Apply after exercise to soothe muscles. Has a stimulating aroma. Apply to back and neck for a soothing aromatic experience. Supports the appearance of healthy skin coloration.

- **Copaiba**. Promotes overall wellness. Supports nearly every system in the body. Also a great skin oil.

- **DiGize**. Top oil for supporting the digestive system. Add two drops, along with a drop of peppermint, to water for a stimulating beverage. Take in a veggie capsule internally. Use with Essentialzyme at every meal to support a wellness regimen.

- **R.C**. Supports a healthy respiratory system. Diffuse for a comforting aroma. Contains eucalyptol. Rub on feet and chest. Encourages an atmosphere of comfort.

How do you order? Simply go to www.youngliving.com, click on "Become a Member," and add my sponsor and enroller number, ~~1879195~~. It's that simple. Welcome to the world of oils!   3735163

A 30-Second Script To Get Someone to Come to Class

You can only hold the average person's attention for about 30 seconds when you are in passing, having a short casual conversation. Online it's about three to four minutes, which is why my online videos are so short! That's how long you have to convince them to get to an oils class. But why would they need it? And how do you unscramble your thoughts when you're standing right in front of them?

I'd really encourage you to listen to them first. Each person has a story and they have a reason why they might use the oils. Some may need it for emotions. Some may need it because they have a smell in their house that they need to get rid of (that was how I hooked my brother!). Try listening to them first, and then responding.

But if that isn't an option, and if I only have a few moments, I always take the chemical-free home angle, because no one wants poison in their house. Oils are a non-toxic way to live.

Below is a quick script you can use to get people to oils classes, without even knowing them. It's important to have a running 30-second script in your head all the time, so you can fall back on it when you only have a few moments to convey the need for oils to someone. This script works WONDERFUL at vendor events, or anytime you're inviting someone to a class or piquing their interest to buy a starter kit.

Script:

The average person applies 300 chemicals to their body every single day, and 80 of those chemicals before breakfast! Most are from four things—soap, makeup, shampoo, and hair care. The biggest pollutants in our home are fabric softener, dryer sheets, air freshener plug-ins, and candles. You are literally poisoning your family every day with the stuff that you can't pronounce in your home, like your bright blue dish soap, the cleaner you use for your kitchen counters, processed food, and more. Health and safety data only exists for 15 percent of all the chemicals out there, even though so many are known to cause asthma or endocrine disruptions.

Essential oils are a better way. They are totally chemical free, steam distilled or cold pressed from pure plants. There's nothing in them but that one oil, whether it is lemon, tangerine, lavender, peppermint, or others. There are over a million uses for essential oils—cleaning supplies, personal care products like toothpaste and deodorant, in the diffuser, oil-infused nutritional supplements. Come to a one-hour class that costs you nothing to learn how to kick the chemicals in your home to the curb. I will walk you through step by step. It's easy, simple, and it's a small change you can make to protect your family and take charge of what's in your house.

I then hand them my business card and collect their information. If I have an event online, I add them to it, and I'm off and running! Don't worry, they'll listen a lot longer when they are in the physical class!

THE OIL ABILITY MARKETING SYSTEM

A simple, free marketing system that works

1) Set up a Facebook event two to three weeks ahead of the class.

   a) In that event, add a banner photo and a punchy description of the class, as well as address and time.

2) Ask three people to invite 50 people to the event and make them a thank you basket.

   a) I like to include some Thieves cleaner, a peppermint roll-on, and some of my DVD's. It costs less than $5 per person to pull that off. Ask them to put one sentence in the event about you to build trust.

3) Grab FDA compliant photos and lines from the 101 Script and market it every single day.

4) After class, tap into your new downline and ask three of them to invite 50 people to the class. Follow steps 1-4 all over again.

5) Rinse and repeat. You have never-ending friend circles without hitting up your family and friends. Make sure you always have at least three people inviting to each class. They need to go into the event and hit "invite friends" for it to work.

6) Then brace yourself for electric growth!

Remember...

Wording matters on your events. Use power-packed action verbs that take them somewhere.

BAD: Please come to my essential oils class. I will have dessert. I will speak for two hours on oils. If you can bring someone, that would be good. We will have NingXia for an extra cost. If you can't come, I will teach another class.

GOOD: Would you like to learn how to kick toxic chemicals out of your home? I'll walk you through step by step and give easy, simple, and affordable tactics anyone can do with the best essential oils on the planet. This class is totally FREE and will blow your mind! I come with an iced NingXia bar for weary mommas! Gear up for a fast-paced, ground-up lecture on everything oils, and have some fun and pampering in the process. I can't wait to see you! I'll have freebies at the door for those that invite 50 friends on the Facebook event. It's time to take control of the yuck in your home and kick it to the curb!

If you need images for your events, go to the "Oil Ability with Sarah" Facebook page for compliant posts.

SIMPLE OIL ABILITY FOLLOW UP CALLING SCRIPT

1) This is (name/rank), calling from your Young Living upline. Thank you SO much for getting a starter kit and being on our team! I was just calling to make sure you've opened the box and are doing okay.

2) Have you tried the diffuser? Do you need help setting it up?

3) Which oils have you used in your kit? What have you not used? Did you know you can use the other oils in your kit for? (Pick just two or three of these oils, based on what they say.)

   a) **Frankincense**: everything. Seriously. Put in on everything. Also one of the top skin oils.

   b) **Lavender**: oil of relaxation. Diffuse for a calming, soothing scent, unwind by adding a few drops to a nighttime bath. One of the top oils to support healthy skin.

   c) **Peppermint**: supports gastrointestinal system, promotes healthy bowel function, enhanced healthy gut function, maintains efficiency of the digestive tract, may support performance during exercise.

   d) **Purification**: diffuse to freshen the air and eliminate odors, add to a carrier and massage on the feet to soothe, add to a carrier to moisturize your skin, use in a spray to enjoy an annoyance-free outdoor experience.

   e) **Thieves**: helps to support a healthy respiratory system, helps to maintain overall wellness when taken as a dietary supplement.

   f) **Stress Away**: promotes wellness. One of the top emotion oils. May be an important part of a daily health regimen.

   g) **Lemon**: enhances the flavor of foods and water, has a citrus flavor, may help support the immune system.

   h) **Pan Away**: apply after exercise to sooth muscles, has a stimulating aroma, apply to the back and neck for a soothing aromatic experience, supports the appearance of healthy skin coloration.

i) **Copaiba**: promotes overall wellness; supports nearly every system in the body; also a great skin oil.

j) **Digize**: top oil for supporting your digestive system, add 2 drops to water with a drop of peppermint for a stimulating beverage, take in a veggie capsule internally.

k) **R.C.**: supports a healthy respiratory system, diffuse for a comforting aroma, rub on the feet and chest.

4) Do you know about Essential Rewards? It's a way of building your oils cabinet by starting to swap out some of the toxic yuck in your home.

This month's Essential Rewards runs through the end of the month, and they are absolutely wonderful! By spending 300 PV, you can basically get (fill in with the freebies of the month).

You can only get on the Essential Rewards program through the Essential Rewards button in your Virtual Office (make sure they know how to log in to their Virtual Office and that they can find the Getting Started.

Your Essential Rewards order ships once a month with oils and other products that you pick. For 190 PV, the Essential Rewards promotion is usually two free oils; 250 PV is usually two free oils and a cash incentive 300 PV is usually two free oils, a cash incentive, and another Young Living product, for example, NingXia nitro or a diffuser.

You can cancel any time, you get to select the products you want, and you can change the date it ships each month. You must spend 50 PV for it to ship. You also get 10% back on all ER purchases, 20% after 4 months and 25% back after 25 months. If you're stocking your Thieves cleaner, laundry detergent, dish soap, you're literally getting paid to stock the cleaning supplies your home! No grocery store I know offers 25% back!

5) One more thing. I have a gift for you! I'm going to give you a little book with some of my favorite recipes—it's called

the Young Living Welcome book—and a new DVD called "Oily Lifestyle" that our leader, Sarah Harnisch, and her five children recorded. It'll go more in depth on how to use your kit and show you some of the other neat products that Young Living has, like the cleaning supplies and supplements! I just want to bless you! I am so thankful you are on this team!

6) If you have ANY questions or need any help setting up Essential Rewards, just call or write me at _____. I am so excited about your oils journey, and I'm here as a resource to walk you through. These oils have changed my life! It's just about making one swap at a time to get away from some of the chemicals. You have a great year ahead!

This is a little document card that the Oil Ability team uses for follow up. Print off these cards as you're connecting with your new members, tape them to a 3x5 card, and keep it in an index file. It's a great way to visually track your team!

Ask them to try 50PV of Essential Rewards for just three months to see how they feel in their chemical-free home journey. In month one talk about cleaning supplies, month two talk about NingXia and supplements, and month three focus on personal care (toothpaste and ART and shampoo and deodorant.)

(Do you need some images to market ideas for Essential Rewards? Check out the ones we made at oilabilityteam.com!)

And you're off and running!

Month 1 Follow-Up

Name_____ Dist#_____

Date _____ Phone _____ Email _____

☆Product User   ☆ Business Builder

❏ If they are a potential business builder to get their oils for free, would they like training? _____
❏ Are they on our team training page? _____
❏ Do they have a copy of the Gameplan book? _____
❏ Do they know how to use the diffuser? _____
❏ Give recipe for respiratory support (10 drops Thieves Vitality, 8 drops Oregano Vitality, 2 drops Frankincense Vitality in a veggie cap as needed); RC in the diffuser, Thieves cough drops as needed, Inner Defense as a supplement for overall immune support, as well as Super C.
❏ Are they on the Oil Ability with Sarah Facebook Page? _____
❏ Invite to class or ask them to host a class. _____
❏ Explain ER, tell them about the promos this month, and how to sign up- tell them you will give them ER ideas via email (mail some of the ER graphics to them from this workbook)
❏ What are the products they want to try? _____

❏ Give them your contact info, an Oily Lifestyle DVD that runs through the kit, and Jordan Schrandt's Welcome Book.
What I mailed or recommended to them:
_____

Month 2 Follow-Up

Name_____ Dist#_____

Date _____ Phone _____ Email _____

❏ How are they using their oils?_____
❏ Give them some ideas for pain: Have they tried Cool Azul Pain Cream or the Deep Relief Roll On?
_____
❏ Ask what products they are most interested in: beauty, personal care, cleaning supplies, oils, or supplements. Then give them some ideas based on the essential rewards cards in the Appendix._____
❏ Give them resources: an Oil Ability DVD or CD, a roll on of a new oil they've not tried, or a sample like NingXia or the Thieves cough drops or Thieves laundry soap.
❏ Explain the various reference guides out there.
❏ Tell them about Essential Rewards, email them some different Essential Rewards ideas cards from the Gameplan Workbook Appendix, and explain the promos for the month.

What I mailed or recommended to them:
_____

Month 3 Follow-Up

Name_____ Dist#_____

Date _____ Phone _____ Email _____

❏ How are they using their oils?_____
❏ What have they not used?_____
❏ Give them recipe ideas for energy and for relaxing:
   o Energy: Super B, NingXia + Nitro, Pure Protein Complete (see the recipe in the Gameplan book for the protein smoothie!), EnRGee oil in the diffuser, or Peppermint.
   o Relaxation oils: Stress Away, Tranquil, Peace and Calming 2, Relaxation Massage Oil.
❏ Tell them about Essential Rewards, email them some different Essential Rewards ideas cards from the Gameplan workbook appendix, and explain the promos for the month.
What I mailed or recommended to them:
_____

CARE PACKAGE MAILINGS: WHAT TO INCLUDE

Every other month or so, I like to take care of the people I have personally enrolled by mailing some new product for them to try out. The goal is to educate them in the oily lifestyle, give them something new to try, and above all, tell them boldly about Essential Rewards.

Each package I mail out has five components to it:

1) A handwritten note

2) Something free for them to try out. (Options: a sample of Protein Powder and my smoothie recipe (find it in Chapter Six), a Thieves cough drop, a small sample of Cool Azul pain cream, a roll on filled with Thieves cleaner as a stain stick, or a packet of NingXia or Nitro.)

3) One of my DVD's. If they are new, I usually pop in the Oily Lifestyle DVD to teach them how to use the kit and also "How to Get Your Oils For Free" (aka "Why Do a Young Living Business")

4) A little booklet to boost their education. I love the "Young Living Welcome book" by Crown Diamond Jordan Schrandt. You can buy that at purposemeetshustle.com. If you want an idea for month 2 or 3 follow up, check out the tiny books at oilrevolutiondesigns.com.

5) The card below (feel free to print it!) and a photo of whatever the promos are for Essential Rewards that month. Let them know how to get free oils and 10% back on their order!

I rotate through my teams every couple of months. If there's a strong leader on that legI sit down with them for an afternoon and train them to do their own follow up (and eat a lot of chocolate!) If there's no clear leader, I'll mail this package out myself. Then a couple months later I may mail a different DVD and sample with a new handwritten note. It's all about building relationships.

ESSENTIAL REWARDS IN CLEAR LANGUAGE

I get asked at least once a day how the Essential Rewards program works, even by leaders, and when I see leaders with 288 PV or 187 PV, I want to kick a wall. So here's a simple explanation (for my own sanity).

1. Freebies

If you spend 190 PV, 250 PV, or 300 PV, you get oodles of freebies! Example: The one this month—a free Everyday Oils Kit—for 300 PV is actually worth $270 (retail). With this amount of money, you can literally restock most of your starter kit, or your cleaning supplies, supplements and oils. It's usually two free oils for 190 PV, two oils and a cash incentive for 250 PV (which makes it worth it to spend 250 PV), and 2 oils, a cash incentive and "something else" (like a diffuser, Nitro, or a whole Everyday Oils Kit) for 300 PV. The freebies change every single month. Look for January's to be released around December 31st. You cannot add to an order from earlier in the month to hit 300PV. It's got to be in one single order.

2. Cheaper shipping

Like a *lot* cheaper.

3. Cash back

For the first three months you're on Essential Rewards, you get 10 percent back. On month 4, you get 20 percent back, and after 25 months, you get 25 percent back. Most of my oils were free this way.

4. Kits only available on ER

The NingXia Essential Rewards kit, for example, costs $1.16 an ounce instead of $1.60 an ounce. Since my whole family drinks it, it's the cheapest way to buy NingXia. The same is true of the Thieves Essential Rewards kit.

5. The requirements

You must spend 50 PV a month to place an Essential Rewards order, and you can always change the date to a better date for you. Then you must check your cart before your ship date and update it. It'll leave the items in your cart from last month. Why? Because most people use this to order the same supplements every month and don't want to keep adding them in month after month. Make sure you have what you want in your cart before it ships out.

Why should business builders be on Essential Rewards? Because you have to spend 100 PV to get your paycheck anyway, which is a good idea because it gets you familiar with the product. If you are on Essential Rewards, you get 10% back. That would mean you're actually only spending $90. And that's better financial stewardship. It's a wiser way to get paid.

3 other Essential Rewards questions I get every week:

1) Where do I order it?

Under the Essential Rewards button only in your Virtual Office. I try to put my entire monthly order on it every month because it's free money back.

2) How do I claim my Essential Rewards points?

Under the Quick Order button. Why there and not under Essential Rewards? You would be earning free points by using your free points. All ER points need to be claimed under Quick Order, not under the Essential Rewards tab.

3) Can I get the freebies under Quick Order?

Yes. Hit the same benchmarks: 100, 190, 250, or 300PV.

Oil Ability Closing Scripts

Here are two strong closes to use at the end of your classes. Start your close after you have gone through the oils in the kit.

NAIL THE SALE

Why oils?

Because you need them in your home as part of a simple, chemical-free lifestyle. When you see what the oils do for your own body and how they help create a chemical free home, it's impossible to walk into the homes of your friends and family members and see their bright blue dish soap or their chemical-laden shampoo that is in their bloodstream in 26 seconds and not speak about what you know! You share it because you love and care for your friends, and you wand want to see them living a healthy life. When you take care of yourself, you can fully do what God created you to do, what you were called to do.

How do you begin?

With a Young Living premium starter kit. I'm a frugal momma, and it's the only thing on the Young Living site that's half off. If you take the diffuser off, you're literally getting 11 bottles of therapeutic grade oil for $70. You can't even get it that cheap at the grocery store. Each bottle has 90 drops of oil in it—that's 90 applications. Who wouldn't pay 6 cents for a drop of Thieves to dull the pain of an aching tooth??

The kit also comes with bottles to share the oils with your family and friends, an AromaGlide roll-on bottle to apply the oils on the go, and samples of NingXia Red for full system support. I want to see every single person in this room on NingXia! It's your first line of defense in immune support!

You also get a diffuser with the kit AND a lifetime wholesale membership. That means 24 percent off your oils FOR LIFE. Every single order you place is 24 percent off. To maintain a wholesale membership, you have to spend $50 in a calendar year of oils YOU select. That's like two bottles of Thieves cleaner, which is the only stuff I use to clean my counters, my stove, my floors, and my windows. Without any chemicals, in one swoop, it eradicated my multipurpose counter spray, my glass cleaner, and my floor cleaner. If you need a small step to start using oils in your home, use them to clean!

Get plugged in to our team resources to learn more about how to use the oils. Join our Facebook page, Oil Ability with Sarah. Get on the newsletter for recipes, the latest science, and the class schedule. www.sarahharnisch.com. Pick up one of our team DVD's—Essential Oils 101, 102, 103, 104—or Oil Purity or Oil Affordability. Get a Teacher Training if you want to learn how to share the oils and GET YOUR OILS FOR FREE! It's not hard to talk about them. They share themselves naturally, because of your love and compassion to see the people around you healthy.

Where do you start?

That's as hard as going to www.youngliving.com, click on "Become a Member," and fill out the form. You'll need a sponsor and enroller number because Young Living is a multi-level marketing company. Many people tell me they can't buy from an MLM, but when you shop at Walmart, you're supporting a CEO's third home. When you shop at a MLM, you're buying local. You're supporting my family business. You're paying for gas in our car or food on our table. It's the best form of business out there, and one of the most important reasons is that you get to see your friends and family financially blessed. The Oil Ability team now has, in two years, more than 3000 members in all 50 states and seven countries. It's because the oils work. A company which sells 100,000 starter kits a month is selling them for a reason! People are tired of the chemical yuck around them, and they are taking control of their homes.

If you look around you—Chipotle is cutting all their GMO's. Panera has placed signs in their restaurants that they're cutting all the chemicals from their salad dressings. Kraft Mac and Cheese has cut their dyes. Heinz Ketchup has cut all corn syrup from their ketchup. People are starting to flip over the backs of the bottles of what they put on their skin, eat, clean their homes with and say "no more." That's where oils come in. Can you live a completely toxic-free life? No, but you can minimize your exposure. You can take control of your laundry soap, your dish soap, your cleaning supplies, your supplements and say, "I want a less toxic life." That's where oils come in. The starter kit literally has 10,000 uses, from cleaning your home, to emotional balance, to personal care products like toothpaste and deodorant, to fitness.

I'd like to issue the three-cabinet challenge. When you get home, I'd like to encourage you to start flipping over the backs of the bottles that you use in any three cabinets in your home, and then read the ingredients on these bottles. If there's anything on there that you can't pronounce, it's time to start swapping it out. I wouldn't slather that stuff on my skin, plug it into my walls and smell it, giving it access to the limbic lobe of my brain! I wouldn't cook with it and ingest it. I wouldn't wash my hair with it and have it in my bloodstream over my brain in 26 seconds. I wouldn't clean my counters and butcher block with it and then eat my food off that same block, or wash my clothes with it. We're at a place where people aren't just taking everything at face value anymore, that is, thinking that a product is safe.

You are the gatekeeper of your home. Only you control what crosses the threshold of your doorway. You alone are responsible for the health and safety of your family within the 4 walls of your house. You can say NO. It's time to start kicking chemicals out of your home. To get a starter kit, we've set up a station where you can sign up right now, and we are here to help navigate the website for you. We will walk you through every step. If you'd like to do it at home, we have bags filled with a picture of the kit so you can see what comes in it, as well as a FREE copy of this 101 lecture on DVD. Take it home, share it with someone who should have been in this class with you. It's my gift to you. Also in the bag is my business card with my contact information, so you have a way to get back to me. Feel free to contact me absolutely any time! It is my job to walk you through this and to be there as a resource for you. There are no dumb questions. Also in the bag is a paper which walks you through how to order online. It's as easy as going to www.youngliving.com, clicking on "Become a Member," and filling out the form.

Thank you for generously giving your time to learn about essential oils! I believe with all my heart that you're about to have the best year you've ever had. You will not recognize your home a year from now, and I am SO excited for you!

You have survived essential oils 101!

THE BOLD CLOSE

(Tweak it and include your story!)

Let me get real with you for a moment as I wrap up—and tell you the true reason I teach so emphatically about this. Why does chemical free living matter so much to me? Because I have seen the other end of a chemical filled lifestyle. And I want everyone to know what they are putting in and on their bodies.

The number 2 cause of death in the United States is cancer. 1,620 people a day die of cancer. 1 in 3 cases in the U.S. are directly linked to poor diet, physical inactivity, weight, or chemical exposure. The American Cancer Society says only 5 to 10 percent of all cancer cases are from gene defects. 5 percent. That means 95 percent of cancer cases are under our control. It's what we allow into our homes.

The National Institute of Occupational Safety and Health studied 2,983 ingredients in our products at home—and found 884 toxic ingredients. 314 of them caused biological mutations. 218 caused reproductive problems. 778 were toxic to the human body. 146 they knew caused cancer tumors—but were allowed in the United States, even though they were banned in other countries around the world. Many of these chemicals are allowed in common cleaning supplies in the United States—things under your cabinets right now.

26 seconds after exposure, chemicals are found in measurable amounts in the human body. The average woman applies 300 chemicals to her body a day—80—before breakfast. The top 10 most dangerous chemicals in our home: air fresheners, like plug ins or candles. Second on the list—chemical cleaning supplies, drain and oven cleaners and furniture polish, as well as dishwasher soap and dish soap. Beauty supplies and personal care products—hairspray, gel, shampoo, and deodorant are laden with chemicals. Most deodorant has aluminum in it, and we slather it on our lymph nodes for 70 years. Many scientists believe aluminum exposure may be linked to Alzheimer's and Parkinson's disease. One of the top pollutants in the family home is laundry soap and fabric softener—you wash your clothes, it sits on your skin, it outgases in your closet all night long. That information, is straight from the government, from the U.S. Environmental Protection Agency's Top 10 Killer Household Chemicals Study.

There are 100-thousand chemicals on the market today. The Toxic Substance Control Act of 1976 grandfathered them in. What does that mean to you? Simply put: these chemicals have not had any safety testing, and we know very little information about their side effects. Dr. Samuel Epstein, chairman of the Cancer Prevention Coalition, says "it is unthinkable that women would knowingly inflict such exposures on their infants and children and themselves if products were routinely labeled with explicit warnings of cancer risks. But they are not labeled."

Since the 1940's, prostate cancer is up 200 percent. Thyroid cancer—155 percent. Brain cancer, 70 percent. And the American Cancer Society estimates a 50 percent rise in cancer rates by 2020. It is no wonder that the quality of air inside your home is 5 to 7 times more toxic then outdoor air quality.

What happens when your body is chemically overloaded? You may see it in something as catastrophic as cancer. But most of us feel it on other ways: lethargy. Inability to focus. Sleep trouble. Chronic inflammation.

Unexplained pain. Skin issues—adult acne. Hot flashes. Stress and fear. If you face any of these issues, it's time to kick chemicals to the curb. You can control what you allow within the walls of your home.

I got invited to my first oils class, got my starter kit, and began right where you are right now, taking this chemical free living thing one day at a time, kicking one chemical out of my home at a time. You can do this. It's about taking small steps, and saying- no more. I will not allow these things in my home. You can't control all the places you are exposed—but you are the gatekeeper of your house.

Learn alongside our team. Let us guide you through the process in simple, easy steps. Step 1 is to start with the starter kit—a diffuser and 11 bottles of oil, some of the most common oils on the earth—for supporting systems of the body. They have just 1 ingredient—lemon is just cold pressed lemon rinds. Frankincense, is resin—properly steam distilled at the right temperature to make essential oil. Lavender—freshly distilled at the peak of the harvest—with thousands of uses in the home. Let us come alongside you and train you how to kick chemicals to the curb. You can DO this. 373 5163

Start by heading to youngliving.com, click on "Become A Member" and enter the sponsor and enroller number of the person who introduced you to the oils. (If you're reading this book and don't have a support system, go ahead and use my number—1879195—in both lines. It's an honor to have you on the Oil Ability team. Welcome. I'm glad you're investing in your family!)

Once you have put in the sponsor and enroller number, it will take you to a second page and ask for personal information where you'll set up your account. Write it all down so you're able to log in later. The third page asks which starter kit you want. My personal favorite is the Rainstone diffuser with the premium starter kit. If your budget is tight, the home diffuser works wonderfully too. I'd also encourage you to sign up for Essential Rewards. You get to pick the oils that come to your door every single month, you switch them out—and you get paid 10% back for everything you order in new oils. That's 10% back on your laundry soap and dish soap and Thieves cleaner—which is all I use to clean my house. It's one of the best choices I ever made. If you'd like to add that to your order, I recommend the Thieves Essential Rewards kit—because in one swoop, it contains just about all you need to get rid of nearly every chemical cleaner in your home. It's simple and easy. And if you're taking chemical free living head on, it's the best place to start.

The final window asks for payment, and you're off and running. We're honored to have you as a part of this team. Look for a welcome package in the mail! Connect with us online at Oil Ability with Sarah on Facebook. Find more resources at oilabilityteam.com. And welcome to the Oil Ability family!

This something you NEED to take seriously. No one is watching your home but you. You are the gatekeeper. And I'd be willing to bet my life that there are things in your home right now that you're exposed to every single day—that could be killing you. And the thing is, it's totally preventable.

What do you do until the box arrives?

Start small. Start slow. Start with what you're convicted on. Let me give you a simple tip. With your food, flip the labels over and start reading the ingredients. If you can't pronounce it, don't eat it. It doesn't mean you can't have ice cream—just go for the ice cream with milk, sugar, eggs, and vanilla instead of an ingredients list of 35 items you can't pronounce.

With your home, start with the biggest offenders first—laundry soap, dishwasher soap, cleaning supplies, candles and plug ins. Toss the candles and plug ins. Swap them out with a diffuser and a pure essential oil. Young Living has oil infused Thieves cleaner, laundry soap, and dish soap—that's affordable and simple to use. Add them to your Essential Rewards order once you have that starter kit.

This is about small, simple, baby steps. Take it one month at a time, and swap things out in your home. Maybe the first month you focus solely on Thieves cleaner and toss your cleaning supplies. You can start that today by grabbing a $22 bottle of Thieves cleaner. Go home and wipe your kitchen down and fall in love—knowing you just gave a boost to your immune system instead of taxing your liver.

The next month, swap out some laundry soap or dish soap. Month 3, focus on your personal care products—deodorant, shampoo. Month 4, beauty supplies—like face wash. Every day you leave your makeup on, your skin ages by 7 days. Use a chemical free option to get it off. The Young Living ART line is my favorite.

I started this journey myself 2 years ago, with a Young Living starter kit, and have never looked back. We use the oils every single day in our home. Every oil you use is a chemical you're not using.

You matter. Your family matters. Your friends matter. And you can take control of your own health. Kick the chemicals out of your life and start living clean.

CHECKLIST SHEETS TO TAKE TO VENDOR EVENTS

Name: _____

Phone: _____

Email: _____

Check a box:

☐ I am interested in having you come teach a FREE class for me and my homies. (This class can be at ANY location)

☐ I am interested in showing up to a class you teach! I will bring my friends!

☐ I would LOVE to get my hands on a premium starter kit and start oiling

☐ Please please please teach me how to use oils! Just contact me and give me info!

☐ If you call or contact me, I will egg your house. But I do want to win that gift basket.

This is the address where you can mail it if I win:

_____

Name: _____

Phone: _____

Email: _____

Check a box:

☐ I am Interested in having you come teach a FREE class for me and my homies. (This class can be at ANY location)

☐ I am interested in showing up to a class you teach! I will bring my friends!

☐ I would LOVE to get my hands on a premium starter kit and start oiling

☐ Please please please teach me how to use oils! Just contact me and give me info!

☐ If you call or contact me, I will egg your house. But I do want to win that gift basket.

This is the address where you can mail it if I win:

_____

Name: _____

Phone: _____

Email: _____

Check a box:

☐ I am Interested in having you come teach a FREE class for me and my homies. (This class can be at ANY location)

☐ I am interested in showing up to a class you teach! I will bring my friends!

☐ I would LOVE to get my hands on a premium starter kit and start oiling

☐ Please please please teach me how to use oils! Just contact me and give me info!

☐ If you call or contact me, I will egg your house. But I do want to win that gift basket.

This is the address where you can mail it if I win:

_____

How to Order a Young Living Starter Kit

Each person that comes to class walks out with an organza bag with an image of the starter kit, my business card, a freebie (like a sample of Cool Azul pain cream), and instructions on how to sign up for a starter kit. This is the sheet I print out and put in those bags:

How To Order A Young Living Starter Kit:

1) Go to www.youngliving.com, click "United States, English"

2) Click "Become a Member"

3) Choose "member" (not retail customer)

4) Use sponsor # _____ and Enroller # _____

5) Pick a user name, password, a 4-digit pin (write it down—you'll need it to log in!)

6) I recommend choosing the Premium Starter Kit with Rainstone Diffuser. What does the kit come with? 11 bottles of oil, a diffuser, NingXia samples, lots of literature on how to use the oils, sharing bottles, oils samples, and more!

7) Choose whether or not you would like to be an Essential Rewards Member. You'll have the oils you choose shipped to your door every month! It's worth every penny!!! Shipping is cheaper, and you qualify for bonus oils if you spend 190, 250, or 300PV. You also get 10% back in free oils (no matter what you spend) for the first 3 months, 20% back after 4 months, and 25% back after 25 months. You must spend 50PV each month to maintain Essential Rewards. You can change the date your order ships each month, and you pick the oils you want.

8) Select "continue shopping" if you'd like to add other items to your cart. I recommend the Thieves cleaner for $22—it's concentrated; you get 20 spray bottles of out of it! That's 50 cents a bottle for organic cleaner!

To learn more about your oils, log into your virtual office at youngliving.com, "sign in" and check out the short videos on the "Getting Started" tab. Welcome to Young Living!

TEACHER TRAINING: HOW TO LAUNCH A YOUNG LIVING LEADER

This section is the super-condensed version of all the leadership training in this book. Use it when you are training your leaders personally.

When I first train a leader, the most important thing is for them to understand where this goes. They have to stack Young Living against their current job and see that it's a better use of their time. Will they be where they want to be five years from now if they keep doing the same things they did today? If you have five minutes, run through the first two paragraphs of "Why Do a Young Living Business" (below) to encourage them to come to a leadership training.

Once they are there I'll go through this whole Appendix with them, which takes about 90 minutes, then cap it off with seven homework assignments (remember Eric Worre's "If I, will you?" training ..."If I train you, will you complete these assignments?) Then end with a Virtual Office tour.

WHY DO A YOUNG LIVING BUSINESS?

Young Living allows you to build a willable income you can leave to your children and family. At a Platinum level, that means my five children will not go hungry like I did! They will have food and a roof over their heads. This isn't a 401k that can run out six months after you're gone, it's like having a storefront with employees in your downtown that continues to generate income even if you're not there.

Other perks to Young Living: there is no income ceiling, you are your own boss, you set your own hours, you can take time off and still get paid, it doesn't matter when you get into the company, the product is consumable and it works! It's easier to share then a pan, some make-up, weight loss pills or books and has virtually no overhead costs, save an affordable starter kit. You get to see people around you experience financial freedom (you cannot put a price tag on seeing your best friend leave a job that's cost her time and stress!), you get to build lifelong relationships with people who care about natural health, you are able to work with your friends and family (you pick your coworkers!), and build time economy, the greatest wealth there is. It does not matter how many people you know and you don't have to be good in sales or speaking. Ready to learn more?

GETTING STARTED

How do you begin a Young Living business? It's easy! Print the 101 Script, open your calendar, grab some friends, and schedule a class! That's it! Rinse and repeat!

Check this out! It's the Young Living income disclosure guide. Need motivation? Here's a good place to start.

YOUNG LIVING 2015 WORLDWIDE INCOME DISCLOSURE STATEMENT

As a direct selling company selling essential oils, supplements, and other lifestyle products, Young Living offers opportunities for our members to build a business or simply receive discounts on our products.

Whatever your interest in the company, we hope to count you among the more than 1 million Young Living members joining us in our mission to bring Young Living essential oils to every home in the world.

What are my earning opportunities?

Members can earn commissions and bonuses as outlined in our Compensation Plan. As members move up in the ranks of Young Living, they become eligible for additional earning opportunities.

This document provides statistical, fiscal data about the average member income, average hours worked per week, and information about achieving various ranks.

RANK	AVERAGE HOURS WORKED PER WEEK	PERCENTAGE OF ALL MEMBERS	MONTHLY INCOME				ANNUALIZE AVERAGE INCOME	MONTHS TO ACHIEVE THIS RANK		
			Lowest	Highest	Median	Average		Low	Average	High
Distributor	3	93.7%	$0	$3,863	$0	$1	$13	N/A	N/A	N/A
Star	8	4.4%	$0	$804	$59	$79	$948	1	12	240
Senior Star	9	1.5%	$0	$2,067	$205	$255	$3,060	1	16	239
Executive	11	0.6%	$0	$12,404	$463	$569	$6,692	1	20	233
Silver	18	0.3%	$306	$27,826	$1,769	$2,221	$26,652	1	22	226
Gold	24	0.1%	$1,952	$39,653	$4,879	$6,042	$72,504	1	50	239
Platinum	33	<0.1%	$5,064	$87,606	$12,630	$14,710	$176,520	2	63	238
Diamond	31	<0.1%	$13,871	$144,369	$29,846	$38,730	$465,000	10	83	221
Crown Diamond	36	<0.1%	$31,699	$204,917	$63,524	$74,335	$892,020	14	91	246
Royal Crown Diamond	37	<0.1%	$63,723	$241,324	$144,985	$141,851	$1,702,212	17	126	290

The income statistics in this statement are for incomes earned7 by all active worldwide members in 2015. An "active" member is a member who has purchased at least 50 PV in the previous 12 months.8 The average annual income for all members in this time period was $28, and the median annual income for all members was $0. Forty-two percent of all members who enrolled in 2013 did not remain active members with Young Living in 2015.

Please note that compensation paid to members summarized in this disclosure does not include expenses incurred by a member in the operation or promotion of his or her business, which can vary widely and might include advertising or promotional expenses, product samples, training, rent, travel, telephone, Internet, and miscellaneous expenses. The earnings of the members in this chart are not necessarily representative of the income, if any, that a Young Living member can or will earn through the Young Living Compensation Plan. These figures should not be considered as guarantees or projections of your actual earnings or profits. Your success will depend on individual diligence, work, effort, sales skill, and market conditions. Young Living does not guarantee any income or rank success.

¹ Based on a count at the end of December 2015.
² Based on a survey of Young Living members in December 2015.
³ Because a member's rank may change during the year, these percentages are not based on individual member rank throughout the entire year. They are based on the average distribution of member ranks during the entire year.
⁴ Because a member's rank may change during the year, these incomes are not based on individual member income throughout the entire year. They are based on earnings of all members qualifying for each rank during any month throughout the year.
⁵ This is calculated by multiplying the average monthly income by 12.
⁶ These statistics include all historical ranking data for each rank and are not limited to members who achieved these ranks in 2015.

YOUNG LIVING
ESSENTIAL OILS

Now, tell them to complete these homework assignments to earn a free gift from you, their leader:

1. Print this Teacher Training and pour over it. Buy a new folder and label it "Young Living Business" and store your training there.

2. Get your hands on a copy of the FDA-compliant 101 lecture notes. Write on them, make them yours (share how you got your starter kit), and call them George. Practice the lecture, and add the notes to your Young Living Business folder.

3. Watch a quick video to get over any fears you have of network marketing. This 4-minute video will give you a leg up on what it really is. Go to Youtube and type this in: "I still think it is a pyramid scheme". (Pyramid Scheme Cartoon by Pat Petrini)

4. Read this paragraph on The FDA: You can lose your entire business if you get flagged by the FDA. The Oil Ability Team offers a comprehensive FDA training on DVD at oilabilityteam.com. (For your first class, just

stick to the compliant 101 script). The FDA is not something to fear, just follow the rules. Do not diagnose or talk about oils for treating disease. Stay above the wellness line. Oils are for supporting systems, not curing cancer. There are thousands of ways of talking about the oils compliantly. People are looking for alternatives to a less toxic lifestyle. Chipotle has cut all GMO's, Panera is cutting chemicals from their salad dressing, Kraft has cut dyes from their mac and cheese, Heinz has cut corn syrup from their ketchup. People are reading labels and paying attention to what they put in their body. Young Living is a solution to that problem, whether it's chemical-free cleaning supplies, pure essential oils, or health supplements like NingXia Red or Pure Protein Complete. Our family's business has tripled in half a year, and even though our classes are taught compliantly. It's about supporting your systems so your body can run like a well-oiled machine, not curing disease.

5. Tour the Young Living Virtual Office. Access it by logging into your account at www.youngliving.com. If you do not know your username and password, call Young Living and they can email it to you. Watch all the videos provided in the "Getting Started" tab at the top of your dashboard and read through the documents on the "Member Resources" tab on the left side of the page. Review the "Rank Qualification" (how you watch you) tab and the "My Organization" (how you watch your team) tab. Then you will understand how to rank up.

6. Set a date for your first class.

HOW TO FILL CLASSES WITHOUT KNOWING PEOPLE

Our team's biggest successes are on FREE Facebook event pages. Under your photo on the header of your Facebook page, click on "More," then "Events" and set up an event. Then ask three people you know to go into that Facebook event and invite 50 people each. Make them a gift basket with some multi-purpose Thieves cleaner, one of my DVD's, and a Peppermint roll on as a "thank you". You'll now have 150 people invited. Of that, 15 to 20 will actually show up if you market in the event once a day.

Market the class for at least two to three weeks before the event. Why? People need a heads up. Standard network marketing numbers are that if you have a class of ten, two or three will get kits.

After that class, find the enthusiast—the one that got the kit and loves it—and ask to teach to their circle of friends. Ask three from the class to go into your next event and invite 50 people each. Always tap into new friend circles, and don't keep speaking to the same people. A word of caution: it grows FAST! If you are tenacious and stick with it, your family business will not look the same one year from now!

TIPS FOR CLASS DAY

1) Have everyone bring a dish to pass. Hungry moms sit still when they have food in their gut. Do not make all the food yourself!

1) Don't take health questions.

2) Pass around a clipboard and collect their names, emails, and addresses so you can follow up later. This is the most important thing you can do! If you don't collect their information, you have lost every contact that came to the class.

3) Keep your lecture under an hour. Start by telling how you got involved with oils. Read the three-page 101 lecture or pop in the DVD if you don't want to speak. End by having everyone smell the oils in the Premium Starter kit and explain how the kit can be used.

4) End with a strong closing script and tell them how to order on the Young Living website. You will not sell any starter kits if you don't tell people where to go. Just tell them where you started your journey. It doesn't have to come off as salesy. It just has to be genuine. Have a laptop set up with internet access so they can order right at the class.

5) Give them an organza bag with a photo of the starter kit, step-by-step information on how to sign up, your business card, and a freebie.

NOW FOLLOW UP!

This is the seventh and final homework assignment: pick up the phone and call the people who came to class! We follow the mantra of 3-10-30. Check in three days after class, ten days after, and 30 days after.

You'll run across people who say they're not interested (drop them), those who say they are interested but got sidetracked (walk them through getting the kit), and those who say they can't afford it right now. (They're actually telling you they don't know they need it.) Find their biggest struggle, and make them something oily that will bless them.

Use the same 3-10-30 motto for people who have gotten a kit. What oils have they not used? Do they know how to use the diffuser? Get the Oil Ability audio CD's or DVD's in their hands, or get them plugged into new classes, and explain Essential Rewards.

THE BIGGEST MISTAKES EVERY STAGNANT BUSINESS BUILDER MAKES

1) Not having a strong close in your lecture

2) Tapping into the same friend circles (use the Oil Ability marketing system!)

3) Not doing follow up

4) Not treating a business as a business (wanting a $10,000 paycheck and holding one class a month)

5) Distractions. Wanting 50 years of aromatherapy knowledge before you feel like you can share oils. Pick up the Gameplan book and read Chapter 23 for encouragement in this area.

COMMISSION CHECK

The first question I usually get after sending this is, "How do I get paid?" You have to spend $100 a month to get a paycheck. I'd encourage you to sign up for Essential Rewards, a once-a-month autoship program (you can change the date and what's in your cart any time you want). Why is that a good idea? Because you'll get $10 back (10 percent of your PV) in free oils! So to get a paycheck, you're actually spending $90, and that's a wiser way to get paid.

Your paycheck is mailed out from the Young Living headquarters on the 20th of the next month. So all of January's sales will be in your February 20th paycheck. In the Virtual Office, you can go to "Member Resources" and "Direct Deposit Instructions For U.S. Members" to have your paycheck directly deposited into your bank account so you don't need to wait for snail mail.

Commission check breakdown:

You get $50 for every starter kit you sell where you are the sponsor and the enroller. That's the starter kit Bonus and the Fast Start Bonus. Then for the first three months, you get 25 percent of everything they buy. That's called Fast Start. (And it is SWEET!)

After three months, you get 8% of all they buy. If they enroll someone, you get a 5% commission of that new person's PV. If that person enrolls someone, you get 4% of that PV. That's called Unilevel bonuses. As a Star, Senior Star, and Executive, you may qualify for the Rising Star Team Bonus Pool, and once you reach Silver, you may qualify for the Generation Leadership Bonus. Both of these are generous shares from the company every month.

Four parts to the check:

Starter kit bonus: $50 on every kit (half is technically the starter kit Bonus and half is the Fast Start Bonus

Fast start: 25 percent on all they buy after the kit (for 12 weeks)

Unilevel: (starts on week 13) 8 percent on those directly under you, 5 percent on your second level, 4 percent on levels third, fourth, and fifth levels

Rising Star Team Bonus (Star, Senior Star, Executive) or Generation Leadership Bonus (Silver through Royal Crown Diamond). The former is based more on volume and the latter is based more on rank.

FIND YOUR NICHE

What if I don't want to stand in front of people? There are many ways of sharing Young Living! Do classes online or blog in an FDA complaint way. Make up samples of the oils and hand them out, then promote the starter kit. Give one-on-one classes over lunch. Recruit people to share the oils and read this training to each person who shares a kit. Mail our Oil Ability DVD's to people and do strong follow up. Our best successes are when you invite four or five people to your living room and give the lecture or pop in the DVD and let Sarah teach, if you don't want to stand in front of people. End by passing around the starter kit and telling them how to buy with your distributor number.

One last tip: Pray and give your business to the Lord. Every good thing comes from the Father of Lights!

Hopefully that answers most of your questions! No question is dumb! Network marketing isn't a lottery—it's a mathematical certainty. Get out there and share, and do it again and again, and you'll grow.

Tell your leader-in-training: When you complete those seven homework assignments, you will have gone from learning the Virtual Office, to marketing, to hosting your own class, to doing thorough follow up that get people their starter kits and onto Essential Rewards. Great job! That is one full cycle of your Young Living business. Since most of the fear in this is just getting through that first initial class, (it's fear of the unknown)—I'm now going to bless you with something that really catapulted my business. It's called the Gameplan book, and it lays out a strategy for what to do next. I just wanted you to see that you can launch your business on your own first, simply with the 101 Script and a starter kit.

God bless you. Time to see some miracles!

ACCOUNTABILITY WORKSHEET

"A dream is just a dream. A goal is a dream with a plan and a deadline." -Harvey MacKay

"A goal without a plan is just a wish." -Anonymous

"Setting goals is the first step in turning the invisible to visible." -Tony Robbins

"People with goals succeed because they know where they are going." -Earl Nightingale

"The plans of the diligent lead to profit as surely as haste leads to poverty." Proverbs 21:5

OIL ABILITY GAMEPLAN ACCOUNTABILITY WORKSHEET

Rules: find a partner, fill it out by the 25th each month, and touch base once a week.

There are only 3 things that grow your business: holding classes, doing follow up, and raising leaders. This chart hones in on those 3 things and helps you set tangible goals and keeps you accountable.

Part 1: Classes

1) Schedule 4-6 classes for the month of: _____

Dates of classes scheduled (place a checkmark next to the class if you have set up a Facebook event and asked 3 people to invite 50 different people to it. This should be done before the end of the month so there is time to market classes early in the month.)

Class 1: _____ □
Class 2: _____ □
Class 3: _____ □
Class 4: _____ □
Class 5: _____ □
Class 6: _____ □

2) Overwhelmed by this schedule? A class a week is a commitment of 2 hours a week. That's 8 hours a month. You are giving 160 hours a month to a full time job. This is the job that gets you out of that job. Commit to at least one class a week to grow fast enough that you'll stick with your Young Living business.

Part 2: Business Benchmark Wish List For This Month

OGV growth:_____

Leg growth:

    Leg 1: _____

    Leg 2: _____

This month I am focusing on these legs:_____

This month I am working with these leaders:
    (write their names and the dates you connected)

Name: _____

Dates: _____ , _____ , _____ , _____

Name: _____

Dates: _____ , _____ , _____ , _____

Name: _____

Dates: _____ , _____ , _____ , _____

Name: _____

Dates: _____ , _____ , _____ , _____

Make sure your leaders get this sheet and also have an accountability partner! Check in with them!

Part 3: Raising Leaders

Write a specific goal on the next sheet for at least two leaders. You should be connecting with your leaders once a week, via phone, text, Facebook, zoom, etc. Tangible goals might be:

- getting the Gameplan book in their hands,
- adding them to your business' Facebook page.
- coming up with a plan to get to convention
- giving them resources like flyers, books, DVD's or CD's
- helping them to teach their first 101 class
- watching them teach a class
- co-teaching a class
- training them to do online classes,
- coaching through their weaknesses
- going through the Teacher Training
- walking them through a Virtual Office tour

- _____
- _____
- _____

Part 4: Follow Up Goals

After each class or Teacher Training, have a plan for following up. For each person that came to class, I make a list of their names and text, call or email them. For each person that got a kit, I mail the package below. For each business builder, I mail the package below. On the back of this sheet, track your mailings.

Sarah's post-class plan (if they get a kit): a Welcome to Young Living book, a Thieves or NingXia flyer, an explanation of Essential Rewards and a list of the Essential Rewards freebies for the month, a DVD or 101 audio CD.

Sarah's post-Teacher Training follow up: the 101 Script in a manilla folder with instructions on how to teach (get 3 people on your couch, read the script, give them your distributor number as sponsor and enroller, rinse and repeat); the Teacher Training in a manilla folder to train them how to raise leaders, the Gameplan book, and links for them to plug in to your team's facebook page and online leadership trainings.

Part 5: Have Set Business Hours

This may not be possible if you have a shift with hours that change, but commit to a certain number of hours worked per week, connecting with leaders, marketing your classes, following up, doing mailings, and teaching classes. Even if you start with 1 hour a week, it's better than no commitment.

Week 1: _____

Week 2: _____

Week 3: _____

Week 4: _____

My best success this month was:

_____

_____

One area I can grow:

_____

_____

My 3-month OGV growth plan:

_____

_____

_____

People that are on my radar (for kits or as leaders):

_____

_____

_____

Congratulations! You made it to the end of the month! Time to start a new accountability sheet!

OIL ABILITY RESOURCES TO CATAPULT YOUR TEAM

Did you know that Oil Ability team resources are open to all crossline, upline, and downline members? It's a policy we have kept in place since the very first class. Classes are free and open to all, and training is free and open to all. Why? Because as your team grows, you'll find it harder and harder to fly or drive out of state to train your own team. We'd hope that Young Living leaders across the nation would allow our team members to sit in their classes—because we truly are one big family. If you want ANY of these resources, order them at oilabilityteam.com

So what resources has our team developed? Check them out here.

Facebook. Our team runs a Facebook page thousands strong called "Oil Ability with Sarah" that's updated several times a day with compliant posts. It's a great place to send your leaders and team members for oily education. Pillage the FDA compliant images for your own pages. (Go ahead! We encourage pillaging!) This is about getting oils into every home in the world—if our page helps you out, go for it. Use the material.

Our website. oilabilityteam.com. is where you can pick up DVD's, Gameplan books, Gameplan Bootcamp resources, and audio lectures. We do offer bulk pricing for leaders that want many copies.

WHAT DVD'S HAS SARAH PUT TOGETHER?

Oil Ability 101: the ground up lecture where it all started; centers on the premium starter kit

Oily Lifestyle: the DVD that shows each new member how to use their kit, explains the other items Young Living sells, and how to get on Essential Rewards. It's a must-have DVD for follow up for any business builder. 30 minutes.

Scavenger Hunt: a hilarious 4-minute icebreaker video for your classes featuring Sarah's 5 kids, showing off what an oil-infused lifestyle looks like. This breaks up your lecture and introduces your audience to a personal tour of a chemical-free home. This video has gotten rave reviews and is a tremendous asset to your teaching!! 3 minutes.

Why Do Young Living As A Business: This little ditty is what helped grow our team to 800 sellers in 18 months. I chase all 101 classes with this. 15 minutes.

Business DVD's:

FDA Compliance Training: A full 30-minute compliance training for those that truly don't want to lose their business. Learn the right speech. 30 minutes.

How to Fill Classes without Knowing People: Our tips on filling classes, no matter where you live! 20 minutes

WHAT CD'S HAS SARAH PUT TOGETHER?

Essential Oils 101. 45 minutes, this is an extremely powerful tool for busy potential oilers to listen to in the car. It's been called the best tool, save Gameplan, that the team has put together.

Gameplan. (You read that correctly. The Gameplan book is now available as an audio CD for your leaders to train in the car!)

WHAT BOOKS HAS SARAH WRITTEN?

Gameplan: A Comprehensive Strategy Guide to go from starter kit to Silver

Gameplan The Workbook: This is a companion workbook that makes the book come alive for your team. It puts action to your dreams and goals. This isn't a fill-in-the-blank workbook. It helps you lay out serious goals chapter by chapter.

(Coming Soon) **Gameplan 2**: a powerful book for Silvers and above—your entire strategy must change!

(Coming Soon) **Silver Bootcamp Gameplan Style** a 5-week guided boot-camp. Let Sarah train your leaders in small group format. Also for personal use!

Find all of this at oilabilityteam.com

YOUNG LIVINGEASE: LEARN THE LANGUAGE

YOUNG LIVING BUSINESS TERMS

Personal Volume (PV): Many products sold by Young Living have a Personal Volume (PV) amount. Not all products are dollar for dollar, so if you're trying to hit a certain rank, make sure you check the PV of an item and not its retail price. (Tax and shipping are not added into PV either). PV is one of the requirements for ranking within the compensation plan, and it accumulates throughout each commission period.

Organization Group Volume (OGV): Organization Group Volume is the entire sales volume of a sales organization. This can be determined by calculating the sum of the PV of all the distributors and customers within a particular organization. OGV accumulates throughout each monthly commission period, and re-sets to zero with the start of a new month.

Personal Group Volume for Silver and Higher Ranks (PGV): For Silver or higher ranks in the compensation plan, Personal Group Volume comes into play. It is determined by the sales volume of the organization directly supported by the distributor. Basically, it's all the volume outside of people who have ranked Silver or above. It is the sum of PV from the distributor down to, but not including, the next Silver or higher rank for each leg of the sales organization. If you are out there selling, you'll not have any problem hitting the 1000PGV requirement once you hit Silver (1000 of your volume must be outside your legs). Let me explain to you how this works. If you have 3 people outside your legs that are spending 300PV each, and you spend 100PV to get your check, you will have 1000PGV. If you have 18 people outside your two Silver legs spending 50PV each, and you spend 100PV to get your paycheck, you will have 1000PGV.

Sales Organization: Also known as a downline, this encompasses all members located beneath a particular distributor. This includes the distributor and all levels within his or her organization.

Level: The position of a distributor within a sales organization. Those distributors who are immediately sponsored by another distributor would be considered the sponsoring distributor's first level. Those distributors who are sponsored by a distributor's first level would be considered that distributor's second level and so on.

Enroller: The person responsible for personally introducing a new distributor to Young Living. Enrollers are eligible to qualify for financial bonuses, including the Fast Start and starter kit bonuses.

Sponsor: A new distributor's direct upline and main support. The sponsor may also be the enroller.

Upline: Any distributor above another distributor in a sales organization.

Customer: A member who chooses not to participate in the Young Living compensation plan but desires to purchase the product at retail price for personal use. Customers need to be sponsored and enrolled by a current Young Living distributor and have purchased an order within the previous 12 calendar months.

Unilevel: Unilevel is a form of commission that is earned through the compensation plan. Qualifying distributors earn 8% on the sales volume, or PV, of each distributor on the first level within their organization, 5% on the second level, and 4% on the third through fifth levels.

Compression: In circumstances where a distributor does not meet the 100 PV qualification to earn commissions, his or her volume, if any, is combined, or "compressed," with all the volume of distributors down to and including the next qualifying distributor in the sales organization with at least 100 PV. For instance, if in the third level a distributor places an order of only 30 PV, then the fourth-level distributor's PV in the organization who has ordered 100 PV compresses up with the third level for payout purposes. This creates a single unilevel to be paid out with a total of 130 PV for that commission period. Compression maximizes compensation in cases where there are inactive distributors in an organization who may not be purchasing regularly but may have others below them who are doing so.

PV Minimum: In order to qualify for retail earnings and enroller-based bonuses, and to be considered "active," a distributor must maintain a monthly order of at least 50 PV. In order to qualify for a paycheck, a distributor must maintain a monthly order of at least 100 PV. If an account becomes inactive by dropping below 50 PV for a period of 12 consecutive months, the account will be dropped.

YOUNG LIVING RANKS

Star: In order to qualify as a Star in the compensation plan, a distributor must achieve 100 PV and 500 OGV within a commission period. As a Star, the distributor qualifies to receive compensation on the volume of 3 unilevels in his or her organization (paid at 8%, 5%, and 4%, respectively) in addition to any retail earnings. Stars may also qualify to receive the Fast Start, starter kit, and Rising Star Team bonuses.

Senior Star: In order to qualify as a Senior Star in the compensation plan, a distributor must achieve 100 PV and 2,000 OGV within a commission period. As a Senior Star, the distributor qualifies to receive compensation on the volume of 4 unilevels in his or her organization (paid at 8%, 5%, 4%, and 4%, respectively) in addition to any retail earnings. Senior Stars may also qualify to receive the Fast Start, starter kit, and Rising Star Team bonuses.

Executive: In order to qualify as an Executive, a distributor must achieve 100 PV, 4,000 OGV, and 2 separate legs with 1,000 OGV each within a commission period. As an Executive, the distributor qualifies to receive compensation on the volume of 5 unilevels within his or her organization (paid at 8%, 5%, 4%, 4%, and 4%, respectively) in addition to any retail earnings. Executives may also qualify for the Fast Start, starter kit, and Rising Star Team bonuses.

Silver: In order to qualify as Silver, a distributor must achieve 100 PV, 10,000 OGV, 1,000 PGV, and 2 separate legs with 4,000 OGV each within a commission period. As a Silver, the distributor qualifies to receive compensation on the volume of 5 unilevels within his or her organization (paid at 8%, 5%, 4%, 4%, and 4%, respectively), personal generation commissions (paid at 2.5%), generation commissions on 2 levels (paid at 3%), in addition to any retail earnings. Silvers may also qualify for the Fast Start, starter kit, and Generation Leadership bonuses.

Gold: In order to qualify as Gold, a distributor must achieve 100 PV, 35,000 OGV, 1,000 PGV, and 3 separate legs with 6,000 OGV each within a commission period. As a Gold, the distributor qualifies to receive compensation on the volume of 5 unilevels within his or her organization (paid at 8%, 5%, 4%, 4%, and 4%, respectively), personal generation commissions (paid at 2.5%), generation commissions on 3 levels (paid at 3%), in addition to any retail earnings. Golds may also qualify for the Fast Start, starter kit, and Generation Leadership bonuses.

Platinum: In order to qualify as Platinum, a distributor must achieve 100 PV, 100,000 OGV, 1,000 PGV, and 4 separate legs with 8,000 OGV each within a commission period. As Platinum, the distributor qualifies to receive compensation on the volume of 5 unilevels within his or her organization (paid at 8%, 5%, 4%, 4%, and 4%, respectively), personal generation commissions (paid at 2.5%), generation 5 commissions on 4 levels (paid at 3%), in addition to any retail earnings. Platinums may also qualify for the Fast Start, starter kit, and Generation Leadership bonuses.

Diamond: In order to qualify as Diamond, a distributor must achieve 100 PV, 250,000 OGV, 1,000 PGV, and 5 separate legs with 15,000 OGV each within a commission period. As Diamond, the distributor qualifies to receive compensation on the volume of 5 unilevels within his or her organization (paid at 8%, 5%, 4%, 4%, and 4%, respectively), personal generation commissions (paid at 2.5%), generation commissions on 5 levels (paid at 3%), in addition to any retail earnings. Diamonds may also qualify for the Fast Start, starter kit, Generation Leadership, and Diamond Express Profit Sharing Pool bonuses.

Crown Diamond: In order to qualify as Crown Diamond, a distributor must achieve 100 PV, 750,000 OGV, 1,000 PGV, and 6 separate legs with 20,000 OGV each within a commission period. As Crown Diamond, the distributor qualifies to receive compensation on the volume of 5 unilevels within his or her organization (paid at 8%, 5%, 4%, 4%, and 4%, respectively), personal generation commissions (paid at 2.5%), generation commissions on 6 levels (paid at 3%), in addition to any retail earnings. Crown Diamonds may also qualify for the Fast Start, starter kit, Generation Leadership, and Diamond Express Profit Sharing Pool bonuses.

Royal Crown Diamond: In order to qualify as Royal Crown Diamond, a distributor must achieve 100 PV, 1,500,000 OGV, 1,000 PGV, and 6 separate legs with 35,000 OGV each within a commission period. As Royal Crown Diamond, the distributor qualifies to receive compensation on the volume of 5 unilevels within his or her organization (paid at 8%, 5%, 4%, 4%, and 4%, respectively), personal generation commissions (paid at 2.5%), generation commissions on 7 levels (paid at 3%, with 1% paid on the seventh level), in addition to any retail earnings. Royal Crown Diamonds may also qualify for the Fast Start, starter kit, Generation Leadership, and Diamond Express Profit Sharing Pool bonuses.

Congratulations

on completing the

GAMEPLAN

Sarah Harnisch, Young Living Platinum

Author of Gameplan

ABOUT THE FOUNDERS OF THE OIL ABILITY TEAM

John and Sarah Harnisch are a husband and wife Young Living team that went from starter kit to Platinum in 17 months, with no prior sales or network marketing experience. Sarah has anchored news for 18 years, has a degree in English and Japanese, and is a homeschooling mom to 5 amazing kids. She loves running, gardening, horseback riding, deep cleaning the house and throwing everything away, and playing laser tag in the dark outside with her sons and daughter. John is a Lego-building software developer that retired from a Fortune 500 company. He is also an avid reader, tech expert, and Minecraft guru. He loves a chilly fall day, family movies with popcorn, and getaways with Sarah. Their passion is raising as many Diamonds as possible.

A MODEL FOR MARRIAGE

Covenant, Grace, Empowerment and Intimacy

JACK O. BALSWICK *and*
JUDITH K. BALSWICK

IVP Academic

An imprint of InterVarsity Press
Downers Grove, Illinois

InterVarsity Press
P.O. Box 1400, Downers Grove, IL 60515-1426
World Wide Web: www.ivpress.com
E-mail: email@ivpress.com

InterVarsity Press® is the book-publishing division of InterVarsity Christian Fellowship/USA®, a student movement active on campus at hundreds of universities, colleges and schools of nursing in the United States of America, and a member movement of the International Fellowship of Evangelical Students. For information about local and regional activities, write Public Relations Dept., InterVarsity Christian Fellowship/USA, 6400 Schroeder Rd., P.O. Box 7895, Madison, WI 53707-7895, or visit the IVCF website at <www.intervarsity.org>.

Scripture quotations, unless otherwise noted, are from the New Revised Standard Version of the Bible, *copyright 1989 by the Division of Christian Education of the National Council of the Churches of Christ in the USA. Used by permission. All rights reserved.*

Figures 3.1 and 3.2 are taken from The Reciprocating Self *by Jack O. Balswick, Pamela Ebstyne King and Kevin S. Reimer. Copyright ©2005 by Jack O. Balswick, Pamela Ebstyne King and Kevin S. Reimer. Used with permission of InterVarsity Press.*

Design: Cindy Kiple
Images: Stockdisc/Getty Images

ISBN-10: 0-8308-2760-9
ISBN-13: 978-0-8308-2760-2

Printed in the United States of America ∞

Library of Congress Cataloging-in-Publication Data

Balswick, Jack O.

  A model for marriage: covenant, grace, empowering, and intimacy
/Jack and Judith Balswick.
   p. cm.
  Includes bibliographical references and indexes.
  ISBN-13: 978-0-8308-2760-2 (pbk.: alk. paper)
  ISBN-10: 0-8308-2760-9 (pbk.: alk. paper)
  1. Marriage—Religious aspects—Christianity. I. Balswick,
Judith
K. II Title.
BV835.B33 2006
  21.8'3581—dc21

        2006020885

P	18	17	16	15	14	13	12	11	10	9	8	7	6	5	4	3	2	1
Y	21	20	19	18	17	16	15	14	13	12	11	10	09	08	07	06		

Mahalo, Don and Joy,

for your generosity in providing

the perfect environment

to write this book.

CONTENTS

ACKNOWLEDGMENTS

WE ARE MOST INDEBTED TO associate editor Gary Deddo, who encouraged and supported us throughout the writing of this book. His scholarship and insight as a trinitarian theologian was crucial when making application to the marriage relationship. In particular, we are grateful to Gary for rewriting chapter two, which will benefit our readers enormously. It has been a deepening process that has expanded our biblical model of marriage and our personal marital relationship as well.

Our thanks to Kathy Daw for typing portions of the manuscript and for most valuable help in preparing the name and content indexes. We also wish to acknowledge Susan Carlson Wood for her thoroughness, attention to detail and helpful suggestions that greatly enhanced the final product. It was satisfying to work with a colleague and friend.

PREFACE

When two people meet as loving adults there is an extended,
deepened sense of self—an experience of being that comes
when there is a joining with the Self of another. Each person is enriched.
Something new is created.

ATHEA HORNER

BEING MARRIED IS ONE OF THE MOST CHALLENGING and rewarding things a person will ever do! Together, spouses create and re-create their relationship through each stage of life. We write this book from a Christian framework, believing that God intends marriage to be the joining of two well-defined persons into a transcendent sacred union.

Marriage has been a transformational process throughout our forty-four years of going through the thick and thin of life together. Our two married children and their spouses have become good friends, and our four grandsons are the source of much delight. During our early marriage we went through the painful and untimely death of our nine-year-old son. Three years later, our teenage daughter, Jacque, and newly adopted ten-year-old Korean son, Joel, challenged us in new ways as we reconstructed our family. These events and many others brought us to our knees time and time again. Our dependence on God and our community of faith, along with the love and support of family and friends, were crucial resources as we journeyed throughout each stage of married life.

Interpersonal spousal dynamics are complex, and we are living proof of how hard it is to balance personal desires with self-giving love. In our attempts to address this monumental challenge we have come to recognize how the trinitarian foundation of our Christian faith provides profound insight for sorting through this very issue. Trinitarian theology has opened the way for us to discover our personal distinctness in and through our mutual interdependence. The relevance of this theme was especially critical through the intensity of graduate school, coparenting, dual careers and our call to family ministry; as well as through the stress and strain of being sandwiched between teenager dilemmas, midlife concerns and elder parent care. Now, as we approach our retirement years we anticipate a new phase of life where the particular issues may change, but not the essential theme of being in right relationship. We are deeply indebted to our couples' support group, which has been a place of community, accountability and empowerment.

Throughout each marital stage we continually have asked the same crucial question, "How do we keep our marriage strong?" in the midst of the hustle and bustle, twists and turns, joys and sorrows of life. As our lives have been inextricably intertwined, our marital union has not only survived, but it has thrived! Our adult children, Jacque and Joel, along with their spouses, Dana and Uyen, and our four wonderful grandsons are a beautiful legacy. Our years of teaching in the Marriage and Family Department at Fuller Theological Seminary have blessed us with students, colleagues and friends over these twenty-some years. Relationship is what's most precious to us. Perhaps our greater achievement is that we have left a mark not only on each other, but on all those special people we have been privileged to know.

We are wholeheartedly committed to the premise of this book, that "two are better than one," as spouses build what we have come to identify as a differentiated unity in marriage. Chapter one explains this dilemma of marriage: the clash between the primary value of individual self-fulfillment and marital fulfillment in relationship. The lofty goal of chapter two is to present a solution to the dilemma by offering a social theology of the marriage relationship. By necessity, this task is based on an integrative process that recognizes the parallel truths of biblical theology and social science knowledge. An analogy drawn from trinitarian theology serves as the foundation for this integrative social theology of marriage. Simply put, trinitarian theology conceptualizes God as three in one, a unity of three distinct divine persons in relationship. In like manner, a social scientific understanding of marriage is seen as a unity formed by two distinctly differentiated spouses. We contend that God has created us to be in a mutually reciprocating relationship as two unique selves in relation to God and to each other. In this way marriage is meant to mirror the trinitarian relationships of holy loving between the Father, Son and Holy Spirit.

Building on this trinitarian foundation, in chapters three to six, we elaborate on four trustworthy biblical guiding principles that contribute to a deeply fulfilling marriage. We present our model for marriage by elaborating on the four relationship principles: covenant (commitment and unconditional love), grace (acceptance and forgiveness), empowerment (mutuality and interdependency) and intimacy (knowing and being known).

In chapter seven we apply the trinitarian model to the process of beginning marriage: *leaving, cleaving and becoming one flesh*. Chapter eight gives an in-depth understanding of the core process within the model: *maintaining a differentiated marital unity*. Chapters nine and ten are devoted to the important marital issues of communication and conflict. In chapter eleven we consider differentiated unity as it evolves and develops through the stages of marriage. Since the majority of couples are dual earner, this is the special focus of chapter twelve. The final two chapters are devoted to *marital sexuality* and *marital spirituality*, respectively.

Although the ultimate goal of this book is to present a social theology of marriage, we believe there is nothing as practical as good theology. Therefore, we apply the trinitarian theology of marriage to practical topics like differentiation in relationship, communication, conflict resolution, dual-earner issues, seasons of marriage, sexuality and spirituality. Differentiation is a key concept we use throughout the book. We define differentiation as developing and defining a secure self, validated in Christ. Our concept of differentiated unity refers to two secure spouses, distinct and unique in themselves, discovering belonging and connection in and through marital unity.

We believe the book will be a helpful resource for couples in the early romantic stage, the grueling middle, the challenging second marriage or the golden sunset years. The common denominator at every stage is to keep the marriage vital and relevant according to its God-designed priority.

1

THE DILEMMA OF MODERN MARRIAGE

THERE IS A DILEMMA ABOUT MODERN MARRIAGE that is getting harder to solve. How is it possible to "become one" without compromising our individual distinctiveness? It would seem that either the unity of the relationship would swallow up the individuals or the uniqueness of the individuals would unravel the unity. Solving this dilemma will help couples stay together happily rather than end in divorce. Learning how to balance individual fulfillment with relationship fulfillment is a relatively new dilemma that has developed during the last one hundred years or so. It is, however, a task that must be mastered if marriage is to continue to be a viable institution in modern society.

The Origin of the Dilemma

If we could transport ourselves back in time one hundred years, it would be enlightening to observe marriages in the days of our great-great-grandparents. Although their lives were difficult in many ways, less than 10% of marriages in any society ended in divorce. The major struggles centered on working long hours to provide the basics (shelter, food, clothing) and to overcome diseases that claimed the lives of every fifth child and the deaths of mothers during childbirth. If our great-great-grandparents could have transported themselves forward in time to observe married life today, they would no doubt be stunned by the modern advances that make life so *easy*. Most would be appalled that so many (approximately 50%) decide to divorce today. How do we explain the seeming contradiction between the high marital success rate during the harder times of the past and the low marital success rate in today's modern world?

While there are complex reasons why people divorce, rising divorce rates over the last one hundred years can best be explained by the changing demands people have placed on marriage by regarding it as a source of self-fulfillment. Back in the 1930s the sociologist Ernest Burgess documented the change he saw taking place in modern, urban, industrialized societies. In the past, he reasoned, people valued marriage as an institution in and of itself, whereas today people value marriage for companionship and fulfillment (Burgess & Locke, 1953). Based on responses to surveys taken between 1939 and 1996, Buss, Schackelford, Kirkpatrick and Larsen (2001) summarize the change in mate selection values as follows, "Both sexes increased the importance they attach to physical attractiveness in a mate. Both sexes, but especially men, increased the importance they attached to mates with good financial prospects. Domestic skills in a partner plummeted in importance for men. Mutual attraction and love climbed in importance for both sexes" (p. 491).

The primary function of marriage regarded as an institution had to do with social and economic arrangements. In a majority of societies around the world in the past, the families of the bride and groom arranged marriages. This practice started to change in modern societies with the emergence of a companionship-oriented focus. The primary reasons people marry in modern times now have to do with romantic attraction, self-fulfillment and ego need gratification (Coontz, 2004). The expectation bar has been raised to include a high level of personal satisfaction. In modern marriage, marital success is gauged by emotional and psychological factors. This change has had an enormous impact on marriage expectations.

It doesn't take a genius to grasp the idea that fewer expectations result in fewer divorces. Neither is it surprising that the focus on personal self-fulfillment increases the demands made on both spouses. In the old days, wives yielded their individual identity and rights. Until the mid-1800s, ownership of any property contributed by the bride's family was transferred to the husband. How astonishing this seems in today's world where individual rights are the focus.

In the twenty-first century, a great change in most societies around the world has to do with women's equal rights in personal, social and legal matters. We applaud this change. Basic security is awarded equally to both spouses. The new challenge in modern marriage is to build a relationship that is mutual, reciprocal and balanced by equal regard for each spouse and mutual sacrifice for the good of the relationship.

A Literature Review of the Modern Marriage Dilemma

The severity of the modern marital dilemma has gotten much attention in the social science literature. For example, an entire issue was devoted to the state of the modern marriage in the professional *Journal of Marriage and the Family* (2004, no. 4). In his article, Andrew Cherlin (2004, pp. 848-61) explains that America has experienced a "deinstitutionalization of marriage," which includes a weakening of social norms that define marriage. He refers to practices like cohabitation, same-sex marriage, individualism and the movement of married women into the paid workforce as examples. In a similar vein, Smock (2004, pp. 966-73) writes about the "retreat" from marriage. Declining fertility, delayed age at marriage, high levels of marital disruption, growing separation between marriage and childbearing, increase in proportion of children being born outside of wedlock, and nonmarital cohabitation are seen as reasons for this retreat. He concludes that a variety of interrelated factors contribute to the decline: economic, social and cultural influences; urbanization and industrialization; social and geographical mobility; redefinition of gender roles; modernity and postmodernity.

In answer to the question she poses in her article "Does Marriage Have a Future?" Ellen Lewin (2004) concludes that it most likely does not have a future if marriage is limited to its present form. In agreement with Lewin, Kathleen Kiernan (2004) writes, "The rise of cohabitation and the recognition of same sex partnerships have in effect, redrawn the boundaries of marriagelike relationships" (p. 985). John Gillis (2004) believes that societal recognition of marriage as the only legitimate conjugal arrangement is "something of an aberration that existed" roughly from 1870 to 1970. According to him, "tolerating a wide range of formal and informal marriage practices" is normative and to be welcomed (p. 990). He concludes, "Seen in the larger historical and global perspective, there is nothing particularly alarming in the tendency. In fact, there is much to recommend it" (p. 991).

Ted Huston and Heidi Melz (2004, p. 943) view contemporary marriages as undergoing two types of change, *normative* and *relational*.

Normative structural change includes nonmarital cohabitation, the increase in the proportion of births that occur outside of marriage, the tendency to marry later in life and the high rate of divorce. Relational change has to do with a heightened emphasis on individualism at the expense of a relational or communal commitment. In his article "Tensions between Institutional and Individual Views of Marriage," Paul Amato (2004) is highly concerned about the intensifying tension these modern trends place on marriage today.

Though many family social scientists are concerned about these modern trends, some hold to a postmodern optimism that embraces alternative forms of marriage. According to them, the outdated, traditional lifelong monogamous marriage needs to be revised. They advocate for alternative forms to better accommodate the diverse needs of a postmodern society, such as same-sex marriage, cohabitation, remaining childless, serial marriage (one marriage after another) and so forth. Some go so far as to suggest that marriage should be thought of as a natural learning process like going to school. Thus, the first marriage is an initiation similar to grade school; the second marriage (high school) gives an opportunity to practice relationship skills; the third marriage (college) offers an advanced level of intimacy. This functional perspective is derived from naturalistic assumptions that society should accept whatever is currently happening as normative and not make value judgments about what marriage should be. Marriage is a relationship of convenience, formed by what the two people decide to make of it.

In contrast to these views, our book is based on the teleological assumption that God has created humankind and designed marriage with an ultimate purpose and meaning in mind. We agree that a hyperindividualistic focus on personal fulfillment has overridden the essential meaning of covenant commitment and relationship values. We need a culture that supports marriage and provides a moral value system that promotes mutual responsibility. We believe the biblical revelation of right relationship offers the answers to the marriage dilemma. In the following chapters, we will show how the biblically grounded trinitarian model of relationship provides a foundation for grasping the biblical principles of marital love that profoundly coordinate the deepest needs of individuals in the context of strong and enduring marriages. Before we do that, however, we give an overview that compares two present competing views of marriage: the traditional and postmodern.

Traditional and Postmodern Marital Ethics

There are two competing sides when it comes to finding answers to the dilemmas proposed earlier in the chapter. Table 1.1 represents a comparative summary of the polar opposite traditional and postmodern

Table 1.1.

TRADITIONAL	BIBLICAL	MODERN
Commitment		
Commitment (to the institution)	Covenant (between partners)	Contract (self-fulfillment)
Coercive	Cohesive	Disengaged
Dutiful Sex (male pleasure)	Affectionate Sex (mutual pleasure)	Self-Centered Sex (personal pleasure)
Adaptability		
Law	Grace	Anarchy
Predetermined (segregated roles)	Creative (interchangeable roles)	Undetermined (undifferentiated roles)
Rigid/Stilted	Adaptable/Flexible	Chaotic
Authority		
Ascribed Power	Empowering	Possessive Power
Authoritarianism (dependence)	Mutual Submissiveness (interdependence)	Absence of Authority (independence)
Male-Centered	Relationship-Centered	Self-Centered
Communication		
Inexpressiveness	Intimacy	Pseudo-intimacy
Pronouncement (legislation)	Discussion (negotiation)	Demand (stalemate)
Nonassertive/Aggressive	Assertive	Aggressive

views. The column on the left represents the traditional view, the column on the right represents the postmodern view, while the center column represents the biblical response to marriage that, although not discussed in this chapter, will form the basis for chapters three to six. We present four important components of the marital relationship—*commitment, adaptability, authority* and *communication*—as a means of contrasting the traditional and postmodern beliefs.

Commitment

It seems obvious that marriage is a commitment! However, it is not so simple to define what it means to be committed—and to what or whom. The traditional view focuses on commitment to marriage as an institution. A couple is to stay married for life out of obligation to family and cultural views that marriage is a sacred institution. A traditional view clearly incorporates a collectivistic emphasis on family and community loyalty over and above individual needs or desires. With the emergence of postmodern thought, the larger collective emphasis has given way to the philosophy that there are many flavors of truth or alternative ways of defining commitment that can be determined by the individual or couple. Since there are many alternative forms of commitment, commitment is relative, based on the persons involved.

In the traditional marriage, our great-grandparents were clear about staying together for life as a commitment to marriage as an institution. Indeed, divorce was rare under the traditional system because it was thought to be morally wrong to break the sacred social institution. To put self-interest above marriage, the family or the good of society was not tolerated by the majority society norms.

The modern/postmodern marriage is about individual rights over relationship rights. To consider lifelong commitment stretches the imagination farther than spouses are willing to go in a culture that honors keeping a variety of options open throughout a lifetime. The intense drive for personal happiness makes spouses skeptical of finding one person who will be able to sustain them over the long haul. Traditional values are sneered at as unrealistic in today's world where multiple divorces are more in vogue. Self-fulfillment is the ultimate gauge for staying married. Of course, the longing for personal fulfillment at all costs places an enormous pressure on marriage and on both spouses in that marriage.

In the 1960s, the counterculture movement led to a rebellion against traditional values. Free love shook the foundation of marriage as an institution. There was no reason for legal marriage; two people stayed together as long as they were both satisfied with the arrangement. Promiscuous sexual behaviors added fuel to the fire, even as social norms shifted to self-fulfillment. The annual divorce rate doubled between the early 1960s and 1970s. Sensitivity and self-help groups were the rage as they promoted the attitude of finding oneself. It wasn't until the early 1980s that the high divorce rate leveled out. It seems when people were unhappy they found divorce as the convenient scapegoat. Their individual right to personal happiness took precedence over staying in the marriage for the sake of the institution.

The postmodern marriage offers a multitude of choices for a person to make. Recognizing there are alternatives, one chooses what is good for oneself at that particular time. As the circumstances change and a person's needs change, the possibilities are many. A major criterion to determine choice is self-fulfillment. A marriage or relationship is considered successful when both partners consider themselves to be happy. We fear that the inordinate amount of free choice leaves one without a sound moral base for taking others into account.

Something vital is missing in both extremes, either commitment to the institution of marriage or commitment to self-interest. There seems to be very little understanding of commitment between persons in which they must consider the best interest of the other as well as themselves and the relationship itself. We believe this is a tragedy because commitment expressed as a covenant promise to the flourishing and welfare of the relationship has lost its deepest spiritual meaning. The problem in the past was too narrow a definition of marriage, limiting it to the survival of an institution, whereas the problem with the contemporary view is too wide a definition of relationship, limiting it to being a means to the individual end of self-fulfillment.

For example, in the area of marital sex, according to the traditional view, sex became viewed as a right to pleasure for the male and a duty to be endured by the female. It is a matter of going through the motions to have children or give pleasure. The wife especially found less satisfaction in this arrangement. In postmodern marriage, people have a vast number of choices in and outside of the marriage bed, with emphasis on the individual's right to personal pleasure. Sex manuals now overflow with a vast variety of techniques promising to give the greatest amount of sexual pleasure. Following this lead, one ends up striving for more and yet being left floundering because sexual relations become more about technique than relationship and communion. Thus, in the process, the real meaning of sexuality is lost.

Role Adaptability

In traditional marriage, roles are *segregated*. The norm is for husbands to assume the role of working outside of the home while wives take on the role of homemaking and child rearing. This is actually a fairly recent phenomenon, since as late as one hundred years ago two-thirds of all families in the United States lived on farms. Marital roles were integrated in home and at work as both husbands and wives worked cooperatively alongside each other in business or farm work.

A postmodern trend calls for *undifferentiated* marital roles. This is to say, various tasks in the home are assigned according to a social exchange formula. This formula is based on the assumption that all relationships involve cost and reward. What one gives to a relationship is experienced as a cost, and what one receives is regarded as a reward. Researchers have found that marriages thrive when the rewards outweigh the costs for each partner. As long as spouses experience getting as much as they give they are satisfied. The formula is this: rewards minus costs bring equal profit.

Let's imagine a couple in a postmodern marriage deciding who will cook the evening meal. Since they both have had a hard day at work, they will need to haggle until the formula works out satisfactorily. If one cooks the other will clean up and take out the garbage. The point is that when roles are undifferentiated it takes bargaining and negotiating skills to work out the equation. Since there are many circumstances to consider and many alternatives to choose from, it takes energy to battle out the final plan for the day to make sure in the cost-benefit analysis that each profits equally.

Parenting is without question one of the most crucial tasks to be performed. In the traditional family the mother does the majority of the parenting while the father plays a secondary role. Roles tend to be rigidly defined with little flexibility as to how they are performed. In postmodern marriages, parenting roles may not be well defined and therefore expectations for children are loosely defined, resulting in confusion or chaos. Without the stability of set routines, the children flounder.

Authority

Authority is a hot topic among Christians these days. Until very recently, authority was exclusively the male domain. Christians and non-Christians alike have adhered to the traditional idea that the husband is head of the home and the wife is expected to submit to his wishes. Postmodern thought rejects male authority and embraces collaboration rather than hierarchy as the ideal. Each partner has authority over his or her personal life. The social exchange model of relating comes into play when it is time to make decisions about any number of necessarily shared issues like money, sex, children, work and so on. It's a quid pro quo system of fair exchange. Each spouse tries to maximize the returns on his or her investments in every area of the marriage. Social exchange theory is built on an assumption consistent with the thought that people are basically self-centered by nature and so each individual needs to look out for him or herself and cannot give another any authority over oneself. There is no such thing as shared authority in this model, but rather two independent authorities competing equally for their own benefit. The relationship becomes essentially competitive and defensive, and so at best opportunistic (I see that the other can benefit me) or antagonistic (I have to watch out that the other does not get from me more than I receive). Promoting self at the expense of the other or the relationship is not the biblical ideal.

Communication

In the traditional marriage, communication tends to take the form of pronouncements rather than dialogue. As head of the marriage, the husband can legislate without considering or consulting his wife. When conflicts arise he can sidestep the issue or act out in angry withdrawal or abuse without challenge from his wife. Communication in the postmodern marriage is characterized as a series of declarations and demands made by both spouses. When conflicts arise, confrontation is the way to get one's needs expressed and met. Although collaboration is the goal, a combative posture and assertion of personal needs can be the demise of the relationship. Spouses may encounter a stalemate instead of finding a satisfying solution.

A Concluding Assessment

Neither the traditional nor the postmodern approach will solve the modern marital dilemma. The debate between traditional and postmodern viewpoints is actually part of a wider societal debate in our world today. Rather than taking sides, we believe it is more fruitful to consider a balanced biblical framework.

A common mistake for Christians is to defend a cultural version of marriage by taking either the traditional or postmodern perspective. We believe it is an exegetical error to regard historical accounts of marriage during biblical times as *normative* rather than *descriptive*. For example, when Genesis 3:16 reads, "and the man shall rule over the women," traditionalists interpret this as normative and prescriptive for marriage. As Bilezikian (1985) and Van Leeuwen (1990) point out, the verse describes what occurred as a result of their fallen condition rather than reflects God's ideal for marriage.

An equally blatant error is to take the naturalist position of accepting the relativistic ethic of postmodernity. In his book *Marriage After Modernity,* Adrian Thatcher (1999) surveyed postmodern writings on marriage in an effort to understand the common features of a post-Christian marital system. He identified *marginalization of marriage* as one of the mindsets underlying postmodern thought. Marriage as a lifelong covenant is no longer considered a core option. The "evacuation of the traditional meanings of marriage" (p. 62) is usurped by individualistic satisfaction derived from a relationship. A related feature is an increased focus upon *individual self-fulfillment*. The irony is that the focus on self-fulfillment sets up high expectations that marriage is unlikely to satisfy, making it less viable. Thatcher notes that an "idolatry of romantic love," makes the feelings of falling in love a "surrogate religion" (p. 63). Personal identity and "Who am I?" questions become a lifelong project in this postmodern, postreligious ethic. Thatcher asserts that this vacuous ethic is incapable of providing what is needed to solidify a long-lasting marriage. He concludes that the postmodern marital ethic fails to take into account marital commitment, the place of children in marriage or any other features that provide a mutual satisfaction gained from the relationship itself.

Summary

We've presented the modern marriage dilemma and the social science literature that attempts to address the problem with secular solutions. We then presented a contrast between the traditional and the postmodern view of marriage. Finding no satisfactory solutions, we offer in the following chapter a trinitarian model of marriage as the needed theological foundation for marriage today. We follow this with chapters presenting the four biblical principles built on that foundation that we believe give the answer to the dilemma, showing how we can learn to live out these God-designed principles, which bear the fruit of satisfaction in the marriage relationship.

A Trinitarian Model of Marriage

WE BELIEVE THAT PART OF THE SOLUTION to the dilemma posed in chapter one is a biblically grounded trinitarian theology. Such a model teaches us about a right relationship, in which neither the individuals nor the relationship of marriage is damaged. The love shared among the persons of the Trinity and the love of the triune God for us provides the best model for our love relationships.

The basis for our seeing the trinitarian relationships as a pattern that can shed light on human relationships may not be apparent. There really are two bases. First, the New Testament revelation bears witness to the fact that our relationships to each other are to be a mirror of God's own relationship to us in and through Jesus Christ and that, in turn, Jesus' relationship to us is a reflection of his own relationship to the Father. Most directly we are told that Jesus has loved us just as his heavenly Father has loved him (Jn 15:9), and then, in the same way that Jesus has loved us, we are commanded to love one another (Jn 15:12).

Our love for each other, therefore, ultimately reflects the very love of the Father and Son from all eternity before there even was a creation. All true love, whether in the trinitarian relationships or among God's human creatures, takes the same shape and so can be compared. True human love is patterned by the divine love in the Trinity. We come to know and recognize the pattern of that love when we encounter God's love for us in Jesus, as he loves us with the same love with which he is loved by the Father. Jesus Christ is our access to the true pattern of love, a pattern that illuminates marital love as well.

Second, we should point out that many theologians have noted the significance of the biblical revelation that we are created in the image of God. "God said, 'Let us make humankind in our image, according to our likeness.' . . . So God created humankind in his image, in the image of God he created them; male and female he created them" (Gen 1:26-27). In this passage, the plural subject—"Let *us* . . . in *our*"—can legitimately be considered to connote the triune Godhead, Father, Son and Holy Spirit, creating humankind. Man and woman are said to be created in such a way that they uniquely bear the imago Dei, the image of God.

It seems, then, that the triune God's intention was for humans— plural, man and woman together—to reflect something of the plurality (us, our) of God's own nature. It should also be noted that Adam and Eve are depicted in Genesis as providing not only the prototype of human beings in general but also of marriage in particular (see Gen 3). So, when we ask what it means for spouses to be created in the image of God, we seem to be directed to draw an analogy from the Godhead to indicate how we are to reflect the image of God in marriage. If there is some kind of plurality, a fellowship or togetherness or communion in God (us, we), then this fellowship and plurality ought to be reflected in marriage itself as depicted in the story of Adam and Eve.

These two revelational insights taken from Old and New Testaments and fulfilled in Jesus Christ, who is the original image of God, when taken together provide the essential foundation for thinking about marriage in light of the trinitarian relationships. The God whose very nature is being in relationship of holy love calls us to love one another in the same way. Human relationships in general and marriage in particular have been given the purpose and privilege of reflecting the plurality, the fellowship of communion within the trinitarian relationships.

In his book *Karl Barth's Theology of Relations,* Gary Deddo (1999) traces out the particular pattern of relationship discerned in the triune relationships. The particular pattern of right relationship is most fully and concretely revealed in the relationships between the Son of God incarnate, Jesus, and the Father and Holy Spirit depicted in the New Testament. The person and life of Jesus is a story of his relationship of holy love with the Father and Spirit. His whole ministry can be summed up as taking us to his Father and giving us his Spirit. This accounts for the fact that Jesus directs his disciples to baptize those becoming his followers in the one name of Father, Son and Spirit.

Deddo then reviews the church's theological reflection on the nature of those trinitarian relationships. Two primary characteristics of the Father-Son relationship came into clear focus. The triune relationships exhibit a unique divine unity of being together as well as an eternal distinction of persons. While the Father and Son are said to be united and one, they can never be confused or collapsed into one undifferentiated divine substance. The divine unity is personal and relational, not static and impersonal. Furthermore, the church came to see that the Father, Son and Spirit are not interchangeable, nor do they refer to three roles or functions of one God without unique abiding personal distinctions and relationships. The God revealed in Jesus Christ is eternally triune. There are eternal and unique divine persons in relationships within God. These persons in relationship in God are essential to who God is. If God were not eternally Father, Son and Holy Spirit, then God would not be God! There never was a time when God was not Father, Son and Holy Spirit. The oneness of God turns out to be a triunity of unique divine persons in unique relationships with each other.

The leaders and teachers of the early church came to recognize that to deny either the unity of the being of God or to deny the plurality of the persons of God was to reject the Christian revelation of the true character of God. These errors would amount to the heresies of tritheism or modalism. God is an eternal fellowship in which the divine unity does not dissolve the abiding reality and relationships of the divine persons, and the eternal persons of the godhead do not threaten or qualify the unity of God's triune being. "There is no way either to reduce the three [divine persons] in their distinctions or to disintegrate the one God into three separate individuals. The unity and the distinction [of persons] are each unimpaired by the other. In fact the differentiations confirm the unity and the unity confirms the differentiations" (Deddo, 1999, pp. 23-24).

So then, if human relationships are to mirror or image something of the divine relationships, then unity with distinction of persons in relationship also ought to characterize human relationships so that maintaining the distinctness of persons does not compromise the unity nor does the unity quench the uniqueness of the persons in communion with each other. That is the shape and task of love itself.

Miroslav Volf (1998), a trinitarian theologian, rightly points out the limits of using the Trinity as an analogy in human relationships.

> Our notions of the triune God are not the triune God, even if God is accessible to us only in these notions. A certain doctrine of the Trinity is a model acquired from salvation history and formulated in analogy to our experience, a model with which we seek to approach the mystery of the triune God, not in order to comprehend God completely, but rather in order to worship God as the unfathomable and to imitate God in our own, creaturely way. (p. 198)

With human limitations in mind, we use trinitarian theology as a model for marriage. Spouses are both distinct (male and female differentiation) and equal (directed to be fruitful and have dominion) in their created purpose. They find ultimate meaning in and through their relationship with God and each other.

Stanley Grenz (1990, p. 47) says it this way: "the creation narratives in Genesis 1 and 2 provide a hint that the plurality of humanity as male and female is to be viewed as an expression of a foundation plurality within the unity of the divine reality." According to Grenz, "Let us make humankind in our image," suggests that the "same principle of mutuality that forms the genius for the human social dynamic is present in a prior way in the divine being" (p. 48). In other words, humankind mirrors the image of God.

Ray Anderson (2004) further explains,

> the original designation of the first human creature in Genesis 1 was the generic term for "man"— 'adam. With the definite article ha- proceeding the common noun "adam," what is designated is neither a particular person nor the typical person but rather the creature from the earth (ha-adama)—the earth creature. Nor is this creature identified sexually. The second chapter presents in narrative form a theological excursus in which the man and the woman emerge simultaneously, not sequentially. The history of man and woman on earth begins at the same point in mutual and corresponding relation, with the relation itself a mirror of the divine image. (p. 9)

Elated in each other's presence, Adam and Eve recognize the exquisite "bone of my bones, flesh of my flesh" distinctiveness in contrast to the animal kingdom. They are human persons relating with bodies, minds, emotions and souls in person-to-person relationship. As Colin Gunton (1993) observes, "Adam can find no true fellow creature among the animals, none that will enable him truly to be himself. It is only when he can rejoice in the fellowship of one who is a true other-in-relation that he is able to transcend the merely *individual* state that is a denial of human fullness" (p. 216). They join together to transcend themselves through their relationship with their creator God and each other.

Charged with mutual responsibility to tend and care for each other and the rest of creation, Adam and Eve create an interdependence derived from their likeness and their difference. The familiarity of their common humanity (similarity) along with unique difference (gender and personality) deepens their experience of knowing and being known. In their meeting, they are intrigued by and drawn to each other. They make room in themselves for the other as they express and explore who they are in relation to each other and to their world. In their mating they give themselves and receive each other emotionally and sexually, discovering profound spiritual meaning in the mystery of their one-flesh unity.

A Theology of Particularity and Relatedness

It is difficult to describe unity together with uniqueness. One way to approach this is to understand the imago Dei both in terms of a *theology of particularity* and a *theology of relationality* (Gunton, 1993; Balswick, Ebstyne King & Reimer, 2005). *Perichoresis* is a term that denotes the mutual indwelling and self-giving between members of the divine Trinity. Gunton expresses the connection between particularity and relatedness as follows, "A concept polar to that of perichoresis is that of particularity, which in trinitarian theology is a way of pointing to the distinctness of the persons. According to the teaching of perichoresis, the three divine persons are all bound up with each other, so that one is not one without the other two" (1993, p. 153).

A theology of particularity emphasizes that the value of uniqueness is inherent in the imago Dei. God exists as three distinct persons—the Father, Son and Holy Spirit. However, the external acts of God cannot be regarded as what differentiates the persons. For if the external acts are what differentiate God, then God is not eternally three, but only becomes externally three in the actions. Theologically, the external acts of God are only apportioned to the particular persons because the biblical depiction shows one or other of the triune persons leading, as in a dance. But their action is a united action. The Trinity does not divide up over the actions, for as Augustine taught early on, "all the external acts of God are undivided." Consequently the persons in the Holy Trinity all share the same authority in each act. Since the three persons do not have separate spheres of authority, the only distinction between the Father, Son and Holy Spirit is the uniqueness of their persons in unique relationship with each other. They share equally in all divine attributes (including authority, power, omnipotence) and all the divine actions (roles, functions). While there may be some reason one divine person is depicted as taking the lead in a certain external act, the act itself does not distinguish them. The Father remains the Father, the Son remains the Son, and the Spirit remains the Spirit; the three remain one. In the fourth-century Nicene Creed, the unique personal identity of each member is named and the divine unity of the Trinity is declared by each being identified as one God or Lord: "We believe in one God, the Father, the Almighty, maker of heaven and earth. . . . We believe in one Lord, Jesus Christ, the only Son of God . . . for us and for our salvation. . . . We believe in the Holy Spirit, the Lord, giver of life, who proceeds from the Father and the Son."

According to Gunton (1993), a theology of particularity points to a relatedness without absorption:

> "In the beginning was the Word, and the Word was with God," thus emphasizing that Jesus was with God the Father in the beginning. John 1:1 concludes with the phrase—"and the word was God." The emphasis is upon unity without absorption of any one part of the Godhead by the other. John is giving testimony to the *distinction between* and *unity of* the Father and the Son. In his own ministry Jesus consistently declares that whoever has seen the Son has seen the Father, that the Son and the Father are one. At the same time Jesus fulfilled his earthly ministry uniquely as the Son in obedience to the Father. In anticipation of his death, Jesus prays *"Abba,* Father, everything is possible for you. Take this cup from me. Yet not what I will, but what you will" (Mark 14:36). (p. 153)

Here we see that Jesus has a unique will, without which his pledge of obedience to the Father would make no sense.

The Holy Trinity is a mystery in which relatedness goes hand in hand with particularity. God is one, yet composed of three distinct members.

The Father, Son and Holy Spirit are distinct but not separate, as they exist with and for each other. They are related without absorption as noted in John 17:21, "As you, Father, are in me and I am in you." The mutual indwelling of the Godhead provides the model for unity in marriage.

The Reciprocating Marriage

The supreme meaning of being created in the image of God is that spouses reflect a relationship of unity without absorption. To be human in the context of marriage is to be a particular spouse in relation—distinct and unique and yet inextricably intertwined and interdependent. God's intention for marital mutuality is reached through a reciprocating relationship in which spouses encounter their own uniqueness in relation to God and each other. Marriage serves as a sanctifying process as spouses strive for unity in the midst of their unique differences.

The relational nature of marriage is analogous in human form to the divine Trinity. As the Father, Son and Holy Spirit (three distinct persons) mutually indwell in a trinitarian fellowship, spouses mutually indwell in the marriage union. *One God* reveals himself to be three persons in unique relationship with each other so that without dividing the Trinity, one person may take the lead in any of the external acts of God such as creation, redemption, glorification, while all three act together in all that God does. To be human is to mirror divine relatedness. As spouses mutually permeate one another they achieve an interdependency (emotional connection) in which neither spouse loses distinctiveness. Unity and distinction coexist. The point is indisputable! Mutual indwelling never negates particularity. As Deddo asserts, "The unity and the distinction are each unimpaired by the other" (p. 23).

Relevant to a trinitarian model of marriage is Gunton's (1993) proposal that human personhood is made up of three different types of relationality. The primary relationship for any human is the vertical, as one exists in relationship with God. Human beings exist in two types of horizontal relationships, consisting of social relationality with other human beings, and what Gunton called nonpersonal relationality, with the nonhuman world. While Gunton's notion of nonpersonal relationality has been used to develop a Christian theology of the environment (Stephenson, 2005), we find his concept of social relationality useful in building a trinitarian theology of marriage. Gunton proposes that the horizontal relationality grows out and takes its shape from vertical relationality. The obvious application to marriage is that husband and wife reflect the imago Dei supremely when they relate to each other in a way that is similar to the relationality in the divine Trinity. Interrelatedness in marriage is evidence of loving mutuality as described in the Gospel of John, "the Son can do nothing on his own, but only what he sees the Father doing; for whatever the Father does, the Son does likewise. The Father loves the Son and shows him all that he himself is doing" (Jn 5:19-20). As Gary Deddo proclaims, "The relational character of the Divine (Father, Son and Holy Spirit) is an unfathomable mystery! God, the source of love, overflows with unconditional grace through salvation in Christ and the Spirit breathes love into us through the Word. Created, reconciled, and redeemed to glorify God and reflect God's character is the ultimate meaning we bring to marriage" (p. 8).

We believe God's intention for marriage is that two spouses become one through a mutual, reciprocating process in which interdependence develops through the coexistence of distinction and unity in relationship. Spouses are transformed into a unity that transcends what either spouse can be alone. An alliance is created in a humble mutual indwelling and making room in self for the other. Spouses who seek to be conformed to Christ, who are open to the Spirit's leading and who offer their gifts to glorify God join together in a sacred venture of discovering their divine purpose both as individuals and as a couple.

Differentiation in unity. The concept of differentiation includes the notion of particularity and unity. In describing *perichoresis* (the reciprocal interiority of the trinitarian persons), theologian Miroslav Volf (1998) comments, "In every divine person as a subject, the other persons also indwell; all mutually permeate one another, though in so doing they do not cease to be distinct persons. . . . those who have dissolved into one another cannot exist in one another" (p. 209). Therefore, it is the distinction (differentiation) rather than fusion (dependency) that leads to vital connection and wholeness. In marital terms, both spouses bring their distinct selves (mutual interiority) while making space for the other (mutual permeation) so they can indwell each other (interdependence) and become an entity (union) that transcends themselves.

Ecclesiastes 4:9-12 proclaims that two are better than one, because two will prevail over one. This passage suggests that two fully formed persons offer united strength to a relationship. You cannot bring warmth to a hurting spouse unless you have emotional and spiritual resources to give. You cannot offer a helping hand unless you are standing on solid (sufficient self) ground to offer stability. Spouses who are holding on to each other for dear life in the midst of a raging river will most likely go down together. But at any particular time in the marriage either spouse has internal resources to give and receive the helping hand providing couple strength. An interdependent bond made up of two strong persons with Christ at the center cannot be easily broken.

Christ at the center. Christ *is* the image of God, while we are *made* in the image of God. The New Testament challenges us to be Christlike in our marriages. While we earnestly desire to love like Christ, it is not so easy in our fallen condition and we must continually depend on the Holy Spirit for strength to follow God's ways.

Deddo writes, "God is He who acts to form and sustain a communion or a fellowship of love. God freely loves us unconditionally and is for us, not against us. In turn, we are created to become spouses who love unconditionally. We then in our humanity are enabled in our existence to become the image of that Image, that is, be a second image in our human to human relationships" (p. 96). Christ is central to our being conformed to the image of God. Rather than deny our humanity, we acknowledge that we need God's help as we are determined to grow into deeper unity and mutuality.

Stages of Consciousness

A social science parallel to the trinitarian model is found in Robert Kegan's model of *The Evolving Self* (1982). Kegan describes the modern self as developing through five stages of consciousness, where each stage of development consists of a temporary solution to the human yearning for *inclusion* and *distinctness*. The human dilemma identified by Kegan—a yearning for inclusion and distinctness—is precisely the dilemma of modern marriage we identified in chapter one. While Kegan's model is meant to give an understanding of the development of the self in general, he refers to the marital relationship as follows, "If spouses construct the self at a different order of consciousness, each will have a different idea of what it means to be intimate, or to be near another 'self'" (pp. 44-45).

Most significant is how Kegan's solution to this human dilemma parallels a trinitarian model of relationality. Persons who are at lower levels of consciousness are unable to simultaneously hold together personal distinctness and inclusion with another. The state of simultaneously maintaining a distinct separate identity and being part of an inclusive relationship is what Kegan identifies as a higher level of consciousness. The move to the highest level of consciousness requires that one put the relationship itself prior to its parts. Married persons at the highest level of consciousness understand that the marriage relationship itself is instrumental in creating each individual partner. Kegan uses terms like *dialectical, interpenetration of selves* and *trans-system* to describe a relationship consisting of persons at the highest level of consciousness. It is impossible to read Kegan's model without comparing it to the theological notion of *perichoresis,* described by theologians as mutual indwelling and interpenetration between God the Father and the Son. The phenomenon he describes is also nearly identical to what social scientists refer to as differentiation.

Differentiated Unity

Differentiation is an important concept in the marriage and family literature. It is defined as the internal ability to have a secure sense of self (differentiation) in relation to significant others. We use the phrase "differentiated unity" to emphasize that differentiation includes a deep sense of belonging as well as an ability to distinguish the self from the family or the marital dyad. Papero (1990) states that differentiation "addresses how people differ from one another in terms of their sensitivity to one another and their varying abilities to preserve a degree of autonomy in the face of pressure for togetherness" (p. 47). Differentiated unity is that process of finding balance, harmony and interdependency.

In marriage, differentiation is seen as the degree to which a spouse has developed a solid self in relation to family of origin (Bowen,1966; Kerr & Bowen, 1988; Schnarch, 1997). The differentiation process has to do with being able to recognize and separate feeling from thinking and make conscious decisions as well as take responsibility for one's choices. For example, a differentiated spouse not only recognizes personal anxiety, but is also able to calm it and to soothe anger and fearful feelings rather than being reactive to or blaming the partner for his or her emotions. He or she is able to recognize and take full responsibility for personal beliefs, values and thoughts while negotiating conflict and intimacy with his or her spouse. Couples who function from a differentiated unity will avoid being caught up in destructive and reactive patterns. In effect, differentiated spouses are able to transcend their personal and even family of origin emotional and thought reactivity for the sake of the marriage itself.

Carter and McGoldrick (1999, p. 35) describe differentiation as a "state of self-knowledge and self-definition" that does not rely on others for acceptance or validation. When validation is centered in Christ rather than in others, spouses look to God as the source of their validation and are accountable to Christ and one another as they live out their relationship to one another.

Table 2.1. Theoretical Parallels to the Trinitarian Model

Particularity	Particularity & Relationality	Relationality
Disengagement	Differentiated Unity	Enmeshment
Independence	Interdependence	Dependence
Selfish	Unselfish	Selfless
Exclusion	Interpenetration of Selves	Inclusion

Table 2.1 is our attempt to provide a summary of differentiation with theoretical parallels to the trinitarian model. The key point of differentiation is having a clearly defined self who establishes meaningful connection with others. In contrast, an undifferentiated spouse lacks a sufficient sense of self and thus is inclined to fuse with others (to be enmeshed or overdependent) at one extreme or to remain disconnected (disengaged), isolated and emotionally cut off. Highly differentiated spouses relate to each other with simultaneous balanced connection and separateness (interdependency), rather than extreme independence or dependence. Us-

ing terms introduced by Stephen Post (1994), *self-centered* describes a spouse who operates solely from a theology of particularity, while *self-less* describes the spouse who operates from a theology of relationality only, that is, there is little self there so the spouse is determined by and dependent on the other. *Unselfish* describes spouses who operate from a theology of particularity and relationality. It has to do with acting out of an unselfish place rather than selfish (self-focused) or selfless (other-focused). Differentiated (unselfish) spouses make the choice of acting for the good of the other as well as to care for self in ways that help them love rightly. For example, a wife makes an unselfish choice when she prevents a violent husband from abusing her and/or their children. She takes responsible action not only for the interest of herself and her children and the relationship, but also for the good of the abusive spouse whose abuse is an abomination to God. In Kegan's model, distinctness and inclusion, particularity and relationality characterize an interpenetration of selves.

It can be expected that persons with similar levels of differentiation marry each other, so those with lower levels of differentiation will struggle with establishing a differentiated unity as a couple. Spouses who are at different levels of differentiation will have unique challenges in their relationship.

Pat Gundry (1980) says it well, "If two people approach marriage feeling that it will make them complete, they are automatically setting themselves up for a disillusioning experience. . . . But, if two whole people come together as a team, a satisfying and realistic relationship can be built." She continues, "Unity can mean different incomplete elements converging to create a complete unit. Or, unity can mean whole and complete-in-themselves units banding together for a common goal. . . . It takes two whole people to have a whole marriage" (p. 185). The extent to which a couple keeps both their *individual* identity and their *couple* identity strong in Christ will determine how they reap the rich rewards of differentiated unity.

3

COVENANT MARRIAGE

The Greatest of These Is Love

CHAPTER ONE POSED A DILEMMA IN MODERN MARRIAGE and then chapter two offered the trinitarian model as a radical solution to the dilemma. In this and the following three chapters we present the biblical principles of *covenant, grace, empowerment* and *intimacy* as the basis for resilient marriage. These relationship principles are evident in the relations of the three persons of the Trinity with us. Unconditional *covenant* is seen in the steadfast love of the Father, culminating in the incarnation, the deepest expression of God's *grace*. In the giving of the only begotten Son, we are reconciled to God through the sacrifice of our Savior. The Holy Spirit bears witness of God's love and claims victory through the resurrection of Christ. The Spirit breaths words of conviction, challenge and transformation to *empower* us to be like Christ. Our Creator knows us *intimately* even as we are being formed in our mother's womb (Ps 139:13-16). Jesus, our Holy Friend, desires communion with us, and the Spirit prompts us with inner yearnings to worship the Lord God. Table 3.1 depicts the circular movement from one principle to the other, illustrating how the four principles are interrelated in an ongoing, deepening process.

What person doesn't want to be loved in faithful and unconditional ways, or to be accepted just as they are and forgiven when mistakes are made? Who doesn't thrive when affirmed and empowered to reach one's full potential? Which one of us doesn't discover a deeper sense of self through intimate giving and receiving of shared love? When spouses live according to the *covenant* principle, "to love and be loved," the *grace* principle, "to forgive and be forgiven," the *empowerment* principle, to "serve and be served" through mutual servanthood, and the *intimacy*

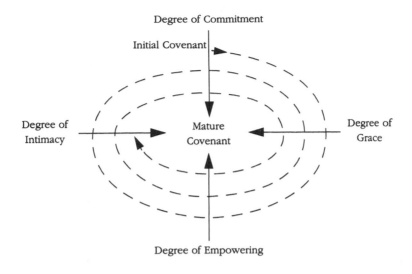

Figure 3.1. A theological basis for marriage

principle, "to know and be known," they will reap the rich rewards of following God's more excellent ways.

God's Way of Loving

Trinitarian theology points us to a God who *is* love and who loves us in trustworthy, steadfast ways. In fact, throughout the Scriptures we find the almighty creator God pursuing the created ones with a "love that will not let us go." God's faithful, always abounding love is sure and secure. In the Old Testament Yahweh establishes a covenant with Adam and Eve, Noah and his family, Abraham and Sarah, Hosea and the children of Israel. The God of the universe covenants to be their God and invites them to be a people of God.

Covenant and grace are inextricably linked together in God's overarching love. Like the story in the New Testament of the father of the prodigal son, God stands with outstretched arms to receive us back after we have gone astray. Through his loving compassion and forgiveness we find our way back to God who loves us and desires to be in intimate communion with us.

The commitment of Yahweh to Israel in the book of Hosea provides a moving example of a covenant love that endures, renews, forgives and restores. God is envisioned as a faithful spouse pursuing an unfaithful lover and as a loving parent who continually pursues the children of Israel. God never gives up on them. In the New Testament, the marital analogy is used to describe Jesus as the groom relating to his bride, the church. Those in the early church are referred to as brothers and sisters in the household of God whom the Holy Spirit indwells and empowers. God's covenant love is freely given along with an expressed desire that we reciprocate.

These truths are exhilarating, yet while God's love is perfect, human love is imperfect. After experiencing a relationship with the Creator in the Garden of Eden, Adam and Eve disobey and hide from their Creator in trembling fear. God comes to them in compassion and provides garments for them to cover their shame. While they suffer the consequences of their disobedience, God's relentless love entreats them and offers them another way.

Spouses have the capacity to mirror these four relationship principles in marriage. Even in our human frailty, the Bible assures us that we can live in conformity to God's ways by the power of the Holy Spirit. We can love our spouse unconditionally, because we have experienced unconditional love from God (1 Jn 4:19). Likewise, we can choose to offer grace to our spouse, knowing we have received acceptance and forgiveness in Christ. Because we are empowered by the same Spirit that raised Christ from the dead, we have power to respond to our spouse with empowering love. Since we know what it is to experience intimate connection with Jesus, we can open ourselves in vulnerable ways of knowing and being known. Practicing these principles in marriage is the greatest gift we can give our spouse.

Characteristics of a Covenant Marriage

The core characteristic of a covenant marriage is commitment, a factor that is profoundly important to marital stability according to research findings. On the wedding day the betrothed eagerly recite their vows, but few seem to truly grasp what covenant commitment entails. Table 3.2 illustrates alternative types of commitment in marriage today. Commitment has two dimensions, one represented across the top of table

3.2, with the first column representing a conditional commitment and the second column representing an unconditional commitment. The second dimension is presented on the left side of table 3.2, with the first row representing a unilateral commitment and the second row a bilateral commitment. Intersecting these two dimensions of commitment in table 3.2 shows four types of commitment.

Table 3.2. Types of Marital Commitments

	CONDITIONAL	UNCONDITIONAL
UNILATERAL	Modern Open	Initial Covenant
BILATERAL	Contract	Mature Covenant

In the bottom left cell of table 3.2, *contract* represents commitment that is bilateral (two-way), but conditional. This is a fairly common view of modern marriage, one in which partners strike a bargain, vowing to stay in the marriage relationship as long as each fulfills their end of the bargain. A grossly distorted view of marital commitment is represented in the top left cell, what we call the *modern open* type of commitment. Commitment is both conditional and unilateral (one-way), meaning the couple views marriage in contractual terms. In the modern open marriage each partner wants the freedom and understanding that they can walk away from the relationship whenever they choose. The unspoken agenda is that one will stay "committed" as long as personal needs are being met. If another relationship looks more fulfilling, commitment should not get in the way of this.

Covenant commitment, represented in the right side of table 3.2, is quite a different matter. God's intention for marriage (bottom right cell) is that both partners (a bilateral commitment) enter with an unconditional commitment to the person, to the relationship and to the institution of marriage. A logical, but hopefully not actual, situation is represented in the upper right cell, where only one partner enters marriage with an unconditional commitment.

We detailed in chapter one how traditional marriage values commitment to the institution of marriage, whereas the postmodern marriage focuses on personal choice and fulfillment. Such partial commitments distort the meaning of covenant. A biblical understanding of covenant love has to do with putting the best interest of the spouse, the relationship and the community as the priority.

Covenant love goes way beyond loyalty to marriage as an institution and far surpasses a self-fulfillment motif. It is a promise to sacrifice for the sake of the relationship. Commitment to the institution results in legalism; commitment to personal fulfillment results in hedonism; commitment that embraces all three (person, institution and relationship) is a commitment to caring for the needs of each spouse, nourishing the relationship itself and upholding the institution of marriage.

The sacred covenant vows made before God, family and friends are for better or worse and till death. The covenant promise is to be faithful, steadfast and sacrificial in love. Covenant love demands a lifelong commitment of intentional investment in the health of the marriage. Flanagan, Clements, Whitton, Portney, Randall and Markman (2002) found that couples who take intentional time for joint activities develop a greater interdependence, which in turn increases commitment between them.

Secure love. One of the most important aspects of unconditional love is security. Being created in God's image, we have basic needs for belonging and bonding. Psychological studies show that children who have been deprived of secure love are at a distinct disadvantage in adulthood. Early attachment disruptions cause anxiety and insecurity that lead to an inability to trust others. A spouse who experienced a significant bonding failure or abandonment early in life is naturally skeptical about forming close connections.

An example from our marriage illustrates this point. I (Judy) had trouble with trusting Jack early on in our marriage. Going back to my childhood for insights into my insecurity, I found that three months prior to the birth of my brother (just twelve months after my birth), my mother arranged for my Aunt Lena and her family to care for me for a few months. This was a rather common practice in those days, and no one imagined it could have a negative impact on me. But that was the beginning of serious abandonment fears. My mother was quite surprised when I cried for weeks after Aunt Lena brought me back home (with a new baby brother in my old crib, I might add). Not only had I managed through broken attachment to my mother, but after reattaching to my aunt, I now felt abandoned by her. It was confusing for a one-year-old child. My secure world had been turned upside down and life seemed quite unpredictable. A reestablished love with my mother certainly compensated for these fears, yet deep down inside I sometimes had unreasonable fears about being left behind.

After marriage to Jack, a faithful, trustworthy husband, I still had unfounded fears that he would leave me. We spend a good amount of time building a trustworthy, secure love. For other couples like us, covenant love may take time to establish due to such attachment fears. An insecure beginning in life can be due to a number of unpredictable circumstances such as death, disease, trauma or disaster.

Unpredictable circumstances that break trust such as affairs, dishonesty and secrets are breaches of trust that also have serious consequences. In this case, the covenant vow has been shattered and trust is shattered along with it. We'll discuss the implications of affairs in chapter thirteen, but suffice it to say that such breaches of trust can only be repaired through a thoughtful process of confession, forgiveness and restoration. Fortunately, most of us were loved unconditionally in childhood and have had a secure start in life. In secure marriages the relationship continues to prove to be a source of secure bonding and belonging.

Secure sex. Covenant commitment will be clearly reflected in the sexual relationship. In traditional marriage, sex was more a right to pleasure for the male and a duty for the female. In postmodern marriage, there are a variety of sexual alternatives determined by the personal desires of each spouse. The biblical approach puts the sexual relationship in the realm of mutual desire, person-to-person engagement and relationship focus.

The security that stems from covenant commitment brings freedom in the sexual relationship. A free-flowing, reciprocal giving and receiving knits together body, emotion, mind and spirit. Being created for relationship, sexual expression is an aspect of marital intimacy that is mutually enjoyable. The security of covenant love encourages vulnerability that deepens the emotional bond. Through sexual intercourse the couple discovers holy meaning that enhances covenant love.

Secure relationship. Covenant love is a love that goes beyond self-interest. In any number of life circumstances, spouses will be called on to give more than an equal share. This is true for our friends the Carters. Devon goes beyond the normal role equality in the personal care he gives his wife, Andrea, who is paraplegic. Andrea gives in other ways to Devon, but much more is demanded of him in terms of physical care and household roles. Andrea attests to living with a husband who shows his covenant love in extraordinary ways to her every day of her life. A covenant commitment means going beyond prescribed roles; it demands sacrificial love in sickness and in health, whether rich or poor, for better or worse, until death.

It is a mark of maturity to know what pleases your spouse and to make the special effort to do what pleases him or her. Being generous with love becomes a positive caring habit. The fruit of the spirit (Gal 5:22-23) speaks of love, joy, peace, patience, kindness, goodness, trustfulness, gentleness and self-control as showing forth God's ways. Untiring care brings relational contentment; sensitive acts of love keep the marriage secure.

Putting Marriage on a Pedestal?

The marriage literature claims that holding unreasonable expectations about marriage actually becomes the demise of the relationship. Unfortunately, when a marriage or spouse is unable to live up to idyllic fantasies in the nitty-gritty real-life marriage, disillusionment looms large! The automatic reaction is to debunk marriage, and divorce becomes an easy exit. It's disheartening to see so many marriages crumble before our very eyes. The divorce statistics, even among people of faith, draw our attention to just how difficult it is to be married today. Listen to the personal testimonies of people who started out with high hopes for their marriage.

Karen told us, "Marriage is a real-life journey that has brought unbelievable life challenges. Our marriage was very fragile after we had three small children in a row. It was so stressful just caring for their every need, and putting a priority on our marriage was the last thing on our minds. We grew distant, we had fights about how to handle the kids, and I lost interest in sex. We were operating with twice as many distractions, which left less time to give to our relationship."

David felt the extreme pressure on his marriage during the raising of teenagers. He was consumed with fears that they would make a serious or "life-threatening" mistake. He had trouble sleeping until the teens were home and felt he had to be on high alert and extremely vigilant about rules. He and his wife disagreed with some of the disciplinary actions, and this kept them on edge as a couple. The teens tested the parental values at every turn, leaving them arguing and doubting themselves. During the turmoil, the marriage was neglected, and David turned to another woman to relieve the tension. The marriage got put on the back burner, and it took a fatal blow.

These stories give us even more reason to keep a constant vigil on the state of our marriage relationship. Even when a couple is grounded in solid theological truth, it is not always so easy to put the biblical ideals into practice. We do not want to be accused of putting marriage on a pedestal of idealism that no one can live up to. But we do offer sound biblical principles that we believe will keep spouses growing into deeper levels of covenant love.

We recognize that marriage is made up of two flawed spouses who must negotiate their relationship in a broken world. Someone has made the observation, "brokenness is not the opposite of wholeness, but the means toward it." Knowing most of us are far from the ideal moves us to humility. While God's love is never emptied in the giving, spousal love is bound to fail and disappoint. Our humanness keeps us ever so humble and in continuous need of God's grace and strength.

Growth-Oriented Love

Covenant love and commitment are what give spouses the ability to counter their human impulse to give up at the first sign of trouble. Our covenant promises that we as spouses stay on equal footing and persistently work out the differences and difficulties that arise.

Living within the realities of a real marriage, spouses must come to terms with their interlocking needs. In the process, we must be able to forsake our needs for the sake of the relationship. Self-denial is not an easy thing for anyone. Covenant love takes an incredible amount of forethought and energy and sacrifice. Covenant love keeps us determined to make every effort to keep the marriage vital. It's a collaborative venture in creating the best marriage possible.

Lewis Smedes writes in his book *Love Within Limits,* "Agape love takes root in our lives . . . as the 'more excellent' way." He says, "we are neither gods or angels, we carry within us a heritage of moral and spiritual failure as part of our invisible baggage" (1978, p. 52). It is an enormous challenge for two imperfect spouses to live in covenant love. However, admitting our failures and brokenness keeps us humble. Recognizing our constant need of the Spirit's prompting and power to live out the extraordinary way of covenant love keeps us dependent on God. Recognizing that as we are willing to face our flawed selves in the context of marriage, God continually transforms us.

To lift up covenant love as an ideal that cannot be achieved in real marriage would be a fatal mistake! Unconditional loving does not come naturally. Our fallen nature is not inclined to put the interest of the other and the relationship first. We must relentlessly rely on God's power to practice these principles in our actions and attitudes. And when we do, the reward will be a spousal bonding of deepening trust.

Advantages of Lifelong Marriage

There are benefits for those who make a lifetime covenant in marriage. Common sense tells us that when spouses are rightfully loved (commitment, acceptance, empowerment and intimacy) they experience a sense of well-being. The Center for Disease Control and Prevention and the National Center for Health Statistics (NCHS) reviewed health data gathered from more than 127,000 adults from 1999 to 2002. They report that marriage has a "protective" effect. Regardless of age, sex, race, education, income or nationality, married adults were least likely to be in poor health, suffer serious psychological distress and smoke or drink heavily (National Center for Health Statistics, 2005).

Linda Waite and Maggie Gallagher (2000), in their book *The Case for Marriage: Why Married People Are Happier, Healthier and Better Off Financially,* found that having a spouse to be accountable to benefits overall health. Married people were less likely to suffer from long-term illness or disability, had better survival rates for some illnesses, better mental health, greater overall happiness, better emotional and physical satisfaction with sex. They report lower levels of domestic violence, solid religious social support and healthy lifestyles.

In her clinical work with thousands of couples, Michele Weiner-Davis (2003) found emotional connectedness and sexual satisfaction give husbands and wives a sense of well-being. Love begets love. Round and round it goes to deeper levels of connection. As spouses give and receive covenant love they are filled with tranquility and vitality.

Summary

We first presented a brief overview of the four overarching relationship principles: *covenant* (unconditional love), *grace* (acceptance and forgiveness), *empowerment* (mutual building up and affirmation) and *intimacy* (emotional and physical closeness). We saw that spouses are either growing toward deeper levels or going in reverse on these four relationship principles. Covenant love and commitment establishes the foundation on which the other principles are built. Gracing assures forgiveness when we fail and encourages us to be compassionate toward each other and our differences. Empowerment leads to individual and couple growth as spouses interact and challenge each other to reach their full potential as God's creation. And intimacy brings safe connection so emotional and sexual bonding takes place, deepening the union. Spouses who form an alliance and wholeheartedly seek to live out these principles are making the relationship a sacred priority and giving their sacred vow to never relegate this most precious relationship to second place.

THE GRACING MARRIAGE

Grace-Full Love

LYRICS FROM A CHILDREN'S SONG RESONATE IN OUR EARS: "I like you as you are, exactly and precisely. I think you turned out nicely, and I like you as you are!" Adults as well as children yearn to be accepted and loved for who they are. Everyone wants to be experienced as special by the ones they love.

Love has been defined as a "queasy feeling in the stomach," "a head-over-heels love" or "an unfortunate state of being," depending on who's talking. Perhaps we can never adequately define or understand the mystery of love. Yet we can identify actions that help us feel loved.

Gracing love is a major component of the mystery. As agents of grace, each spouse participates in reciprocal interaction of talking and listening, giving and receiving, honoring differences and affirming giftedness, forgiving and being forgiven. The far-reaching effects of gracing love culminate in a deeply satisfying relationship. Acceptance and forgiveness are the bedrock qualities of gracing love, because the inevitable disappointments and failures of human relationship demand a love that is full of grace.

God's Unrelenting Grace

As fragile, imperfect beings, spouses are acutely aware of how hard it is to love unconditionally. However, having received grace through Christ, we know we are accepted just as we are and forgiven just as we are. Drawing upon God's grace, we can offer grace to our spouse. Joe makes this comment about living with a "grace-filled" wife: "Even when I really messed up and felt like a total failure as a husband, my wife had an amazing ability to unleash my guilt with her compassionate understanding and forgiveness. My honest confession opened up a new intimacy between us providing me with the incentive to go forward and pursue needed change." Living in an atmosphere of grace erases guilt and shame, wipes the slate clean, gets beyond the mistakes, gives impetus to change, and moves spouses forward in renewed commitment.

Naked and Not Ashamed

In their nakedness, Adam and Eve felt no shame (Gen 2:25)! But in choosing to do things their own way rather than God's way, they broke ties with their Creator (Gen 3:7-8). Now they were exposed! They attempted to be gods rather than depend on the creator God. Can you imagine how their hearts pounded with fear when God called out to them in the garden? They were ashamed! Their immediate impulse was to hide from God, so they made a feeble attempt to cover up their nakedness with fig leaves. They didn't have a clue how to repair the disconnection.

How foolish it is for the created ones to hide from their Creator. There is nowhere to hide from God. When hiding didn't work, they tried to defend their actions by putting the blame on others rather than take personal responsibility for the breach in their relationship to God. They needed the courage to face God, confess their disobedience and accept the consequences of their actions and ask for forgiveness.

Accepting and Forgiving Versus Shaming and Blaming

Grace-full love is neither selfish (thinking only of self) nor self-less (never considering self), but shows itself in selflessness (focusing on the relationship). In a mutually gracing love the couple decides to make decisions for the sake of the "Us." The richest form of "two are better than one" is mutual commitment to "Us." It is out of grace that we continuously stretch beyond self-interest to incorporate the spouse.

Marriage is the closest kind of living and it is extremely demanding. No matter how hard spouses try to love like God, they are fallible and will fail to love perfectly. Therefore, forgiveness and acceptance are essential every step of the way through every stage of marriage. Grace is infectious, so when a spouse receives forgiveness and acceptance it inspires a gracious and generous loving back.

Blaming and Shaming

Judgmental attitudes are guaranteed to crush love. You can fill in the blank, it goes something like this: "I'll love you if . . . !" or "I'll love you when . . ." These conditional judgments bring on an automatic defensive stance to withhold yourself in body, mind and spirit. It's excruciating to be *unacceptable* because it strikes the very core of where it hurts! The shaming message says there's something radically wrong with you and unless changes are made you will not be acceptable. It's a harsh blow! Shame shatters confidence and makes us feel we *are* a wrong. This is in contrast to guilt, which we feel when we've *done* a wrong. Shame takes a personal toll on self-esteem. No wonder shame-based comments are so toxic and elicit such reactivity. The blaming makes one feel inadequate and deficient.

Shame is a deficit-based judgment that breeds distrust, suspicion, inferiority and uncertainly. Grudges and resentment get magnified in a vicious cycle that gets increasingly nasty. Spouses begin to calculate counterattacks, condemning each other in a destructive game of nonacceptance. Barriers are constructed to keep each other out, but they also keep out any chance of love getting through. It's a sad state of affairs. In the depths of painful reactivity no one wins.

If one has come from a shaming family system (perfectionist), one learns that the only way to deal with the shame is to *blame* someone else. In marriage, the spouse becomes the target of blame. Pointing a finger at your spouse may alleviate the shame of personal failure, but it unfairly undermines your spouse. In addition, it leads to the habit of not being responsible for one's actions and thus solving nothing. Unless one can admit fault, a defensive stance is the only option. To blame one's spouse can be a defensive projection similar to the biblical example of seeing the speck in another's eye, while not seeing the plank in one's own eye. We need to take a second look at what we're really saying.

I (Jack) grew up in a shaming home and learned early on that being "less than perfect" meant I was unacceptable. Though I didn't realize early on what was happening, the most natural thing to do when things went wrong in our marriage was for me to conveniently blame Judy for the problem. For example, whenever we got lost while driving it was quite clear that Judy had given bad directions. This blaming, in turn, dampened Judy's spirit and put distance between us. After a few years of marriage, Judy spoke up about this negative pattern. Then when I took a serious look at what was behind the blaming, I realized as a child I did anything to avoid those shaming "eye messages" from my mother. I got into the habit of denying and lying rather than admit I was wrong. Now, as a married adult, I needed to understand I could admit mistakes without jumping to the conclusion that I was a woebegone reprobate. Judy was willing to accept me, blunders and all! Being differentiated with a strong self means you can acknowledge mistakes, receive forgiveness (from self and spouse) and make responsible changes.

Nonacceptance puts marriage on an unequal footing. When Jack blamed me (Judy), it placed me in a one-down position. An unequal partnership also left Jack feeling the heavy burden of having to know and do everything right. I often struck back out of frustration. The critical spirit between us broke our cherished connection, leaving both unhappy. We needed to revisit the biblical concept of covenant and grace for our marriage time and time again.

Differences, Not Deficits!

Each spouse enters marriage with a unique personality, gender, family history, value system, cultural tradition, religious tradition and so on. These differences can enrich or threaten the marriage relationship. Spouses may be attracted to each other precisely because of the differences (traits, qualities, personality) secretly wishing to compensate for an underdeveloped part of themselves. However, the very quality that caused the initial attraction too often becomes an irritant in marriage. Spouses need to honor their differences rather than treat differences as deficits. The meeting and blending of two selves is part of the refining process that brings out the best in each person.

I hate to admit it, but it's true that I (Judy) secretly thought I would be able to change the things I didn't like about Jack after we were married. Many people marry with this unspoken thought. Jack, too, did his share of trying to change me early in our marriage. How presumptuous of us! How I remember some twenty years later when discussing this idea with our son, Joel, who was serious about a young woman at the time. He told us he would change the things he didn't like about her after they married. I remember telling him, "Don't let yourself be deceived, what you see is what you get!" I went on to share how this idea back-fired on us.

It isn't that the person we marry won't change, because they will! Change is something we can count on in life. Although we can request and even encourage change in each other, ultimately change must come from within—assisted by the inner urgings of God. Having a personal agenda to change one's spouse can only end in disillusionment and a dis-heartened spouse. The message clearly indicates nonacceptance. Thus, when one spouse is invested in changing the other, it's quite natural for that spouse to resist. In fact, it's fodder for a huge battle of defensiveness, anger, frustration and distancing tactics. Power and inadequacy issues get triggered in these futile attempts. When you think about it, wanting to change your spouse is usually self-serving. We want our spouse to be something we want them to be for our own purposes. Making demands for change due to self-centered needs undermines the spouse.

Mutual Acceptance

Equal-partnership marriage thrives on mutual acceptance. Showing ap-preciation and respecting unique differences is a graceful thing to do. A gracing attitude opens up all kinds of creative possibilities in marriage. There is more than one way (my way) to approach life, and who says this way is the right way? As June told us after several months of marital therapy, "I no longer want him to become anything other than what he is. . . . we've both let go of worn out expectations. Now I accept the person I wake up beside for who he is that very morning." In this case, her husband, Gary, must now be responsible for himself and his own growth. Knowing he is accepted and appreciated will do more for him in the long run.

Appreciating Gender Differences

Gender is an essential part of our distinctiveness according to Genesis 1. Male and female are created for each other. Perhaps why so many mar-riage books focus on gender differences is because spouses intuitively resonate with common tendencies. Whether by nature or nurture or both, males and females bring unique gendered selves to the marriage.

We may wonder about God's intention in creating male and female. Referring to Karl Barth's work, Theologian Gary Deddo (1999) writes, "there is a theological meaning, an ontological significance for our being male and female. . . . it plays an essential part in our being and becoming who we are as we engage in relationship with persons of the opposite gender. We exist in this essential polarity for the sake of human communion" (p. 115).

Being male or female impacts how we relate to each other as spouses. When we relate as gendered persons, we see ourselves in contrast to each other, giving us a clearer definition of self. Deddo (1999), gives additional insight on this point, "The marriage relationship is uniquely an image in that the otherness of the partners, and so the obviousness of one having and being what the other is not (male and female), and of one being able to reflect to the other that which the other cannot of itself know or see in its own self-reflection, is acknowledged and structurally represented in a unique way in a life-long relationship of faithfulness" (p. 141).

Gender differentiation through contrast and comparison affirms our sense of masculinity and femininity. Through our interaction we discover more about our distinction and similarities. By affirming uniqueness and commonality spouses can achieve the God-intended interdependent unity as Deddo (1999) claims. "They cannot be dissolved or interchanged because each needs the distinctiveness of the other to fully realize itself and enable the other to be fully realized as well" (p. 115). We can surmise how appreciating our gender differences draw us to interdependence. The fact is, we need each other.

Appreciating Collaborative Roles

In traditional marriage, as we noted in chapter one, roles tend to be clearly defined and segregated. One would be hard pressed to argue, on the basis of either history or biblical evidence, that woman's place is in the home and man's place is outside the home. Yet marital roles tend to be rigidly defined by traditionalists.

Modern/postmodern marriages base roles on multileveled criteria. Once again, there are many ways of doing things, and spouses must negotiate the roles. The costs and rewards formula is used to assure that

things are strictly equal in role responsibility. Whenever it appears one
is doing more than the other there is trouble. Bargaining for one's position often results in competition and conflict. Advocating for self easily
turns into a battle of score keeping. As you can imagine, disaster looms
when spouses have different ways of determining role expectations.

A gracing marriage emphasizes exchangeability of roles through mutual agreement. The couple considers the unique needs of each spouse
in working out a cooperative plan about who does what when. Roles
are flexible but clearly determined as a collaborative venture. Because
each spouse is capable of doing any particular task (no male or female
distinction), the couple can easily exchange tasks when needed. The
husband enjoys cooking, so takes charge of this arena, while the wife is
good at record keeping and takes on the financial duties. When deciding
on role responsibilities the focus is on giftedness, desire and convenience. There is a sense of pride in working together in their respective
roles for a united purpose.

Appreciating Personality Differences

Personality differences are a given in marriage. Every day of married life
we bump up against the "different strokes for different folks" reality.
These differences both attract and exasperate us! It is so essential to
show grace by valuing and accepting our natural differences. The covenant love that urges us to put our spouse as the priority means we must
make every effort to respect personality differences.

While spouses are initially drawn to each other's unique personality,
that same personality can cause struggles after marriage. Some spouses
may be quite similar in certain personality qualities, while others are extreme opposites. Most of us are somewhere in between, having a combination of similar and opposite traits. Whatever the situation, personality traits can bring harmony or cause disruption in marriage.

Every couple needs an extra dose of grace in working out the dynamics of their contrasting personalities. Spouses who fail to admit their frustrations about differences undoubtedly become resentful. In order to
find creative solutions to honest personality differences, spouses must
be able to identify both the strengths and limitations of various personality traits. Next, the couple needs to consider the impact of these traits

on their interactive patterns. Finally, they need to determine how to utilize their differences to their advantage.

We have found the well-known Myers-Briggs Personality Type Indicator (Myers, 1962) useful in understanding how a couple can use their personality differences and similarities to strengthen their marriage. Many are familiar with the archetypes initially described by Carl Jung (1971) and popularized by David Keirsey in the book *Please Understand Me II* (1998). It is revealing to acknowledge our own style, as well as that of our partner, in an effort to navigate differences in how we think, communicate and behave.

We approach personality traits as general tendencies or preferences in how a person approaches others and the environment. Most agree that these personality traits are developed through a combination of biological and environmental factors.

The four major categories of the Myers-Briggs personality typology are *Extroversion/Introversion* (E or I), *Sensory/Intuitive* (S or N), *Thinking/Feeling* (T or F) and *Judging/Perceiving* (J or P). Each pair of descriptors represents a personality continuum with the two terms as polar ends. Extraversion is explained as outward directed and expressive, while introversion is inner directed and reserved. Sensory has to do with the concrete ability to take in or observe the surroundings, while intuition has to do with introspection and drawing from an imaginative mind. Thinkers are focused on their mind and objectivity, while feelers on their feelings and others. Judging is a category that can be confusing because it is not about making judgments. Rather, it has to do with being organized and routine oriented, while the perceiving person looks at alternatives and focuses on opportunities. While most of us lie somewhere between the extremes on these four categories of polar opposites, it's the amount of difference between spouses in any one or all four categories that becomes the biggest struggle for the couple. We will describe each of these traits briefly and indicate how they might affect the marriage relationship.

Extroversion/Introversion

Perhaps the most identifiable of the personality dimensions is the *extroversion* and *introversion* scale. Although most persons feel they have a fairly good understanding of these two personality traits, it is important to understand the basic differences. In general, the *extroverted* person relates more easily to the outer world of people and things, while an *introverted* spouse relates more easily to the inner world of ideas. Table 4.1 contrasts some of the major qualities of each trait.

Table 4.1. Differences Between Extroversion and Introversion

Extroversion	vs.	Introversion
Outward		Inward
Sociable		Private
Expressive		Reflective
Breadth		Depth

We illustrate the differences in terms of a couple attending a social event where they will meet and mingle with acquaintances and strangers. The outgoing extroverted spouse looks forward to the occasion and is energized by it, while the introverted spouse may dread the event because it takes so much energy to interact with a large number of persons. The introverted spouse enjoys people, but it takes a lot out of him or her. Introverts are misunderstood when they spend more time processing ideas and concepts, and they are expected to acquire extroverted skills to function in society. The posture of the extroverted spouse is *sociable* and easily engages with others, while the introverted spouse takes time to develop relationships at a more *reserved* pace. The introverted person may be experienced as a *private person* who is somewhat hard to approach, while the extroverted spouse is seen as a *people person* whom others may enjoy or may want to avoid due to their over-exuberance and enthusiasm.

Note the difference between the two in conversation at the party. The extroverted spouse is verbally expressive while the introverted spouse is more passive and quiet. It will take a while to settle down after the party for the extravert while the introvert is exhausted and drained of energy. As you can see, this couple will need to negotiate how often they attend such social gatherings. Extroverted spouses must make room for the introverts by recognizing their need for silence and recovery time. The introverts must understand their spouse's enjoyment of social stimulation and being "the life of the party."

In terms of friendship networks, the extroverted spouse tends to have many friends while the introverted spouse has few but deeply loyal friends. In other words, extroverts have a breadth of friendships while introverts have depth in their friendships. The following story from our marriage is an example of how we tried to change each other's natural personality differences to no avail.

In the beginning, I (Jack) found myself enthralled with Judy's natural tendencies to be friendly and outgoing. In fact, it was what drew me to her. As an introvert and rather shy around women, I felt comfortable with her easygoing way of conversing and how she was so accepting. Judy's father was a shy, reserved man and therefore she was very comfortable with the same mannerisms in me. We felt well matched as a couple and enjoyed our couple interaction. Judy says my more thoughtful way of expressing myself intrigued her, while her freely expressed emotions helped me open up to her. All fared well for those courting days. However, after marriage, some of these natural traits became more of a challenge. I remember how embarrassed I felt in public with Judy's uninhibited ways. Judy, on the other hand, didn't like the shy way I responded in social situations. The very things we found attractive in each other initially had become areas of dissatisfaction. Judy tried to get me to talk more by turning the conversation toward me in social situations, only to irritate me to no end! I tried to dampen Judy's emotional exuberance by nonverbal shaming messages. You get the picture. The nonacceptance turned into hurtful criticism. Only when we got a better grasp on our personality differences were we able to accept and affirm each other.

Sensory/Intuitive

The sensory personality trait has to do with *practicality* as compared to *intuition*. The sensory spouse would rather work with concrete facts, while the intuitive spouse looks for possibilities. Table 4.2 contains a list of contrasting adjectives describing these traits.

We can see a good example from marriage in the way each spouse

Table 4.2. Differences Between Sensory and Intuitive

Sensory	vs.	Intuitive
Practical		Imagining possibilities
Details		Patterns
Present		Future
Routine		Variety

approaches a task like assembling a picnic table. The sensory spouse will begin by carefully reading the detailed instructions. Meticulously following the diagrams, this spouse counts out the bolts and nuts and proceeds in a step by step, orderly fashion. The intuitive spouse ignores the instructions altogether, looks at the parts and tries to detect a pattern to assemble the whole table. Disagreements are likely to ensue around whose way is the right way. One spouse believes it's best to follow set procedures and sequential steps, while the other spouse finds this a waste of time and considers it more fun to follow hunches. The sensory spouse looks for routine (conserves) whereas the intuitive spouse looks for variety (change); the sensory spouse uses perspiration while the intuitive spouse uses inspiration. One can see how these differences would bring disharmony.

In the first years of our own marriage we initially took turns doing the dreaded income tax forms every other year. We were each capable, but it was inefficient in the long run because we got rusty in the in-between year. In working out a harmonious interdependency on these differences, we have divided the task up to take advantage of our personal strengths. Judy, the more structured and detail-oriented one, neatly organizes all of the supportive information needed. I (Jack), being more comfortable with the big picture, complete the annual tax return. This has saved a good bit of turmoil over the years.

Thinking/Feeling

The thinking/feeling dimension refers to how one makes decisions. Thinkers base judgments on impersonal analysis and logic, while feeling persons base judgments on personal values and emotional considerations. See the list in table 4.3 contrasting thinking- and feeling-oriented personalities.

Table 4.3. Differences Between Thinking and Feeling

Thinking	vs.	Feeling
Head		Heart
Logic		Personal Conviction
Truth and Justice		Harmony in Relationships
Critiques		Appreciates

Take the example of a couple making an important decision about their family. The thinking spouse goes right to the *head* to consider all the implications, while the feeling person leans more on the *heart*. The thinker influences through objective logic, while the feeler follows subjective personal conviction. While the thinking spouse can be convinced by precise facts, the feeling spouse is moved by persuasive emotion. The thinking spouse values and appeals to truth and justice, while the feeling spouse is more concerned about relationship harmony. The tone taken by the thinking spouse can be cool and detached, while the feeling spouse exudes emotion. In responding to others the thinker tends to critique, while the feeler tends to appreciate. The basis of judgment for the thinking spouse is principles, but for the feeling spouse it is personal values.

A typical struggle may be in the area of parenting children. Differences may put parents at odds when it comes to discipline and rules. The logical parent may be good at sticking to the rules but shows little feeling, while the feeling parent may relax the rules due to emotional considerations. Distress arises when spouses judge each other about parenting. However, by combining their strengths, they will make a parenting decision based on a balanced view.

Judging/Perceiving

A final personality dimension involves personal adaptability. At one end of this continuum is the need for structure (called *judging*), and the trait at the other is called *perceiving*. Judging spouses like it when there is a

clear order to life, while perceiving spouses prefer an open, spontaneous way of life. Table 4.4 gives an overview of the differences between
structured and flexible spouses.

Table 4.4. Differences Between Judging and Perceiving

Judging (structured)	vs.	Perceiving (flexible)
Ordered		Go with the flow
Clear limits		Freedom to explore
Security in closure		Security in remaining open
Plans in advance		Last minute rush

To gain an insight on how this set of personality traits affects a marriage, think about how a couple makes vacation plans. The structured
spouse likes things planned far in advance: knowing where they will
stop each night, having motel rooms reserved and activities preschedu-
led. This spouse is peaceful when things are set in stone with no unexpected surprises to disrupt the plans. In contrast, the perceiving-
oriented spouse loves to go with the flow, and actually takes great
delight in the unexpected surprises that occur along the way. Decisions
are made on the spot, so when everything is preplanned it spoils spontaneity. Holding off the final decision keeps things exciting. Being locked
into a plan means they will miss out on the many delights in life. One
spouse feels security in closure, whereas the other feels closed down.

This is the dilemma. One will plan and pack well in advance, while
the other throws things together in a last minute rush. How will this couple find a happy balance? Both will need to forgo their ideal to create a
balance between planned and spontaneous experiences.

In our marriage I (Judy) have gone outside my normal desire for structure in order to incorporate Jack's desire for spontaneity. This has resulted in some wonderful surprises and opened up a world to me I otherwise would not have discovered on my own. Traveling and living in
other cultures is just one example. On the other hand, giving way to my
more structured nature has lessened Jack's frustration in a number of situations where his desire for nonstructure has ended in chaos.

Achieving Harmony

Marriages come in all combinations—as spouses weave together multi-dimensional strands of personality, gender and cultural differences into a unique partnership. Every couple must integrate their differences into a creative unity. When honest differences are honored and embraced, differences function as strengths rather than deficits.

We encourage spouses to pay serious attention to areas of difference so they can have a deeper understanding and appreciation for each other. Go back to our example of my discomfort when Judy was too exuberant. Recognizing that my nonacceptance dampened Judy's spirit, I took an honest look at myself, realizing that the problem was more about me than about Judy. My personal growth came by stretching beyond my comfort zone and ability. At the same time, Judy's awareness of my discomfort of her extraverted personality gave her impetus to monitor her responses, giving me more space to enter into conversations. This mutual appreciation for each other's unique way of being became a significant stepping stone for personal and relationship growth.

As a rule of thumb, couples will be more conflicted when there is significant polarization in a number of areas. Differences weaken the relationship if (1) either spouse defiantly asserts a right to be "who I am" at the expense of the *us* or (2) when the *us* is emphasized at the expense of each spouse being true to his or her own self. When a couple accepts and harmonizes differences, they are on their way to a thriving interdependency.

Have you ever gotten out on a dance floor with your spouse, each going in a different direction? Jack will often ask me to lead since he never learned to dance, but when I do he isn't inclined to follow. Or, he tries to lead while I refuse to follow. How can we be in step when we are battling each other's every move? It's much easier to dance separately and make your own moves. But moving out of sync in a close embrace is awkward. The dance becomes a turbulent mismatch of disturbing tension.

Self-focus, control and resistance creates jerky, chaotic moves. Asserting self over the synchrony of us means we've lost touch with each other. Sometimes we need to take a break, sit out the next dance until we can be in tune with each other and can achieve a graceful rhythm of interdependency. His foot goes back and mine goes forward; my body leans into his and we sway together; he swings me out and I come back in the joy of moving together as a team.

The trinitarian model promotes two uniquely differentiated spouses becoming a united whole. Equilibrium and balance are the fruit of interdependency. Mutual gracing and forgiveness are indispensable aspects of creating a fulfilling differentiated unity. There is power in being accepted as you are and being forgiven when you fail. Spouses flourish in an atmosphere of grace because they can be authentic rather that pretend to be what their spouse wants them to be. When differences are embraced, spouses can be confident that their uniqueness is not only valued, but even brings complementary strength to the relationship. As spouses incorporate their differences into a creative unity, they can gladly appreciate and take pleasure in their mysterious and beautiful one-flesh interdependency.

THE EMPOWERING MARRIAGE

Mutual Empowerment and Mutual Servanthood

"'TILL DEATH DO US PART' SHOULD NOT BE A LIFE SENTENCE," quips family therapist Carl Whitaker (in Neill & Kniskern, 1982). Yet turmoil is a natural part of marriage. Spouses must navigate the murky power dynamics that arise in the day-to-day complexities of life. Marriage can sometimes seem like a life sentence under the stress of relationship demands. It takes extraordinary resolve to relinquish personal rights for the good of the marriage.

In this chapter, we introduce the concept of power in marriage. We compare secular models of marital power with biblical notions of power. We propose a model that has mutual empowerment and mutual servanthood as core dimensions.

Power Dynamics in Marriage

In his classic book *Love and Will* (1969), Rollo May identified five ways power can be used: (1) to *exploit*—influence through brute force; (2) to *manipulate*—influence through devious means; (3) to *compete*—influence through personal resources; (4) to *nurture*—influence through care; and (5) as *integrative influence*—using personal power for another's sake. The biblical definition of power, to use May's terminology, is integrative influence. Hereafter, when we use the term *empowerment,* we mean to connote power that is *for* another.

Marital power, simply defined, is the ability to influence. Most research on power focuses on the *use* of power to influence or control a spouse (Levine & Boster, 2001; McDonald, 1980; Scanzoni, 1979). An underlying conclusion derived from research is that spouses devise a number of ways to be powerful in marriage. A difficulty in assessing marital power, according to Tichenor (1999, p. 649), is that you must account for hidden power in qualities like nurture, communication skills, gender ideologies and family structures.

In social science literature, power is treated as a commodity of limited supply. Therefore, marital power is based on personal resources in terms of what the spouses need, desire and/or value. If resources are not valued, they become a valueless commodity, putting power in the hands of the spouse who possesses the resources that are most valued. It is easy to see how this secular view leads to a vicious scramble to increase power by whatever means necessary—manipulation, coercion, control and competition.

When partners live and breathe by the law of quid pro quo, they become invested in gaining power. Let's take one hundred percent units of power, with each spouse competing to get a ten to twenty percent advantage. Such tactics lead to extreme power struggle standoffs. When spouses insist on their own way, marriage becomes a dreadful place of vying for power. Physical and verbal abuse, manipulative ploys and withdrawal threats become recurrent strategies used to get one's way. Badgering a spouse into submission is a hollow victory indeed! Marriage becomes nothing more than a "life sentence" of tolerating an intolerable state of being. Someone once said, "the relationship wins or the spouse wins!" If winning means being the most powerful, both spouses lose.

This mistaken idea of power is the death decree of meaningful relationship. The spouse who yields out of ignorance or weakness becomes a victim, while the spouse who bullies and wields power at the expense of the other is feared and avoided. This polarization ends in extreme isolation for both spouses, denying them the satisfaction of mutuality, emotional bonding and interdependence.

Alternative Views of Authority in Marriage

In chapter one we contrasted the postmodern with the traditional view of marital authority. Here we extend that contrast before applying the trinitarian model to marital authority. In the postmodern world, marital authority revolves around the concept of *personal power*. Each spouse maximizes personal resources in order to gain influence in marriage. The social exchange template described in chapter one explains how spouses attempt to maximize the return on their investment. Personal resources like money, sex, nurture and protection become important sources of influence.

The traditional view places marital authority in the inherent position of the husband. According to this view decisions having to do with marriage and family life are ultimately determined by the husband. The corresponding implication is that the wife takes a submissive role. Traditionalists come in two types: hard patriarchy or soft patriarchy.

Hard patriarchy advocates adherence to a rigid structure of male ascribed authority. Husbands make critical and final decisions while wives submit without question. This chain-of-command view puts the husband in a one-up position, while the wife is left with one of two options—either to willingly give in or to find indirect ways to influence. Christian books written to women in this position, such as *The Total Woman, The Surrendered Wife* or *Fascinating Womanhood,* give advice on how to outsmart her husband who is actually the weaker one. The irony is that she can have her way through sweet talk, finesse and sexual enticements. In subtle and not-so-subtle ways she becomes dishonest and gains power through manipulative actions. If the husband's masculine security is based upon his wife's submission, the truth is that she can reduce his power to zero with the right moves. Power founded on inequality has the potential for abuse and manipulation.

Soft patriarchy places final authority with the husband but emphasizes a suffering servant role in which a husband's leadership is to be fashioned after Christ, who laid down his life for the church. In this case he shows concern for his wife's needs and consults her about issues. Although he still has the final authority, there is more of a belief in complementary roles. When this kind of leadership is practiced the wife has little problem submitting. However, proponents of this position continue to advocate ascribed power in which the roles are predetermined.

We believe that legitimizing self-sacrifice on the part of the wife only is unbiblical, and historically it leads to abuses of power against women throughout the world. While affirming the servant leadership model of soft patriarchy, we challenge how complementary is defined, especially in terms of limitations put on women. There is a substantial body of literature using a biblical hermeneutic that challenges these interpretations (see, for example, Christians for Biblical Equality website: http://www.cbeinternational.org).

Marital Authority and the Trinitarian Model

Evangelical theologians differ in their conclusions about marital authority. Proponents of both *marital equality* and *marital hierarchy* draw on biblical texts and the doctrine of the Trinity. The following discussion draws heavily upon Kevin Giles's excellent book *The Trinity and Subordinationism: The Doctrine of God and the Contemporary Gender Debate* (2002).

Evangelical theologians arguing for male headship seek to base their position in the argument that the Son is eternally subordinated to the Father. Evangelical theologians arguing for gender equality and mutual submissiveness in marriage seek to base their position on equality within the holy Trinity. Theologians representing each position can draw upon a selected battery of Bible verses to support their respective claims.

Those arguing for male headship in marriage usually begin with Paul's assertion in 1 Corinthians 11:3 that just as the head of Christ is God, so should the man be head of the woman. They also refer to texts like John 4:34 or 5:30, in which Jesus states that he has been sent to do the Father's will. Romans 5:18-19 and Hebrews 5:8 describe the obedience of the Son to the Father. In John 14:28 Jesus specifically states, "the Father is greater than I." Taken together, subordinationists argue that since Scripture clearly teaches that the Son is subordinate to the Father, the clear implication of trinitarian theology is that the wife is to be subordinate to the husband.

Proponents of gender equality point to the many Bible verses in which the Son is spoken of as God, such as in John 1:1, 20:28; Romans 9:5 and Hebrews 1:8. Furthermore, Philippians 2:6 states that the Son is *equal* with God, while Ephesians 1:22 and Colossians 2:10 point to the Son as being *head over all things*. Giles (2002) points out that in more than two hundred scriptural references the Son is referred to as *Lord*—the title used in the Greek translation of the Hebrew Bible to render the Old Testament name for God *Yahweh*.

The solution to this seeming contradiction, according to Giles, was given more than 1600 years ago. St. Athanasius wrote that the whole scope of Scripture gives a double account of the Son of God, "one of his temporal and voluntary subordination in the incarnation, the other of his eternal divine status" (Giles, 2002, p. 15). Scriptural texts that speak of the Son's equality with the Father refer to the eternal relationship between the holy Trinity. Texts that speak of inequality between the Father and the Son have one thing in common—they all refer to the Son taking on human form to give his life for the salvation of humankind. This subordination was voluntary and temporarily a part of the Son's incarnate ministry.

The lesson to be learned from St. Athanasius is that the verses on subordination within the holy Trinity must be understood within their historical context. It is unfortunate that some contemporary theologians, apparently for the sake of bolstering support for a hierarchical position in marriage, ignore how the vast majority of theologians through history have understood subordination within the holy Trinity (Giles, 2002).

Building upon the consensual view of theologians through the history of the church, we propose that the equality found in the holy Trinity can indeed serve as a model for equality in marriage. Marriage is to be a relationship of equals. There are two biblically based models of marital equality: *mutual submission* and *equal regard*.

Mutual submission. Proponents of mutual submission base their model on Ephesians 5:21, "Be subject to one another out of reverence for Christ." Bible scholars contend that verse 21 should be part of the paragraph that follows, which then entreats husbands to love their wives as Christ loved the church and gave himself up for her, and for women to submit out of reverence for Christ (Bilezikian, 1985; Fee, 2005; Garland & Garland, 1986; Grenz, 2001; Liefeld, 2005; Marshall, 2004). These verses are not to be understood in a hierarchical sense in which the husband lords it over his wife, but rather in sacrificing oneself for his wife. She submits out of love and honor as well. The priority of the other is clearly upheld since both husbands and wives are to follow Christ's example of self-giving in a suffering-servant role.

Equal regard. Don Browning (1997) promotes an ethic for marriage based on "equal regard." His expressed concern is that the language of submissiveness and self-sacrifice opens the door to personal abuse of power. Recognizing how the self-sacrifice message has been misused against women, he proposes a morality of "equal regard" in which the other is treated as one wants to be treated. A mutual-regard philosophy radically changes the way spouses operate in their marriage. Both are highly regarded by each other. Although this view is open to the concept of self-sacrifice in love, it is interpreted as being "derived from equal regard" (pp. 283-84).

While we agree with the equal regard position in substance, we also affirm the concept of mutual submission and personal sacrifice. We suggest there might be something to be learned in the trinitarian model from the Son's voluntary and temporary submission to the Father. First, it is not inappropriate to think of marriage as a relationship in which *each*—husband *and* wife—are called upon to subordinate their will and needs to the other. This we take as the thrust of what Paul writes in Ephesians 5:21: "Be subject to one another out of reverence for Christ." Special circumstances like mental or physical incapacity requires unequal sacrifice of one spouse. In this case, one spouse is challenged to give much more than an equal share. Placing the "best interest of the other" as a priority is the essence of the "extraordinary" way of the cross and covenant love.

Thus marriage may reflect the Son's *unilateral* temporary submission to the Father. Besides temporary physical incapacity, emotional stress or distress, there might be a yielding to the greater knowledge or wisdom of the spouse in a specific area. God gifts each of us in different ways. In marriage, gifts can be used in mutual, yet complementary ways. In our own marriage we have learned, often the hard way, when it might be wise for one of us to submit to the greater wisdom of the other. We turn now to the complex marital process of *complementarity without hierarchy*.

Complementarity Without Hierarchy

We reject both the traditional and postmodern views on authority as inadequate because they have accepted a secular view of power as a limited resource. Both models are based on the assumption that human beings are self-centered and therefore power issues need to be regulated. Although we acknowledge we are a fallen people in need of accountability, we also believe God offers us a way of achieving mutual empowerment and mutual servanthood.

As a starting point, in Christian marriage, both spouses are first and foremost to submit to the lordship of Jesus Christ and then to one another. We agree with Browning that inequality diminishes women and therefore a partnership of equal regard has the greatest potential for spousal satisfaction. We also agree that the mutual submission position is an important perspective. So we incorporate the themes of mutual empowerment and mutual servanthood into a model of complementarity without hierarchy. For a comprehensive overview of this model see *Discovering Biblical Equality: Complementarity Without Hierarchy,* edited by Ronald Pierce, Rebecca Groothuis and Gorden Fee (2005).

In this proposed model, both spouses are challenged to empower *and* serve one another, as imitators of Christ. *Mutual empowerment* has to do with each spouse reaching his or her full potential by having full access to personal and relational resources. The good news is that the power of God is available in unlimited amounts! One can be filled with the Holy Spirit and receive unlimited power in terms of the fruit of the Spirit: love, joy, peace, patience, kindness, goodness, fidelity, gentleness and self-control (Gal 5:22-23; Eph 4:13). God's resources are inexhaustible!

In promoting our case for a mutual empowerment, we refer to the Greek word for "authority," *exousia,* which literally means "out of being." It refers to a type of influence that is not dependent upon any personal strength, achievement or skill, but which comes forth "out of the being" of a person. The Greek word for "power," *dynamis,* is the word from which *dynamo* is derived. The authority of Jesus flowed from his personhood. It was dynamic.

Jesus empowered others throughout his earthly ministry in the form of a servant. Rejecting the idea that power means ruling over people, he emphatically declared that he had *not* come to rule but to be a servant to all. Through his teachings and actions, Jesus used his power to lift up the fallen, to forgive the guilty, to encourage maturity in the weak. Most notably, he honored those who occupied a marginal status (women and children) in the patriarchal culture of New Testament times. He was an empowerer of people (Spencer, 2005).

The apostle John puts it this way: "But to all who received him, who believed in his name, he gave power to become children of God, who were born, not of blood or of the will of the flesh or of the will of man, but of God" (Jn 1:12-13). Ray Anderson (1982) exegetes this text by noting that power "of blood" is power in the natural order; "the will of the flesh" is conventional power derived from tradition, duty, honor and obedience; while Jesus gave personal and spiritual power to the children of God.

Each spouse is given gifts in full measure. God calls spouses to give of their lives out of fullness, not out of deprivation. Spouses who are for each other want the best for each other, not less than the best. Both spouses have power and neither lords it over the other. They use their personal resources for the relationship in marriage, work, coparenting roles, life goals and service to the Lord. It is neither a matter of yielding to the wishes of the other nor does it mean having one's own way; rather, it is joining forces to become one.

Mutual empowerment is a reciprocal process of building up, equipping, supporting, encouraging, affirming and challenging. Philippians 2 urges us to look to the interests of others with the same mind as Christ. First Corinthians 7:1-5 promotes marital agreement. Just as an orchestra makes harmonious music when each instrument contributes its own unique part, there is marital harmony when two unique spousal voices join together with a centered vision and mutual investment in their common future.

Seeking to be Christlike, *mutual servanthood* becomes a higher calling, a giving oneself up to God's high calling (Eph 5:21-33; Col 3:18-19). Mutual self-sacrifice is a benefit for both spouses. In a very real sense, dying to self places marriage in God's care. By offering their relationship to God, spouses acknowledge they belong to God as they seek to be Christlike in mutual servanthood.

Empowering Versus Enabling

The following story from our marriage illustrates how empowerment differs from enabling. We spoke earlier of personality differences. Jack, being an introvert, became quite dependent upon me, the extravert, in social situations. What was easy for me was difficult for Jack, who was a bit awkward and timid around people. Whenever we were visiting friends, I automatically took on the role of social broker, that is, excusing ourselves when it was time to go home. We had it perfected! I picked up on Jack's ever-so-subtle nonverbal signals (eye contact or a glance at the clock) and would then dismiss us from the occasion. It worked like a charm!

However, after a few years of marriage, it became a drag. I began to protest the arrangement. "Why don't you speak for yourself, Jack?" Despite my request, Jack continued to depend on me, and when I failed to respond to his signals he became irritated and disgruntled. One evening it all came to a head. While sitting around a table with three other couples, Jack repeatedly gave signals—and I repeatedly ignored him. In fact, I felt quite powerful at this point. After several desperate attempts and a few loud yawns, he stretched his leg under the table and gave me a gentle kick. Frustrated with the situation myself, I said out loud for everyone to hear, "Jack, why are you kicking me?" Needless to say, it led to a rather heated "discussion" in the car on the way home.

In the end, this disruption became the impetus for change. Jack no longer could "hide" behind my natural ability and had to develop social skills. Mutual empowerment means each spouse becomes competent instead of getting trapped in enabling patterns. Mutual support enhances, while overdependency constrains personal and relational growth.

Relationship Power: The Fruit of an Empowering Marriage

Mutual empowerment and mutual servanthood is devised on the premise of equality. Herein lies the greatest challenge for a couple: the transforming of personal power into *relationship power*. It is a daunting task for two unique, self-confident individuals to become one. Two equally empowered spouses, fully developed and clearly differentiated, choose to surrender the "I" for the "Us." Spousal resources are being used *for* each other and the good of the relationship. This does not mean that spouses blindly yield to the wishes of the other, but they willingly regard the spouse's desires as equally important. They gain power by encouraging full potential, affirming each other and building on each other's gifts, as they become all that God intended them to be—both individually and as a couple.

In an empowering marriage, spouses collaborate through interaction and responsiveness. Spouses are stretched in unimaginable ways toward personal and relational growth in the process. Secure and self-confident in who they are, each spouse has a perspective that contributes to the relationship. Being eager to understand each other's perspective, spouses tolerate a certain amount of anxiety until couple clarity is achieved. Strongly believing that two perspectives are better than one, they express themselves honestly and without hesitation. Mutual exchange becomes the catalyst for thriving marriage.

Mutually empowering marriage places the locus of authority in the relationship, adding a dimension of mutual accountability and responsibility. Spouses gain an overarching balance in their mutual giving and receiving throughout the years. The inevitable sense of satisfaction at the end comes from knowing each spouse has put forth one hundred percent in terms of self-giving and mutual empowering. In the end, mutual empowerment and mutual servanthood prove to be success factors in their marriage. Empowering is covenant love in action! When spouses experience a secure covenant love, gracing acceptance and empowerment in marriage, they undoubtedly will develop intimacy—the topic we turn to next.

6

THE INTIMATE MARRIAGE

Knowing and Being Known

THERE IS NO SUCH THING AS INSTANT INTIMACY! Intimacy is born out of trust and safety—an increasing scarcity in our world of suspicion and distrust. We read in 1 John 4:18, "There is no fear in love, but perfect love casts out fear." However, while God's love is perfect, human love is imperfect. There is plenty of fear in human loving. In fact, most people find it quite terrifying to give themselves wholeheartedly to another, even in marriage. The dread of being rejected keeps people from the richest possibilities of intimate knowing.

The only perfectly secure relationship is with God, the one who loves us unconditionally and is solely deserving of our trust. Yet even in this relationship we run and hide from God until we are nudged by the grace extended in Jesus. Then when we respond to God's personal invitation of love, we are received just as we are and found fully acceptable in Christ. The Holy Spirit enters in and communes with us, assuring us that we are the children of God.

Spouses who are willing to journey together in the worthwhile adventure of knowing and being known will deepen their marital bond. Spousal intimacy strengthens marital commitment, increases grace-full loving and fosters empowerment, contributing to even deeper levels of intimacy.

A Biblical Perspective on Intimacy

The intimate connection between the members of the Holy Trinity shows solidarity in unity and purpose. The Father's love for the Son and the Son for the Father is seen throughout the earthly ministry of Jesus. In the most agonizing times when Jesus is in the desert and the garden, the intimate communion between Son and Father is striking. Jesus draws on the Holy Spirit to do the Father's will. The relationship between the three members of the Holy Trinity demonstrates intimate connection.

In terms of the relationship between the Godhead and human beings, the creator God knows us before we are knit together in our mother's womb, according to Psalm 139:13-16. A trustworthy covenant maker, God pursues us with unrelenting grace; Jesus gives his life to redeem us; and the Holy Spirit bonds us to God as his adopted children. We are called to know God in a personal way and in that knowing be made whole. Romans 8:1-2 assures us, "There is therefore now no condemnation for those who are in Christ Jesus. For the law of the Spirit of life in Christ Jesus has set you free from the law of sin and of death." Later in that chapter Paul exclaims, "Who will separate us from the love of Christ? . . . For I am convinced that neither death, nor life, nor angels, nor rulers, nor things present, nor things to come, nor powers, nor height, nor depth, nor anything else in all creation, will be able to separate us from the love of God in Christ Jesus our Lord" (Rom 8:35, 38-39). Precisely because we are no longer condemned, we freely give ourselves to God, knowing he will never leave or forsake us.

What an awesome truth! Our almighty Creator entreats us into fellowship, friendship and communion, "Listen! I am standing at the door, knocking; if you hear my voice and open the door, I will come in to you and eat with you, and you with me" (Rev 3:20).

The Intimacy Principle

In the idyllic Garden, Adam and Eve are unabashedly open to each other in their meeting (Gen 2:23-25). Being naked and not ashamed refers to much more than their physical encounter; it has to do with all aspects of knowing each other. There is no need to wear masks for they reveal themselves without fear or pretense.

What a radically divergent picture is found in Genesis 3 after the Fall. Now Adam and Eve are hiding in the shadows, ashamed of who they are and what they have done. Their love without fear has been drastically disturbed. Now there is enmity between them—they cover up, blame each other and are unwilling to be accountable to God or each other for what they have done. Out of fear they deny, defend and distance themselves from each other and from God.

The ultimate motivating force behind marital intimacy is the longing to be fully known in the safety of covenant love. Spouses intuitively understand that revealing their innermost selves, even their darkest interior, is part of intimate knowing. The secure belonging that comes from knowing each other in profound and endearing ways enhances intimate connection. Mutual revelation leads to self and spousal discovery. Spouses choose to share because they want to be known, and they are eager to listen out of a desire to know their spouse.

Too Risky to Share

While this deep level of knowing sounds inviting, self-disclosure is risky business and many factors keep spouses from intimate sharing. For instance, in the traditional marriage there is little focus on personal or emotional expression due to ascribed authority. The couple's sexual intimacy is primarily focused on the husband's rights rather than the wife's desires. In postmodern marriage the self-focused expressions lessen interactive intimacy, and spouses concentrate on personal sexual pleasure rather than relationship-focused sex. Both perspectives stifle couple intimacy.

It takes courage to share in vulnerable ways even to a spouse. It is scary to reveal when you're unsure that what you share will be handled with care. Under conditions of conditional loving, shaming, controlling and distancing, the tendency is to hold back and to cover up. The spouses are riddled with concerns like, "What if he disapproves?" "What if she condemns?" "What if he's filled with disgust by my secrets?" "What happens if I can't accept the truth?" The apprehension closes them down. Even when they ache for a spousal connection that will break through their loneliness and pain, they simply cannot take the risk.

If what we are is not acceptable, it seems best to stay hidden in the safety of one's own secrets. If deceit is more tolerable than exposing oneself, it leads spouses to hide behind masks of pretense. They put on false fronts, covering up their true selves. The safest policy is to put on a happy face, pretend all is well even when it isn't, and soon their whole life is pretty much a fake. Those who stop being honest with themselves stop being honest with their spouses. Being continually responded to with disrespectful disregard or blame automatically shuts a person down. Barriers are constructed and it becomes increasingly difficult to penetrate the protective walls. Until there is safety, intimacy is not an option. Spouses will not risk exposing their loneliness, opening up their heart, expressing fears, revealing dreams or connecting at a deeper emotional level.

Secure Attachment and Intimacy

Bonding is essential if intimacy is to thrive, according to attachment theorists Winnicott (1986), Bowlby (1969, 1973), Ainsworth (1978), Greenberg and Johnson (1985, 1988) and Marion Solomon (1994). Secure attachment in childhood is a building block for intimate relating, just as insecure attachment is a barrier for intimacy in marriage. Those who have been loved unconditionally (accepted, affirmed, empowered) in childhood will find it easier to develop close ties in marriage.

In line with this body of psychological literature is the Scripture verse, "we love because he first loved us" (1 Jn 4:19). Experiencing God's love helps us love others. Predictable, faithful love is the basis for the capacity to be predictable and faithful in loving others. Consider how important it is for parents to lovingly attend to their newborn infant. The baby feels secure when parents respond appropriately to the basic needs for nourishment, comfort, protection and bonding. When life is experienced as a trustworthy place, the secure attachment grounds a child to become a trustworthy adult.

Secure attachment is a strong predictor of healthy differentiation, just as unstable attachment predicts low levels of differentiation. Insecurely attached persons react in one of two extreme ways: either avoidance, withdrawal and disengagement or clinging, dependency and enmeshment (see chapter eight for a fuller discussion of this issue). An inability to form a healthy connection with others is quite understandable in light of childhood deficits.

A relevant example was given in chapter three about how Judy's early attachment disconnection left her with irrational fears of abandonment later in life. She was afraid she would be left behind in a busy department store, she had difficulty spending overnights with a friend, she literally clung to her mother rather than step out and trust new relationships. Her fears kept her cautious and dampened her ability to reach out to others. As an adult she found the piece to her insecurity puzzle in her mother's own words: "I am feeling so bad because little Judy [11 months old] is crying and I can't seem to comfort her." This is a crucial developmental stage, and the problem in establishing a secure attachment had resulted in a deficiency. In our early marriage, Judy's overly dependent reliance on and need for my reassurance become a burden to me and I responded with distancing maneuvers. She was looking to me (other validation) rather than developing an internal differentiation (validation in Christ). By understanding the problem, however, we have been able to rise above it. Judy addressed this deficiency by developing a differentiated self; I helped her by staying connected through a compassionate understanding of her past. This opened up the possibility of mutual love and trust.

Healing Leads to Heightened Intimacy

People bogged down by a painful past sometimes wonder if it's possible to develop an intimate relationship as an adult. Mental health professionals believe that even one meaningful relationship can make a difference in a person's life. In their research on dating couples, Hammond and Fletcher's study (1991) found that a positive relationship with a friend, therapist or mentor was enough to bridge the gap created by the old hurts. A secure relationship with one who is steadfast, sensitive and empowering can begin the important process of trusting others. We believe God uses important relationships, like marriage, to assist in the healing of childhood deficits.

Hopefully, our spouse is a person who conveys God's love to us in our physical, everyday world—being for us a "God with skin on"—and so brings positive change in our life. It is a wonderful blessing when our spouse offers a secure place of belonging. Our spouse can be a healing instrument by listening, supporting, understanding and loving us in predictable, trustworthy ways.

When someone listens to us with sensitivity, it opens the door to honest scrutiny, confession and self-disclosure. When we speak freely, even about shameful areas of pain, we become more fully known. Heightened awareness keeps us attuned to each other. The logic is simple! Strong emotional bonds increase intimate knowing. Knowing each other's emotional worlds creates secure connection.

Emotional caring begets emotional healing. Deep childhood wounds take time to heal, and when a spouse listens with empathy, speaks words of kindness and validates those childhood experiences, it truly makes a difference. It opens spouses up in a way that keeps them reaching out again and again to ultimate connection. There are many levels of self-truth, so when spouses pay attention to the brokenness, shed their masks, reveal their pain and confess their fears, it satisfies that deep yearning to be known at deeper levels.

While God is the author of healing, it's real people, in the flesh, who convey God's love.

Intimate Marriage

Thomas Oden (1974) defined intimacy as a mosaic of two persons putting together moments of personal closeness that are unique to the two of them. The heart of Christian marriage is to form a relationship bond in which "two are better than one."

Married couples sometimes lose their impetus to stay emotionally close. After the honeymoon is over it's all too easy to get caught up in the throes of everyday life. The Clinebells (1970) have identified the following areas of intimacy for a couple to enjoy in marriage:

Commitment intimacy: Ongoing growth of the relationship
Emotional intimacy: Sharing personal values, beliefs and meaning
Sexual intimacy: Sensual sexual expression and engagement
Intellectual intimacy: Exploring ideas, thoughts and opinions
Aesthetic intimacy: Sharing the arts, the beauty of nature, travel
Creative intimacy: Creating home, family, future, history, traditions
Recreational intimacy: Being playful, having fun, planning activities
Work intimacy: Common shared tasks and mutual goals
Crisis intimacy: Facing life difficulties and coping with stressors of life
Service intimacy: Dedication to common causes and giving to others
Spiritual intimacy: Involvement in faith, worship and God
Communication intimacy: Receptive listening, dialogue and understanding
Conflict intimacy: Discovering creative solutions to conflicts
Attachment intimacy: Being in tune with desires, pain and joy

Intimacy is multifaceted and expands our lives in multifaceted ways.

An accountable relationship accesses both our emotions and our minds. Spouses must understand how these two aspects fit together and need to use all their resources to develop an intimate bond. It is natural for a couple to go through a rhythm of closeness and distance in these various areas of marital intimacy, but making the investment to be intimate companions throughout life brings rich rewards.

Sexual Intimacy

Emotional intimacy is inextricably related to sexual intimacy! Since chapter twelve is entirely devoted to this topic, we simply introduce the importance of the sexual relationship to the broader intimacy principle. "Men want sexual intimacy; women want emotional intimacy." This often-quoted statement suggests that men experience closeness through the sexual encounter, while women experience closeness through emotional sharing. While it may be generally true that sexual intimacy helps men feel emotionally close, just as emotional connection opens women up to sexual intimacy, every couple must find a good balance between the two.

The one-flesh concept in Genesis is not merely a reference to genital connection, but to emotional connection as well. Couples have the best of both worlds by attending to both aspects of intimacy. Paul Ricoeur notes, "When eros is mated with tenderness and fidelity, authentic happiness and spiritual fulfillment follow" (1994, p. 73). If sex is the only emphasis and emotional and spiritual bonding is lacking, the couple ends up with a distorted intimacy. Spouses intuitively know something crucial is missing because sex alone just doesn't cut it.

Keeping both sexual and emotional intimacy alive in marriage increases the likelihood of mutual satisfaction, according to Duncombe and Marsden (1993). When women realized that erotic energy moved their spouses toward deeper emotional connection and men made a stronger link between sexual and emotional intimacy, the couple intimacy increased. Mutual interdependence has also been found to be incredibly important in all aspects of intimacy. Steil and Turetsky (1987), in a longitudinal study of 130 husbands and wives, report that equality was positively related to sexual intimacy. Rampage (1994) found that martial intimacy is most achievable when there is equality between part-

ners, empathy for each other's experience and a willingness to collaborate around both meaning and action. The ability to express a full spectrum of feelings as well as engage freely in the sexual encounter gives
the couple the best of both worlds.

A comfortable balance of being close sexually and sharing at deep
emotional levels brings couple security. In a beautiful essay titled "Sleeping like Spoons," John Giles Milhaven writes about the intimacy he feels
when he curls up with his wife at the close of the day: "Our feeling for
each other is not only sensual pleasure, but sensual trust. Wrapped together in our bodily trust we slide into the abyss" (1994, p. 89).

Spiritual Intimacy

Chapter thirteen deals in depth with marital spirituality, but here we take
a moment to consider how spiritual intimacy is an essential part of a
Christian marriage. Sacred bonding includes knowing and being known
spiritually. A profound connection is made when spouses share in the
spiritual realm. Bringing ourselves before God as a couple is a sacred
commitment to our faith.

Spouses come to know and understand themselves more fully
through the sharing of their spiritual journeys. Being open about spiritual highs as well as the lows keeps spouses in tune with one another.
Input from a spouse gives perspective in moving toward spiritual depth.
By praying for and with each other, spouses sense a tender connection.
Even in agonizing circumstances, unanswered prayer and confusion
about God's will, prayer keeps spouses united. We certainly have experienced this in our marriage and in the raising of our children. Taking
them to the Lord in prayer kept us united and gave us strength to face
the difficult times throughout our marriage. Research suggests that difficult life circumstances negatively impact the marriage relationship. However, we believe common faith keeps the couple strong when confront-
ing life's battles.

Knowing each other spiritually completes the picture of "two are better than one." At times one spouse does the praying because the other
is discouraged and vice versa. Listening to each other's spiritual perspective clarifies our own thoughts, feelings and values. In isolation there is
no solace, but through spiritual intimacy we are no longer alone.

Crisis Intimacy

One of the deepest healings in our life as a couple had to do with the untimely death of Jeff, our nine-year-old son, of bone cancer. It had all happened so fast. It started with a simple complaint of leg pain, then a visit to the pediatrician, a rushed trip to the hospital for x-rays, the discovery of a tumor, surgery the next day, a diagnosis of bone cancer, a month's treatment at NIH research center and finally the devastating blow, "There is nothing more we can do for your son." The next four months rushed by, and our hope that a miracle would bring healing was dashed: God was going to take him. Before we knew it our son had died. It was finished! We were terribly sad and lonely. We had the comfort of each other while each of us worked out grief in our unique ways. We often clung to each other in the quiet of our bedroom, drawing comfort and strength, for no one loved Jeff more than either of us. When the whole world was crashing down on us, we felt the deep presence of the Lord. Psalm 34:18 came to mind, "The LORD is near to the brokenhearted, and saves the crushed in spirit." This particular intimate moment with God brought a healing peace that was far beyond human understanding. With God as our strength and with each other by our side, we could face life together without our beloved son.

This is interdependence at its best. In such transforming moments of vulnerability, spouses take a step closer to couple connection. In a crisis it's natural to reach out to God for wisdom and comfort and to turn to each other for courage and understanding. Together, in our pain, we are brought to our knees in humble agony. Together a couple can turn to God for strength to get through the difficult time. Together a couple can receive God's gracious love and peace.

Interdependency is woven into the fabric of an intimate relationship. Giving and receiving in mutually vulnerable ways draws us deeper into God's truth. Mutual self-disclosure becomes part and parcel of relationship growth. Together spouses build a relationship that can withstand the difficulties they face in life.

LEAVING, CLEAVING AND BECOMING ONE FLESH

BEGINNING AND GROWING A MARRIAGE RELATIONSHIP involves a process full of transitions: "Therefore a man leaves his father and his mother and clings to his wife, and they become one flesh" (Gen 2:24). The three action verbs in this verse will be our point of reference in discussing the transitions from the initial *leaving* one's family of origin, into the intermediate mate selection that can be described as *cleaving,* to the eventual *becoming one flesh* in marriage.

Leaving

Genesis was written in the context of a patrilocal culture in which women left their family of origin to join the man's family. It is noteworthy that the verse indicates that the *man* is to leave mother and father. The original audience assumed the woman leaves her parents. In other words, both persons are to achieve a level of differentiation from their parents. Marital and family therapists agree that developing a healthy degree of differentiation from family of origin is a necessary step in establishing a solid marital union. Ultimately they must leave physically and emotionally so they can establish a boundary around their spousal relationship. Today loyalty for the marital union takes precedence over loyalty to family ties in Western cultures and increasingly elsewhere too. While couples honor their parents, the marital relationship is the higher priority. A couple maintains a close and responsible relationship with their parents and brings the best of both families into a distinct system of their own.

The trinitarian model is crucial in helping us understand the social processes of leaving, cleaving and becoming by which two spouses form a differentiated unity in marriage. It is so important for a couple to establish the firm foundational relational structure that promotes growth as individuals and resilience as a couple. It is also vital that we recognize the difference between relationality in the Holy Trinity and relationality in marriage. While marriage consists of two separate individuals who *become one* through their relationship, the Father, Son and Holy Spirit *are one* from the beginning (Jn 1:1-2). Nevertheless, we believe the trinitarian model of relationality—that two become one without absorption—is God's ideal for marriage.

We can also learn a great deal about God's ideal for relationality by paying attention to how God relates to us throughout the Scriptures. As we have already detailed in chapter three, God's unconditional love is freely given for us to receive. When Israel goes astray, God holds them accountable for their actions, yet continually offers a grace-filled way back through reconciliation and restoration. In a similar way, spouses who are sufficiently differentiated are able to balance unconditional love and accountability. They have the relational capacity to give and receive each other in mutual, reciprocal ways.

Cleaving

If you ask someone why he or she married their spouse, most will reply they were "in love." Given the importance of romantic love in our world today, social scientists have attempted to determine just what romantic love has to do with it. Romantic love leads to rather dramatic changes in one's character. New studies suggest that an area of the brain known as the caudate is associated with romantic passion. Neuroscientists have produced brain scan images of this fevered activity prior to long-term commitment. Brain imaging reveals that only pictures or thoughts of the object of one's desire is capable of "lighting up" certain areas of the brain. Based on these findings, Fisher, Aron, Mashek, Li and Brown (2002) suggest that what we call romantic love develops over three sequential stages, starting with *lust* (sexual drive), then *attraction* and finally *emotional attachment*. Such "falling in love" is a romantic attachment that is different from one's relationship with family or friends. It actually involves physiological changes such as the body increasing the production of hormones known as peptides, vasopressin and oxytocin (Fisher, 2002; Fisher et al., 2002). Romantic love is similar to drives like hunger, thirst or drug craving in comparison to emotional states like excitement or affection. During this intense time in life, disparate emotions may go from euphoria to anger to anxiety, and can become even more intense when it is withdrawn or rejected. As a relationship deepens, the neural activity associated with romantic love alters to long-term attachment.

One ambitious study identified three dimensions of romantic love: *commitment,* the cognitive component; *intimacy,* the friendship factor and emotional component; and *passion,* the physical motivational component (Sternberg, 1986). The corresponding biblical concepts are *agape,* self-giving covenant commitment; *philia,* a deep friendship of emotional sharing; and eros, physical desire or sexual passion (Balswick & Balswick, 2006). A generous portion and balance of all three types of love will be present in mutually reciprocating relationships.

Erich Fromm, in his book *The Art of Loving* (1956), believes that most people mistakenly refer to love in terms of being loved rather than giving love. He viewed love as an art that must be practiced through discipline, concentration, patience and supreme concern for the other. Romantic love must move from a mushy feeling in the pit of the stomach to an act of commitment, intimacy and secure bonding.

Becoming One Flesh

Sociologists use the term *assimilation* to refer to the social process of two groups or cultures becoming one, while *accommodation* refers to the social process of two cultures accepting the differences while retaining separate identities. As a social process, the trinitarian model promotes accommodation (individual distinctiveness maintained within unity) as the ideal for marriage. The metaphor of Christ as groom in relationship to the church as bride has a similar connotation. The believer becomes one with Christ yet does not lose his or her personal identity and uniqueness in the process. Rather, we are directed to be imitators of Christ as we live our unique lives in relationship to others and our world.

Therefore, becoming one involves two distinct persons forming an interdependent union. Neither spouse is to give up his or her personhood for the sake of the other because their differences are part and parcel of becoming one. Two fully developed persons show Christlike behavior by humbly expressing who they are as they each make room in themselves for their partner. Through reciprocal giving and receiving they humble themselves in mutual submission, empowerment and intimacy.

Mate Selection

Mate selection, in most modern societies, is an exquisite conscious and unconscious process in which persons select the person they eventually marry. In a self-selecting marital system the individual has the task of finding one's own mate. Since choosing a spouse is one of the most important decisions a person will make, one seeks to obtain the very best person possible. Although the criteria may differ and all sorts of unconscious needs must be factored in, each person attempts to strike the best bargain possible. Criteria should include the potential mate's degree of differentiation, which is generally possible for each partner to come to know when adequate time and attention is given to the courtship process. In addition, people looking for a mate consider many other factors. First, we will discuss important conscious factors that serve as filters in the courtship process, then unconscious factors that may be part of the attraction to a potential marriage partner.

Conscious mate selection factors. A number of conscious factors that influence mate selection can be classified as *like marrying like*. People tend to marry someone who is quite similar to them in a number of ways. *Endogamous* factors that draw people together are similar backgrounds like race, ethnicity, religion, education, occupation and geographical proximity. *Homogenous* factors that draw people together are personal characteristics and interests such as moral values, religious and political beliefs, hobbies, intelligence, height, weight and physical appearance.

Kerckhoff and Davis (1962) use *filter theory* to explain how factors of endogamy, homogony and complementary are involved at different stages of the courtship. Endogamy (similarity of background) is the initial filter; as the courtship advances, homogony (similar personal characteristics and interests) plays an important role in refining the choice.

In the advanced courtship stage, complementary needs become the final filer used to choose a mate. Most of these factors are conscious and external, but some are unconscious.

Unconscious mate selection factors. Unconscious factors in mate selection are based on the notion that *opposites attract*. Nurturing persons marry persons who need nurturing, extraverts marry introverts, and so on. Based on *complementary needs,* there seems to be an unconscious desire to find qualities in a mate that one does not possess. It's as if a person is trying to complete a perceived deficiency by choosing someone who can make up for what is lacking.

Unconscious factors having to do with family of origin dynamics are considered extremely important by marital and family systems therapists. In his book *Getting the Love You Want,* Harville Hendrix (1988) theorizes that a person chooses a mate to replicate family of origin interaction patterns. He speculates that marital choices are based on unconscious factors in which childhood strengths and deficits will be fulfilled. Therefore during courtship, people find mates who emulate qualities of those who raised us, hoping that person will compensate for childhood wounds. For example, if mother coddled her son, he will most definitely be attracted to a woman who is nurturing. However, if a wife's nurture becomes like his overprotective smothering mother, he resents it.

In general, mates are usually drawn to familiar qualities that make them comfortable with a person. I (Judy) was attracted to Jack because he was a hard worker, and I assumed he would be a faithful provider like my father. He was also a quiet, introverted person like my reserved father who never expressed his affection or affirmation. I hoped Jack would make up for this childhood deficit, but Jack, as an inexpressive male, also found it difficult to express emotional feelings. Jack, too, had expectations that I would be accepting and nonjudgmental to make up for the shaming messages from his mother. When I offered a suggestion or questioned Jack, he interpreted it as criticism. Each of us sought a mate who would fill in the gaps of our childhood, and we were disappointed when this didn't happen quite the way we hoped. However, once we were aware of these expectations, it became an impetus for differentiation and couple growth.

It has been said that you don't really know somebody until you know his or her parents. By understanding the childhood wounds that trigger reactivity, there is great potential for healing. Having compassion can give spouses an opportunity to behave differently than the parents. Although we can't make up for the childhood pain, showing empathy for past hurts can promote healing. Mutual awareness, attention and validation are powerful connectors that empower spouses to move beyond the old wounds and develop new patterns of relating. Change happens! It's a matter of responding out of genuine care.

Six in the Marriage Bed

What a strange idea! What is meant by "six in the marriage bed" is that all four parents enter the marriage in the sense that each spouse's relationship with their parents is deeply imprinted on them. Family-of-origin influences, messages, attitudes, beliefs and values seep into our hearts and minds. Our perspective is shaped by family background, cultural heritage, religious persuasions, experiences in childhood, and parental and sibling relationships.

Spouses who have a good relationship with their parents and siblings enter marriage with a fairly clean slate and little emotional baggage to bog them down. Yet no one has a perfect childhood, and family relationship dynamics will become part of every couple encounter. Earlier we gave the example of how I (Judy) expected Jack to meet my unfulfilled emotional needs. These expectations left Jack feeling inadequate. It wasn't until I dealt with my own father issues in therapy that our relationship dynamics improved. In time I was able to speak directly to my father about my hurt feelings, which freed me from the bitterness that had haunted me for years. This healing led to a more differentiated self, which opened up doors for Jack to relate from his true self, rather than trying to make up for past deficits that belonged to my father.

Boundaries

Appropriate boundaries around the marital relationship help establish the spousal relationship while maintaining a respectful relationship with in-laws. Some parents make demands that undermine the newly established unit. If a spouse cleaves to his or her family of origin it can wreak havoc on the marriage.

Is this really about me or your mother? a spouse may sometimes rightfully wonder. It may surprise us when our spousal relationship triggers something from our past relationship with a mother or father. When a husband feels belittled, slumps his shoulders and shrinks in a corner during a marital argument, you can picture a little boy being scolded by a mother. Or when a wife rages in retort to the suggestion by her husband that she is overspending, you see a little girl who reverts back to a memory of her father expecting her to order the lowest priced item on the menu. The extreme reactivity gives a huge clue that family of origin dynamics are involved. It takes a great deal of emotional, intellectual and spiritual maturity to stay connected with one's family while keeping healthy boundaries around the spousal dyad.

Cast of Characters: Multidimensional Roles

The roles spouses play are multidimensional. Marriage is a stage on which an entire cast of our internal characters performs. We introduce the concept of a cast of characters to identify the aspects of the personality within each spouse. For over thirty years in clinical practice, I (Judy) have found it helpful to think about the complex pattern of internal parts within each spouse. Recognizing the complex multiplicity of the mind, Richard Schwartz (1995) has defined three categories of parts that he refers to as *managers, exiles* and *firefighters*. In addition, I have identified a category of *resilient* parts that aid a person. The *leader* (differentiated self) coordinates and directs these parts that make up the core of one's being. *Exile* parts have to do with childhood wounds such as hurts, fears and anger. The *manager* parts try to divert the pain of the exiles by functioning in superhuman ways. They look very competent and together on the outside but they can be judgmental and critical. The *firefighter* parts attempt to distract from or numb the painful parts (exiles) by various means such as food, alcohol or drugs, overwork, sleep and so on. The *resilient* parts (wise, spiritual, courageous) bring perspective and resources to counteract the extreme behaviors.

Since each spouse carries family-of-origin dynamics into marriage, an extreme reaction to one's spouse means he or she has most likely triggered something painful in one's childhood experiences. Our manager parts function to protect these vulnerable childhood wounds by keeping them at bay and taking charge of things. They put on an external front that disguises the underlying pain. Until there is healing of past wounds, however, this disguise will be ineffective. For example, when wounded parts (exiles) emerge, they need to be acknowledged, addressed, understood and comforted. In marriage, if there is no understanding of these parts, spouses tend to react emotionally with anger, accusation and blaming, which only escalates misunderstanding, distrust and distance.

Acknowledging these complex internal parts helps spouses take responsibility for their own cast of characters, allowing their differentiated self to take leadership of the parts. The internal work is to create balance and harmony within, so one interacts with one's spouse as a clearly defined self. When both spouses are in tune with their internal parts, they can share these deeper parts of themselves with each other. This brings intimacy because it allows for compassionate understanding. The goal is for two differentiated selves to share and relate "I" to "I."

In childhood, most of us feel overwhelmed by the big people in our lives. Common themes include abandonment, incompetence, inferiority, not being fully loved, engulfment, coercion or abuse. When a spouse has a strong emotional reaction to his or her partner, we can be assured that he or she has encountered internal wounds. Most of us are aware of the little boy or little girl part that has been carefully tucked deep down inside. And these exiles (wounded parts) come out at the most unsuspecting times. Often triggered by fear, distrust, sadness or a sense of being overwhelmed, under stress these parts come to the forefront in more extreme forms of emotional reactivity or silent withdrawals.

Identifying internal parts increases spouses' ability to address the pain from the past, gain insight and provide a place to sort out the emotional upheaval. Spouses who share and listen to each other with compassion will help soothe the wounds of the past and provide new experiences of healing. A differentiated spouse has the capacity to be responsive rather than reactive. A husband can remain steady during a wife's emotional outburst because he does not take it personally and can respond with appropriate empathy and connection. He becomes a calming presence by responding with a comment such as, "I didn't mean to be critical, but what I said evidently struck a chord deep inside that opened up a deep hurt. How can I understand what that pain is about?" In a relationship sense, trust is being established because the spouse has shown an interest in what contributed to his wife's pain. Because he is able to stay emotionally connected rather than backing away or retorting with a defensive remark, he becomes part of the healing process.

Being aware of the cast of characters in yourself and your partner can provide insight into internal parts that trigger negative or positive responses in the relationship. As one develops a more clearly differentiated self, one learns to soothe and center oneself and so can act in balanced and responsible ways. Being differentiated means one is not only aware of the parts and the extreme reactivity, but is also able to draw on internal resources and calm oneself. By understanding and monitoring the more extreme parts, one learns to lead with a solid, differentiated self. A differentiated spouse no longer needs to blame the partner or needs the soothing of the partner, for he or she has taken full responsibility for self. The relationship is a secure place of belonging in which personal sharing of past pains has become part of the healing process. Clearing out past baggage allows for more compassion, connection and communion in the interdependency of the union. No longer do spouses expect to fix or fill or heal the other, but the interaction proves to be a healing balm.

Now both spouses see themselves and each other in a less extreme way (when parts were so pronounced) because they are balanced within themselves. Their differentiated self is able to acknowledge the extreme reactivity of internal parts without being overwhelmed or acting out. The spouse is able to show compassion for their own parts without moving to extreme measures. In fact, they gain perspective by paying attention to all their parts, discover ways to diminish the extreme aspects and temper them with resilient resources for a balanced response. Resourcing the internal spiritual parts and looking to external resources in the Godhead, spouses are differentiated in Christ.

By tuning in to each other's inner parts, one can more easily share experiences, memories, sufferings and struggles. Through these respective experiences, spouses are understood and validated at the core of their being, fostering authenticity of self as well as intimate connection. When both spouses are differentiated in Christ, they have so much more to offer their one-flesh union. Developing internal and external resources creates a spiritual interdependence that becomes a place of personal inner healing and relational healing.

Parents as Role Models

Spouses naturally implement styles of relating derived from their families of origin. A good predictor of how well a person will be able to get along with a spouse is the nature of his or her parents' marriage. Children learn how to be a husband or wife by watching their parents in this role.

Modeled behavior is a strong conditioner. If a mother expressed strong anger toward her husband, a daughter will be inclined to lash out in a similar way. The husband who sees his father being inconsiderate will most likely behave in a similar manner. Without being fatalistic, we believe that recognizing these tendencies can help spouses resist repeating these patterns. Defeatist remarks such as, "My wife wants me to communicate about my feelings, but I'm an introvert like my Dad," keep one stagnated and controlled by these beliefs. Awareness is the key to making a concerted and conscious effort to change for the sake of the new relationship.

Spousal Roles

Shakespeare said the whole world is a stage, and we all have our entrances and exits as players upon it. Marriage is a stage on which each spouse learns to play a role in relationship to the other. The concept of marital roles is useful because it provides a way to conceptualize marital unity without forfeiting individual uniqueness. A role is *anticipated* (role taking), *learned* (playing at a role) and *played* (role playing).

Role taking. Before two people marry, they formulate in their minds a role for themselves and for their spouse. They engage in role taking by anticipating the role they will assume after they marry. In fact, we fantasize a great deal about what it will be like to be married to a particular person. Expectations are set up as we create imagined roles in our mind. One of the adjustments early in marriage is to understand the roles anticipated by your spouse.

Playing at a role. Once married, spouses assume the roles they imagined prior to the wedding. *Playing at a role* is the self-conscious beginning of actual role-playing. How well we remember attending a small church just three days after we were married and were completely caught off guard when asked to introduce ourselves to the entire congregation. Without thinking, Judy reverted to her maiden name rather than her newly acquired married name, while Jack quickly explained to a befuddled crowd that we had "just gotten married." We play at a role over and over again as each new situation presents itself, for instance, becoming a provider or a parent or a stepparent. When we finally assume the role, we discover it's quite different from what we imagined. We begin marriage by playing at a role until we eventually become more spontaneous in that identity. It is always awkward when first learning the new role, but over time we become comfortable and natural with our roles.

Role making. The role of husband or wife is objectively defined by one's spouse, family, church, community and society at large. However, the role is subjectively defined by the person experiencing and performing the role as well. There is rarely a one-to-one correlation between these two definitions. Spouses play out the role of husband or wife according to their own distinctive taste and style; thus all role playing is also *role making* since each individual acts out his or her role in a unique way. In healthy marriage each spouse creates a uniquely personal role that is congruent with the couple's sense of God's intended purpose in their marriage.

Role Conflict

Since expectations do not always match reality, there can be role conflict in any stage of marriage. Differing preconceived definitions and expectations are likely to bring conflict. Being emotionally attached to the fantasy we hoped for means we must deal with disappointment. A husband may enter marriage assuming he will never be expected to scrub out a toilet while the wife considers this part and parcel of his role in the home. Similarly, a wife may assume she will be responsible for managing the budget the way her mother always did, but the husband expects it to be part of his role.

Role conflicts can become a serious area of disruption in marriage.

However, couples who are able to make adaptations by adjusting the fantasy role to a reality-based role will be able to resolve differences quite easily. Role conflicts serve as refining tools toward a mutually co-operative mode of operation that enhances the relationship.

Marital roles, unlike dramatic roles, are dynamic and ever changing. Role definitions appropriate in the beginning stages of marriage may become outmoded two or three years later. In the daily act of meshing spousal roles together, the couple is responsible for updating roles to be in the best interest of the relationship as they navigate changes throughout the life cycle.

The most troublesome adjustments have to do with dissatisfaction with a role or responsibility. Consequences for everyone concerned must be considered all along the way. At one time things may be going smoothly, while the next year circumstances make it rocky. The stepfamily may work out nicely in the beginning, but confrontations with an ex-spouse can quickly change things. It's always back to the drawing board to consider new solutions.

Role Flexibility

Marital trouble will surely occur if either spouse holds to a rigid definition of what the other's role should be. Modifying role expectations honors personal differences and preferences so spouses are free to develop roles that suit them. This, in turn, contributes to relationship unity. Flexibility is absolutely necessary! Circumstances may be such that one spouse intentionally chooses to forego his or her own personal needs out of concern for the other. Such a decision clearly indicates that one is differentiated in Christ. The spouse is not just thinking about or defending self, but looking toward the good of the spouse and the marriage.

Each spouse can derive satisfaction with chosen roles especially if they know changes will be made according to the relationship needs. One spouse does not have to be stuck in a particular way of doing things because routine evaluation is part of the bargain. In this arrangement, there are no hidden agendas or built up resentments. Out of their commitment to the relationship the healthy couple will be open to each other to make changes as needed.

Discerning of God's Will

Mate selection quite clearly includes an incredible mixture of conscious and unconscious factors. In terms of biblical faith, we believe that God is at work in this process as well. Marriage is pivotal to the psychological well-being of individuals, the social well-being of family life, the economic well-being of communities and the well-being of society itself. Therefore, taking marriage seriously means the Christian will also want to discern God's will.

Three guidelines are helpful in seeking God's direction about marriage. First, seek God's will directly through prayer, biblical truth and reflection as a couple. Second, seek premarital counseling. David Olson's "PREPARE/ENRICH" (Olson & Olson, 1999) inventory identifies couple strengths and weaknesses; the relationship areas of personality differences, family of origin dynamics, communication and conflict patterns; and compatibility in terms of finances, parenting, sexual, social and couple expectations. It has proven to be 80-85% accurate in predicting couples that eventually divorce (Fowers, Montel & Olson, 1996). Third, seek affirmation from your family, friends and faith community. Those who know your strengths and weaknesses can give honest feedback and wisdom that will be invaluable to you.

Discerning the will of God can be likened to bringing a boat safely into harbor in the dead of the night. When the captain was asked how he knew where to enter, he explained about the three guiding lights into the harbor. "When they are all lined up in a row, I confidently sail right in!" When the couple's spiritual and personal discernment line up with premarital counseling factors and with affirmation by family, friends and faith community, the couple can proceed with assurance.

8

DIFFERENTIATED UNITY

WEAVING TWO LIVES TOGETHER INTO A THREEFOLD CORD with Christ at the center is the ultimate goal of differentiated unity:

> Two are better than one, because they have a good reward for their toil. For if they fall, one will lift up the other; but woe to one who is alone and falls and does not have another to help. Again, if two lie together, they keep each other warm; but how can one keep warm alone? And though one might prevail against another, two will withstand one. A threefold cord is not quickly broken. (Eccles 4:9-12)

Spouses offer themselves to each other to form a sacred union that is not easily broken when grounded in biblical faith. Through mutual support and empowerment they discover the delicate balance between separateness and togetherness. Equal partnership is pivotal to harmonious interdependence. It's impossible to achieve this goal without sufficient personal differentiation.

In a trinitarian model of marriage, *differentiated unity* is not only warranted by a theological interpretation of Genesis, but also by the New Testament and the teachings of Jesus in particular. Here are a few of the many proclamations by Jesus that aptly point to the differentiated unity of the Godhead:

> "You know neither me nor my Father. If you knew me, you would know my Father also." (Jn 8:19)

> "The Father and I are one." (Jn 10:30)

> "But if I do [the works of my Father], even though you do not believe me, believe the works, so that you may know and understand that the Father is in me and I am in the Father." (Jn 10:38)

"Whoever believes in me believes not in me but in him who sent me. And whoever sees me sees him who sent me." (Jn 12:44-45)

"If you know me, you will know my Father also. From now on you do know him and have seen him." (Jn 14:7)

"Whoever has seen me has seen the Father. How can you say, 'Show us the Father'? Do you not believe that I am in the Father and the Father is in me?" (Jn 14:9-10).

Jesus likewise points to the believer's relationship with God as a differentiated unity. He prays "that they may be one. As you, Father, are in me and I am in you, may they also be in us" (Jn 17:21). Unlike salvation in eastern mysticism, the human self continues to exist as a differentiated self.

Differentiation describes a person who has a clear sense of self and the maturity to form an effective interdependent relationship. Paradoxically, the more spouses know themselves as distinctly different, the greater their capacity for intimate connection. Sometimes described as "self in relation," differentiation is to be distinguished from independence (which implies one does not need to depend on others) or overdependence (which implies one is fused with others).

A Self in Relation

Being a self in relation is a key concept in the trinitarian model of marriage. Uniquely created by God, each spouse is an individual in his or her own right who is accountable to God. The Holy Spirit indwells each spouse, empowering each to develop a character and meaning that is unique to him or her. Created to be in relationship, two unique spouses form an interdependent union in which they also develop meaning as a couple.

In order to be sufficiently differentiated, one must have a clearly defined "self." Becoming a differentiated self is a lifelong process that occurs in the context of our most intimate relationships. In marriage each spouse brings their personal resources into the union to work together for the good of the whole. In her book *An Unfinished Marriage,* Joan Anderson (2002) puts it this way: "It's through trial and error, yielding and resisting, retracing and reinventing, dependence and interdependence we assemble our lives together. Love's deep realization is in the growing, struggling, longing and reaching toward what is possible and living fully in the here and now" (p. 138).

Differentiated in Christ

When we use the idea of being differentiated in Christ, we mean that each spouse centers his or her life in Christ and attempts to live according to biblical truth. Therefore, our actions are determined by obedience to Christ rather than defined by culture, family or even one's spouse. We are accountable to God for our actions and strive to live according to God's word to the best of our ability. Being ever aware of our human proneness to sin, we acknowledge our dependence on God alone to accomplish this. We are a work in process, eagerly looking for God to grow us into maturity as a Christian husband or wife. Lewis Smedes, in his book *Love Within Limits* (1978), makes the following observation on the statement in 1 Corinthians 13:4 that love is not jealous:

> Jealousy becomes the more cruel the more intense are the expectations of eros and the threats to its fulfillment. If we have nothing else in the world to live for but our lover, we are vulnerable to the worst fits of jealousy. The person who tells someone else, "I can't live without you," is threatened at his deepest selfhood when the one with whom he cannot live without has to be shared in the *smallest* way. Such a person always suspects the worst, and this very suspicion prods him to cruel reaction. Agapic love is the power to diminish the pain of jealousy because it keeps us from expecting too much from another finite person. Agape does not let us give our souls to idols, not even to the idol of the ideal husband or wife or friend. Agape keeps eros from expecting everything in this life. So agape will not let us be so deeply threatened that our very existence seems at stake. (p. 26)

Being dependent on Christ alleviates an overdemanding concentration on the spouse to meet our needs. Colossians 3:2-3 reminds us, "Set your minds on things that are above, not on things that are on earth, for you have died, and your life is hidden with Christ in God." In a spiritual sense, we surrender our will to the will of God when Christ is the center. Being a child of God is our core identity and therefore we embrace the notion that "he must increase, but I must decrease" (Jn 3:30). Being differentiated in Christ means we are focused on God's validation and less focused on our spouse's validation.

God Validation

Our validation is gauged in terms of pleasing God rather than pleasing self or spouse. It's easy to lose perspective when our validation is centered on our spouse rather than God. When we are overly invested in spousal validation we become entrapped and reactive to their responses. When we are so externally focused on spousal approval we have less ability to make room for them internally. In contrast, when both spouses are ultimately invested in what God wants for their relationship, they are more open to their spouses as well.

It's not that we take self completely out of the formula! In 1 John 4:7-21 we read that we are to love others because God first loved us. Without an awareness of self it is virtually impossible to give up the self for the sake of others. Being differentiated in Christ means each spouse holds on to convictions they believe are right according to the Bible. We are willing to challenge each other about things that are contrary to God's best for the relationship. It requires a strong, healthy self to stand up as well as give up self for differentiated unity. Being differentiated in Christ keeps us dependent on God to live out covenant love, grace, empowerment and intimacy in marriage. Once we are no longer enslaved by self-focus or other-focus, we are able to be God- and relationship-focused.

The couple has the greatest potential for achieving spiritual and relational unity when both spouses are centered in Christ. The highest goal of mutual covenant is to draw upon God's spirit for relationship strength. During inevitable struggles spouses ask God to calm their fears, to keep them from defensive reactivity and to keep them persistent in their mutual covenant commitment. Being anchored in Christ means they can tolerate personal anxiety in order to stay connected during conflicts. Spouses seek the help of the Holy Spirit to resist self-centered tendencies in order to achieve mutually satisfying outcomes. Differentiated spouses listen wholeheartedly to each other's unique perspective by setting aside personal agendas. Honest self-disclosure brings vitality, and collaboration brings hope. Differentiated unity is the culmination of two authenticated differentiated selves becoming one. Grounded in Christ, harmony is a reward that passes human understanding.

Family of Origin Differentiation

Murray Bowen emphasized that every person needs to be *emotionally* differentiated from one's parents so he or she can maintain a healthy balance of individuality (separateness) and togetherness (connectedness) in marriage (Bowen, 1978; Kerr & Bowen, 1988). In fact, this tension of individuality and togetherness is an ongoing critical task throughout each stage of marriage. Interdependency is accomplished by acknowledging individual perspectives while remaining emotionally connected as the couple forms a united stance.

Each family, in a sense, hopes their son or daughter will ensure that their family traditions are carried on. Parents may even become rivals over whether their children will carry on the important family, cultural and religious values they have ingrained in them. It is natural that parents are invested in having their legacy passed down through the next generations. It becomes a matter of family loyalty! For example, Swedish parents may accuse their adult son of disloyalty when he marries an Italian woman who serves a pasta dinner instead of the traditional smorgasbord for Christmas. The challenge for the couple is to differentiate from their family of origin in such a way that they blend the best of both cultures into their unique union, while adding their own touches along the way.

During stress in their relationship, it is typical for spouses to revert back to the familiar ways of their family of origin. Spouses simply repeat what worked for them as a child, whether it was to withdraw, manipulate, pout, scream or control. Understanding family of origin dynamics will help spouses see how they bring less than perfect childhoods into the marriage. Whether our childhood experiences are positive or negative, it's crucial that spouses understand their origins. Marriage can either be a source of healing for childhood wounds or a place of rewounding. By telling our childhood stories, our spouse is able to enter the other's world of hurts and confusion, and it becomes an opportunity for healing and differentiation.

After several years of marriage, Regina finally broke down after an unsuccessful attempt at sexual intercourse. She began to tell Chris about the abuse she had suffered as a child. Would he blame her for her uncle's action? Would he think less of her? Would he reject her or find her undesirable now? These fears ran through her mind, but she reminded herself that Chris had proven over and over his unfailing love. She risked divulging her secrets through agonizing tears. Chris was angry about what had happened to his beloved wife, but kept his feelings to a minimum so he could listen to her story of horror. He never loved her more. Utmost in his mind was how to support her through this deep pain in her soul. In this moment, Chris held on to himself (differentiation) in a way that promoted healing. Over time, Regina found release from the shackles of the past trauma in the safety of Chris's love and acceptance. His ability to stay differentiated and not be emotionally reactive made room for her to grow in personal differentiation. This, in turn, deepened the trust and intimacy and increased the sexual and emotional satisfaction in their marriage.

God can use the marriage relationship as a tremendous healing force. No earthly relationship has more potential for transformation than marriage. When we are sufficiently differentiated, we can be a comforting presence in the midst of past wounds. An undifferentiated husband may have lost the opportunity to serve as an agent of healing by giving in to his feelings of rage. That would surely distance him from his wife who needed to feel safe to tell her story. In this case Chris provided a safe environment by being fully present to her in the moment. This enabled Regina to open up her heart without hesitation.

Levels of Spousal Differentiation

Behind the "two are better than one" Scripture is the idea that two independent persons have unique strengths to offer each other and the relationship. Humanly speaking, when two people are overly dependent on each other, they fail to develop aspects of themselves. Settling for dependency, one fails to grow. Of course, temporary dependency is another matter altogether. There are times when dependency is necessary due to unique circumstances. But generally, it balances out over a lifetime.

The level of spousal differentiation has an impact on the quality of the marriage. High levels of individual differentiation result in high marital differentiated unity. Likewise, low levels of individual differentiation will result in low levels of marital quality.

As illustrated in table 8.1, level of self-differentiation is represented on a curvilinear continuum ranging from low at the left, high in the middle, to low at the right. This means that low self-differentiation comes in two types: at the extreme left is the *disengaged* self with an independent relationship style. This person has a protected self that disconnects from others. Closed boundaries result in a fortressed self. Due to low ego strength, this person is self-centered and relies upon narcissistic validation. In its extreme form this person presents in a self-confident way that borders on cockiness. In reality this is a misleading portrayal since underneath the person is actually insecure.

Table 8.1. The Curvilinear Dimensions of Self-Differentiation

Level of Self-Differentiation		
LOW ⟵——————— HIGH ————————⟶ LOW		
Self/Other Relationship		
Disengaged Self	Congruent Self	Enmeshed Self
Style of Relating		
Independent	Interdependent	Dependent
Boundaries		
Closed	Strong, yet Permeable	Weak or Nonexistent
Source of Validation		
Narcissistic Validation	God/Self Validation	Other Validation
Ego Strength		
Selfish	Unselfish	Selfless

Represented on the extreme right in the continuum is the *enmeshed* self with a dependent relationship style. Such persons have a fragile self that gains validation through the opinions others have of them. They become dependent on others for definition and therefore their boundaries are wide open. This person readily allows others to invade their space. Low ego strength shows itself in selfless actions that accommodate others. In exact contrast to the independent attitude, this person has a clinging personality, latching on to others for the ego strength they lack.

The person with a highly differentiated self is represented in the center of table 8.1. This person possesses a *congruent* self and is comfortably assertive and outgoing. He or she has no desire to withdraw from others or any need to fuse with others. This person has an interdependent style of relating, choosing collaborative interaction rather than relying solely on self or others. The self has strong, yet permeable boundaries, allowing for self-care while still being open for engaging others. Drawing upon self-/God-validation, the person with a high degree of differentiation is internally rather than externally validated. Sufficient ego strength allows this person to act unselfishly towards others.

In presenting this chart, we have described stereotypes of polar opposites. Our composite descriptions are obviously over the top, and we contend that most people are actually somewhere in between, working toward the middle. Now we focus on three different types of low-differentiated marriages and then on the well-differentiated congruent marriage.

The Enmeshed Marriage: A Delusion of Fusion

Marriages in which both partners have enmeshment tendencies end in spousal fusion. Some hold to the false notion that dependency is ideal, the idea that I need you to be whole. Actually, clinging to a spouse because you aren't able to stand on your own two feet weakens the relationship. When partners look to each other to complete themselves, the tendency is to hang on to each other for dear life. Depending on the spouse for strength weakens one's ability to develop personal strength. Rather than growing into two whole persons who contribute to the union, they lean on each other for wholeness. It is tempting to romanticize with comments like "we can't live without each other." Yet in reality both spouses in such a relationship are underdeveloped.

Recall, for example, how in our early marriage the human insecurity in Jack and in me kept us overly dependent upon each other. In a social situation for instance, I used my social skills in a way that kept Jack totally dependent upon me. I felt smug about his needing me, but under closer scrutiny we both realized we had created a counterfeit security. Unfortunately, mutual dependency tends to move us to use power *over* our spouse. Out of the desire to be needed, we keep our spouse dependent rather than helping him or her become competent.

During the courtship dance, lovers take intense delight in losing themselves in each other. It's quite natural to be completely absorbed in each other's lives, soaking up the undivided attention during the initial coupling stage. This fantasy fusion does not last long, however, for soon the unique personalities become apparent as one progresses in the relationship. By acknowledging and appreciating their differences, they make room for the unique self of the other as they progress beyond the courtship dance.

In second marriages, persons also enjoy the romantic aspects of getting to know each other. The second adolescent "being in love" charm and candlelight dinners don't last long before reality sets in, though. Soon the couple gets down to the brass tacks of living together. There are many areas to negotiate, such as finances, children, in-laws, career and household considerations, which very quickly become part of their lives. When both partners have achieved a mature level of differentiation, they can be more forthright about their limitations as well as their strengths. There is less chance they will be overly dependent and fused at this point in their lives.

A good friend of ours who recently married for a second time at the age of sixty told us about the day she met with her intended on the beach. They each had a list of what they wanted the other to know about themselves before they married. Back and forth it went, "I can be a real witch! . . . I'm hard to get along with at times. . . . I have very strong opinions. . . . I'm not ready to give up my career. . . . Our children need to approve. . . . I'm a grouch before I have my cup of coffee in the morning. . . ." They were entering marriage as two strongly defined persons forming a covenant of interdependency.

The Disengaged Marriage: A Misfortunate Misconnection

Marriage between two persons who tend toward disengagement will find intimate connection difficult. In a marriage between disengaged spouses, for example, self-sufficiency keeps them working independently side-by-side rather than toward an interdependency. It should be noted that the disengaged marriage is the norm in some cultures (societies that promote marriage as an institution).

In the case of the disengaged marriage, spouses will need—for the sake of the relationship—to stretch beyond their natural tendencies to be separate. It was normal for Bill to distance himself from any inkling of dependency in his new marriage. He had learned to keep himself removed from his family members and friends most of his life. He was intelligent and successful according to outward standards of success, but when it came to relationships he was superficial. Although he enjoyed the sexual relationship, he did not allow himself to be emotionally vulnerable. He married Sophie, a young woman shy by nature, who had developed a self-sufficient internal life that kept her removed and sometimes aloof in her relationships.

The two didn't demand much of each other in terms of emotional intimacy, but if they were honest both could admit feeling lonely in their marriage. Neither had very much connection with their family of origin, and there were no models in the family to help them learn how to make significant emotional connection. Due to their dissatisfaction in their relationship they sought help in therapy. Being willing to risk asking more from themselves and each other, they faced their fears about being emotionally close. As they developed safety in their relationship, they could admit distancing maneuvers and could make intentional choices to increase their emotional connection.

The Polarized Marriage: Codependency

Polarized marriage takes place between persons with low levels of differentiation who are at opposite ends of the continuum, that is, the spouse who needs to be cared for marries one who wants to be a caregiver. Thus, spouses who have a tendency toward disengagement and fusion marry each other, forming a codependent relationship. It may appear to be a perfectly complementary union, but due to each spouse's low level of differentiation things are more complicated than that. The underdeveloped and overdeveloped selves feed off each other in order to feel complete.

Sheila, who wants to be cared for, looks to Steve, the caregiver, to meet all her needs. While confident in the role of caretaker, protector and provider, he is incompetent when it comes to satisfying her emotional dependency needs. These voids leave a huge breach between them. Sheila feels rejected and Steve feels inadequate, weakening their marriage. What they each need is a good dose of differentiation! Sheila must develop skills so she can take care of herself, while Steve needs to develop emotional strengths to fill out his deficits.

There is a certain degree of deception during courtship as both mates put their best foot forward to the extent each can portray a false self that is quite different from the real self. For example, Jose and Juanita presented themselves as self-assured in courtship. Juanita was attracted to Jose because he exuded confidence, while he was impressed with her level of self-sufficiency. Underneath Jose was actually quite insecure and Juanita quite dependent. Each of them was looking to the other to make up for their own weaknesses. You might say they fell in love with the other's false public self rather than their real self, each hoping to draw strength from the other. After marriage, they were forced to get beyond the external presentation and confront their real selves.

It is an illusion to think that the spouse can make up for one's weakness. In some codependent marriages it can be very difficult for either spouse to acknowledge his or her weaknesses. So both continue to live the illusion of their false selves, never admitting their polarized positions. A marriage based upon polarized codependency sinks under the strain. Grabbing on to each other for wholeness puts the relationship in an extremely precarious place. Both spouses must build personal strengths and balance their resources as a couple, so they stand firmly on the solid ground of interdependency.

The Congruent Marriage: A Differentiated Unity

In the congruent marriage, our internal and external resources keep us strong in the joys and torrents of married life. Differentiated spouses have the extra reserves and perspective to create a reciprocating interdependency. By being solidly grounded as spouses and as a couple, they confidently keep their relationship on higher ground.

Of course, there is no such thing as two perfectly differentiated persons. Even in the best circumstances of growing up and developing a mature self, differentiation is an ongoing process throughout our lives. God created us to be in a marriage where both spouses are continually transformed and differentiated through the intensity and intimacy of marriage.

Making secure but permeable boundaries is a mark of differentiated unity. Mature spouses show deep regard for each other's personal boundaries without intruding or distancing. They modify behavior as needed to respect personal boundaries and also carefully guard the boundary around their relationship as a couple.

Facing each other for real, in a real-life marriage, means spouses are willing to tackle real issues head on. Their covenant commitment means they solemnly refuse to duck out of their responsibilities of mutual regard when the going gets tough. As disillusionments pop up along the way, they face their struggles and hardships by joining forces to persevere through the thick and thin of marriage. Differentiated spouses seek to be mate-worthy. Each pays attention to the unique needs of his or her spouse, knowing this is the most effective way to make meaningful connection. Being oriented to the "other" expands their possibilities. Below is a summary of what it means to form a differentiated unity in marriage.

DIFFERENTIATED UNITY

We have a separate identity in Christ.
We have high regard for self, spouse and the relationship.
We seek God-validation as opposed to self- or spousal-validation.
We express ourselves honestly and directly.
We earnestly listen to and take each other seriously.
We choose interdependency rather than dependency or independency.

Deciding to be the right partner is a sign of differentiation. It takes a great deal of maturity to be a self-giving spouse. Being differentiated in

Christ means we choose to live the exceptional life of selflessness. We practice self-giving love by going the second mile and turning the other cheek. Our character is formed as we are transformed by the Holy Spirit who empowers us to be the spouses God wants us to be.

Actually, marriage can be a sanctifying experience, as we will suggest in chapter fourteen. None of us enters marriage as fully mature persons, but we are challenged to grow in the context of this intense relationship. The ultimate goal is to fit our lives together outwardly and inwardly after God's way. In marriage, God sharpens and matures us as we serve and empower each other into a differentiated unity that brings out the best in each other. Because God has created us for a special purpose as a couple, we take delight in accomplishing that purpose. The incentive is to live for the Lord, to reach our God-given potential and to seek the Lord's will for our life.

Spouses grow by keeping their individual lives and couple relationship strong in Christ. In the next two chapters we offer practical advice on two crucial ways spouses build a differentiated unity through communication and conflict resolution.

COMMUNICATION, CONNECTION, COMMUNION

IN A BEAUTIFULLY WRITTEN PASSAGE, Elizabeth O'Connor (1987) expresses the essence of communication: "The deepest craving of every heart is to be laid bare, to be known, to be understood. . . . If ever we take the time to know another life, we will be experienced as godly—as one 'who cares.' When we are listened to and understood, the clouds roll back, the dawn breaks, Christ comes" (p. 40). Communication is so much more than learning a few techniques—it's about truly listening and being understood. Ultimately, spousal bonding occurs in the mutual vulnerability of self-disclosure, emotional sharing and compassionate understanding. As spouses make room in themselves for each other (indwelling), they become known in the Christlike presence of their beloved.

The mutual indwelling of the members of the Godhead models synchronous communication, connection and communion. The Holy Spirit is the breath of God indwelling the Son. The Father sends the Holy Spirit in the form of a dove as a blessing descending on the Son. In anticipation of his death on the cross, Jesus communicates his agony to the Father in the garden and then, in the next breath, submits to the Father's will: "yet not what I want, but what you want" (Mt 26:39). The Spirit raises Christ in victory over death, and the Son joins Abba Father in eternity. The communion between the members of the Trinity is foundational to oneness.

In a similar way, spousal interaction takes the couple beyond the narrow lens of two separate persons into a deeper one-flesh unity. Through communicating and listening to each other, they make a place in their heart for emotional connection. We challenge couples to move beyond communication patterns that distort understanding and cause distance. Creating communication habits that enhance connection and enliven communion is what this chapter is about.

Dying to Self

When we asked our friends Gene and Virginia Lowe the secret of their fifty-year marriage, Gene teased, "You have to be willing to give up!" We laughed a little about the way his answer could be interpreted, but his statement was actually quite profound. This is exactly what it takes to be a good communicator! While it's never easy to die to self, it's the secret to listening with wholehearted attention. Our covenant vows provide impetus for sacrificing self for the good of the relationship.

Philippians 2 describes Christ as emptying himself and taking on the form of a servant. In the same way, spouses can choose to go this second mile. They empty themselves by putting their own agenda on the back burner so they can remain calm and stay emotionally connected during their encounter. In an act of conscious submission, they devote themselves to a relationship-centered marriage.

Kegan (1994) explains how we can do this even in the midst of emotional turmoil. The point is to understand what is being said without moving away from our spouse emotionally.

> We can provide company to our partners in their unhappiness or discontent (even their unhappiness or discontent with us) because at some level we are aware that our closeness to them does not require us to be made up by their experiences ("I am not her experience"), and at some level they are aware that the other is the maker of her own experience ("she is not made up by her experience"). (p. 127)

The point is that when we die to self, we have a deeper capacity to be present to our spouse. We do not take on our spouse's experiences or emotions, but respectfully listen in a way that brings clarity and hope.

Spouses draw close through open and vulnerable interaction. Sensitive listening and the ability to understand how things look from the spouse's point of view promote understanding. Elizabeth O'Connor puts it this way:

Dialogue is more than your giving me space to say my words, and my giving you space to say yours. It involves our listening. We are all very different. We cannot have dialogue unless we honor the differences. How can I build a bridge across the gulf between me and you unless I am aware of the gulf? How can I communicate with you unless I see how things look from your side? Dialogue demands that I leave the place where I dwell—the landscape of feelings and thoughts that are important to me in order to dwell for a time with your thoughts, feelings, perceptions, fears, hopes. I must deny myself—forsake the familiar, give up my life—in order to experience your life. (O'Connor, 1987, pp. 39-40)

Differentiation *and* Emotional Bonding: Two Sides of the Same Coin

Strong marriages are founded on both differentiation and emotional bonding. To ask which is more important in marriage is like asking if the right or the left wing of an airplane is more important. We believe differentiation opens up the deepest possibilities of emotional intimacy, while emotional bonding establishes the greatest possibilities of becoming a differentiated self.

The "two are better than one" passage indicates how differentiation and emotional connection are two sides of the same coin. When one spouse is floundering, the other is steady; when one is sad, the other brings comfort; when one is battling a demon, the other brings hope. When Vanessa is shaking with fear, Jerry offers a steady hand to calm her fears. When Peter walks through a painful loss, he is nurtured by Annette's loving presence. When Liz is struggling, Carlos maintains his inner strength to stabilize the situation. In other words, developing a solid sense of self gives spouses the capacity to embrace each other's experiences in an empowering, supportive way.

Differentiation is the backbone of self-giving actions. A differentiated spouse puts aside personal feelings in order to listen to and understand his or her partner's world of feelings, perspective and desires. Being genuinely invested in each other's well-being, each spouse creates a place of caring that elicits honest disclosure. The integrity of the relationship is upheld as spouses mutually acknowledge each other's internal world without becoming entangled in it.

Low levels of differentiation correspond to low levels of couple intimacy. Take the example of a wife asking her husband about something she thinks needs changing in their relationship. If he automatically gets defensive, taking her request as a personal affront, we would assume he has a low level of differentiation. He responds as an injured husband who has been severely criticized. Since his self-worth is so wrapped up in her validation of him, such a question is interpreted as an attack. A lack of differentiation leads to a faulty (self-centered) perception that he is being judged or blamed for the problem. This simple request for change elicits an extreme emotionally reactive response that disallows any possibility of working for positive changes. In contrast, a highly differentiated husband would be receptive to his spouse's desire for change, eager to listen to her ideas, willing to make suggestions of his own and ready to participate with her in improving the relationship.

In a reciprocal rhythm that deepens the relationship connection, it is important for spouses to attend to the other in a way that empowers. In our early marriage, codependency kept us from a deeper emotional connection. When Jack was discouraged as a doctoral student, my anxiety about his situation heightened his fears. What he needed instead was someone who could listen with compassionate understanding as he shared his vulnerable feelings. He needed the assurance that he could express his disappointment without my adding to his worry. I was so emotionally fused with him at this point in our marriage that my fearful emotions spilled out on top of his. In that situation the only thing he could do was pretend to be strong for my sake. My emotional reactions shut his emotions down. Later in our marriage, when we were more differentiated, we were able to listen to each other without being emotionally entangled in ways that prevented us from lending support to the other.

Differentiation gives spouses the capacity to set aside personal feelings (die to self) so they can listen well and be a source of stability. This maturing of selves draws spouses closer because they can be safely vulnerable with each other's inner and outer worlds.

Differentiated spouses have high regard for each other and for their relationship interdependency and unity. Together the couple stands firm in difficulties, bringing to each situation something bigger than either of them can be alone. They can communicate without fear of spilling into each other's lives in an unhelpful way. Differentiation gives spouses the freedom to challenge and confront each other, speak their desires, honestly examine what is being expressed, take rightful responsibility for their actions and work together for change that enhances the relationship. Regard for differentiation and emotional connection moves the couple toward the more excellent way.

Having a self "differentiated in Christ" means that our validation is centered in Christ. Although we care deeply about what our spouse thinks and feels, we are not dependent upon their feelings and experiences for our validation. Therefore we do not need to be responsible for the experiences and feelings of our spouse. Instead, we remain close by, listening in a nondefensive, nonreactive stance. We empathize responsively when our spouse discloses. In this way, both spouses take responsibility for relationship growth and harmony.

Connecting Through Communication

Communication has become the buzzword in marriage today. Virginia Satir (1967), along with Miller, Nunnally and Wackman (1975), were among the first to focus on what has now become known as active listening skills. Markman, Stanley and Blumberg (1994) more recently have developed the PREP (Prevention and Relationship Enhancement Program) model to assist couples in learning communication skills. Spouses take turns in the speaker position, where they are taught to give short, direct statements, and in the listener position, where they paraphrase what has been said, until understanding is reached. It is an effective way to clarify and keep emotions from escalating. In a book written for Christians, Scott Stanley et al. (1998) emphasizes the importance of commitment, forgiveness and restoration as important dimensions of communication and connection.

Having emotional awareness and learning how to express feelings effectively is the goal. Using "I" instead of "you" messages helps one take responsibility rather than place blame. A husband who feels angry towards his wife is taught to say, "I am angry because . . ." (fill in the blank) and "I would like . . ." (fill in the blank). In this way he acknowledges his own feelings, expresses a concrete request and takes responsibility for his desire for change.

Certainly there are enormous benefits in learning how to communicate well. Knowing how to accurately express and reflect is incredibly important, yet something much more crucial is at stake! It's all too easy to see solutions in terms of right techniques. Therapist Susan Johnson (2004) uses an emotionally focused approach to help spouses share in a way that brings the emotional bonding so desired.

It takes humility to enter into this emotional sanctuary of sharing, requesting and responding. Sharing can be risky business because vulnerability comes with the territory. The one who shares may be misunderstood, rejected or judged; the one who listens may fail in his or her response. But this is the very essence of knowing each other more deeply. Honest disclosure brings out the greatest possibility of being understood and known. It's really what spouses are longing for; it's a risk worth taking.

Seek First to Understand, Then to Be Understood!

It has been said that listening is far more challenging than talking. Listening with genuine, heartfelt interest opens the door to sharing at the depths of who we are. Being attentive to what your spouse is saying and demonstrating sensitive understanding creates communion. A spouse naturally keeps sharing from the deepest levels of his or her being when feeling validated by the other's listening posture and engaging questions. There is great reward in relationship intimacy returns.

It's quite obvious when someone is only pretending to be listening! While they are looking at you, they don't really see or hear you because they are chomping at the bit to give a rebuttal or promote an agenda of their own. As soon as they have a chance to speak, the counterpoints come blasting forth in a barrage of defensive statements. Under the pretense of listening, they have been preparing their own argument.

It takes tremendous effort to truly understand another person. As we said earlier, it requires that we die to our own agenda, give up the desire to defend ourselves or counter what is being said so we listen with full attention.

Just being listened to with understanding is a validating experience. So develop the habit of listening with understanding. It can become second nature, and practice makes perfect. The idea is to respond in a way that enhances spousal connection and keeps communication going. *Re-*

flection is the term used to describe repeating the other person's words as well as acknowledging their feelings as if you are a mirror. Your spouse feels validated simply because they know you got the message and feelings right. If the reflection is not accurate, on the other hand, the spouse can reiterate or explain further so you understand more clearly where they are coming from.

Reflecting with accurate empathy is one of the most affirming things we do. Every spouse longs to be truly understood, so it is absolutely crucial to repeat both the words as well as the feelings behind the words. Notice the feelings attached to the words by paying attention to the body and voice cues as well as the feeling words your spouse uses. Reflecting at this deeper level brings deeper understanding. For example, in reflecting back to one's spouse you would simply say, "I sense the hurt behind your tears and the frustration in your voice. Your coworker's comments that you were not up to the task were really humiliating and hurtful." Because you got the innuendoes as well as the words, your spouse feels validated by your compassionate understanding. So don't simply give the words back, which can appear wooden and uninvolved. Work at "getting it" at a deeper feeling level.

Every effort you make to get it right pays off. The way you get it right is to continually check out with your spouse to make sure you are on track. Simple statements like, "Let me see if I understand what you said" or asking, "Did I get it right?" ensure you are working toward understanding. The concerted effort both spouses make to engage each other in meaningful dialogue will do wonders for the relationship.

Don't Just Do Something, Stand There!

When a spouse presents a problem, it takes a lot of discipline to "just stand there!" Yet the most important thing a spouse can do is *listen* without interpreting or interrupting. Though the desire to alleviate a spouse's stress comes out of a good motive, resist the temptation to offer solutions. A common complaint of wives is the husband's tendency to take on her problem with a vengeance and in doing so completely miss attending to *her.* Eagerness to fix the problem only makes things worse! In fact, doing so undermines your belief in her ability to solve her own problem (differentiation). The solver modality puts the spouse in a one-up position and the relationship in a one-down position. Doing tends to disconnect, while being there makes connection.

Listening empowers! The best gift you can offer your spouse is a listening presence and accurate reflection. By standing there, attuned to your spouse, you provide a place of safety for your spouse to express feelings, sort out thoughts, gain perspective and maximize creative solutions.

Be a patient, persistent listener. Listening is a privilege that invites us into cherished moments of connection. Jennifer remembers how Don held her through her anguished tears after the sudden death of her mother. He could not change what had happened, but he could be with her in her grief. Responding in this way drew them close. He put aside his temptation to take charge of things. There would be plenty of time for making arrangements later. He could not alleviate her loss, but he could engage in this intimate connection.

Listening Under the Words

When strong reactive emotions emerge during spousal interaction, it is usually a sign of wounding earlier in life. Extreme emotions that are aroused in the context of your relationship most likely come from unresolved relationship issues with parents or other family members. This is why it is good to share childhood experiences. It gives spouses an ability to be compassionate and sensitive when something is triggered from the past. The following story illustrates this well.

The alcoholism of his father led to Frank's early cut-off from his family. Betty, an only child, was very connected with her parents and felt a great deal of responsibility for them. An emotional breach came when Frank openly admitted to Betty his jealousy and anger about the amount of time she spent with her family. He was feeling cut off from her. Hurt by his comments, Betty responded with an outburst of uncontrollable tears that surprised them both. They both realized there were deeper issues behind their reactions. After they took enough time to calm down, they came together again for deeper understanding of what had happened. Frank was able to express how lonely and isolated he was and how it triggered his fear of losing her. Betty admitted her being overwhelmed by her concerns about losing her parents. By delving into their childhood experiences they came to a new understanding of each other.

Their mutual understanding united them and brought solidarity in how they would proceed.

When a spouse feels continually misunderstood, discounted, betrayed or ignored, it is natural to pull away. Disillusioned and hopeless, the spouse detaches by becoming an island of invulnerability. It is a protective maneuver in which apathy looms large. For example, when a wife vows to never let her husband hurt her again, the discounted wife deadens any feelings to the point where the husband can no longer penetrate her life. Unfortunately, this barrier prevents the connection that is so desperately needed.

Erin comments, "I can tell you exactly the day I deadened myself to Craig. I felt utterly abandoned by him when he didn't come home for the umpteenth time without bothering to call. I was suspicious he was having an affair. He treated me like I didn't matter. After that night I pulled away big time. I vowed I would never trust him again. The sad thing is he didn't even seem to notice. I've seen a lawyer and I'm pretty sure he'll be shocked when I tell him I want a divorce." Apathy deadens feeling, making it almost impossible to break through.

Never let your marriage get to this point of no return! Sound the alarm when you're in a hard place or "too busy" to communicate. You need a wake-up call! Don't settle for apathy, a dead marriage or divorce! In the next chapter we discuss conflict, an aspect of marriage that can actually predict divorce or temptations for an affair. The time you make for spousal conversation and connection can turn the tide.

Communication that connects is the highest priority. Regular communication keeps toxic interaction from destroying your marriage. Commit yourselves to daily communication time as the most important appointment on your day planner.

"Two Becoming One" Communion

Can you walk in your spouse's shoes? Can you see the world from your spouse's experience? Can you imagine how life looks through the lenses of your spouse's gender, culture, family of origin, religion and life experience? Can you put yourself in his or her place to such an extent that you truly comprehend with compassion and understanding? When you do, you enter a sacred communion in which two differentiated spouses experience one-flesh union. It is a place in which spouses mutually engage in emotional warmth, interpersonal affection and intimate connection.

Without doubt, team-centered unity requires personal sacrifice. A shared covenant faith and common worldview are core components of meaningful couple communion. Admitting fault, apologizing, renewing vows, choosing to forgive and be forgiven demonstrate gracing love. Mutual empowerment and differentiation in Christ promote communication, communion and connection as a lifelong process.

10

CONFLICT

The Fertilizer of Growth

"CONFLICT IS THE FERTILIZER OF LIFE! While not very fragrant, it is necessary for optimal growth," quips family therapist Carl Whitaker (quoted in Neill & Kniskern, 1982, p. 200). Since there is no such thing as a completely compatible couple, conflict will be an inevitable part of a relationship as intimate as marriage. In fact, if a couple claims never to have conflicts, we can make one of several assumptions: they haven't been married very long; they don't talk to each other very much; one spouse has all the power and the other has none; or they are in denial. Sorry to say, to deny conflict is to deny an opportunity to grow.

The marriage relationship becomes a crucible in which conflicts can heat things up to the breaking point or can be a refining process of transforming growth. In other words, conflict can either make or break the marriage. Research indicates that increases in conflict and emotional distress are one of the precipitating factors that can lead spouses toward extramarital involvement (Allen, Atkins, Baucom, Synder, Gordon & Glass, 2005, p. 103). On the other hand, dealing effectively with conflict opens spouses up to new levels of differentiation and intimate connection.

All couples must consider the serious ramifications of not addressing conflicts and anger in a manner that leads to relationship growth. Good marriages are not those that never experience conflict, but rather those that, when conflict arises, deal with it in a manner that facilitates the growth of the relationship. In this chapter we present a biblical perspective on anger, offer constructive guidelines for dealing with conflict, identify five common conflict styles and indicate how couples can collaborate on a style that works best for them.

A Biblical Perspective

Since the topic of marital conflict can be subsumed under marital communication, all we said in the previous chapter about trinitarian relationality applies here as well. Although it is theologically inconceivable to think of conflict between persons of the Holy Trinity, it might be fruitful to reflect on why this is so. As noted in chapter two, Volf speaks of *perichoresis* (the Father is in the Son and the Son is in the Father) as "the reciprocal interiority of the Trinitarian person." It is precisely this reciprocal interiority that allows Jesus to avoid a potential conflict with the Father. In anticipation of his agonizing death, Jesus prays, "Father, if you are willing, remove this cup from me; yet, not my will but yours be done" (Lk 22:42). While the text indicates a *will* residing in both Jesus and the Father, Jesus submits his will to the Father's, avoiding any possibility of conflict. In chapter five we drew upon Giles's excellent book *The Trinity and Subordinationism: The Doctrine of God and the Contemporary Gender Debate* (2002) in utilizing the trinitarian model as a basis for mutual submission in marriage. When both spouses approach marital conflict with a posture of mutual submission, they make room for the other's point of view, and they desire as well as keep the best interest of the relationship as the priority.

Assuming that a marriage reflects trinitarian relationality, scriptural passages such as Ephesians 4:26 provides practical wisdom on the subject. To be angry (the emotion) is not a sin, but how you deal with negative expression of anger in a relational conflict can be a sin. This should persuade spouses to see their emotions as a powerful signal alerting them that something is wrong between them. Only when we pay attention can we bring about change. Jesus displayed anger in response to sin and injustice. Righteous anger helps us right the wrongs in our world and our relationships. Accepting anger as a God-given emotion gives us cause to attend to our feelings in a constructive manner.

Scripture provides many gems of wisdom on how to express anger in a way that keeps the integrity of the relationship intact. Ephesians 4:25-27 instructs to "speak the truth. . . . Be angry but do not sin; do not let the sun go down on your anger, and do not make room for the devil." These principles help us deal with anger in an honest and timely manner so that it doesn't fester or escalate. Ephesians 4:29 tells us how to approach our spouse when angry: "Let no evil talk come out of your mouths, but only what is useful for building up . . . that your words may give grace to those who hear." Ephesians 4:31-32 keeps us accountable for how we express anger: "Put away from you all bitterness and wrath and anger and wrangling and slander, together with all malice, and be kind to one another, tenderhearted, forgiving one another, as God in Christ has forgiven you."

There is a lot to unpack in these few verses. Most importantly, we are admonished to deal with our angry feelings while treating each other with utmost respect. We are not to let our anger turn into bitterness, hatred or revenge. We are not to deny anger, but to approach others in a way that builds them up. By following these words of wisdom, we will preserve our relationship connection and make the kind of changes that will transform our relationship for the good.

Conflict That Destroys

While we strongly believe that dealing effectively with conflicts can lead to personal and couple growth, we must acknowledge that wrongful expression of anger can be destructive to relationships. The inability to deal well with conflict can end in inconsolable isolation, deep bitterness and hateful attitudes. Harmful expression of anger ignites violence and hideous escalation that turns to retaliation. Many spouses have witnessed violence in their homes growing up as children and have firsthand knowledge of the irreparable damage that can be done by anger gone awry. These experiences tend to keep them from acknowledging anger because they believe when anger is exposed it cannot be controlled.

Unfortunately, reluctance to deal with conflict usually leads to smoldering, long-term resentments and revengeful actions that also do harm. Withdrawing from conflict doesn't settle it. Wanting peace at all costs doesn't stop passive aggressive behavior. The following psychological mechanisms are ways people learn to ignore angry feelings:

> *Denial:* pretending there is no problem when there is one
> *Displacement:* expressing anger to the wrong person
> *Disengagement:* separating yourself from your anger
> *Disqualification:* discounting anger by minimizing it

"Sweeping problems under the rug" only leaves a huge bulge that spouses trip over every day. Hidden anger heats up beneath the surface and eventually erupts in a volcanic explosion that destroys anyone in its path.

It is essential that spouses acknowledge and learn to deal with the conflicts that come up in the normal course of their relationships. It is a well-researched fact in the domestic violence literature that emotional connection inhibits violence, whereas disconnection is a cause of violence. Steven Stosny (2004) views domestic violence as a crisis of disconnection. He found that fathers who are emotionally connected with their wives and children instinctively want to protect rather than harm them. The single most important factor that prevents violence in the home had to do with fathers holding their spouses and children in high esteem.

Inability to Deal Effectively with Conflict Predicts Serious Marital Trouble

Researchers claim they can predict whether a marriage will succeed or fail just by observing how spouses engage in conflict. John Gottman (with Silver, 1994), the top researcher in the field of marital conflict, identified four toxic behaviors that are deadly to marriage. The first is *criticism* or *scathing sarcasm;* the second is *defensiveness;* the third is *contempt* or *hostility;* and the fourth is *stonewalling* or *angry withdrawal.* Distancing maneuvers such as rolling the eyes with disgust or giving an indignant cold shoulder are ways of showing hostility. Endless bickering, judgmental accusations, derogatory labels and blow-by-blow critical encounters inflict wounds. Reciprocal and escalating negative emotions are the most consistent indication of unhappiness in couples.

A crucial finding from Gottman's (1994) research was the importance of cooling down during a heated argument. Heart rates were monitored while couples were arguing. When the spouse's heart rates rose above 100, the researchers interrupted the fight with the false explanation that their equipment was malfunctioning. Couples took a break for about a half-hour (when their heart rates were down) before they resumed their fight. The change it made in terms of how they approached each other after the break was remarkable.

Under heightened emotional reactivity couples tend to escalate, regress and rarely use positive communication skills. Caught up in the heat of things, it's hard to make room for the other or to die to self. Men in Gottman's study (1994) were more likely to be negatively impacted by highly emotional conflicts physiologically, and it took at least 20 minutes before the nerve centers could be quieted. It seems the rise in heart rate and rush of adrenaline creates havoc with their ability to process information. Time is needed to recover from the emotional upset and to reestablish safety. So by taking time out (at least an hour break), the body cools down, emotions de-escalate, relationship dynamics change and the couple can resume reconciliatory conversation.

It was interesting to note how husbands and wives differ during conflicts (Gottman, 1994). Husbands more than wives resorted to belligerence and withdrawal, which is exactly the behavior that had the most negative impact on the wives. On the other hand, wives most frequently resorted to harsh start-ups and blaming (critical) comments, which most adversely affected husbands. Husbands were most open to their wives when they were approached with a soft start-up (nonaccusatory), while wives were most open when their husbands responded nondefensively during an argument.

Gottman (with Silver, 1994) describes three common conflict couple types. The *volatile* couples value openness and honesty and are emotionally expressive. Since they express both positive and negative emotions, their relationship can be emotionally volatile, but when there is a strong ratio of positive to negative emotions expressed, volatile couples are usually able to grow through their conflicts. More moderate in their emotional expressions are the *validating* couples. Validating couples use softening techniques when bringing up a disagreement, are sensitive to their spouse's feelings, and focus on the good of the relationship. The third pattern identified is the *conflict-avoiding* couple. If conflicts are not avoided altogether, they are addressed in a low-key fashion. Although the conflict-avoiding couple may deny conflict, Gottman believes they can build a satisfying relationship without much marital conflict when they are empathic and relationship focused. Gottman also recognized mismatched couple types have more difficulty dealing with marital conflict than couples with the same style.

These studies make it clear that incorporating some basic principles into marital conflict will bring a more satisfying outcome. Taking a break is absolutely necessary when a conflict escalates. Both spouses need to get centered (differentiate), soothe their emotions and allow their bodies' reactions to de-escalate. An important aspect of differentiation is the ability to process information through the head (self-talk) and the heart (emotion-talk) in order to de-escalate the emotions. Differentiation helps spouses take a step back to calm anxious thoughts and feelings in order to take a step forward with a balanced head-and-heart perspective. Self-regulation gives them the ability to proceed respectfully and to approach each other with a calm, revitalized presence that facilitates relationship unity.

Removing oneself from the intense emotional energy opens the way to thoughtful reflection. It may be necessary to actually expend physical energy by going for a walk, taking a shower or getting one's thoughts and feelings out on paper during the break time. Invite God into the process, ask for spiritual wisdom, draw on Scripture and prayer for perspective.

After spouses have recuperated physically and emotionally during the break, they are ready to come back to the conflict in a renewed state of being. Having a clear sense of self gives them freedom to accurately express their feelings and wishes; in the role of compassionate listener, the spouse is able to "die to self" while listening respectfully to the partner. Both spouses can take responsibility for holding the relationship as the primary focus.

Engaging in this way—even about a conflict area—empowers spouses to be mindful of positive qualities. Koerner and Fitzpatrick (2002) found that accurately decoding relational positive affect, and distinguishing it from nonrelational negative affect is related to marital satisfaction. In other words, spouses who hold a positive view of each other and the relationship and who recognize that and distinguish it from their negative feelings about a particular issue can take a hopeful stance founded on mutual regard, relationship resilience and covenant commitment. In light of relationship unity, they are willing to forthrightly face the issues that constrain their harmony. Mutual growth as the common goal means they choose to work cooperatively in smoothing out the rough edges and collaborate in making the crooked ways straight.

Believing that God transforms them into the likeness of the Son through this crucible of growth helps spouses move outside themselves toward a mutual indwelling.

Fighting Fair in Marriage

Is there marital conflict "till death do us part," you may ask. The answer is Yes! Judy remembers the day her mother, married for over fifty years, threatened to leave her father after an angry encounter. These flashes of anger, even at eighty-five, are apt to flare up at any age. While there tends to be less active conflict in later married life, conflict happens throughout the stages of marriage.

During marital conflict the spouse so often is seen as the enemy. In the heat of an argument, it's tempting to draw lines and focus on winning the battle by defeating the opponent. This attitude keeps spouses antagonistic, defensive and distant. The idea of fight fair rules is to approach conflict with rules that will ensure productive conflict.

One of the oldest approaches to martial conflict is George Bach and Peter Wyden's book, *The Intimate Enemy: How to Fight Fair in Love and*

FIGHT FAIR RULES:

1. *One issue only.* Identify the issue and don't veer from it.
2. *Choose the time and place.* Agree on a neutral place and time.
3. *Be prepared.* Know and abide by the rules. Bring a proper attitude.
4. *The past is past.* Refuse to "throw up the past" in a current fight.
5. *No surprise punches.* Emotion-laden areas are off limits.
6. *No hitting below the belt.* Sensitive areas divert the issue.
7. *Don't dismiss.* Don't be flippant or make light of problems presented.
8. *No Why questions allowed.* Blame or accusation often lies behind the why questions.
9. *Dyad vs. triad.* Keep it between the two of you—no third person allowed.
10. *Don't ridicule.* Ridiculing is rude. No put-downs or name-calling.
11. *Veto power.* Signal technical error when rules are broken.
12. *Break at the end of each round.* Short breaks ensure bodily rest.

Marriage (1969). The authors use the metaphor of a boxing match to help couples incorporate fight fair rules. For example, a boxing match is scheduled by a mutual agreement, the time and place are arranged, and boxing rules are adhered to at all times. Here are some important fight fair rules to follow (see text box on p. 124).

These fight fair rules are safety measures to ensure a fair fight. Technical fouls can be called when unfair tactics are used. Either spouse can call "foul" by indicating a "T" with their fingers to note that a technical has been committed. For example, if one is forced into a corner, the natural response is to put up the dukes in a defensive stance and come out swinging. In this case the technical reminds the spouses to come back in the center of the ring. The couple must approach conflict with rules that will ensure fairness.

We certainly don't advocate that the couple "duke it out" to determine a victor. We do advocate common courtesy and mutually agreed upon rules so spouses engage in a clean fight that leads to a good end. Veering from the rules takes you off course. Taking breaks between rounds rejuvenates both physically and mentally, and having a contained place and time frame provides a sound boundary.

The idea behind scheduling a time and place to have conflict is extremely sensible. A "morning person" will have the advantage early in the day, whereas a "night person" has more energy late in the evening. By scheduling their conflict in the middle of the day, spouses honor their differences. Deciding on a neutral place (two easy chairs in the living room or the dining room table, etc.) puts spouses on equal footing. Agreeing to follow the rules and sticking to one issue at a time keeps things focused. The goal is to make progress through common courtesies that bring resolution, rather than for one to win or lose a fight.

While everyday disagreements may be irritating, they can usually be handled with less emotional investment. It's important to remember that some conflicts don't usually get resolved in one or two rounds or even in a series of rounds. It's perfectly acceptable for some conflicts to be put "on hold" or in "cold storage" or even "put to rest" by personal agreement. Differences in conflict style, mannerisms, personality, politics and religion are examples of factors that can continually surface in conflicts (Roloff & Johnson, 2002). On some issues spouses may need to agree to disagree and for the time being not bring up the topic.

Mutually satisfying solutions take time. Since there are always issues stirring in the wings, it helps to prioritize conflicts in terms of their impact on the relationship. Conflicts that end in relational disconnection require special attention. Not attending to these issues heightens relationship anxiety and takes a toll on the relationship. Therefore, be persistent by taking regular time each week to work on specific issues that come up regularly, rather than leaving the issues to be dealt with only when circumstances force you to attend to them.

Common Conflict Styles

One of the more fruitful advances in interpersonal conflict is the identification of common conflict styles. Labels for these styles first originated in the business world, but they can be applied in helpful ways to marital conflicts. The five conflict styles are presented in table 10.1. We will introduce each conflict style, indicating the positive and negative qualities in terms of marital conflict. As spouses identify their particular style and that of their partner, they have a better chance of understanding how they typically respond when conflict arises. When a couple can adapt their particular styles in relation to one another, they can create a unique couple style that works well for their unique relationship.

Naturally, spouses use a style they believe is best in helping them deal with marital discord. They tend to bring a conflict style to marriage that they learned earlier in life. However, a style that worked well within their particular family may trigger negative reactions in a spouse. So just

Table 10.1. Five Styles of Conflict

Winner		Resolver
	Compromiser	
Withdrawer		Yielder

doing what comes naturally often gets them in trouble with a spouse. What is good in one situation may not work in another.

There is no perfect conflict style! In fact, we'll give examples from the life of Jesus to indicate how he used all five styles. Each style has aspects that may hinder achieving what the couple wants. While some persons use the same conflict style in all situations, others vary their styles according to the circumstance. It's better not to get locked into any one style, but most likely each spouse has an immediate preference for one style. Spouses will need to be adaptable so they can take advantage of what works best in their marriage. We are looking for combined styles that keep relationship connection while having open dialogue so the couple can reach a satisfying conclusion.

The withdrawer. The natural response for a withdrawer (represented in the lower left corner of table 10.1) is to avoid conflict at all costs! The first thought in a withdrawer's mind is to leave the scene as a way to stop the ramifications of the conflict. This is not just taking a necessary break, according to Gottman's research, but it is the way the person keeps peace. The withdrawer does need to get away to get perspective, and he or she usually returns in a relaxed mood because the conflict is over in his/her mind. However, the problem has not been solved, nor has the spouse been engaged in the process. Therefore the conflict is left in limbo land.

As you might imagine, the biggest challenge for the withdrawer is to come back after getting perspective and be willing to engage with the partner over their conflict. When withdrawers fail to take this step, they have abandoned their responsibility to their spouse and the relationship. The mandate is to initiate connection and follow through after they have taken leave.

Avoidance was not the usual way Jesus handled things, but there were times he chose to withdraw, for example, when his life was in danger, when crowds pressed upon him, when he needed perspective, when he needed to commune with the Father (Mt 12:14-15; Lk 5:15-16; 22:39-41). These are legitimate reasons to withdraw.

The yielder. The conflict style of the yielder is represented in the lower right side of table 10.1. The natural response of the yielder is to accommodate one's spouse without expressing personal desires. Yielding is the chosen way to keep peace. However, one may yield due to fears of rejection or wanting to be liked, which is more a cop-out. The ability to assert oneself is a problem a yielder readily admits. Those married to a yielder tend to respond angrily when their spouse fails to stand up for themselves, because others (partner included) tend to take advantage and walk all over them.

To truly yield, to go a second mile or turn the other cheek, takes a strong person who acts out of a sacrificial choice. Yielders fail the relationship when they fail to express themselves. How can "two be better than one" when a spouse never speaks up or has voice?

The greatest conflict facing Jesus was the cross, to which he yielded himself (Mt 26:50-53). After the soldiers seized Jesus, he didn't resist or allow his disciples to protect him. However, he boldly requested that the cup be removed (honest human voice) yet he yielded and gave himself as a sacrifice for all. The yielding was out of strength and conviction, not out of inability to express his desire or assert needs.

The challenge for a yielder is to voice his/her opinion. A yielder usually needs time to process internally because it is hard to think spontaneously, especially when there is tension in the air. The yielder must take responsibility by spending time to process a conflict (writing things down first gives words for verbal expression later), sort out feelings and thoughts, and then use the written notes as a prompt to assert themselves.

The winner. The winner style is in the top left corner of table 10.1. It is natural for a winner is to assert personal views and desires in a most persuasive way. Winners are verbally astute and tend to be in occupations that highly value verbal ability. Speaking truthfully does not mean disrespectful or demanding talk, put-downs or hurtful words. Going for the jugular to win a point destroys the heart of the marriage. The winner style can feel harsh and diminishing to the spouse. In their eagerness to win the argument, winners can easily overtake a spouse with persuasive arguments. The more the winner tries to convince through logical arguments, the more the partner turns a deaf ear. The spouse simply refuses to do battle, knowing they can't stand up to a spouse who cleverly uses every angle in their argumentation. The winner wins the battle (the point) but loses the war (the relationship).

We see Jesus adopting the winner style when he challenged the Pharisees. Out of righteous anger he drove out the moneychangers in the temple to keep the temple a holy place of honor for the Father (Mt 21:12-13; Jn 2:13-16). Jesus acted authoritatively and decisively out of strong convictions.

The most important challenge for a winner is to stop talking and listen. Strong convictions bring a lot of energy, and winners need to tone down so spouses will talk. Taking on the role of listener means reflecting back the message until the spouse feels accurately understood. Refrain from persuasive arguments and concentrate on your spouse's point of view. A discipline used to break the old pattern is to take one day as the listener without any verbal or nonverbal responses. The whole point is to listen! After a day or two, the winner takes the spotlight and is allowed to express desire without using persuasive talk. In this way the winner is forced to make concerted effort to understand the spouse's point of view and consider its merits. This exercise empowers the partner to express freely, knowing the time is theirs alone and there will be no interruptions. The winner is humbled in practicing the art of dying to self as a servant. Then, when the winner gets a chance to talk a day or two later, the intense energy has lessened and the message is softened. Taking into account the partner's ideas and feelings brings a needed closeness that winners seldom experience. The couple has the wisdom of two perspectives clearly iterated; therefore they can form a mutual plan of action. The relationship wins!

The compromiser. Represented in the center of table 10.1 is the compromiser, who gives as well as gets through negotiation. The natural inclination of a compromiser is to care about what the spouse wants as well as to clearly express personal wants. Cooperation in finding a mutually satisfactory solution is the goal. It is assumed that one will give in order to get, but over time this balances out. Negotiation is a practical, realistic way to deal with conflicts for a compromiser. Conflicts are settled quickly even though both spouses may have to settle for less than what either really wants. It is important to note that compromisers do not compromise their personal values even though they regard the spouse's values as important. They are optimistic about finding practical solutions, even if ideals are not met.

Though not a compromiser when it came to doing the Father's will,

Jesus amazed the crowds with parables and with the answers he gave when the Pharisees tried to trap him, for example, "Give therefore to the emperor the things that are the emperor's, and to God the things that are God's" (Mt 22:21). He evaded the critics by giving directives that brought a solution, "Let anyone among you who is without sin be the first to throw a stone" (Jn 8:7).

A major challenge for compromisers is to carefully consider the consequences of compromise. They must resist the urge to make decisions too hastily. Take time to consider the deeper implications of what is good for the relationship. Settling for second best may not be the best in the long run, and giving in too easily fails to persist toward a more satisfying outcome. It may not be worth the sacrifice a compromiser pays for peace, especially if the relationship gets the short end of the deal.

The resolver. Represented in the upper right corner of table 10.1, the resolver will stay with the conflict until a couple comes to an ideal resolution. Intensely committed to the relationship, resolvers work hard toward a win-win situation. Maximizing satisfaction for both spouses is the ultimate goal. Since compromising is viewed as a defeat, the resolver persists for as long as it takes to find a resolution that is the best for both spouses and the relationship. This style takes a lot of emotional energy, but most resolvers seem to have an unlimited supply of stick-to-it-iveness. They never give up! They pursue to the end.

During his earthly ministry, Jesus responded sensitively to the relational needs and desires of his disciples. John 21 depicts the way Jesus let his disciples know what he desired of them and challenged them toward excellence. When the disciples were not catching fish, Jesus told them to throw the net to the other side. They responded and were greatly rewarded with an abundance of fish. In like manner, Jesus asked Peter three times, "do you really love me?" (Jn 21:17). This conversation gives Peter the chance to affirm his love for Jesus and to receive Jesus' affirmation in his commission to serve him. These interactions between Jesus and his disciples allowed the past hurt to be cleared away. Moreover, Jesus pursues the sinner by sacrificing his life, one of the best conflict resolutions we can ever experience.

A major challenge for resolvers is to be able to tolerate the anxiety felt when their spouse isn't as engaged in working toward the ideal solution.

The intensity of the pursuit and idealistic relationship goals may drive the spouse away. They must resist the heavy pursuing, take a step back once in a while and give up unrealistic idealism.

Resolvers tend to be relentless in their pursuit, and the partner may rebel by ignoring (withdrawer/winner) or giving in (yielder/compromiser). At this point, the resolver must back off, slow down and give the spouse a break from the emotional persistence. Resolvers need to prioritize the issues worth pursuing and let go of those that have little impact on the health of the relationship. This requires distinguishing the important from the less important. Differentiation helps resolvers utilize personal resources to reach personal ideals and manage their lives without dragging their spouse into every issue. As the resolver engages in personal self-care and validation of the spouse, the partner will be more willing to engage in the relational remedies that matter.

Collaborative Combinations

Each of the five conflict styles entails a level of concern for self, spouse and the relationship. There are fifteen potential combinations of conflict styles that bring a unique dynamic to the couple during spousal conflict. A yielder married to a winner, a compromiser to a resolver, a withdrawer to another withdrawer and so forth. The combined couple conflict style has its own chemistry and provokes unique problems. In order to successfully navigate during conflicts, a couple must identify their styles and learn how to unlock their particular gridlocks. Some styles are complementary while others are competitive or constrictive. We describe just a few of the combinations to illustrate the relational process necessary to work out a couple conflict style that is effective for them.

We begin with the proverbial *resolver-withdrawer* combination. Picture Jonathan, a resolver, trying to work out a conflict with Jill, a withdrawer. In this marital conflict, Jonathan pursues while Jill distances. It's a cat-and-mouse game that leaves them at odds with each other. The more Jonathan pursues, the more Jill withdraws. The challenge for this couple is to adjust their styles so they work for the relationship. Jonathan must relax and stop pursuing so intently, while Jill must be more willing to engage with him.

In order to break the pursuer-withdrawer pattern, spouses must try something different. The vicious cycle repeats, intensifies, subsides and is put back into motion over and over again. Each reacts to the other without thinking. Polarized positions lead to rampant blaming. Unless each spouse is committed to doing something different things will only get worse! So the resolver promises to stop pursuing while the withdrawer decides to take more responsibility to care for the relationship, thus breaking established patterns.

This was true of our relationship in our early marriage. Jack's typical response was to withdraw while I (Judy) was constantly going after him for some relationship problem. This made Jack squirm and run just as he remembered his father doing. When a conflict arose between his dad and mom, Orville (a withdrawer) would leave the house in a huff, slam the door, and run a strip of rubber as he escaped in his '48 Ford. After a few hours, he returned cool, calm and collected, and the conflict was over in his mind. Unfortunately, his wife, Frances, (a yielder) swallowed her anger, never said another word, but her body kept score through many physical ailments. Her anger turned inward because she was not able to deal directly with her husband.

However, as a resolver I was not willing to let Jack get by with withdrawing like his father. I waited for him to come home so we could talk it through. I wanted to hear his perspective as well as express my thoughts and feelings. I granted him time to cool down, but he had to promise to come back to reconcile and negotiate a solution. Making these simple adjustments helped us reconnect and work on a mutual solution.

The Huangs, who represent a *winner-compromiser* combination, had a conflict about where to live. Peter, a winner, was convinced that they should find a house in the heart of the city where they both worked. His persuasive reasoning didn't convince Anita, who had her heart set on finding a twenty-acre plot of land in a rural area just outside the city. When Peter changed his tactic of interrupting and persuading, he listened to her deep desire to get away from the pressure of her job through nature. Peter actually loved the sounds of the busy city, but he understood Anita was rejuvenated in peace and quiet. Peter resisted his tendency to convince, while Anita was receptive and respectful of his needs as well. When they considered all the ins and outs of this decision, they decided to buy a house in the suburbs with enough yard space to create a peaceful garden area in the backyard.

Donald and Deborah were both *yielders*. Neither had strong opinions about anything, and there was little passion between them in a rather humdrum marriage. They were both steady persons and went about their work and marital roles in faithful ways, but they had become extremely routine and apathetic about their marriage. Their constant "I don't care, you decide" messages left them at an impasse. Years of disappointments, unmet expectations and unresolved conflict lead to emotional alienation. Donald and Deborah had moved to a place of apathy where neither invested in the marriage. Their marriage had come to an emotional death of disconnection.

After a religious conversion, Donald talked to his pastor about the state of the marriage. Encouraged to do something different, he began to make new attempts at connecting with Deborah. She was quite skeptical at first, but his kind and loving gestures got her attention. She began to respond little by little. His faith gave him a new lease on life. No longer content with the way things were, his hopeful perspective moved their relationship to a level that opened up new possibilities for them. They began making efforts to identify their needs and desires and, despite their discomfort with conflict, to learn to communicate and work toward positive change.

The Impact of Marital Conflict on Children

It is not surprising that children are a source of marital conflict nor that children are alert to their parent's martial tension. In a decade review of the literature, Mari Clements (2004) concludes that marital conflict increased the risk of children developing a variety of difficulties. Not only were children negatively impacted by the frequency and duration of their parents' conflicts, they were acutely aware of and stressed by conflict between their parents. The research shows that a highly conflicted marriage is neither good for the marriage nor a good environment for children. Clements's summary advocates that parents work out their conflicts in a timely fashion for the sake of the emotional security of the children.

In their study, Buehler and Gerard (2002) found that marital conflict was associated with both ineffective parenting and children's maladjustment. Research by Cummings and Davies (1994) found that chronic un-

resolved conflict between spouses left children feeling insecure, unable
to regulate their emotions and hypersensitive. Crockenberg and Forgays
(1996) found that hostility and anger between parents was associated
with withdrawal and avoidance patterns in children. Children were emotionally invested in the parent's conflicts, tried to diffuse them or inter-
vene because they tended to blame themselves for the problems between parents. It is important that parents demonstrate to their children
they can work out their conflicts without their children's intervention.
What can be more important than to model positive conflict skills for the
sake of one's marriage and children?

An enduring debate centers on the wisdom of conflictive couples
staying together for the sake of the children. Based on their research,
Booth and Amato (2001) conclude that "the dissolution of low-conflict
marriages appears to have negative effects on offspring's lives,
whereas the dissolution of high-conflict marriages appears to have
beneficial effects" (pp. 197-212). This research dictates that every couple take seriously their responsibility to deal effectively with their conflicts, not just for the sake of their marriage but also for the sake of their
children.

Growing Through Conflict: A Concluding Comment

We believe problems are solvable! Honoring conflict styles, learning
communication skills, following fight fair rules and upholding relationship commitments are essential ingredients of the conflict challenge. It's
amazing how dealing effectively with conflict leads to creative solutions
and places the relationship on higher ground.

Gottman (1994) found that a formula of five positive affirmations to
one negative predicted marital stability. Couples who exude qualities of
affection, humor, interest, support, listener-back communication chan-
nels, kindness and generosity are happiest. They can readily repair the
damage done during conflict because they have learned to accentuate
the positive and eliminate the negative.

A strong marital coalition of shared power equips the couple to be
kind in their firmness, caring in their confrontation, self-confident in
making requests and proactive in marital solutions. Practicing principles
of covenant love, grace-full interactions, mutual empowerment and ser-

vanthood, while staying emotionally connected creates an environment in which spouses can deal safely and responsively with their conflicts. Conflicts can be approached with confidence and a renewed spirit, bringing clarity in attitude, manner, purpose and perspective.

11

THE SEASONS OF MARRIAGE

WHEN WE LEAD MARRIAGE RETREATS, Jack will unnerve the audience by saying. "I've been involved in seven marriages in my life . . . all to the same woman!" Then I chime in, "And aren't you glad we've changed over the years?" Marriage is far from being static! It is a mysterious one-flesh relationship that a couple creates and re-creates as they move through each season of life together. Each new stage of marriage challenges the couple to transcend themselves and reconfigure their relation as a team.

Circumstances have a way of bringing surprises and challenges to marriage, requiring an ongoing revision of dreams and goals. Through the shifting realities of each new stage, it's the marital bond that provides the solid foundation for entering a new stage with imaginative possibilities. In the "two are better than one" analogy, spouses count on each other through the unexpected realities brought by each stage.

Maintaining a balance of marital unity and spousal differentiation is the central theme throughout the stages. Structural change can push spouses towards greater codependency, separate them through disengagement or grow them into a more resilient interdependency.

Seasons of Marriage

The stages of marriage are based on contextual markers (aging, children, unexpected stress) that occur along the lifeline. Table 11.1 lists the *season of marriage* in the left-hand column, the corresponding type of *stressor* in the center column and in the right-hand column the important *developmental tasks* required in this season of marriage. Difficulty occurs when a couple is unsuccessful in dealing with the challenges at any one stage, making it more difficult to navigate the next stage. There is a domino effect: what happens in one stage affects the next stage either posi-

Table 11.1. Seasons of Marriage, Stressors and Developmental Tasks

Season of Marriage	Stressors	Developmental Tasks
Honeymoon Marriage	Differences, Roles	Accept Differences, Mesh Roles
First Child	Displacement	Incorporate Parenting Role
No Children	Infertility/Choice	Spousal Focus
Young Children	Busy, Lack of Time	Develop Priorities
Teenage Children	Dual Identity Crisis	New Relationship with Children
Divorce/Remarriage	Loss/Adjustments	Reconstructing Lives
Remarriage	New Roles	Establishing Boundaries
Reconstituted Family	Multiple Adjustments	Establishing New Family
Launching Stage	Leaving Home	Letting Go
Emerging Adulthood	In-between Place	Establishing Independence
Post-launching Stage	Role Loss	Relate to Children as Adults
Retirement	Always Together	Find Meaning in Retirement
Sunset Years	Insecurity, Illness	Learn to Age Well

tively or negatively. For instance, an inability to develop good communication in one stage adversely affects the couple's ability to negotiate conflict that comes up in the next stage. Cohan and Kleinbaum (2002) found that "spouses who cohabited before marriage demonstrated more negative and less positive problem solving and supportive behavior compared with spouses who did not cohabit" (p. 180). So even patterns established during courtship or cohabitation impact the relationship.

We acknowledge that there are a variety of ways to travel through the marital journey. A couple may feel "out of sync" for any number of reasons (late marriage, divorce and remarriage, deaths or illness, etc.) at any season of marriage. With that said, table 11.1 presents structural changes along with common issues that typically accompany these stages.

The Honeymoon Marriage

God's elegant design seems to urge lovers through initial attraction. The powerful mechanism of romantic love (attraction) combined with an urgent sex drive moves people toward bonding. The intense preoccupation between the lovers, referred to as narcissistic love, is ego gratifying. Nothing else matters except being together.

Most newlyweds begin marriage with the love of their life, yet neither is entirely prepared for the enormity of what marriage requires of them. It can be a rude awakening when the honeymoon is over and the couple faces the demands of married life. It can feel overwhelming to deal with a multitude of tasks like setting up a household, negotiating roles, dealing with differences, managing family of origin boundaries, working out dual-earner dynamics and friendship priorities.

In addition, the personality traits that were so attractive during courtship may be a source of irritation in day-to-day living. Her outgoing personality is now defined as aggression; his shyness is now condemned as ineptitude. After marriage, spouses are not as tolerant of each other and no longer see each other as "godlike." Disappointments are voiced when expectations are not met. Sexual passion cools down in light of these realities.

Researchers find that unrealistic expectations may be one of the most devastating blows to early marriage. Romanticized ideas of love carry unbelievable expectations. Real marriage can never live up to the fantasies developed during the romance. When disappointments surrounding conscious and unconscious agendas begin to raise their ugly heads, things heat up like they never did during courtship, raising serious discontent and doubt. "Is this the same man I fell in love with?" "Is she the same woman who was so kind and gentle when we were dating?"

Spouses must develop roles and routines that enhance their couple goals. This is the perfect time to enjoy and explore the sexual relationship, to focus on emotional intimacy, to develop communication and good conflict skills, to establish oneself in career or work goals, develop couple friendships and meaningful worship patterns. The couple is forming an interdependency that honors distinctiveness and unity. In the honeymoon, marriage unity is idealized and individuality begins to challenge that unity.

A major theme and task of the honeymoon marriage is individual and couple differentiation. Questions emerge about how close we can be without suffocating each other. How separate can we be without being too distant? Spouses are becoming more clearly defined in the context of their relationship.

And Then There Were Three

Anticipating parenthood is an exciting prospect for most couples. This is especially true when a differentiated unity has formed a firm foundation for bringing up a child. The challenge in this season of marriage is to make room for the new member while maintaining a strong marriage.

By its very nature, the dynamic of a triad is much different than a dyad. The child becomes a new priority. Major adjustments are about to occur. Work and career aspirations will be evaluated and prioritized. There may be less income and more expenses. While having a precious baby in the home is experienced as a blessing, the responsibility of caring for the child siphons off energy from the couple relationship.

Each spouse will feel slightly less important when baby takes center stage. Sleep deprivation enters in big time, leading to shortened tempers (Shapiro, Gottman & Carrere, 2000).

Resentments can occur if the stay-at-home parent does all the grunge work or if the spouse working outside the home is jealous of the special relationship established between the stay-at-home parent and the child. Jan spoke about the reverse situation with her husband, Dan, who was so enamored with their new baby that she felt shut out. Dan wanted to do everything and make all the decisions about their daughter. Jan began to doubt her ability to be a good mother and resented her daughter, creating a wedge between the spouses.

The challenge is to balance the baby's needs with the couple needs so neither is neglected. It is crucial to create a place in the triad for *both* spouses, and this means agreeing upon new mother and father roles. Neither spouse must be made to feel like the third party in the triad. Fathers as well as mothers can bond in loving connection with children throughout life. Parents who are committed to coparenting take on a special place in the lives of their children. Coparenting practices unite the couple through shared meaning, responsibility and joy.

Not Having Children: Choice or Infertility

Whole books are written on this complex issue. Whether a couple chooses not to have children or has difficulty conceiving, it will cause stress. Family and friends and even strangers tend to be insensitive to a couple without children, causing much pain and anger. When spouses face these issues together with compassion and support, they can form a united front that brings unity. It makes a huge difference to have a supportive community who understands and accepts your choices.

Approximately one in twelve marriages are affected by infertility, a figure that has not changed significantly since 1960. There are various paths to take, and going through the process of determining and seeking treatment can be a grueling process. Which course to follow is not a casual decision, and it requires tremendous patience and cooperation as a couple. Dealing with disappointments is a heart-rending experience that can distance spouses. Research conducted on couples that enter fertility programs shows them to be psychologically well adjusted, but the waiting game causes a great deal of stress. No doubt, infertility is a stressor that affects both husbands and wives, even though they experience the problem differently. Jordan and Revenson (1999) found that women use their social support networks to a greater degree than men. Counseling can provide a safe place to deal with the emotional and sexual struggles that often accompany this process.

Married with Young Children

Childrearing years serve as a magic link in the lives of many couples, yet they also bring new stress to the marriage. Investing so much time and energy as parents is sometimes done at the expense of their marital relationship. Once a couple has children there is usually a spread of about nine years between the birth of the first and last child. When the ages are concentrated together it will be a very busy and active family.

Debates about discipline—Whose way is the best way?—often trigger conflict. A couple must stand firmly together on major things while accepting the unique ways each spouse engages the children. By holding on to a style that fits him or her, each parent will be more genuine in the unique relationships they have with their children. By consulting each other and honoring each other's perspective, spouses will achieve a united wisdom.

Parenting can be a tremendous bonding experience for spouses. Watching a relationship develop between each child and your spouse opens you up to them in ways never imagined. Their love warms your heart and deepens your love. Parenting is among the most demanding things a spouse will ever do, but it can also bring the greatest joy.

It is a wise saying that the best thing a father and mother can do for their children is to love each other. Don't abandon your spouse for your children. Children learn about love and commitment by watching their parents care for and take time for each other. Stay attuned and affirm each other. Mutual kindness and thoughtfulness model respect and good intentions to the children. It delights children to hear their parents tell couple stories, talk in the night, laugh and enjoy each other's company.

One way to care for the spousal relationship is to establish a clear boundary that children are not allowed to intrude. For example, at the end of a demanding day it is appropriate to tell children, "You'll need to watch a video for the next hour on your own, because Mommy and Daddy are taking time for each other," or "No, you can't interrupt our special talk times, because we love each other and want to listen to each other."

Keeping the sexual relationship vital secures a spousal boundary that protects the sacredness of the one-flesh union. Research reveals that the frequency of sexual intercourse diminishes after couples have children. The sexual connection can suffer at any stage, but young children take so much out of spouses that it's more troublesome. Our friend Karen, stay-at-home mom of three young children, made this comment, "When Greg comes home I do not want him to touch me or ask anything of me. All day long I have been giving to my kids and now I need to get some space, to be alone. I need to get in touch with myself as more than the Mommy. So when he comes home [tired after a hard day's work, she acknowledges] I need him to get involved, to take over the parenting duties, to put effort into household chores. If I just have personal time for peace and quiet I am more open to engage with him after the kids are in bed." Even if it's just cuddling, it is satisfying to stay close in the comfort of each other's company.

In this stage of life, spouses are being formed and transformed in the deepening love for children. These activities join a couple together in one of life's most meaningful purposes.

Teenage Years: Dual Identity Crisis

By mid-life, marriage has hopefully ripened in terms of spousal differentiation and interdependency. These qualities are highly desirable when facing the turbulent teenage years. Referred to as a *dual identity crisis,* two things are often happening simultaneously: teenage children are on the growing edge while parents are into midlife dilemmas. Parents are acutely aware of physical decline while teenagers are approaching their physical prime. I (Judy) vividly remember that ominous day when, walking down the sidewalk with my beautiful teenaged daughter, the whistles from the passing car were obviously for her. She was developing into a young woman, as I was becoming the wise older woman. To top it off, she reminded me to "hold my stomach in!" I retorted in defense, "It is in!" Jack, too, remembers the first day our son Joel legitimately beat him in tennis. While we take great pride in the development of our teenagers, it also reminds us that we are on that downhill slope.

There are particular stressors related to raising teenage children, especially in a culture where sex, drugs, music, media and Internet accessibility have such a claim on them. In their process of establishing a separate identity, they tend to negate parental values and embrace peer values. It can be a scary time in the lives of both parents and teens. It's hard to determine if rebelliousness is a normal part of the adolescent's search for a self or a destructive struggle that leads to serious consequences.

Healthy adolescent behavior is a beginning stage of differentiation. It is a time when they are developing autonomy, interpersonal relationships and purpose in light of becoming a responsible member of society. They are working out relationships with parents and other family members, teachers, adult authorities and mentors, and friends. They are developing a sexual self and interacting with the opposite sex in dating. They are learning tolerance for those of different faiths and cultures while searching for personal religious meaning, career goals and ultimate purpose. Life is a whirlwind of homework, extracurricular activities, church events and community involvement.

Parents who are sufficiently differentiated will be better prepared to stay connected to their teens in their process of individuation. They will be less reactive in personal matters but more forceful in taking appropriate action when necessary. In fact, wise parents will be part of their teenagers' differentiation process by giving them a chance to think out their positions through open discussion. Differentiated unity in the parental dyad can serve as a healthy model for teenage children to emulate. It gives them room to develop a solid self that is both separate from their family while maintaining a close relationship. Parents' behavior can even have a profound affect on how their teenage children relate to their friends. Cui, Congers, Bryant and Elders (2002) found that teenagers with supportive parents have closer friendship ties and less hostile relationships with other teenagers.

Keeping the marriage strong offers a secure place for teens who are coming into their own sense of self in relation to the family. While not perfect, spouses have modeled a covenant love that will not let them go, a gracing atmosphere that lets them be unique and an empowering attitude that builds them up to reach their full potential. Keeping closely connected assures them that intimacy is worth pursuing in their relationships.

Divorce

Divorce, though never expected, is an unfortunate experience for nearly half of all married persons. The ending of the marriage is inevitably a painful process of dealing with a failed relationship and the tremendous loss for everyone involved. Special consideration must be given to children who are part of the family.

When assessing the relative importance of relational skills and marital commitment in explaining divorce, Amato and DeBoer (2001) found commitment to be the more important factor. They also made the sobering discovery that children of divorced parents "have an elevated risk of seeing their own marriage end in divorce because they hold a comparatively weak commitment to the norm of lifelong marriage" (p. 1038). So commitment in marriage not only affects spousal stability but also has an influence on the potential stability of their children's future.

Graham's (1997) research on postdivorce parents noted a number of relational adjustments. Over time, a gradual relational progress was made when both parents were committed to caring for the children. Emotionally charged issues disrupted progress and impeded adjustment. Destructive patterns included a disjointed, erratic cycle in which the quality of the relationship with children fluctuated and eventually deteriorated when parents drifted apart.

Emotions experienced in the divorcing process are similar to the loss and grief during the death of a loved one: denial, anger, bargaining, depression and acceptance (Kübler-Ross, 1970). Price-Bonham and Balswick (1980) present a typical four-stage sequence of divorce as follows: the first stage, which begins prior to separation, is characterized as the *erosion of love;* the second stage is the *actual separation,* which typically entails bargaining, depression, anger, ambivalence, guilt and regret; the third stage is the *period prior to legal divorce,* in which legal issues, economic readjustments, coparenting arrangements, reorientation of lifestyle and renewed focus on personal identity and emotional functioning occur; the final stage is the *period of adjustment,* which brings a forward look toward new activities and goals. Acceptance of the divorce opens the way for personal recovery and restructuring a stable life. At this point, the divorcee is open to a new relationship and the potential of remarriage.

Remarriage and the Reconstituted Family

It should be recognized that remarriage occurs after the death of a spouse as well as after divorce. Statistics indicate that approximately three-fourths of all divorced persons remarry. Unfortunately, statistics also indicate that remarriages have an even higher divorce rate than first marriages, pointing to the unavoidable stressors involved in second and third marriages.

Since most remarriages involve the children of at least one of the partners and more likely both, a considerable amount of research has been conducted on the impact of children on remarriages. Visher, Visher and Pasley (2003) report that remarriages with children experience a multitude of stressors such as power and boundary issues; competing loyalties; custodial and visitation arrangements; working out relationship dynamics with children, parents and remarried spouses; discipline issues surrounding parenting stepchildren; and various structural changes (living arrangements, family of origin relationships, financial considerations, etc.).

In the beginning, stepfamilies are apt to be in a *fantasy stage,* with idealistic expectations about the newly formed family relationships, similar to that portrayed by *The Brady Bunch* (Papernow, 1993). This view is usually shattered in the *immersion stage,* when feelings of confusion, resentment and jealousy emerge as family members try to make sense of the boundary complexity and role ambiguity in their new family. Beyond this there is much variation in the trajectories of remarriages with children.

In research based on interviews assessing changing feelings over the initial four years of marriage, Baxter, Braithwaite and Nicholson (1999) report that 31% of stepfamilies rapidly progress to feeling family cohesion, 27% slowly progress toward family cohesion, 14% fail to develop a cohesive feeling, 6% start out feeling like a family but steadily decline in these feelings, and 22% fluctuate drastically in feeling like a family. It is hopeful news that families who will stick it out for at least four years get better for everybody. Some key principles that help remarried spouses get through the rough years until better relationships emerge include releasing themselves from high expectations; choosing to get along with stepchildren; having the biological parent discipline his/her own children until an appropriate transition is made; keeping a strong boundary and priority around the newly established marital relationship; having flexible boundaries that allow for extended family accessibility; and working cooperatively with ex-spouses for the best interest of the children.

The differentiated unity principle is highly applicable and indispensable to those who remarry. When remarried spouses have a developed sense of self, they will be less reactive (not taking things personally) with the stepchildren. As both spouses maintain a strong unity, they will stand together and not allow stressors of the remarried family dynamics to circumvent their marital vows. Maturity will give them a head start in knowing that flexibility is key in dealing with the emotional and structural upheaval that is an inevitable part of remarriage. They will adapt as needed to accommodate the many needs of this newly formed family. Braithwaite, Olson, Golish, Soukup and Turman (2001) identified three important factors in remarriage success: *boundary management, solidarity* and *adaptation*. These factors certainly fit with differentiation being a key determiner in the eventual success or failure of remarriage.

Launching Stage

This is the stage when children are preparing to leave home. The major factor contributing to the ease or discomfort of this event is the degree of *differentiated unity* that has been achieved by the couple. If adult children find it difficult to leave at a culturally appropriate time, it is likely they lack confidence (differentiation) to make it on their own—for example, grown children living at home still dependent on their parents for everything (food, shelter, finances). It may be that the parents have a need for their adult children to be dependent on them. Unless parents are willing to pull some of the feathers out of the nest, their children will not be inclined to become less dependent.

To assure a smooth transitioning through the launching stage, a married couple needs to focus on four areas: (1) the marriage relationship; (2) establishing an adult-to-adult relationship with children; (3) if the child marries, the development of good relationships with the child's spouse and his or her family; and (4) resolving issues with aging parents (Blacker, 1999; McCullough and Rutenberg, 1989). This leaving home stage is usually a transition in which adult children are preparing for their future, whether college, work, marriage or military service. It is a stressful time due to a frenzy of activity that accompanies their leaving. It's a big change for everyone in the family! Focusing on the future makes everyone at bit uneasy because it raises fears, regrets, sadness and sometimes anger. It is a big deal, and spouses need to take it seriously. Good planning helps move the process along at a pace that is right for all concerned.

Spouses will need to anticipate adjustment in their marriage. Undoubtedly, the kids will be missed, but the couple needs to think proactively about how their lives will go on after the leaving takes place. Much of their lives have revolved around the children, and therefore it can be a lonely time. Along with the loss, negative issues between spouses can resurface. The focus once again returns to the marriage relationship.

This is an opportune time to work on revitalizing the spousal relationship. It won't be such a huge chore for couples that established a differentiated unity earlier, but this stage can be especially difficult for couples who have not done so. Either way, after the children have been launched, loss of focus on the children can leave couples floundering when it comes to their relationship. On the other hand, freedom can also bring a new spontaneity that feels exhilarating. There is time to deepen friendships and develop new community support; enjoy things you've always wanted to do such as hobbies, classes, sports or travel; volunteer for meaningful service or church activities; downsize into a smaller home or redecorate. In this season the spousal relationship is revitalized and deepens in terms of couple meaning.

Emerging Adulthood Stage

Adult children who come back home after they have left are referred to as *boomerang children*. This is a fairly new phenomenon due to a variety of circumstances, such as loss of or inability to find a job, marital troubles, financial struggles and addictions. In 2002, a poll reported that 62% of graduating college seniors planned to move home for a period of time, and it is predicted that nearly 40% of children will return home at some point (Ianzito, 2004). Ianzito reports that Gordon and Susan Morris Shaffer refer to this gap between fledging self-sufficiency and confident adult status as "adultescence." When done right, those adult children will pull their weight in the home by using their gifts and resources for the good of the family.

In many cultures it's customary for adult children to live at home during the in-between times, especially prior to marriage. Likewise, parents who value interdependency will do what they can to provide support for adult children during such transitions without thinking of it as a failure. Communicating as respectful adults, working out mutually agreeable living arrangements and adopting empowerment principles will go a long way in making this a positive experience. The conditions under which adult children return to the home will be clearly stated as parents and their adult children work out matters of fiscal responsibility, paying rent, doing laundry, cooking meals, contributing to the running of the household, interacting in positive ways with others in the home, repayment of loans and courtesies of living together.

When giving this transitional support, a couple needs to consider the difference between enabling, which fosters dependence and unhealthy patterns, and empowering, which provides support while encouraging growth, personal responsibility and healthy interdependence. Savvy parents will be able to keep a healthy attitude so the adult child finds this to be a stepping stone toward independent living. It is a different world than it was in our generation, so flexibility will be a key to making the needed adjustments during this transition. By focusing on respectful interdependence, parents and adult children can co-create a positive plan to work out areas of tension and establish an appropriate time frame for the arrangement. Living together in an attitude of trust and love will enhance the relationship.

Post-Launching/Empty Nest Stage

When the nest is clearly emptied at last, the marriage truly becomes a dyad again. For most couples this is a time to refocus and invest more time on the spousal relationship. This availability for each other, combined with the fact that many marital conflicts center on parenting issues, probably explains why the rate of marital happiness increases somewhat after children leave the home (White & Edwards, 1990). When the marriage relationship has matured through a transforming differentiation process, the empty nest period can be a time of satisfying companionship.

What goes on during earlier stages of marriage may have much to do with ease or difficulty during the empty nest stage. For some couples the empty nest period is a difficult time. This perhaps explains a rise in the divorce rate that occurs after twenty-five years of marriage. In a study of over 5,000 women, Heidmann, Suhomlinova and O'Rand (1998) found that divorce is much higher among couples that entered their empty nest years after only 25 years of marriage when compared to those who became empty nesters after 35 years of marriage. The researchers speculate that those who become empty nesters after only 25 years of marriage probably had children soon after they married, depriving them of time to develop a solid marriage dyad. On the other hand, couples that enter their empty nest years after 34 years of marriage probably had their children later in marriage, after having a sufficient amount of time to adjust to each other and form a solid relationship.

Pryor (1999) reports that couples who experience difficulty in the empty nest years had experienced difficulties during the earlier stages of their marriage. This fits with our differentiated unity model; the couples that had low levels of cohesion, high levels of conflict and marital boundary issues had more trouble sustaining a viable marriage. It might very well be that some couples in troubled marriages stay together for the sake of their children, only to divorce when they leave home.

For some empty nest couples, the term *sandwich generation* applies, a concept coined to refer to couples who are sandwiched between the financial and emotional responsibilities they still have for adult children and an increased responsibility for their elderly and dependent parents. For those over sixty years of age, individual well-being has to do with feeling competent and in control of several dimensions of life—relationships with each other, immediate family members and friends; personal safety; personal economic conditions; health; housing; transportation; daily activities and work.

Most often, couples in this stage are able to invest more time in work or career, deepen friendships, spend time with grandchildren and increase involvement in ministry or voluntary activities. While they are continuing to leave their mark on the world, perhaps the greater achievement for spouses is that they have left a mark on each other. Blessed and delighted to have meaning and purpose as individuals and as a couple, they continue to bear the fruit of a fulfilled life.

Retirement Years: The Best for Last!

The past and future meet in the retirement stage. Retirement can be anticipated with a nagging dread or great excitement, depending on how it's perceived. Viewing retirement as moving forward rather than removing ourselves from life gives a new purpose. Blessed to have come to this point and assured of their enduring love, spouses can enter the retirement journey with positive resolve.

In some ways, retirement can be seen as the prime of marital life. Spouses are wiser and hopefully content with what they have accomplished in life. Though the physical body is declining, mature differentiation has created a bolder self. No longer needing to prove oneself to anyone, we are free to follow our unique heartbeat. In an interview, Maya Angelou (2005) said it well: "I put a big red flower in my hair, wear the colors I most enjoy whether they're in fashion or not, put a swing in my hip and move into the world with the confidence of who I am" (p. 57). She notes that people advised her to take the flower out of her hair and buy some new clothes, but for her it's just as natural and exciting to be herself, as she is.

In terms of health, most of us are aging well. We don't have to assume a downhill road with the many medical advances that help relieve the normal aches and pains and keep us generally healthy. People are not only living longer, but most adults over 65 are in good health, according to Robert Butler (1988), who found a ripping 71% report that their health is excellent, very good or good.

Still, health issues are a concern for many in this phase of life. Enter a room with people in their sixties and you will hear the topic of health issues come up. There are physical realities that must be dealt with. Lifestyle and health practices are critical. How spouses respond to physical ailments or disease impacts the relationship. Since mind and body are intricately linked together, psychological factors (attitudes and emotions) affect the physical just as the physical affects our emotional life. Older persons need to pay close attention to good nutrition, low calorie and cholesterol intake, moderate use of alcohol, regular exercise and sleep patterns.

A major change for a retired couple is the huge amount of discretionary time. Spouses not only have time on their hands, but a lot of time together. Spending so much time together can cause tension between spouses if they have neglected their relationship. We recall the comments of a wife in one of our marital seminars: "Since Henry's retirement he is around all the time, I don't know what to do with him. I wish he would find some outside activity so I can spend more time with my female friends." In such a case, further differentiation is needed for the couple to become interdependent rather than overly dependent on each other at this stage. Each spouse can enjoy personal activities, friendships and meaning as well as couple activities, friendships and meaning.

Retirement is a time of changing gears. Just like the other stages, it opens up an opportunity to expand and determine future goals. It brings much joy to engage with children, grandchildren and great-grandchildren. Umpteen ministry opportunities can keep our lives fulfilling. It vitalizes the marriage for spouses to enjoy meaningful activities together such as being involved in missions, traveling, church and community service. It's about living the breadth as well as the length of life.

Sunset Years: Blissful and Blessed

Someone once said, "The great thing about getting older is that you don't lose all the other ages you've been." By this stage, spouses have been through an incredible journey together. The life they've lived is no doubt radically different than the one they imagined on the day they were married. But having come through it all together, they can move into this last stage with confidence. Their previous years contain a reservoir of memories to draw upon as they continue to find meaning in the sunset years.

For many over eighty, health has declined and spouses may be caring for each other. Some will live in retirement communities, others in health care facilities to assist them in their waning physical and mental health. The resources given by family and friends will continue to be an incredible blessing.

Dickson (1995) found that couples who have been happily married for fifty years or more have three things in common: (1) They treat each other with mutual respect and dignity. (2) They have established a comfortable level of closeness. (3) They have a shared vision and course of action. In her book *Lasting Love: What Keeps Couples Together,* Judy Pearson (1992) found that couples married for fifty years perceive themselves in more optimistic terms than reality would suggest. They report that disagreements are infrequent, and conflicts, though rare, don't seem to have a negative impact on their relationship. They are ready to forgive, keep negative attitudes at bay and have a positive outlook on life. Laughter and humor are an important part of their relationship. They enjoy recounting fond memories of their courtship and the positive memories over the years.

Radiant faces of old love emerge through the rich marital history of commitment, differentiation and devotion. Most likely they have forgiven each other millions of times and have learned to smile rather than grimace about their differences. By now they have learned the fine art of "giving up self" for the good of the marriage. Indeed, they are companions to the end, grateful for their intimate love as they reach out for a gentle touch at the end of the day.

The movie *On Golden Pond* gives a glimpse of a couple at this stage of life. Kathryn Hepburn, in her role as Ethel, affectionately refers to Norman, played by Henry Fonda, as the "old poop" when his pessimism gets the better of him. In turn, he pokes fun of her eternal optimism. Their basic personalities have not changed after all these years, and their mutual acceptance is seen in the humorous bantering. We begin to realize an uncanny interdependency between them as they enter the uncertainties of aging, illness, impending death and the unknowns of their future. They have come to overlook the unessential and hold on ferociously to the essential bond of their togetherness. The sweet scene at the end of the film shows them holding each other (two are better than one) at the end of that long journey of two shared lives.

THE DUAL-EARNER MARRIAGE

An Elaborate Balancing Act

DUAL-EARNER HOMES ARE THE MOST COMMON FORM of marriage in the United States. Although the proportion has been declining since 2000, the Bureau of Labor Statistics (2005, p. 2) reports that 50.7% of married-couple families in 2004 were dual earner. In addition, only 7% of the families are considered traditional arrangements where the mother stays home with the children

It is truly an elaborate balancing act for spouses to keep their relationship and their family a priority as a result of "circuit overload." The couple who decides that they will both work outside the home must think of how to accomplish this in the most satisfactory way, with the best interests of every family member in mind. We believe the couple must proactively establish and maintain a rightful balance of work and family. When spouses hold equally high commitments to work and home life, they must balance the demands of both. In wanting to do it all, sooner or later something gives, whether it's work, the marriage, parenting or the emotional health of the spouses themselves

The trinitarian model may provide a helpful perspective. The concept of mutual indwelling *(perichorisis)* suggests that women and men's work roles need not be as bifurcated as in the past. Following biblical principles of covenant love, both spouses contribute to the good of the whole while fulfilling their unique needs and desires. Grace recognizes and accepts unique personalities and abilities. Mutual empowerment urges spouses to maximize the development of their potential. Unity in decisions about work and family roles binds their lives intimately for the common good. Their complementary meaning in work and family is based on their life in Christ and their honoring God in all they do.

In a dual-earner marriage spouses share the role of provider and homemaker, whereas in the single-earner marriage one spouse is designated as the provider and the other as the homemaker. When spouses are satisfied with these arrangements all is well, but dissatisfaction will be a source of stress and potential conflict.

Balancing Work Roles and Home Roles

It takes agility to juggle work and family roles! We believe it challenges differentiation in spouses and can be an opportunity to attend to the desires of each spouse while keeping the marriage strong. We offer a perspective that takes into account many different dual-earner stances to assist spouses in their elaborate balancing act at different stages of marriage.

Table 12.1 illustrates the different ways couples balance commitment to work and family. The horizontal continuum represents commitment to the home, ranging from low commitment at the left to high commitment at the right. The vertical continuum represents commitment to work, ranging from low commitment at the bottom to high commitment at the top.

The most conflictive balancing style is the *adversaries* (top left side of

Table 12.1. Balancing Commitment to Work and Family Life: Alternative Strategies Used by Dual-Earner Couples

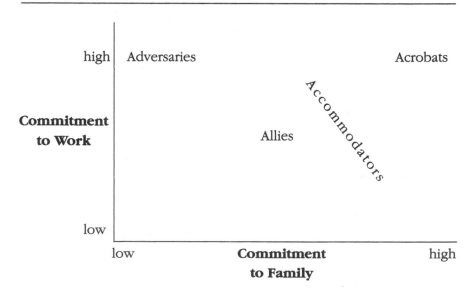

table 12.1). In this case neither spouse wants to be the homemaker, so each tries to persuade the other to do it. A less adversarial pattern is when both spouses choose to put 100% into work and homemaking roles. In order to successfully meet the high demands in both arenas, they need the agility of an *acrobat* (top right side of table 12.1). While *acrobats* think they can do it all, when they run short of the time and energy to do it all, the stress takes a toll on the marriage.

Represented in the middle of the table are the *allies,* who blend their commitment to work and home. They are allies in the sense that they truly share responsibility for home life and are willing to sacrifice advancement at work for the sake of the marriage and family. Both spouses may choose to take part-time work so both can be involved in the nurturing of their children.

Accommodators agree to take turns in the home and work roles at different times throughout the family life stages. Neither spouse is expected to carry the entire load in either the area of earning money or managing the home. Over time, as demands in either area change, they switch the balance. The husband may pull back from his career commitments in order to increase time given to family life because his wife is at a crucial stage in her career. Spouses function as teammates by clarifying these roles and prioritizing the essentials from the nonessentials in making these decisions. Honoring each other's gifts and taking circumstances into consideration, they work toward the good of the whole family.

Accommodators agree to be different in their work and home priorities. In this arrangement each spouse chooses to take a majority role in either work or home according to preference and circumstances. While *allies* stress equality in work and home roles, *accommodators* complement each other in their unique role strengths and preferences. For example, a wife loves the homemaking and mothering role while the husband enjoys the work world, so they happily agree to take on these major roles. Even when the homemaker spouse is employed, she/he has the more flexible work schedule—for example, works out of a home office to be with the children during illness or see that they get to their activities at unusual hours and so forth. This couple works together for the good of the whole family.

Allies and *accommodators* work out a balancing act based on a complementary model, recognizing that roles may need to be altered due to crucial life circumstances in career or homemaking responsibilities. When a career requires extensive traveling or when young children demand more attention, spouses will be flexible enough to do what is needed at that point in time.

Dual-earner marriages need an extra dose of flexibility. Spouses change roles as circumstances change in work and in the home. They must learn tremendous skills to manage spillover from both worlds. Dual-earner couples who do it well have perfected an amazing balancing act. By bringing the best of both spouses in both areas of life, everyone gains.

Household Chores: A Big Dilemma

For either spouse who has a full-time job outside the home, taking on household chores and family responsibilities is like a second shift! The dilemma can be especially pronounced for women since they end up doing more of the second-shift work. Research finds that women who earn *less* than their husbands do more housework as compensation, yet those women who earn *more* also do more second-shift work to alleviate guilt about their higher wage. It's a no-win situation whatever way you look at it. Reynolds (2005) reports that conflict at work or home makes women want to decrease the number of hours they work outside the home whether the conflict originates at home or at work. Men, on the other hand, only want to decrease their hours at work when the conflict is at work, with only some choosing to increase their hours at work, presumably as a way to escape the reality of the home conflict.

It's true that both spouses have limited energy for the second shift when they expend a vast amount of time and energy working outside the home. Yet in the majority of cases, it's the women who carry the major burden of household and family matters. In fact, when calculating the additional work performed by the average wife, it amounts to an extra month each year. No wonder women crash from the exhaustion of working not one, but two full-time jobs.

When asked, both husbands and wives agree that housework should be shared, but the truth of the matter is that husbands *think* they help out more than they actually do when they keep track of hours spent in these activities. The more complicating fact is that both husbands *and* wives believe the second shift is the *wife's* responsibility. So even when husbands do share household chores, it's usually the wives who take on the *responsibility* of managing and organizing the tasks.

While husbands in dual-earner marriages actually do help out more in the home when compared to single-earner husbands, the time spent in the home averages less than one hour per day. In addition, husbands are selective about what tasks they are willing to do. For example, few men assume responsibility for washing dirty clothes, cleaning toilets, scrubbing floors and a host of other unpleasant tasks. While they agree to help out with caring for the children, don't ask them to change a diaper or clean up vomit. Fathers are prone to play with their children rather than take on the nitty-gritty tasks.

One should not be surprised that the issue of marital equality is especially pronounced in the dual-earner marriage. Rabin (1996) notes that western-influenced societies hold beliefs about marriage that range on a continuum from *traditional* at one end to *egalitarian* at the other. However, many marriages today are *transitional,* falling at neither extreme but somewhere in the middle. Rabin notes that the transitional marriage is characterized by greater conflict because spouses must negotiate new behaviors and roles during the in-between transition times. This adds a significant amount of stress to the marriage.

Recent research confirms that perceived fairness is related to the division of labor for women in equalitarian and transitional families but not in traditional ones. For equalitarian women, a more segregated division of labor is linked directly with lower marital quality (Klute, Crouter, Sayer & McHale, 2002). These studies point to the importance of gender ideology in understanding satisfaction or dissatisfaction in traditional and equalitarian dual-earner marriages and how this affects marital quality and satisfaction. Traditionally oriented dual-earner wives value *conformity* more and tend to be less discontent with division of household tasks based on gender, while equalitarian oriented dual-earner wives value *self-direction* more and are discontent when family roles are not shared equally.

In their research, Gottman and Silver (1994) found that husbands who do housework have better health, better sex lives and happier marriages.

Both husbands and wives benefit when household cleanliness standards and parenting expectations are reasonable. He concludes, "Men would be well advised to be vigilant for inequities in child care and housework, and to ask their wives if there is a problem—women are unlikely to bring it up until their mounting frustration leads to an explosion. And men will get many points for their thoughtfulness" (pp. 157-58). Note that it was also important for husbands to be validated for their involvement in household and child-care activities. Of course, expressions of appreciation are important for all family members and when given enhance the relationships.

Mutuality of shared roles increases satisfaction for both husbands and wives at work and at home. In her research on peer marriages, Pepper Schwartz (2004) found that when spouses make a successful effort to divide chores fairly, they both benefit. It allows the wife, in particular, to find fulfillment in work, marriage and mothering. Inequalities in household and child-care activities, on the other hand, have profound negative consequences, adversely affecting satisfaction and quality in marriage.

One of the important findings in Hochschild's (1989) study was that a couple's inability to work out shared responsibility of household duties resulted in marital tension, whereas couples who worked out equitable sharing were the happiest. Spouses agreed that getting to an equitable arrangement was a difficult but rewarding journey. The ability to work out a satisfactory division of family and home responsibilities may be just as important as the fact that they agree to share these tasks. When there is a perception of fairness, appreciation and unity, satisfaction increases.

Tension About a Wife's Employment

A husband's lack of support for his wife's employment has consistently been found to be a significant source of tension in marriage. Not only is a lack of support from the husband linked with depression among dual-earner wives (Ulbrich 1988), but lack of fit in work schedule has been found to lead to psychological distress (Gareis, Barnett & Brennan, 2003). Depression was a common complaint among employed wives when husbands were either opposed to or had a negative attitude about their employment. Indeed, the husband's attitudes about work roles, marital roles and personal roles determined his reaction to her status as a wage earner. The degree of congruency between his beliefs about *what is right* and the reality of *what is* greatly impacts the couple's degree of satisfaction or dissatisfaction.

Spouses must take seriously the discrepancy between what a husband believes about his wife being a wage earner and the realities of the marriage. When the wife of a husband who holds to the traditional model of marriage works full time, his image as sole breadwinner is challenged. Her employment smacks his male ego with the message that he is insufficient as the sole provider. Even when he agrees that her salary helps pay the bills, it can be a point of contention since it is inconsistent with how he thinks things *should* be. This places his wife in a difficult situation because her employment in his mind defines him as a failure. She inadvertently becomes the brunt of his discontent.

Though many husbands are glad when their wives find personal fulfillment in work, their masculine identity may be threatened when her work is an economic necessity. When his masculinity is based on role stereotypes, his self-worth is at risk. One study found that husbands who were aggressive, dominant and emotionally tough helped out less than men who were expressive toward their wives (Nyquist, Slivken & Spence, 1985). They were more comfortable assuming the traditional male tasks like mowing the lawn, taking care of the car and making minor household repairs.

Some husbands not only fail to appreciate their wife's financial contribution, but actually devalue her employment status. It's as if the hours she puts in at work produces a zero return in her husband's eyes. On the other hand, if the wife has no interest in being employed but does it grudgingly, she is apt to minimize herself and her work. In fact, if a woman gets caught midstream between a traditional marriage ideal and the reality of having to work to make ends meet, her frustration is likely to be disrupting to the marriage.

Not surprising, husbands who were more flexible in their masculine self-identity believed in equalitarian roles. They assumed more responsibility for housework than husbands who held rigid, traditional attitudes about manhood. That's how it worked when Curt and Susan changed from traditional roles to a dual-earner marriage. When they found themselves in financial straits, Susan found a job to help with the income. Curt admitted to being a bit threatened when she brought home her first pay-check. He feared she would have less respect for him and it would di-minish his power. These fears were allayed through intentional dialogue about their mutual decision. They agreed together how to manage their dual-earner home: Susan had more say in how the money was spent—a nice reward for earning money—but Curt had more say as they made decisions about parenting and other family matters.

Their mutual desire to take joint leadership in their home helped them redefine their previous notions of power. Curt realized that a cooperative model meant he no longer felt the sole burden of providing for the fam-ily. In working out the cooperative details, each spouse's unique strengths were recognized and affirmed. They showed appreciation for each other in a way that helped them feel mutually powerful. Their dual-earner home served to enhance their relationship rather than disrupt it.

Costs and Benefits of Dual-Earner Marriage

The most common stressors for dual-earner husbands are physical and emotional overload, decrease in leisure time, increased time spent on household tasks, decreased sexual activity due to exhaustion or lack of time, decreased opportunities for career placement, multiple role de-mands and less time for emotional life with one's wife. The benefits for men in a dual-earner marriage are increased income, greater content-ment of the wife and an emergence of her independent identity, the wife's greater opportunity for social interaction, less pressure on him to provide economically and greater rewards from parenting.

Often overlooked is the benefit to men who rethink this area of life and are therefore liberated from culturally restrictive definitions of man-hood. Men who break free from a narrowly defined view of masculinity enrich their potential to expand themselves. A dual-earner marriage pre-sents an opportunity for increased intimacy with spouse and children. Husbands discovered that taking on these roles enhanced relationship dynamics. In the mutual giving and receiving, satisfaction is found through the oneness achieved.

When the inevitable pressures from both work and family threaten to pull the marriage apart, this mutual agreement to be equally involved in work and family responsibilities protects the union. Working together to balance the multiple challenges and demands of the dual-earner marriage deepens marital covenant, enhances differentiated unity, increases emotional intimacy and shared meaning. Putting the priority on interdependence keeps spouses focused on growing together rather than growing apart in all aspects of their lives.

Coparenting Benefits

Research indicates that coparenting benefits parents and children alike. Marital quality is also related to coparenting quality (Floyd, Gilliom & Costigan,1998). Coparented children do better in a number of areas when compared to those who are parented by one parent. Children who have closer relationships to both parents are more secure, do better in school, adapt better in social discrimination skills, display greater creativity and moral development, have less animosity toward the other gender and develop strong friendship bonds with opposite-sex children (Ehrensaft, 1990; Stright & Neitzel, 2003).

Change always disrupts the status quo. When trying on new roles, both spouses will have to make adjustments for the long-range impact to take hold. After Judy started graduate school, I (Jack) remember how hard it was to follow through on the decision to be a coparent. I was responsible for the children and cooking evening meals while Judy was taking classes. One evening while I was settling an issue between our two children, Judy came in the door and rushed over to help settle the argument. I asked Judy to back out of the situation. In order for me to effectively take on the role of disciplinarian, Judy had to stay out of it. Judy struggled to let go of an old role, while I was taking on a new role. Yet she recognized the importance of letting me deal with such situations myself as we adapted. By respecting the different ways mothers and fathers deal with children, we came up with a more congruent coparenting plan.

Doing It Well

In order to do it well, dual-earner couples need to develop a *proactive* plan for work and family life. When couples have a *reactive* response to circumstances, they merely respond to the pressures and tensions created in the moment. A proactive response means they agree about goals and decide how they will deal with pressures they will face. In this way, a couple establishes, to the best of their ability, a back-up plan for when unexpected circumstances occur. Being intentional helps a couple anticipate obstacles and issues, rather than letting circumstances control them.

A first step in taking a proactive response is to distinguish between what can be changed and what can't. Reinhold Niebuhr's prayer expresses a wise strategy: "God, grant me the serenity to accept the things I cannot change, courage to change the things I can, and wisdom to know the difference." The second step is to identify existing and potential resources for the marriage. Children are resources when they take a cooperative participant role. Studies show that giving appropriate responsibility to children in the home actually builds qualities of responsibility in their character. One unintended positive consequence of dual-earner marriage may be that as children take more responsibility for household tasks, they become more responsible children. Extended family, friends and neighbors can also provide back-up resources and support. The family-friendly workplace also provides resources that are in the best interest of the family and their businesses.

A Personal Note

Our dual-earner marriage began about the time our children reached school age. It took a while for Jack to get the idea that he was not merely helping out, but that he was to assume equal coresponsibility for home and children. When we encountered differences about household cleanliness standards, Jack decided that vacuuming once a month would do, whether the rugs needed it or not! This wasn't good enough for me; I wanted the rugs to at least be vacuumed several times a week. We compromised, and Jack faithfully vacuumed every week—whether needed or not!

Since affirmation was important in his new role, I (Judy) was glad to show appreciation. I stepped outside my comfort zone as well by taking the car to the garage to get repairs. I learned to assert myself when communicating to the mechanics. Coresponsibility meant that we both had to give up something in order to gain the benefits our new roles offered.

We found marital equality foundational to maintaining a rightful balance of work and family (Balswick & Balswick, 1995). Rather than merely reacting to life circumstances and pressures, we were intentional in forming an equal-participation marriage. Here are some important points we learned from our dual-earner marriage: establish a close relationship; be flexible and adaptable to life circumstances; agree on priorities; focus on the essentials; and draw upon all the resources you can muster to help meet the demands of parenting and family life.

It took discernment, wisdom and practice to juggle work and home-making roles. It was necessary to set priorities. For example, rather than letting ourselves be overly concerned about the specks of dust under the bed, we were more reasonable about cleaning standards. Our relationships with our kids and each other would be more important priorities. We no longer fixed gourmet meals, but found efficient, nutritional recipes for the family. We settled for being *good-enough* jugglers, and when things got out of balance we learned from our mistakes, made changes and continued on. The benefit to both of us was enormous. We wouldn't be teaching and writing today on a professional level without the major shift early on in our marriage. We are forever grateful that we are in it together and reaping the rewards; our two grown married children and four grandsons are doing well, as are we!

SEXUALITY IN ITS SPLENDOR

One-Flesh Mystery

THERE IS NOTHING MORE FULL OF SPLENDOR than marital sexuality that is a reflection of trinitarian relationality. Inversely, marital sexuality without a meaningful relationship is terribly disconcerting. The Genesis account of the one-flesh union is rooted in the mystery of the Triune God. As Ray Anderson (2004) comments, "Human beings, in some inexplicable way, image divine being, particularly in being man and woman. . . . the biblical story is a mirror, not a myth, disclosing to us the soul of humanity as a reflection of the soul of God."

Adam and Eve immediately recognize their likeness, "bone of my bones and flesh of my flesh" (Gen 2:23), and in the same moment are intrigued with their distinctiveness. Their gender and sexual distinctiveness as male and female opens up incredible possibilities in coming to know themselves and the other in the context of their mysterious one-flesh relationship. Knowing and becoming known encompasses every aspect of their being. The reality of becoming "one flesh" entails much more than a mere sexual knowing; it is an all-inclusive knowing (emotional, intellectual, spiritual) that brings ultimate meaning in forming their union. Adam and Eve form an interdependent alliance in responsive obedience to God's command to have dominion over all things and to replenish the earth. According to Ray Anderson (2004), it is in their human encounter as man *and* woman, as well as in their distinctive task of being a man *or* woman of God, that they affirm the divine image.

God created us as sexual beings and pronounced it good. By design our sexual nature moves us toward intimate knowing. Through mutual exchange and engagement, our sexuality deepens relationship meaning. Ultimately, two distinct individuals mesh their lives together—body, mind and spirit—in the giving and receiving, creating a uniting purpose for their lives together. It's not merely the sexual encounter that drives us; it's the complete one-flesh experience of two persons becoming one through mutual vulnerability and responsiveness. The free-flowing interchange in which two whole persons intermingle to form a mystical one-flesh union is deeply satisfying emotionally and intellectually and spiritually.

Phyllis Trible (1987) writes about the erotic expression between the lovers in the Song of Solomon: "Neither escaping nor exploiting sex, they embrace and enjoy it. Their love is truly bone of bone and flesh of flesh, and this image of God as male and female is indeed very good" (p. 161). Their attraction leads to an enthusiastic expression of person-centered love. They offer themselves wholeheartedly as lover to the beloved. It goes beyond sexual desire; it is a longing for the beloved him or herself.

Emotional transparency is an essential part of such person-centered intimacy. Exposed in every way through the sharing of their lives, spouses are making room for each other as they form an interdependent union. Being fully in tune with each other, they engage in well-choreographed expressions of love. And the reciprocal giving and receiving of selves culminates in a unity that transcends them both. They have discovered the splendor of emotional, physical, psychological and spiritual unity.

Differentiation and Person-Centered Sexual Expression

The capacity for achieving person-centered intimacy corresponds to one's level of differentiation. Differentiation is that ongoing, lifelong process (described in chapter eight) of achieving a balanced awareness of self, spouse and relationship in which interdependency flourishes. Trible (1987) explains that "leaving and cleaving are interrelated. . . . the man does not leave one family to start another; rather he abandons familial identity for the one flesh of sexuality" (p. 104).

In fact, the sexual relationship acts as a grindstone that sharpens spousal differentiation (Schnarch, 1997). Undifferentiated spouses tend to hold back out of reluctance to reveal too much of themselves. It is a frightening prospect to be vulnerable when validation is wholly dependent on the spouse's approval. While they may enjoy the pleasure of physical sex, they cheat themselves out of the deeper meaning that comes from a person-centered sexual bonding.

Low levels of differentiation lead some spouses toward engulfment and others toward disengagement. In either case, the relationship is kept at a superficial level. Lacking the ability to create person-centered connection, spouses either try to fill that emotional deficit through frequent sex for reassurance or little sex to stay safely disengaged.

Well-differentiated spouses, on the other hand, are able to form a gratifying emotional bond without suffocating or distancing. They hold each other without clutching and release without cutting themselves off emotionally. They grow into two fully formed persons who continue to develop a rewarding person-centered intimacy in their sexual encounters. Because they focus on each other as whole persons, their sexual engagement is a person-centered engagement without the need for fantasy diversions or distractions. There is a quality in the person-centered sexual encounter in which mutual desire determines the frequency. It's the meeting of two persons (I to I) who give themselves to each other completely that creates the sexual splendor.

Cornerstone Principles of Marital Sex

The four biblical principles of *covenant, gracing, empowering* and *intimacy* can deepen sexual meaning in marriage. Spouses who practice these principles will move toward more profound levels of emotional and sexual bonding. Conversely, responding to each other with the opposite behaviors—conditional love, shaming, controlling and distancing—will inhibit the couple's capacity for achieving intimacy. This reverse cycle results in broken trust, unforgiving spirits, constant criticism, and withholding or controlling tendencies that keep them distant and removed emotionally and sexually.

Covenant love secures sexual trust. Covenant love promotes security in the sexual relationship. According to Barry McCarthy (2003), the role of marital sexuality is to energize the marital bond of respect, trust and intimacy. Research has found that both husbands and wives invest themselves more fully in sex when they feel secure in the relationship. When trust is broken, suspicion and jealousy emerge as defenses that automatically shut down sexual responsiveness. Later in the chapter we'll discuss the destructive impact of sexual and emotional affairs on the marriage, the most destructive breaches of all.

The vast majority of Americans are monogamous and happy about it, according to studies on sexuality (Laumann, Gagnon, Michael & Michaels, 1994). Marital commitment proves to be an important aspect of sexual openness. Waite and Joyner (2001) report that for both men and women, sexual exclusivity is strongly related to emotional satisfaction in marriage. Married persons who express satisfaction with their sex lives also indicate that emotional commitment enhances their sexual relationship. Covenant love provides a secure foundation in which sexual intimacy is able to thrive.

Of course, all spouses struggle to be consistently unconditional in their love. It is not an easy task! It takes commitment and fortitude to live according to such high ideals. But when doing so, covenant love opens spouses up to the delights of erotic passion and free abandonment. Confident in themselves and their spouse, they are free to give and receive the mutual tender touches of affection.

Gracing love secures sexual safety. While covenant offers security in terms of trust, grace establishes security through actions of acceptance and forgiveness. In order to accept our spouses just as they are, it is necessary to understand their sexual value system and how it informs their sexuality. In grace-full actions, spouses who show compassion for each other's sexual idiosyncrasies and limitations will be seen as Christlike. The grace-full marriage is a safe sanctuary to share past sexual hurts and mistakes. When painful past experiences have occurred, such as sexual abuse, rape or addiction, it takes extraordinary understanding and compassion to support each other. But knowing the spouse's sexual history brings understanding that can result in kindness, consideration, forgiveness and support that eventually deepens the relationship connection.

A spouse's sexual value system is developed through early childhood experiences, family, cultural, religious and societal influences. Every couple is challenged right from the beginning of their sexual relationship to grapple with these personal values. For instance, if either spouse is uncomfortable with some aspect of their sexual relationship, it is imperative that he or she can speak honestly about it rather than hold back out of fear of being judged or shamed. Labels like "prudish" or "overly sexed" have no place in this discussion. Personal sexual preferences must be understood and honored in light of different underlying beliefs and values.

Grace-full love gives the impetus for following a pathway toward deeper bonding. Together a couple will determine the sexual practices that enhance their sexual relationship. When honest differences emerge, each spouse must be willing consider what is best for the relationship, whether this is to relinquish a sexual preference or to stretch beyond a comfort zone for the sake of the other. As spouses keep the good of the relationship in mind, neither will try to persuade or coerce the other in these matters. Instead, both will choose to honor as well as to please their spouse in their sexual preferences.

Grace will also be practiced when it comes to gender differences. A common tendency is for men to feel emotionally close through sexual intimacy, while women open up to sexual intimacy when they feel emotional connection with their spouse. While men bask in emotional connection just as women enjoy sexual encounter, spouses must acknowledge differences and create a balance in sexual and emotional intimacy. Sexual appetite usually deteriorates when emotional intimacy is lacking, just as emotional connection deteriorates when sexual interest loses its vigor. Sexual differences can cause turmoil, but gracing responses will help spouses get beyond their differences in order to mutually enjoy their sexual relationship.

Forgiveness is a gift of grace that softens the sharp edges of sexual misunderstandings and human blunders. Making mistakes in the sexual arena requires honest confrontation and the ability to forgive and be forgiven, which then clears the way for restoration and renewal.

Empowering love enhances sexual potential. The empowering principle seeks the full sexual potential of each spouse through a synchronous rhythm of interaction and interdependence. The principle of differentiated unity is noted in 1 Corinthians 7:3-5, "The husband should give to his wife her conjugal rights, and likewise the wife to her husband. For the wife does not have authority over her own body, but the husband does; likewise the husband does not have authority over his own body, but the wife does. Do not deprive one another except perhaps by agreement for a set time, to devote yourselves to prayer, and then come together again, so that Satan may not tempt you because of your lack of self-control."

In this passage, Paul holds up full mutuality and equality as the highest ideal in marital sexuality. Each spouse is encouraged to express personal preference while honoring the spouse's preference as well. It's not a matter of either spouse promoting personal needs but of negotiating mutual satisfaction. One spouse should never seek to override the other, since the ultimate goal is what's best for the relationship. Just as a symphony makes harmonious music when each instrument contributes its unique part, so the married couple reaches sexual harmony through mutual agreement.

In contrast to empowerment, controlling maneuvers are fundamentally at odds with sexual fulfillment. Engaging in sex should never be a mandate but an invitation. If one spouse initiates sex and the other is unresponsive, it is often interpreted as a personal rejection by a spouse who is undifferentiated. In reaction to those feelings, that spouse may resort to belittling or demanding sex, which makes matters worse. In contrast, a differentiated spouse is not inclined to take the partner's disinterest as a personal rejection. Having a solid self allows the initiating spouse to accept a *no* gracefully, understanding there are many legitimate reasons a spouse may not feel like engaging in sex. The more important thing for differentiated spouses is to have a willing partner who fully participates in the sexual encounter rather than one who says *yes* without really engaging. The ideal of person-centered sex is full participation of both spouses. So, respecting an honest *no* also guarantees that when the spouse says *yes* you know the spouse is responding out of choice and enthusiasm.

Negative feelings between spouses can affect their sexual desire and responsiveness. In a study of couples in their first years of marriage, anger was shown to have a negative effect on sexual satisfaction (Henderson-King & Veroff, 1994). Unresolved anger may get acted out in terms of a sexual power struggle. For example, a wife who wants to have a baby may seduce her husband into having sex without using birth control, or a husband may refrain from sex because he does not want to risk a pregnancy. Intimacy is sabotaged and sex becomes a battleground of manipulation and control. Indirect methods like turning silent, failing to respond or angry withdrawal only dampen intimacy. Spouses must be forthright rather than harbor bad feelings. It behooves a couple to work out conflicts without bringing them into the marriage bed.

A vital, person-centered sexual relationship is undoubtedly mutually empowering and mutually gratifying. In fact, numerous studies have shown that an active positive sex life is actually good for one's physical and mental health—longer life, better heart health, improved ability to ward off pain, a more robust immune system and protection against depression and even certain cancers. So staying sexually healthy is good for the spouses as well as the relationship.

Sexual knowing promotes emotional intimacy. Marital sexuality is designed to be woven into a wider fabric of knowing and being known. Sexual intimacy is only as good as the emotional intimacy achieved between spouses. The ability to know and be known sexually deepens emotional bonding. Spousal disclosure and vulnerability—whether sharing about past sexual history, well-kept secrets or any number of feelings and attitudes regarding sex—heighten awareness of our inner selves and promote healing and bonding.

Sexual delight comes in the still of the night through pillow talk, gazing, nuzzling and cuddling. While there are multitudes of ways to communicate love, most spouses shy away from talking directly about their sexual relationship. In this matter, there is no room for guessing. If a particular kind of touch inhibits rather than enhances pleasure, honesty is crucial. The mistaken idea that a spouse should know intuitively what a spouse enjoys sexually fails every time. Verbal expression about what one desires is crucial to sexual communication. No matter how risky, honest sharing is the best policy. Our body language (eyes, lips, face, posture and general body movement) mirrors our sexual and emotional language.

Taking the spectator role during sex (removing self mentally by focusing on performance and/or fantasy) diminishes person-centered sex. Whenever spouses remove themselves from the immediate experience something essential is missing, and it's that person! Being concerned about performance or indulging in fantasies distracts from the immediate experience. It's not only the spouse that's missing, but the person-centered focus is also lost. The rich interaction of being present through sight, touch and involvement that enhances relationship bonding is absent.

Sex therapist David Schnarch (1997) is known to ask spouses if they really "see" their spouse during sex (eye to eye and "I" to "I"). It is the blessed few, he claims, who are sufficiently differentiated to experience such person-to-person intimacy. In each other's presence, in the giving and receiving of two whole selves, spouses become acutely aware of and lost in each other's embrace as they reach deeper levels of knowing in their sacred union.

More Than Technique

In bookstores you can find an entire section devoted to sex. Perusing these books reveals the extent to which couples are interested in improving their sex lives. Living in a technologically oriented society, we are given detailed instruction about sexual techniques as a means of enhancing sexual pleasure. Marriage suffers under the illusion that mastering a set of sexual techniques is the best vehicle for intimacy. In fact, reducing sex to body maneuvers leaves the couple with nothing more than a few complex body contortions. It isn't long before these couples realize that it's not the mechanics of sex that makes sex satisfying, but engagement with one's partner. So what is important to couples when it comes to their sex life?

Laumann and colleagues (1994) reported that nearly 40% of married people said they had sex once or twice a week and nearly three-quarters of wives enjoy orgasm during sex. This study also concluded that sexual frequency is less important than the quality of sex experienced by both spouses. The desire for security and long-term bonding is especially satisfying for women when they engage in sex.

Sexual arousal is part of our chemical makeup. Testosterone, estrogen and oxytocin, along with brain chemicals such as dopamine, serotonin and norepinephrine, have a role in sexual arousal. The complex interaction of hormones and neurotransmitters govern a spouse's arousal system. It has been found that oxytocin is related to the bonding response in humans. Referred to as the "cuddle hormone," it surges when fathers hold an infant, mothers nurse a baby or the couple cuddles in a romantic moment.

Gender differences in sexual arousal show that while both men and women are aroused by visual stimuli, men are more affected by sight alone and have ten times the amount of testosterone. Women's arousal is affected by hormonal levels and is closely paired with the overall quality of the relationship. Sexual arousal is a fairly straightforward biochemical response, while sexual desire is somewhat more complicated!

The brain is uniquely involved in sexual desire. If the mind is preoccupied with worries about children, responsibilities, work or the relationship, it inhibits sexual thoughts from entering. Numerous studies indicate that women experience desire in the context of how they feel about themselves and their partner, how secure they are in the relationship and how closely attached they are to their partner.

The Desire to Be Desired

The active enjoyment of being erotically attracted to and stimulated by a spouse is ego gratifying and mutually stimulating. When we are desired, we feel desirable. Henderson-King and Veroff (1994) found that spouses thrive on affirmation during their first years of marriage, and this is correlated with their sexual satisfaction. A study of Korean American couples found that higher levels of self-esteem, positive regard, communication and cohesion were all associated with sexual satisfaction (Song, Bergen & Schumm, 1995). A study of 48 married couples found that having a shared purpose and common goals was associated with higher levels of sexual enjoyment (McCann & Biaggio, 1989). These studies indicate how qualities in the marital relationship impact sexual satisfaction.

Sexual Embers

Not long ago a client blurted out his frustration in the counseling office: "Can you help us get the passion that we once had back into our marriage?" Ironically, they remembered how hard it was to contain the fiery passion in their early marriage, but after ten years the fire had fizzled. Both spouses tried to rekindle the flame in different ways. Beverly fixed scrumptious dinners with all the romantic accouterments (candles, china and crystal, soft music playing in the background) to set the mood. She was sure this would get the sparks flying, but to her dismay Chuck didn't pick up on any of it. He had other ideas about how to spice up their sex life with videos he thought would do the trick. Beverly was appalled, leaving him feeling rejected. Things only worsened. They retreated into complacency, accepting a bland sex life.

Boredom diminishes sexual embers. Sexual routines become ruts of dissatisfaction. It is noteworthy that in response to advice columnist Ann Landers's question "Has your sex life gone downhill after marriage? If so, why?" that she received over 140,000 replies, with 80 percent indicating that sex after marriage was less exciting—the most used adjectives being *boring, dull, monotonous* and *routine* (as reported by Cox, 2002, p. 245). In *The Gift of Sex,* Cliff and Joyce Penner (2003) encourage couples to keep the flame through creativity, inventiveness, fun loving and openness to new experiences.

It goes without saying that every couple experiences a normal ebb and flow of marital passion. However, a lack of sexual desire and involvement should be a warning sign to couples (Donnelly, 1993). In a national sample of 6,029 married persons, factors that predicted sexual inactivity were unhappiness with the marital relationship, lack of shared activity, increased age and poor health. It behooves a couple to pay attention when either spouse experiences decreased interest in sex. This includes checking out medical concerns that could be contributing to the lack of desire such as hormonal levels, as well as life or relationship stressors that may be contributing to the lack of desire.

Infertility can present a problem in the sexual life of a couple. It is estimated that approximately 1 out of 5 married couples face infertility problems at some point in their relationship, while between 10 and 15% are unable to have children. In serious pursuit of getting pregnant it is easy to lose sight of each other. When sex becomes a means to an end, relationship spontaneity is hard to retain. When the medical professionals enter into the privacy of a couple's sex life it can feel like an invasion. In addition, all these activities are a constant reminder of the emotional pain of being infertile. To circumvent these problems the couple needs to make as much effort as possible to remain emotionally close. Openly sharing their vulnerabilities, working through the disappointments and losses, connecting in the common goal, seeking God through prayer and having the support of a loving community will help the couple deepen their bond during this difficult time.

All couples experience dry spells in their sexual relationship. The stressful combination of busy schedules, work demands, child-caring responsibilities, household tasks, and family and social obligations can diminish sexual responsiveness. Here is where unconditional love and accepting grace can provide momentum for addressing sexual issues. Sharing each spouse's perspective honestly and asking for what is desired to keep sex fresh and alive is the pathway toward renewed sexual vigor. It is not a matter of one spouse complaining and the other succumbing, but of both spouses making a concerted effort to enhance the sexual relationship.

Duncombe and Marsden (1993) found that intentional steps made by couples to keep sexual and emotional intimacy alive pay off. When women take greater responsibility for being open to sex and men make a stronger link between sexual and emotional intimacy, couple intimacy satisfaction increases. Even simple steps can make a difference, like agreeing to have sex at least once a week and to take turns initiating every other week, planning regular talk times for couple connection or weekly dates.

When a wife asked her husband if he thought the spark had gone out of their twenty-year marriage he responded, "A spark lasts only a second. It lights a fire. When the flame burns down, we are left with the hottest part of the fire, the embers, which burn the longest and keep the fire alive!" Relationship quality is the ultimate power of passion that lasts a lifetime.

Desire Discrepancy

A frustrating complaint for both spouses is that one spouse desires sex more often than the other. Make efforts to bridge the gap between the differing desires and actual frequency; both spouses will need to take part in the solution. Spouses with less desire can put themselves in a frame of mind that keeps them open to sex. They can make efforts to stay in tune with their bodies through exercise, nutrition, massage, taking time for self and paying attention to personal appearance. They can intentionally engage in activities that keep them mindful of their sensuality through intimate conversations with their spouse, reading novels, enjoying music, watching movies, setting a romantic atmosphere and so on. Spouses with less desire will need to take personal responsibility for finding ways to be receptive.

Spouses with high sexual desire can divert some of their sexual energy into relationship-focused activities, for example, romancing one's spouse, buying small presents of appreciation, doing special things that alleviate personal stress like helping with household chores, engaging in intimate conversations, being interested in what the spouse is thinking and feeling. It is their relational responsibility to keep the lines of emotional connection open. They will need to respect the spouse's different frequency needs and concentrate on quality when they engage in sex. They augment sexual desire by knowing and reaching out in ways that engage their spouse's responsiveness to sexual pleasuring.

The relationship itself may need some special tending. In the busyness of life, a couple's relationship may have gotten neglected. Being more alert to a spouse's needs, moods, emotions and desires may combat feelings of neglect. Communicating verbally and nonverbally through expressions of tenderness and affection will show a spouse that he or she is desired and desirable. Overt behaviors like giving a gift or card, writing a love letter or poem can be a special way of expressing love and appreciation. Although they are disastrous as poetic art forms, I (Judy) am more than responsive to the love poems Jack has written to me over the years. Actions do speak loudly! Covenant vows involve being in touch with your beloved. If marriage is a sacred priority, spouses need to do everything in their power to keep it precious.

Unfaithfulness in Marriage

One extensive review of the infidelity research reports that the first five years of marriage is an especially risky time for affairs (Allen et al., 2005). In a survey of 3,432 adults, New York sociologists discovered that a married woman's likelihood of straying is highest in the first five years, while men have two high-risk phases, one during the first five years of marriage and another after the twentieth year.

During the wedding ceremony, the bride and groom unreservedly promise to be faithful and true and fully committed. Yet the self-sacrifice required to keep these marital vows is not always so easily achieved. Marital bliss fantasies may leave spouses disillusioned when things don't go as planned, triggering a lingering appetite for the flirtation and the sexually charged attention they received while single. Lacking sufficient skills or maturity to deal with the normal life stressors of marriage opens up the question of whether one married the wrong person. The temptation to escape or find someone else to soothe personal doubts and relationship inadequacies may open one up to infidelity as an escape.

While there are a myriad of reasons spouses have affairs, we propose that level of differentiation contributes to this decision. In early marriage spouses are in the midst of working out differentiation from their families of origin. They are in the beginning phase of discerning the difference between independence and dependence in their effort to achieve balanced interdependence. Not long out of the romance stage, spouses still want to be adored, yet become less enamored with each other in real-life marriage roles. In addition, unreasonable marital expectations shake their confidence in self and other, bringing feelings of inadequacy.

Further neglect may occur when children enter the scene. Lack of effective communication and conflict skills leaves them unable to honestly deal with their issues. Then, as spouses lose their intimate connection, they are tempted to soothe their wounded egos elsewhere. If spouses have not established a solid sense of self, the culmination of these factors hits hard.

Denial and distraction become a common theme. Some spouses never have an affair with a person, but resort to mental affairs by secretly engaging in pornography or Internet sex. Online chat rooms, computer screens and private emails are the epitome of non-person-centered sexuality. In the consumption of pornography or Internet sex one relates to a fantasy—rather than a real live person—to bring sexual arousal and ego gratification. In the false intimacy of two anonymous persons, anything is possible. One does not have to relate to a spouse in the reality of marriage, but rather exists in a world of pretense. This supposedly innocent behavior (that can become a full-blown and life-threatening sexual addition) is truly a betrayal. The spouse has no access to the other's secret life and is therefore kept in a one-down power position with the potential of becoming irrelevant. The spouse is no longer the priority but replaced with a fantasy person. The covenant vow is broken and the sexual union has become contaminated, distorting what God intended for sex and marriage.

Affairs can happen at any stage of marriage. While it's impossible to explain the complex reasons spouses have affairs, one striking truth revealed by researchers is that those who have affairs make a *clear choice every step of the way* (Allen et al., 2005). Denial comes into full swing, judgment is warped, enormous risks are taken, and little consideration is given to the impact infidelity will have on the marriage.

One serious caution made by Shirley Glass (2003) is that spouses be mindful that proximity in the work place can be a brewing ground for sexual or emotional affairs. Because people are drawn close together, in a familiar atmosphere and spend many hours of the day together, it becomes a viable opportunity for affairs. A sexual relationship is often preceded by emotional intimacy, and therefore sharing with a compassionate coworker about your personal and marital life is the perfect set-up. In addition, the spouse is kept out of the loop, which puts him or her at a distinct disadvantage. When the workmate offers comfort, you have chosen the wrong person to soothe you or assist you with your marital problem. It's the spouse who needs to hear the vulnerable personal sharing, and it's the spouse who must be included in solving the marital issues. Secrets breed deceit! Secrets keep the important person out. Secrets break marital vows.

Any time can be risky for an affair in our sexually charged society where spouses have easy access to getting their needs met outside the marriage. Lack of societal values that ordinarily reinforce faithfulness adds fuel to the fire. It's difficult to combat these temptations when the spouse is not sufficiently differentiated or does not hold strong moral values to support marital vows. Sylvia tells the following story that illustrates how denial can lead to secret fantasies or liaisons.

"I couldn't believe it. I received an e-mail from an old high school boyfriend. He asked questions about my life these many years later. I was flattered and excited. We discussed careers, kids, hopes and dreams, but it was not long before we exchanged complaints about our lives. He was a compassionate friend who listened and seemed to care about what I was going through. Then a secret flirtation started, and we revealed more about our personal desires. I felt a sexual chemistry when he said he had a wonderful dream about me. It stroked my ego. I was hooked on these e-mails and became so eager to hear from him that it was all I could think about during the day. Then, at night, I would secretly make the connection. I couldn't tell my husband, Jake, because I knew he would be jealous and ask me to stop. I told myself it was innocent and I would never consider meeting him, but secretly this idea

begin to intrigue me. That's when I got scared, took a good look at myself and asked God for the strength to reveal what was happening. Jake
was quite shocked by what I was telling him, but once the secret was
broken I could become real about what had happened. I wanted to
share my intimacies with my spouse—the real person I lived with—
rather than an anonymous person who only saw one side of me. My secret had created distance, and it was time to confess and reconnect. Now
we had to face my fear of sharing openly, and my husband had to recognize his part in not making our marriage a safe place."

Most offending spouses fail to recognize the serious ramifications infidelity will have on their marriage. The truth is that an affair breaks marital trust (the covenant vow) and has a decidedly catastrophic impact on
the marriage. The good news is that when spouses deal courageously
and honestly with this painful situation, it can be an occasion to differentiate and strengthen the marital ties. Marriages that have been damaged by an affair can be transformed through the repairing of the relationship. With the help of a skilled therapist, even very unhappy couples
can persevere in the face of betrayal, according to Allen et al. (2005).
The couple must do everything they can to reconcile and not allow an
affair destroy their marriage.

The Work of Reconciliation

Keeping secrets is, in itself, a huge breach of trust. Breaking the silence
is the first step toward reconciliation. It may be the hardest thing to do,
but truth telling levels the plain, so to speak. Honesty is the best policy.
Now, the resolute spouse is no longer denied access to the liaison, but
is brought into the equation. The revelation of an affair is an enormous
shock, usually followed by explosions of anger and emotional chaos that
can last for months. It is a crucial time of asking questions, dealing with
self-doubts, and most of all grappling with being deceived and ex-
cluded. The couple has a crucial need for a place of safety to deal openly
with the issues and conflicts while keeping a connection. A professional
therapist or trusted mentor brings the safety and perspective necessary
to transcend the affair and repair the relationship.

There is no magic formula to resurrect trust. After deciding that the
marriage is worth fighting for, both spouses must invest in looking in-

ward as well as outward to the current relationship and what they want for their future. The toughest step for the aggrieved partner may be granting forgiveness when they are still experiencing hurt, mistrust and pain. A willingness to talk about the betrayal is critical. It takes persistence to fully express and finally let go of anger and disappointment in light of the shame that is experienced. A personal decision to preserve both love and marriage is key.

After working with many couples, Michele Weiner-Davis (1992) concludes that healing of affairs is not a straight but a jagged line within which honesty brings the best hope for eventual healing. The unfaithful partner must be willing to talk about the affair over and over again to the satisfaction of the resolute spouse. And at some point, the resolute spouse must be willing to forgive and also consider their part in the relationship dynamic. Over time a couple weans away from the need to focus on the affair. Even when flashbacks or dreams bring the affair back to consciousness, the resolute spouse can choose to find ways to soothe these fears and get beyond them, which is a sign of increased differentiation. Recovery demands endurance, patience and compassion.

Affairs do not have to be the death toll of the marriage! Perhaps it's fair to say the affair is never really forgotten because it is part of the couple's martial history. But forgiveness means the couple can put it aside, no longer let it have power over their marriage, and go forward with renewed vigor. A decision to forgive and to create a healthier relationship leads the couple through a differentiation process that ends in an even greater intimacy.

Lewis Smedes (1976) reminds us that God's intention for marital sexuality involves more than what he calls negative fidelity:

> A man or woman can be just too busy, too tired, too timid, too prudent, or too hemmed in with fear to be seriously tempted by an adulterous affair. But the same person can be a bore at home, callous to the delicate needs of the partner—too prudish to be an adventuresome lover, too cowardly to be in honest communication and too busy to put oneself out for anything more than a routine ritual of personal commitment. One may be able to claim to have never cheated; but may never have tried to grow along with their partner into a deep personal relationship of respect and regard within marriage. Their brand of negative fidelity may be an excuse

for letting the marriage/relationship fall by neglect into dreary conformity to habit and, with that into dull routine of depersonalized sex. I am not minimizing the importance of sexual fidelity, but anyone who thinks that morality in marriage is fulfilled by avoiding an affair has short-circuited the personal dynamics of fidelity. (pp. 168-69)

In Colossians 1:17 Paul tells us that the risen Christ exists before all things, and in him all thing hold together. A couple needs God's help to keep sexuality a positive force in their lives. It's one thing to have a spiritually grounded sexuality; it's quite another to live up to the promises. The couple's religious faith can be a source of restoration and healing as they recommit their sacred vows.

Summary

In the trinitarian model, members are loyal to each other and faithful to the oneness of the Godhead. The reciprocal interaction and communication between the members safeguards the good of the whole. One member does not act without the knowledge of the other in the relentless work for the good of the whole. In like manner, a mutually differentiated couple puts loyalty, mutuality and reciprocity at the core of their oneness.

Monogamous, lifelong marriage has always been the ideal context for sex. In marital sex, spousal vulnerability reflects God's self-giving grace. The marital relationship is a refining crucible of growth as well as a comforting container of trust. The two are protected by their covenant commitment and wrapped together in bodily trust. In the depths of emotional and sexual intimacy, each spouse has a sense of well-being in the context of their mysterious one-flesh union.

Our earlier citation of John Milhaven's description of "sleeping like spoons" might beneficially be quoted further here: "The resistance goes out of me. . . . All of me falls. . . . Nothing holds back. . . . It is a blissful giving way by bodily self to itself. A sweetness of complete relaxing, of luxurious letting go of muscles, skins, nerves, and all. An effortless, sensuous shedding of all concerns, worries, even thoughts . . . as I slope down with Julie to sleep, thoughts float off. I don't think, I enjoy" (1994, p. 88). Falling asleep in the arms of your spouse in the comfort of being known, accepted and trusted is what marriage is all about. "If two lie together, they keep each other warm"; "two are better than one" (Eccles 4:11, 9).

14

Marital Spirituality

Roman Catholic tradition considers marriage a sacrament and quite naturally emphasizes the importance of spirituality in the life of a couple. But the topic of marital spirituality is too often neglected, and so we end this book by addressing this central issue. In elaborating on the sacramental nature of marriage, Gisbert Greshake (1995) identifies what he calls the "fundamental structural elements of marital spirituality." They are *togetherness* in their faith, engagement in a continual process of *reconciliation, faithfulness* in lifelong fidelity, *living God's love* as a reciprocal process and *being a cell of the church*.

In his practical book *Marriage Spirituality* (1989, p. 21), Paul Stevens describes marital spirituality as "simply being intentional about the development of our relationship with God through Christ as a response to his grace throughout lives." Stevens identifies the ten disciplines that enhance marriage spirituality as *prayer* (a special intimacy), *conversation* (listening to the heart), *worship, retreat* (sharing solitude), *study* (hearing God speak), *service* (partnering in ministry), *sexual fasting, obedience* (doing God's will), *confession* (the surgery of forgiveness) and *mutual submission*.

We certainly agree that these are important practices of couple spirituality, and here we present trinitarian theology as an overarching integrative foundation of marital spirituality. Within a trinitarian perspective on relationality, the core aspect of marital spirituality centers on a couple achieving a *differentiated faith*. Differentiated faith in a marital context involves three aspects: first, each spouse's differentiation (identity) in Christ; second, both spouses establishing spiritual differentiation in the context of their marriage; and third, spouses developing a meaningful couple spirituality that is unique to them.

In this chapter we show how a trinitarian model informs our ideas about marital spirituality. We follow with a discussion of what it means to be differentiated in Christ, and how spiritual differentiation is an important aspect of marriage. Building on these discussions we offer practical ideas for how a couple can establish and maintain a couple spirituality. We close the chapter with an emphasis on couple spirituality embedded in a community of faith and small care group.

A Trinitarian Model of Marital Spirituality

In his book *After Our Likeness* (1998), Miroslav Volf utilizes a trinitarian theology to develop a model of the church as a Christian community. We draw upon Volf's insights as we develop a relational model of marital spirituality. Volf explains *perichoresis* as the reciprocal *interiority* of the divine persons mutually indwelling and permeating one another. He writes that "internal abiding and interpenetration of the Trinitarian persons . . . determines the character both of the divine persons and of their unity" (p. 208).

In a similar way, a couple's spiritual character is defined and developed through the internal interdependence and mutual indwelling (interpenetration) of their spiritual lives. Just as the members of the Godhead do not cease to be distinct persons in their unity, neither do spouses cease to be distinct spiritual persons in their union. As Volf (1998) further explains, "the distinctions between them are precisely the presupposition of that interiority, since persons who have dissolved into one another cannot exist in one another" (p. 209). In other words, differentiation makes interiority and interdependency possible. If spouses absorb into each other spiritually, they cease to be a distinct spiritual presence to each other when it comes to spiritual matters. At the other extreme, when the spirituality of either spouse has little or no impact on the other (disengagement), spiritual interiority and interdependence is nonexistent.

While we must be mindful of the limits of using the trinitarian analogy in human relationships, we believe that this model of mutual interaction and indwelling of two spiritually differentiated spouses brings the best hope for meaningful couple spirituality. When spouses dissolve into each other (enmeshment) they cannot offer a unique spiritual perspective, just as when they distance or disengage from each other spiritually, they cannot draw on the spiritual resources that could enrich their spiritual lives as a couple. Spiritual differentiation within and between spouses gives potential for spiritual depth and vitality in marriage.

Differentiated in Christ

In chapter eight we discussed the concept of being *differentiated in Christ,* referring to the New Testament emphasis on each believer finding their identity and reference in relationship with Christ rather than other humanly derived sources. Surrendering one's personal will to the will of God places Christ at the center of each spouse's identity. As the Spirit enters a person, the self becomes less self-centered and more Christ-centered. John the Baptist expressed it this way, "he must increase and I must decrease" (Jn 3:30). Each spouse's personal relationship to Christ and growth in the Spirit (salvation, sanctification, transformation) enhances couple spirituality. Mutual commitment to spiritual transformation keeps both spouses consciously aware of how God is working in and through each of them.

An important aspect of marriage, according to Mark Lau Branson (1984), is sanctification (to be set apart, to be holy). He claims, "God's goal for us is Christlikeness, and that requires powerful and persistent means. The brokenness within us, resulting from our own sin and because we have been sinned against, requires drastic measures. If health is to be restored and new growth made possible, God has to reach deeply into our souls" (p. 10). In other words, spousal spiritual transformation transforms the marriage just as the marriage transforms each spouse's spiritual life.

Spiritual growth is an ongoing and sometimes painful journey that occurs in the context of marriage. Marriage serves as a crucible (a resilient vessel) in which a metamorphosis process occurs. Our relationship becomes the catalyst in which we see ourselves more clearly in response to each other. We become more fully differentiated through marital tension when we understand ourselves more clearly and take responsibility for our own spiritual growth. Marriage is that crucible where we encounter our spiritual differences and become acutely aware of our human frailties as we relate to one another. We recognize individually and as a couple that we need God to be part of our healing and change. We recognize that God's covenant love for us is what urges us toward a faithful covenant love for each other. This, along with grace, keeps us hopeful when our human tendency is to give up or bail out.

Sanctifying situations unfold over the lifetime of marriage. Gary Deddo (1999) comments, "In the covenant relationship of marriage a man and woman live out a mutual and ordered relationship in which each mirrors and may discover the meaning of creaturely, lifelong history of union and the meaning of the polarity of their being in relationship as man and woman" (p. 141).

Marital spirituality is an evolving process that corresponds to the major developmental issues in marriage. During the early stages of marriage spouses create the beginnings of their spiritual practices; after the arrival of children they are immersed in teaching and modeling the faith to their children; after grown children leave home they must navigate their role as adult children differentiate in the area of faith; later in life, a couple's faith is solidified in grandparenting and elder care roles and ultimately facing the finality of death. At each stage of marriage both spouses are sanctified through their struggles and united in their joys.

Spiritual Differentiation in Marriage

Acts of covenant love and grace are a driving force in the couple's spirituality, and acts of empowerment serve to transform them through the power of the Holy Spirit to be conformed into the image of Christ. While spouses are responsible *to* each other spiritually, it is not to be assumed they are responsible *for* each other spiritually. It's important to make this distinction. Spiritual differentiation between spouses means each spouse is responsible to God alone for his or her individual spiritual growth. In the case of an enmeshed marital spirituality, if one spouse experiences spiritual trials or doubts, the other spouse may be threatened to such an extent that their own faith is questioned. Being overly dependent on their spouse's spiritual life leads to the desire to control how and what their spouse believes. Honest differences in spiritual practices or beliefs are not tolerated and if admitted lead to a negative mode. Such a state of spiritual fusion puts both spouses under duress. Thus, we make the distinction between spiritual *overdependence* and spiritual *interdependence*.

The opposite extreme of spiritual fusion is spiritual disconnection and indifference. In this case, a low level of spiritual differentiation leaves spouses cut off from each other's spiritual lives. Spiritually disengaged spouses keep their spiritual lives private. They are rather apathetic about their spouse's beliefs and practices. Unfortunately, since their spiritual life (joys and struggles) remains internal, it separates rather than connects them in the spiritual realm. They are missing a crucial avenue of spiritual meaning that occurs when spouses share their beliefs and vision. In this case, we draw the distinction between spiritual *independence* and spiritual *interdependence*.

The spiritually differentiated couple, in contrast to spiritually fused or disengaged couples, shares their spiritual lives in a way that *expands* and *connects*. The relationship becomes a place of adult growth because their spiritual differences become a catalyst for differentiation. Their personal faith holds firm regardless of what's happening in their partner's spiritual life. Yet it also serves as a cause for personal self-examination before God. They show interest in and concern for their partner's spiritual life by being a compassionate listener and calming presence. They offer a balanced perspective and empowering support when spiritual doubts or struggles are shared. Their own faith is not jeopardized by their spouse's spiritual dry spells nor do they feel slighted by their spouse's spiritual devotion. Instead, their spiritual lives have a positive impact on each other.

During Jesus' time of greatest spiritual anguish, he let his disciples know, "My soul is overwhelmed with sorrow to the point of death" (Mt 26:38 NIV). He reprimanded them for falling asleep rather than joining him in prayer. In his humanity, Jesus sought comfort and support from his disciples. After they failed him, Jesus prayed, "My Father, if it is possible, may this cup be taken from me" (Mt 26:39 NIV). Jesus then faced the gut-wrenching anguish of being torn to the breaking point. He desperately wanted to be relieved of the upcoming suffering, but also agonized about being separated from his Father in death. In the intimate connection of prayer and assurance of his Father's love, he willingly submitted, "Yet not as I will, but as you will." Here we have a glimpse of the differentiated spiritual unity between God the Father and God the

Son. The text reveals that the Son and the Father have their own separate wills. Yet the Son prayed that his will be one with the Father's will. Did the Father feel the anguish and the "sorrow unto death" of the Son? We have no doubt that he did! In a fatherly sense he certainly died with Jesus and was very present through his love. However, it was the Son, not the Father, who physically died. In a spiritual sense the Father was there for the Son, without depriving the Son of his spiritual purpose. And in the end, after the resurrection, Christ is fully transformed as he becomes one with God.

Marital Spirituality

Paul Stevens (1989) writes, "Marriage is not only parallel to our journey toward God but one of its main paths" (p. 18). Our spiritual lives are not lived in isolation but in the context of our couple journey. The biblical injunction, "Be still, and know that I am God" (Ps 46:10) is both an invitation and a command. A couple's spirituality develops through an awareness of God, reading and listening to God's Word, reflecting on God's great creation, seeking God's will in prayer, worshipping and actively participating in the life of a faith community.

The all-knowing and ever-present God is the couple's spiritual dwelling place. John 15:5 promises that when we make our home in Christ, as Christ is in God, we will bear fruit and have abundant joy. The trouble, says Henri Nouwen (1986), is that few of us spend time in the presence of the Divine. However, he makes this astute observation, "The great paradox of the spiritual life is that precisely because we have a home and belong to the Lord, we can be in the midst of the network of wounds and needs without being pulled apart and destroyed" (1986, p. 10). Couples who make their home in Christ will find spiritual nourishment and strength that will bind them together into a blessed union.

In sharing their spiritual journeys and revealing their spiritual desires, spouses will come to know and be known at an intimate spiritual level. Laying down defenses opens up spiritual connection. Expressing spiritual vulnerabilities, confessing failures, admitting guilt and disclosing fears unlocks the door for relationship healing, forgiveness and restoration. Steadfast in their desire to be conformed to God's will, the couple is able to admit moral failure and look to the Divine potter to mold them into the image of Christ. They take great comfort and joy in the James 5:16 passage, "Therefore confess your sins to one another, and pray for one another, so that you may be healed. The prayer of the righteous is powerful and effective."

You may have heard the adage "a couple who prays together, stays together." While this is not a magic formula, prayer does bring solidarity. The touch of the Spirit is experienced when spouses share their concerns and spiritual requests with each other. Precious moments of closeness unite them as they pray together for wisdom, strength and guidance. And when they pray, they experience God's loving presence; "For where two or three are gathered in my name, I am there among them" (Mt 18:20). In the intimate corners of their spiritual lives they are becoming more fully known.

Creating a meaningful spiritual structure undergirds the marriage. Integrating spiritual values into everyday life affects how spouses relate to each other, raise children, spend time, use money, interact with family, friends and coworkers, and serve others. Practicing spiritual disciplines at home, like prayer at bedtime or in the morning, keeps Christ a central focus in their daily lives. Attending spiritual retreats, incorporating religious rituals in the home, engaging in religious traditions during sacred holidays are ways a couple puts Christ at the center of their home and lives.

Couple spirituality is also a call to generative faith. Common spiritual goals inspire a higher calling that extends beyond immediate family. Together they consider how their couple faith commitment affects their work, church, community and wider world involvement. Active participation in church activities, involvement in acts of service, giving time and money for religious and humanitarian efforts are spiritually life giving. As the couple attempts to bring every aspect of their lives in line with their spiritual values, they will reap the rewards that come with having a united spiritual vision and purpose.

The uniting premise is that God desires to bless and use them in their mutual indwelling as a couple. Viewing their marriage as a gift to be used for God's kingdom on earth, the couple depends on God's Spirit for strength to live out their faith to the glory of God.

Dealing with Differences in Faith

In this section we acknowledge that not all spouses have similar religions or faith commitments. While it is a mistake to assume the lack of a common faith automatically negates couple spirituality, it will certainly be more challenging. Differences in faith can seriously limit or leave couples at a distinct disadvantage when it comes to spiritual togetherness. We believe that spiritual differentiation is especially important for these couples. Depending on how you look at it, levels of spiritual differentiation will either exasperate or be a means of enhancing mixed-faith marriages.

When spiritual differentiation is low, enmeshed spouses will naturally be threatened by faith differences. Insecurity about spiritual differences tends to set up defiant and hostile attitudes toward each other. Out and out disdain for the other's faith may tempt a spouse to ridicule or put down the partner's beliefs. There may be nasty attempts to cajole or coerce the partner. There may even be an uncanny need to punish the partner for not conforming to what one needs the spouse to be in order to feel good about oneself.

Alternatively, disengaged spouses tend to take a "hands off" policy in the name of respecting faith differences. Although such an evasive tactic succeeds in eliminating religious conflict (each goes their independent ways spiritually), it does little to enhance couple spirituality. Consciously ignoring the spirituality of the partner, spouses become as two ships passing in the night. Holding the spiritual part of their lives separate from their relationship keeps them from commingling their spiritual resources.

When there is a high level of differentiated spirituality, it is possible for spouses of different faiths to openly accept their partner's spirituality in a way that enhances rather than constricts marital spirituality. Spiritually differentiated spouses openly share their spiritual journeys and have high regard for their partner's spiritual beliefs and practices. Mutual indwelling means giving and receiving each other's spiritual faith and integrating their unique spiritual selves into a united whole.

Even when different spiritual perspectives heat up the marriage crucible, spouses tolerate the anxiety they feel about their differences in these moments because they are confident that even their differences will lead to heightened differentiation and understanding. Although each partner's "ground of being" is not identical, they find common spiritual ground that connects rather than disconnects them.

A good evangelical friend of ours recently married a Roman Catholic man. It has been delightful to see how Kathy's evangelical beliefs and Keith's Catholic tradition have complemented rather than threatened each other's faith. Keith has come to value the emphasis on lay participation in worship in Kathy's tradition, while Kathy has appreciated the rich spiritual disciplines of Keith's tradition. Their unique spirituality and spiritual traditions have increased their individual faith and enriched their couple spirituality.

Marriages Embedded in Supportive Community

While couples may be able to survive on their own spiritually, we believe they will never thrive on their own without a supportive community. It's incredibly difficult for two people to stand against the onslaught of the spiritual distortions of a secular society. The deep undertone of hyperindividualism in modern society is an enormous barrier to faith. It is nearly impossible to hold on to community values in a society that promotes the *I* and the *me* over the *we* and the *us*. In fact, community words like *cohumanity, reciprocity, interdependence* and *mutuality* are undervalued and rarely used.

This self-focused mentality goes against the Christian ideal of forsaking self for the sake of other. This in itself is a compelling reason to join a community of faith that upholds biblical principles. We need all the help we can get to be relationship centered! Being part of a community of care is not just a wise thing to do, but is a necessary spiritual discipline. In our experience we have found that flourishing marriages are embedded in a church community as well as a more intimate support group.

A community of faith. As we noted in chapter two, the relationality exemplified in the holy Trinity is a model for congregational life as well as marriage. Miroslav Volf (1998, p. 16) utilizes the trinitarian model to give a "theologically appropriate ecclesiological response to the challenge of modern societies." He goes on to declare that if the church is truly a reflection of the divine Trinity, relationships will be *reciprocal* and *symmetrical,* with all members expressing their gifts for the good of all others. Secure identity in Christ at the congregational level means a healthy degree of *connectedness* as well as a healthy degree of *separation*. Permeable boundaries show respect for individual, couple and family needs as they participate in the life of the church. In such a community, themes of reconciliation, transformation, restoration and spreading peace and justice are lived out.

Church members reflect the trinitarian model by maintaining a differentiated identity in Jesus Christ. Paul explains in Galatians, "I have been crucified with Christ; and it is no longer I who live, but it is Christ who lives in me. And the life I now live in the flesh I live by faith in the Son of God, who loved me and gave himself for me" (Gal 2:20). In Romans 6:6 we are reminded that our *old self* has been crucified with Christ, so a *new self* can be alive in Christ. Being differentiated in Christ means we are therefore ultimately empowered by and accountable to God Almighty. Yet as members of the body of Christ, we live by the faith of the risen Lord and are therefore accountable to love, forgive and empower one another in all our relationships.

A faith community is to be invested in the spiritual maturity of all believers (1 Cor 12:7-12). Being baptized by one Spirit into one body, members acknowledge their interdependency and mutual submissiveness (Eph 5:21). When one stumbles, everyone is affected, just as the healing of one brings blessing to the entire congregation. Members are called to accountability for destructive patterns of relating and are empowered through care and challenge. The church is a place where a couple's differentiated faith is nourished and preserved. It supports the making and keeping of our vows to our spouse and our family. Through its multiple resources the church supports a couple's growth with instruction and enrichment opportunities for couples.

Michael Vasey (1996) points out that "the Jewish and Eastern tradition understands marriage as a gift. . . . an aspect of human life, with its own inherent potentialities and responsibilities, that comes to us from the hand of the creator" (p. 181). The gift of marriage then is offered to the community as a mutual blessing and responsibility for both the couple and the community. Just as individual healing best takes place within marriage, so healing of marital wounds sometimes best takes place within the context of the Christian community. Colossians 3:12-15 provides a model for the church:

> As God's chosen ones, holy and beloved, clothe yourselves with compassion, kindness, humility, meekness, and patience. Bear with one another and, if anyone has a complaint against another, forgive each other; just as the Lord has forgiven you, so you also must forgive. Above all, clothe yourselves with love, which binds everything together in perfect harmony. And let the peace of Christ rule in your hearts, to which indeed you were called in the one body. And be thankful.

A healing community. Ray Anderson refers to the church as a hospice because "it's where we can die with dignity" (1986, p. 157). In the beginning of life we're baptized/dedicated, and the community pledges to protect, instruct and be part of our growing process. In the healing services of baptism and the Eucharist we acknowledge our need for God and one another. It is in the church that we humbly understand the essence of being forgiven and restored through the confession of sins and through serving each other. And in our sorrow, pain and even death, the community comforts us with hope in Christ that passes all understanding.

A caring-couple community. Social science research (Pattison, 1984) has discovered that while membership in religious congregations serves an invaluable role in providing faith plausibility structures (Berger, 1967), something more is needed. In particular, marriages need the *support* and *accountability* of a small committed group. Even when groups become as large as a dozen, they begin to tax the degree to which each member is able to develop and maintain an intimate relationship with each other member of the group. We (Jack and Judy) have been part of a couple's caring group for most of our married life. It's the most important thing we do for our marriage. The group not only provides support and accountability, but is also a place of healing and hopeful possibilities.

We vividly remember the day Karen called to let us know Greg had accidentally cut his leg to the bone with a circular saw. Hearing his agonizing screams, Karen ran to the backyard to find Greg sprawled in the grass, both hands clutching the bleeding wound. She called 911 and soon the paramedics came to his rescue. When they tried to pry his hands apart to tend to his wound, his instinct was to hold on. This truly was the right thing to do to halt the bleeding so the surgeon could eventually repair his leg. In a similar way spouses are inclined to protect themselves when trouble comes. The tendency is to keep ourselves together until someone trustworthy shows up to help. We have found that our couple's support group does this for us. As a group we are committed to being there for each other through the blood-curdling times of life. Most importantly, we offer a safe, intimate place for healing to occur. Through unconditional acceptance, especially in our broken condition, we are challenged, empowered and held accountable.

First Peter 3:8 reads, "Finally, all of you, have unity of spirit, sympathy, love for one another, a tender heart, and a humble mind." This is the motto of our couple's group. We meet every week for two hours, primarily focusing on real-life couple issues. The frequency and small number (only four couples or at most five) establishes familiarity. Admittedly, our fears of being exposed, rejected or misunderstood deter growth, and this is why a pledge of confidentiality is absolutely crucial. Only when we are willing to admit our struggles and confess our failures will the group be truly effective. There have been many sad and painful stories shared together. We have learned through each other's experiences and have been encouraged in times of hopelessness. As 2 Corinthians 1:3-4 states, "Blessed be the God and Father of our Lord Jesus Christ, the Father of mercies and the God of all consolation, who consoles us in all our affliction, so that we may be able to console those who are in any affliction with the consolation with which we ourselves are consoled by God."

Each couple and individual spouse plays a unique role in our spiritual lives. We take great delight in sharing how God is working in our lives. Our laughter, tears and joys help us celebrate life together. We search for God's mysterious ways of working in and through our marriages. This small caring group has been an inner sanctuary in which we have come to know each other and be known more intimately.

Marriage mentoring is another avenue of couple support and accountability (Parrott & Parrott, 1995; Hunt, Hof & DeMaria, 1998). The younger couple meets with a mature couple for an agreed upon period of time in a structured or unstructured way. We've had the privilege to meet with a younger couple from our congregation, and it has been a delight to share openly from our personal experiences and spiritual lives. The focus is primarily on the mentored couple, and they set the agenda. The most important thing is to listen carefully, to share honestly and to pray faithfully with and for the couple.

Summary

Jesus proclaims in John 17:22-23, "The glory that you have given me I have given them, so that they may be one, as we are one, I in them and you in me, that they may become completely one, so that the world may know that you have sent me and have loved them even as you have loved me." We are convinced that the living Christ dwells in each spouse, working through his or her unique spiritual gifts and the couple's united faith as a powerful witness of God's love. Christ, the cornerstone of faith, is the grounding force that permeates our marriage with sacred meaning. Mark Lau Branson (1984) puts it like this, "There have been times when Christian marriages provided a profound witness for the Kingdom. . . . marriages provide a glimpse of the salvation offered by life in Christ: partners bearing witness to wounds that have been healed, priorities that have been rearranged, suffering that has been redeemed, lifelong relationships that furnish love and hope" (p. 13).

In a sense, marital spirituality represents the various ways that marriage is meant to reflect trinitarian relationality. Thus, the foundational element of marital spirituality is covenantal love, in which shortcomings are responded to with grace, and personal gifts and strengths are used to mutually empower, resulting in an intimate relationship. Marital spirituality is not a static state to be achieved, but a relational process to be lived out that balances the *I* and *us*. The process of developing and maintaining a vital marital spirituality involves effective patterns of communication that can grow through conflicts and change over the seasons of marriage. The measure of marital spirituality is found in the imago Dei—the simultaneous unity and uniqueness found in the Holy Trinity characterizes the marital relationship.

BIBLIOGRAPHY

Ainsworth, Mary D. Salter. (1978). *Patterns of attachment: A psychological study of the strange situation*. Hillsdale, NJ: Lawrence Erlbaum.

Allan, Graham. (Ed.). (1999). *The sociology of the family: A reader*. Oxford: Blackwell.

Allen, B., Atkins, D., Baucom, D., Synder, D., Gordon, K., & Glass, S. (2005). Intrapersonal, interpersonal, and contextual factors in engaging in and responding to extramarital involvement. *Clinical Psychology: Science and Practice, 12* (2), 101-30.

Amato, P. (2004). Tension between institutional and individual views of marriage. *Journal of Marriage and the Family, 66* (4), 959-65.

Amato, P. R., & DeBoer, D. D. (2001). The transmission of marital instability across generations: Relationship skills or commitment to marriage? *Journal of Marriage and the Family, 63,* 1038-51.

Anderson, Joan. (2002). *Unfinished marriage*. New York: Broadway Books.

Anderson, Ray S. (1982). *On being human: Essays in theological anthropology*. Grand Rapids, MI: Eerdmans.

Anderson, Ray S. (1986). *Theology, death, and dying*. Oxford: Basil Blackwell.

Anderson, Ray S. (2004, November 1-5) Why can't a woman be more like a man? *The Semi* (Pasadena, CA: Fuller Theological Seminary), pp. 1, 9.

Anderson, Ray S., & Guernsey, Dennis B. (1985). *On being family: A social theology of the family*. Grand Rapids, MI: Zondervan.

Angelou, Maya. (2005, February). Love's exquisite freedom. *The Oprah Magazine* (New York: Hearst Communication), p. 57.

Arking, Robert. (1991). *Biology of aging: Observations and principles*. Englewood Cliffs, NJ: Prentice Hall.

Bach, George & Wyden, Peter. (1969). *The intimate enemy: How to fight fair in love and marriage*. New York: Morrow.

Balswick, Jack O., & Balswick, Judith K. (1995). *The dual-earner marriage: The elaborate balancing act*. Grand Rapids, MI: Revell.

Balswick, Jack O. & Balswick, Judith K. (2006). *The family: A Christian perspective on the contemporary home.* (3rd ed.). Grand Rapids, MI: Baker Books.

Balswick, Jack O., Ebstyne King, Pamela, & Reimer, Kevin. (2005). *The reciprocating self: Human development in theological perspective.* Downers Grove, IL: InterVarsity Press.

Balswick, Judith K. (2005). Cast of character counseling. In Karen Helmeke & Catherine Ford Sori (Eds.), *The therapist's notebook for integrating spirituality in counseling.* New York: Haworth Reference.

Barna Research Group. (2001). Born again adults less likely to co-habit, just as likely to divorce, August 6. Retrieved November 5, 2003 from http://www.Barna.org/cgi-bin/Page Press release.

Bartchy, S. (1984, May). Issues of power and a theology of the family. Paper presented at the Consultation on a Theology of the Family, Fuller Theological Seminary, Pasadena, CA.

Barth, K. (1975). *Church Dogmatics.* Vol. 1/1. (G. W. Bromiley & T. F. Torrance, Trans.). Edinburgh: T & T Clark.

Barth, K. (1963). *Church Dogmatics.* Vol. 3/4 (G. W. Bromiley & T. F. Torrance, Trans.). Edinburgh: T & T Clark.

Baxter, Leslie A., Braithwaite, Dawn O., & Nicholson, J. H. (1999). Turning points in the development of blended families. *Journal of Social and Personal Relationships, 16,* 291-313.

Berger, Peter L. (1967). *The sacred canopy: Elements of a sociological theory of religion.* Garden City, NY: Doubleday.

Bilezikian, Gilbert G. (1985). *Beyond sex roles: What the Bible says about a woman's place in church and family.* Grand Rapids, MI: Baker Book House.

Blacker, L. (1999). The launching phase of the life cycle. In Betty Carter & Monica McGoldrick (Eds.), *The expanded family life cycle: Individual, family, and social perspectives* (3rd ed., pp. 287-306). Boston: Allyn and Bacon.

Booth, A., & Amato, P. (2001). Parental predivorce relations and offspring post-divorce well-being. *Journal of Marriage and the Family, 63,* 197-212.

Bowen, Murray. (1966). The use of family therapy in clinical practice. *Comprehensive Psychiatry, 7,* 345-74.

Bowen, Murray. (1978). *Family therapy in clinical practice.* New York: Jason Aronson.

Bowlby, J. (1969). *Attachment and loss:* Vol. 1. *Attachment.* New York: Basic Books.

Bowlby, J. (1973). *Attachment and loss:* Vol. 2. *Separation: Anxiety and anger.* New York: Basic Books.

Braithwaite, Dawn O., Olson, L. N., Golish, T. D., Soukup, C., & Turman, P.

(2001). "Becoming a family": Development processes represented in blended family discourse. *Journal of Applied Communication Research, 33,* 159-88.

Branson, Mark Lau. (1984, March/April). Marriage as sanctification. *Radix Magazine.* pp. 11-13.

Brennan, M. Bridget, & Shen, Jerome. (2004). *Claiming our deepest desires: The power of an intimate marriage.* Collegeville, MN: Liturgical Press.

Browning, Don, Miller-McLemore, Bonnie, Couture, Pamela, Lyon, K. Brynolf, & Franklin, Robert. (1997). *From culture wars to common ground: Religion and the American family debate.* Louisville, KY: Westminster John Knox.

Buehler, C. & Gerard, J. (2002). Marital conflict, ineffective parenting, and children's and adolescent's maladjustment. *Journal of Marriage and the Family, 64,* 78-92.

Burgess, Ernest & Locke, Harvey. (1953). *The family: From institution to companionship.* New York: American Book Co.

Bureau of Labor Statistics. (2005). Employment characteristics of families summary, released June 9, 2005. Retrieved December 12, 2005 from http://www.bls.gov/news.release/famee.toc.htm

Buss, D., Shackelford, L., Kirkpatrick, L., & Larsen, R. (2001). A half century of mate preferences: The cultural evolution of values. Journal *of Marriage and the Family, 63,* 491-503.

Butler, Robert. (1988). Aging well. In J. J. F. Schroots, J. E. Birren & A. Svanborg (Eds.), *Health and aging: Perspectives and prospects* (pp. 143-53). New York: Springer.

Carnes, P. (1992). *Don't call it love: Recovery from sexual addiction.* New York: Bantam Books.

Carter, Betty, & McGoldrick, Monica (Eds.). (1999). *The expanded family life cycle: Individual, family, and social perspectives.* (3rd ed.). Boston: Allyn and Bacon.

Cate, R., Levin, S., & Richmond, L. (2002). Premarital relationship stability: A review of recent research. *Journal of Social and Personal Relationships, 19,* 261-84.

Cherlin, Andrew. (2004). The deinstitutionalization of American marriage. *Journal of Marriage and the Family, 66* (4), 848-61.

Clements, Mari L. (2004). For the sake of the children: Effects of marital conflict in intact families. *Journal of Psychology and Christianity, 23* (1), 58-62.

Clinebell, Howard J., Jr., & Clinebell, Charlotte H. (1970). *The intimate marriage.* New York: Harper & Row.

Cohan, C., & Kleinbaum, S. (2002). Towards a greater understanding of the cohabitation effect: Premarital cohabitation and marital communication. *Jour-*

nal of Marriage and the Family, 64, 180-92.

Coontz, S. (2004). The world historical transformation of marriage. *Journal of Marriage and the Family, 66,* 974-79.

Cox, Frank. (2002). *Human intimacy: Marriage, the family, and its meaning.* (9th ed.). Belmont, Calif.: Wadsworth.

Crockenberg, S., & Forgays, D. K. (1996). The role of emotion in children's understanding and emotional reactions to marital conflict. *Merrill-Palmer Quarterly, 42,* 22-47.

Cui, M., Congers, R., Bryant, C., & Elders, G. (2002). Parental behavior and the quality of adolescent friendships: A social-contextual perspective. *Journal of Marriage and the Family, 64,* 676-89.

Cummings, E. Mark, & Davies, Patrick. (1994). *Children and marital conflict: The impact of family disputes and resolution.* New York: Guilford Press.

Deddo, Gary W. (1999). *Karl Barth's theology of relations: Trinitarian, Christological, and human: Towards an ethic of the family.* New York: Peter Lang.

Dickson, F. (1995). The best is yet to be: Research on long-lasting marriages. In Julie Wood & Steve Duck (Eds.), *Understudied relationships* (pp. 22-50). Beverly Hills, CA: Sage Publications.

Donnelly, D. (1993). Sexually inactive marriages. *Journal of Sex Research, 30,* 171-79.

Duncombe, J., & Marsden, D. (1993). Love and intimacy: The gender division of emotion and "emotion work": A neglected aspect of sociological discussion of heterosexual relationships. *Sociology, 27,* 221-41.

Ehrensaft, Diane. (1990). *Parenting together: Men and women sharing the care of their children.* Urbana: University of Illinois Press.

Fee, Gordon. (2005). Male and female in the new creation: Galatians 3:26-29. In Ron Pierce, Rebecca Merrill Groothuis & Gordon Fee (Eds.), *Discovering biblical equality: Complementarity without hierarchy.* Downers Grove, IL: InterVarsity Press.

Ferder, Fran, & Heagle, John. (2004). *Tender fires: The spiritual promise of sexuality.* New York: Crossroad.

Fisher, H. (2002). Lust, attraction, and attachment in mammalian reproduction. *Human Nature, 9,* 23-52.

Fisher, H., Aron, A., Mashek, D., Li, H., & Brown, L. (2002). Defining the brain systems of lust, romantic attraction, and attachment. *Archives of Sexual Behavior, 31,* 413-19.

Flanagan, K. M., Clements, M. L., Whitton, S. W., Portney, M. J., Randall, D. W., & Markman, H. J. (2002). Retrospect and prospect in the psychological study of marital and couple relationships. In J. P. McHale & W. S. Grolnick (Eds.),

Retrospect and prospect in the psychological study of families (pp. 99-126). Mahwah, NJ: Lawrence Erlbaum.

Floyd, F., Gilliom, L., & Costigan, K. (1998). Marriage and the parenting alliance: Longitudinal prediction of change in parenting perceptions and behavior. *Child Development, 65,* 1461-79.

Fowers, B. J., Montel, K. H., & Olson, D. H. (1996). Predicting marital success for premarital couple types based on PREPARE. *Journal of Martial and Family Therapy, 22,* 103-19.

Fowers, B. J., & Olson, D. H. (1992). Four types of premarital couples: An empirical typology based on PREPARE. *Journal of Family Psychology, 6,* 10-21.

Francis, J. (1996). Children and childhood in the New Testament. In S. Barton (Ed.), *The family in theological perspective.* Edinburgh: T & T Clark.

Fromm, Erik. (1956). *The art of loving.* New York: Bantam Books.

Gareis, K., Barnett, R., & Brennan, R. (2003). Individual and crossover effects of work schedule fit: A within-couple analysis. *Journal of Marriage and the Family, 65,* 1041-54.

Garland, Diana S. Richmond, & Garland, David E. (1986). *Beyond companionship: Christians in marriage.* Philadelphia: Westminster Press.

Gilbert, Lucia Albino. (1985). *Men in dual-career families: Current realities and future prospects.* Hillsdale, NJ: Lawrence Erlbaum.

Giles, Kevin. (2002). *The Trinity and subordinationism: The doctrine of God and the contemporary gender debate.* Downers Grove, IL: InterVarsity Press.

Gillis, John. (2004). Marriages of the mind. *Journal of Marriage and the Family, 66,* 988-91.

Glass, Shirley. (2003). *Not "just friends": Protect your relationship from infidelity and heal the trauma of betrayal.* New York: Free Press.

Gottman, John M. (1979). *Marital interaction: Experimental Investigations.* New York: Academic Press.

Gottman, John M. (1994). *What predicts divorce: The relationship between marital processes and marital outcomes.* Hillsdale, NJ: Lawrence Erlbaum.

Gottman, John M., with Silver, Nan. (1994). *Why marriages succeed or fail: What you can learn from the breakthrough research to make your marriage last.* New York: Simon & Schuster.

Graham, E. E. (1997). Turning points and commitment in post-divorce relationships. *Communication Monographs, 64,* 350-68.

Greenberg, Leslie S., & Johnson, Susan M. (1985). Emotionally focused couples therapy: An affective systemic approach. In N. S. Jacobson & A. S. Gurman (Eds.), *Handbook of clinical and marital therapy.* New York: Guilford Press.

Greenberg, Leslie S., & Johnson, Susan M. (1988). *Emotionally focused therapy for couples*. New York: Guilford Press.

Greil, A., Porter, K., & Leitko, T. (1989). Sex and intimacy among infertile couples. *Journal of Psychology and Human Sexuality, 2,* 117-37.

Grenz, Stanley J. (1990). *Sexual ethics: An evangelical perspective*. Louisville, KY: Westminster John Knox.

Grenz, Stanley J. (2001). *The social God and the relational self: A trinitarian theology of the imago Dei*. Louisville, KY: Westminster John Knox.

Greshake, Gisbert. (1995). Spirituality of the permanent sacrament. Retrieved June 29, 2005 from http://www.housetop.com/courses/extra4.htm.

Gundry, Patricia. (1980). *Heirs together: Mutual submission in your marriage*. Grand Rapids, MI: Zondervan.

Gunton, Colin. (1993). *The one, the three and the many: God, creation, and the cultural of modernity*. Cambridge: Cambridge University Press.

Hammond, J., & Fletcher, G. (1991). Attachment styles and relationship satisfaction in the development of close relationships. *New Zealand Journal of Psychology, 20,* 56-62.

Hart, Archibald D., & Morris, Sharon Hart. (1994). *Safe haven marriage: Building a relationship you want to come home to*. Nashville: W Publishing Group.

Heidmann, B., Suhomlinova, O., & O'Rand, A. M. (1998). Economic independence, economic status, and empty nest in midlife marital disruption. *Journal of Marriage and the Family, 60,* 219-31.

Henderson-King, D., & Veroff, J. (1994). Sexual satisfaction and marital well-being in the first years of marriage. *Journal of Social and Personal Relationships, 11,* 509-34.

Hendrix, Harville. (1988). *Getting the love you want: A guide for couples*. New York: H. Holt.

Hendrix, Harville, & Hunt, Helen LaKelly. (2004). *Receiving love: Transform your relationship by letting yourself be loved*. New York: Atria Books.

Hendrix, L. (1997). Quality and equality in marriage: A cross-cultural view. *The Journal of Comparative Social Science, 31,* 201-25.

Hochschild, Arlie Russell. (1989). *The second shift*. New York: Viking.

Horner, Althea. (2005). *Being and loving: How to achieve intimacy with another person and retain one's own identity* (3rd ed.). New York: Jason Aronson.

Hunt, Richard A., Hof, Larry, & DeMaria, Rita. (1998). *Marriage enrichment—preparation, mentoring, and outreach*. New York: Brunner/Mazel.

Huston, Ted, & Melz, Heidi. (2004). The case for promoting marriages: The devil is in the details. *Journal of Marriage and the Family, 66,* 946-58.

Ianzito, Christina. (2004). Full houses: When kids move back home. *Washington Post,* C09.

Johnson, Susan M. (2004). *The practice of emotionally focused marital therapy: Creating connections*. New York: Brunner-Routledge.

Jordan, C., & Revenson, T. A. (1999). Gender differences in coping with infertility: A meta-analysis. *Journal of Behavioral Medicine, 22,* 341-58.

Jung, Carl G. (1971). *Psychological types*. Princeton: Princeton University Press.

Kegan, Robert. (1982). *The evolving self: Problems and process in human development*. Cambridge, MA: Harvard University Press.

Kegan, Robert. (1994). *In over our heads: The mental demands of modern life*. Cambridge, MA: Harvard University Press.

Keirsey, David. (1998). *Please understand me II: Temperament character intelligence*. Del Mar, CA: Prometheus Nemesis Book Company.

Kerckhoff, A., & Davis, K. (1962). Value consensus and need complementarity in mate selection. *American Sociological Review, 27,* 295-303.

Kerr, Michael E., & Bowen, Murray. (1988). *Family evaluation: An approach based on Bowen theory*. New York: W. W. Norton.

Kiernan, K. (2004). Redrawing the boundaries of marriage. *Journal of Marriage and the Family, 66,* 980-89.

Klute, M., Crouter, A., Sayer, A., & McHale, S. (2002). Occupational self-direction, values, and equalitarian relationships: A study of dual-earner couples. *Journal of Marriage and the Family 64,* 139-51.

Knudson-Martin, C., & Mahoney, A. (1998). Language and processes in the construction of equality in new marriages. *Family Relations: Interdisciplinary Journal of Applied Family Studies, 47,* 81-91.

Koerner, A., & Fitzpatrick, M. (2002). Nonverbal communication and marital adjustment and satisfaction: The role of decoding relationship relevant and relationship irrelevant affect. *Communication Monographs, 69,* 33-51.

Kübler-Ross, Elisabeth. (1970). *On death and dying*. New York: Macmillan.

Laumann, Edward O., Gagnon, John, Michael, Robert, & Michaels, Stuart. (1994). *The social organization of sexuality: Sexual practices in the United States*. Chicago: University of Chicago Press.

Lederer, William J., & Jackson, Don D. (1968). *The mirages of marriage*. New York: W. W. Norton.

Levine, T. R., & Boster, F. J. (2001). The effects of power and message variables on compliance. *Communication Monographs, 68,* 28-46.

Lewin, Ellen. (2004). Does marriage have a future? *Journal of Marriage and the Family, 66,* 1000-1006.

Liefeld, W. (2005). The nature of authority in the New Testament. In Ronald Pierce, Rebecca Merrill Groothuis & Gordon Fee (Eds.), *Discovering biblical equality: Complementarity without hierarchy*. Downers Grove, IL: InterVarsity Press.

Loyd, F., Gilliom, L., & Costigan, C. (1998). Marriage and the parenting alliance: Longitudinal prediction of change in parenting perceptions and behaviors. *Child Development, 69,* 1461-79.

Mahler, Margaret S., Pine, Fred, & Bergman, Anni. (1975). *The psychological birth of the human infant: Symbiosis and individuation.* New York: Basic Books.

Mansfield, P., McAllister, F. & Collard, J. (1992). Equality: Implications for sexual intimacy in marriage. *Sexual & Marital Therapy Special Issue: Couple Therapy, 7,* 213-20.

Markman, Howard, Stanley, Scott, & Blumberg, Susan L. (1994). *Fighting for your marriage: Positive steps for preventing divorce and preserving a lasting love.* San Francisco: Jossey-Bass.

Marshall, I. (2004). Mutual love and submission in marriage. In R. Pierce, R. M. Groothuis & G. Fee (Eds.), *Discovering biblical equality: Complementarity without hierarchy.* Downers Grove, IL: InterVarsity Press.

May, Gerald G. (1993). *The awakened heart: Opening yourself to the love you need.* San Francisco: HarperSanFrancisco.

May, Rollo. (1969). *Love and will.* New York: W. W. Norton.

McCann, J., & Biaggio, M. (1989). Sexual satisfaction in marriage as a function of life meaning. *Archives of Sexual Behavior, 18,* 59-72.

McDonald, G. (1980). Family power: The assessment of a decade of theory and research, 1970-1979. *Journal of Marriage and the Family, 42,* 841-54.

McCarthy, B. (2003). Marital sex as it ought to be. *Journal of Family Psychotherapy, 65,* 1-12.

McCullough, P. G., & Rutenberg, S. K. (1989). Launching children and moving on. In B. Carter & M. McGoldrick (Eds.), *The changing family life cycle: A framework for family therapy* (2nd ed., pp. 285-309). New York: Gardner Press.

Milhaven, John Giles. (1994). Sleeping like spoons: A question of embodiment. In James B. Nelson & Sandra P. Longfellow (Eds.), *Sexuality and the Sacred: Sources for theological reflection.* Louisville, KY: Westminster John Knox.

Miller, Sherod, Nunnally, Elam W., & Wackman, Daniel B. (1975). *Alive and aware: Improving communication in relationships.* Minneapolis: Interpersonal Communication Programs.

Myers, Isabel Briggs. (1962). *Manual: The Myers-Briggs Type Indicator.* Palo Alto, CA: Consulting Psychologist Press.

National Center for Health Statistics. (2005). Fertility/infertility. (Vital and Health Statistics, series 23, no. 19.) Retrieved June 29, 2005, from http://www.cdc.gov/nchs.fastats/fertile

Neill, John R., & Kniskern, David P. (Eds.). (1982). *From psyche to system: The evolving therapy of Carl Whitaker.* New York: Guilford Press.

Nelson, James B., & Longfellow, Sandra P. (Eds.). (1994). *Sexuality and the Sacred: Sources for theological reflection.* Louisville, KY: Westminster John Knox.

Nichols, Michael P., & Schwartz, Richard C. (2001). *Family therapy: Concepts and methods.* (5th ed.). Boston: Allyn and Bacon.

Nouwen, Henri J. M. (1986). *Lifesigns: Intimacy, fecundity, and ecstasy in Christian perspective.* New York: Doubleday.

Nyquist, Linda, Slivken, Karla, & Spence, Janet. (1985). Household responsibilities in middle-class couples: The contribution of demographic and personality variables. *Sex Roles, 12,* 15-34.

O'Connor, Elizabeth. (1987). *Cry pain, Cry hope.* Waco, TX: Word Books.

Oden, Thomas. (1974). *Game free: A guide to the meaning of intimacy.* New York: Harper & Row.

Olson, David H., & Olson, A. K. (1999). PREPARE/ENRICH program: Version 2000. In Rony Berger & Mo Therese Hannah (Eds.), *Preventive approaches in couple therapy* (pp. 196-216). Philadelphia: Taylor & Francis.

Papernow, Patricia L. (1993). *Becoming a stepfamily: Patterns of development in remarried families.* New York: Gardner.

Papero, Daniel V. (1990). *Bowen family systems theory.* Boston: Allyn and Bacon.

Parrott, Les, & Parrott, Leslie. (1995). *The marriage mentoring manual.* Grand Rapids, MI: Zondervan.

Pattison, M. (1984, May). Intimate, personal, and social networks. Paper presented at the Consultation on a Theology of the Family, Fuller Theological Seminary, Pasadena, CA.

Pearson, Judy. (1992). *Lasting love: What keeps couples together.* Dubuque, IA: W. C. Brown.

Penner, Clifford, & Penner, Joyce. (2003). *The gift of sex: A guide to sexual fulfillment.* Nashville: Word.

Pierce, Ronald W., Groothuis, Rebecca Merrill, & Fee, Gordon D. (2005). *Discovering biblical equality: Complementarity without hierarchy* (2nd ed.). Downers Grove, IL: InterVarsity Press.

Post, Stephen G. (1994). *Spheres of love: Toward a new ethics of the family.* Dallas: Southern Methodist University Press.

Price-Bonham, S., & Balswick, J. O. (1980). The noninstitutions: Divorce, desertion, and remarriage. *Journal of Marriage and the Family, 42,* 959-72.

Pryor, J. (1999). Waiting until they leave home: The experiences of young adults whose parents separate. *Journal of Divorce and Remarriage, 32,* 47-61.

Rabin, Claire Low. (1996). *Equal partners—good friends: Empowering couples through therapy*. London: Routledge.

Rampage, C. (1994). Power, gender, and marital intimacy. *Journal of Family Therapy Special Issue, 16* (1), 125-37.

Reynolds, J. (2005). In the face of conflict: Work-life conflict and desired work hour adjustments. *Journal of Marriage and the Family, 67,* 1313-31.

Ricoeur, Paul. (1994). *Oneself as another* (Kathleen Blarney, Trans.). Chicago: University of Chicago Press.

Rodin, J. (1987). Personal control through the life course. In R. P. Abeles (Ed.), *Life-span perspectives and social psychology* (pp. 103-19). Hillsdale, NJ: Lawrence Erlbaum.

Rogers, S., & DeBoer, D. (2001). Changes in women's income: Effects on marital happiness, psychological well-being, and the rise of divorce. *Journal of Marriage and the Family, 63,* 458-72.

Roloff, M., & Johnson, K. (2002). Serial arguing over the relational life course: Antecedents and consequences. In A. Vangelistic & H. Reis (Eds.), *Stability and change in relationships* (pp. 107-28). New York: Cambridge University Press.

Satir, Virginia. (1967). *Conjoint family therapy: A guide to theory and technique*. Palo Alto, CA: Science & Behavior Books.

Scanzoni, J. (1979). Social processes and power in families. In W. Burr (Ed.), *Contemporary theories about the family* (pp. 295-316). New York: Free Press.

Schaumberg, Harry. (1997). *False Intimacy: Understanding the struggle of sexual addiction*. Colorado Springs, CO: NavPress.

Schnarch, David. (1997). *The passionate marriage*. New York: W. W. Norton.

Schwartz, Pepper. (2004). *Peer marriage: How love between equals really works*. New York: Free Press.

Schwartz, Richard. (1995). *Internal family systems therapy*. New York: Guilford Press.

Segrin, Chris, & Flora, Jeanne. (2005). *Family Communication*. Mahwah, NJ: Lawrence Erlbaum.

Shapiro, A. F., Gottman, J. M., & Carrere, S. (2000). The baby and the marriage: Identifying factors that buffer against decline in marital satisfaction after the first baby arrives. *Journal of Family Psychology, 14,* 59-70.

Sittser, Jerry. (1985). *The adventure: Putting energy into your walk with God*. Downers Grove, IL: InterVarsity Press.

Smedes, Lewis. B. (1976). *Sex for Christians*. Grand Rapids, MI: Eerdmans.

Smedes, Lewis. B. (1978). *Love within limits*. Grand Rapids, MI: Eerdmans.

Smock, P. (2004). The wax and wane of marriage: Prospects for marriage in the

21st century. *Journal of Marriage and the Family, 66,* 966-73.

Solomon, Marion. (1994). *Lean on me: The power of positive dependency in intimate relationships.* New York: Simon & Schuster.

Song, J. A., Bergen, M. B., & Schumm, W. R. (1995). Sexual satisfaction among Korean-American couples in the Midwestern United States. *Journal of Sex and Marital Therapy, 21,* 147-58.

Spencer, A. (2005). Jesus' treatment of women in the gospels. In Ron Pierce, Rebecca Merrill Groothuis & Gordon Fee (Eds.), *Discovering biblical equality: Complementarity without hierarchy.* Downers Grove, IL: InterVarsity Press.

Stanley, Scott, Trathen, Daniel, McCain, Savanna, & Bryan, Milt. (1998). *A lasting promise: A Christian guide to fighting for your marriage.* San Francisco: Jossey-Bass.

Steil, Janice M. (1997). *Marital equality : Its relationship to the well-being of husbands and wives.* Thousand Oaks, CA: Sage.

Steil, Janice M., & Turetsky, B. (1987). Is equal better? The relationship between marital equality and psychological symptomatology. *Applied Social Psychology Annual, 7,* 73-97.

Stephenson, B. (2005). Nature, technology and the Imago Dei: Mediating the nonhuman through the practice of science. *Perspectives on Science and Christian Faith, Journal of the American Scientific Affiliation, 57* (1), 6-12.

Sternberg, R. (1986). A triangular theory of love. *Psychological Review, 93.* 119-35.

Stevens, Paul. (1989). *Marriage spirituality: Ten disciplines for couples who love God.* Downers Grove, IL: InterVarsity Press.

Stosny, Steven. (2004). Compassion power: Helping families reach their core value. *Family Journal: Counseling and Therapy for Couples and Families, 12* (1), 58-63.

Stright, A., & Neitzel, C. (2003). Beyond parenting: Coparenting and children's classroom adjustment. *International Journal of Behavioral Development, 27,* 31-40.

Thatcher, Adrian. (1999). *Marriage after modernity: Christian marriage in postmodern times.* New York: New York University Press.

Thatcher, Adrian. & Stuart, Elizabeth. (1996). *Christian perspectives on sexuality and gender.* Grand Rapids, MI: Eerdmans. (See section 4, Sexuality and marriage, pp. 169-209.)

Tichenor, V. (1999). Status and income as gendered resources: The case of marital power. *Journal of Marriage and the Family, 61,* 638-50.

Trible, Phyllis. (1987). *God and the rhetoric of sexuality.* Philadelphia: Fortress.

Torrance, J. (1989). The doctrine of the Trinity in our contemporary situation. In A. I. C. Heron (Ed.), *The forgotten Trinity: Study commission on trinitarian doctrine today*. London: British Counsel of Churches.

Ulbrich, P. (1988). The determinants of depression in two-income marriages. *Journal of Marriage and the Family, 50* (1), 21-131.

Van Leeuwen, Mary Stewart. (1990). *Gender & grace: Love, work & parenting in a changing world*. Downers Grove, IL: InterVarsity Press.

Vasey, Michael. (1996). The family and the liturgy. In S. Barton (Ed.), *The family in theological perspective* (pp. 169-85). Edinburgh: T & T Clark.

Visher, E. B., Visher, J. S., & Pasley, K. (2003). Remarriage families and stepparenting. In F. Walsh (Ed.), *Normal family processes: Growing diversity and complexity* (3rd ed., pp. 153-75). New York: Guilford Press.

Volf, Miroslav. (1998). *After our likeness: The church as the image of the Trinity*. Grand Rapids, MI: Eerdmans.

Volf, Miroslav. (1996). *Exclusion and Embrace: A theological exploration of identity, otherness, and reconciliation*. Nashville: Abingdon.

Waite, Linda J., & Gallagher, Maggie. (2000). *The case for marriage: Why married people are happier, healthier, and better off financially*. New York: Doubleday.

Waite, Linda J., & Gallagher, Maggie. (2005). *The case for staying married*. Oxford: Oxford University Press.

Waite, Linda J., & Joyner, K. (2001). Emotional satisfaction and physical pleasure in sexual unions: Time horizon, sexual behavior and sexual exclusivity. *Journal of Marriage and the Family, 63*, 247-64.

Weiner-Davis, Michele. (1992). *Divorce busting: A revolutionary and rapid program for staying together*. New York: Fireside/Simon & Schuster.

Weiner-Davis, Michele. (2003). *The sex-starved marriage: A couple's guide to boosting their marriage libido*. New York: Simon & Schuster.

Whitaker, Carl A., & Bumberry, William M. (1988). *Dancing with the family: A symbolic-experiential approach*. New York: Brunner/Mazel.

White, L., & Edwards, J. N. (1990). Emptying the nest and parental well-being: An analysis of national panel data. *American Sociological Review, 55*, 235-42.

Willingham, Russell. (1999). *Breaking free: Understanding sexual addiction & the healing power of Jesus*. Downers Grove, IL: InterVarsity Press.

Winnicott, D. W. (1986). *Home is where we start from*. New York: W. W. Norton.

Internet References

Christians for Biblical Equality: http://www.cbeinternational.org

Couple communication: http://www.couplecommuniction.com/

Employment characteristics of families summary, 2005. *Handbook of Labor Statistics*. http://www.bls.gov

PAIRS: Practical application of intimate relationship skills: http://www.pairs.com

PREP: Prevention and Relationship Enhancement Program: http://www.prepinc.com

Name Index

Subject Index

Scripture Index